W9-DEI-170

# SALEM COLLEGE
## LIBRARY

Purchased Through The

Louise Horton Barber C'11

Memorial Book Fund

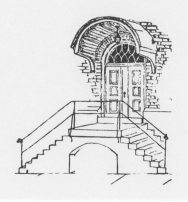

Gramley Library
Salem Academy and College
Winston-Salem, N.C. 27108

# Dante

Nick Havely

**Blackwell**
Publishing

Gramley Library
Salem Academy and College
Winston-Salem, N.C. 27108

© 2007 by Nick Havely

BLACKWELL PUBLISHING
350 Main Street, Malden, MA 02148-5020, USA
9600 Garsington Road, Oxford OX4 2DQ, UK
550 Swanston Street, Carlton, Victoria 3053, Australia

The right of Nick Havely to be identified as the Author of this Work has been
asserted in accordance with the UK Copyright, Designs, and Patents Act 1988.

All rights reserved. No part of this publication may be reproduced, stored in a
retrieval system, or transmitted, in any form or by any means, electronic, mechanical, photocopying, recording or otherwise, except as permitted by the UK
Copyright, Designs, and Patents Act 1988, without the prior permission of
the publisher.

First published 2007 by Blackwell Publishing Ltd

1   2007

*Library of Congress Cataloging-in-Publication Data*

Havely, N. R.
Dante / Nick Havely.
p. cm.—(Blackwell guides to literature)
Includes bibliographical references and index.
ISBN 978-0-631-22852-3 (hardcover : alk. paper)—ISBN 978-0-631-22853-0
(pbk. : alk. paper)   1. Dante Alighieri, 1265-1321.   2. Authors, Italian—To
1500—Biography.   I. Title.

PQ4335.H384 2007
851′.1—dc22
[B]
2006034809

A catalogue record for this title is available from the British Library.

Set in 10/13 pt Galliard
by SNP Best-set Typesetter Ltd, Hong Kong
Printed and bound in Singapore
by Markono Print Media Pte Ltd

The publisher's policy is to use permanent paper from mills that operate a sustain-
able forestry policy, and which has been manufactured from pulp processed using
acid-free and elementary chlorine-free practices. Furthermore, the publisher ensures
that the text paper and cover board used have met acceptable environmental
accreditation standards.

For further information on
Blackwell Publishing, visit our website:
www.blackwellpublishing.com

**For**

*Alvin Pang*
*Amy Shearer*
*Cristina Figueredo*
*Danuta Borucka*
*Emily Kleboe*
*Hayley Longster*
*Helen Lacey*
*James Wade*
*Julia Straub*
*Kenneth Kwok*
*Lei Ying Goh*
*Leonardo Lisi*
*Mark Balfour*
*Massimo Cantagallo*
*Mel Duckworth*
*Sarah Pringle*
*Shengpei Ong*
*Trev Broughton*
*Wei Wei Yeo*

*and many other friends and students of Dante at York*

# Contents

# Plates and Diagrams

## Plates

## Diagrams (drawn by Richard Bennett)

# Acknowledgements

'Who is that man with the beard?' 'He is a friend of my father.' This slightly sinister dialogue (perhaps involving a couple in a café?) is from an exercise in Kathleen Speight's *Teach Yourself Italian*, which helped me to get started on my reading of Dante and so deserves to be acknowledged first. Questioned on the subject of learning Italian, my first teacher of Dante, the late Colin Hardie, (with a sharp intake of breath) replied: 'The motto of Oxford, Mr Havely, is: *you are expected to know*.' So I fulfilled that expectation – after a fashion – and was able then to benefit from his immense knowledge.

At York, from 1971 onwards, I was lucky to be able to start teaching (and learning about) Dante with the late Alan Charity. At Cornell in 1977–8, the learning continued, with Giuseppe Mazzotta, Pete Wetherbee and the late Bob Kaske. Since then, I have been fortunate to share conversations about Dante with a large number of scholars, friends and colleagues in Britain, Ireland, Italy and the USA: the late Peter Armour, John Barnes, Piero Boitani, Santa Casciani, Caron Cioffi, Lilla Crisafulli, the late Charles Davis, Carlo Delcorno, Steve Ellis, Ron Herzman, Chris Kleinhenz, Alastair Minnis, Corinna Salvadori, Bill Stephany, Jeremy Tambling, David Wallace and Barbara Watts, and many others – including students at York. None of these, however, is in any way responsible for any of the mistakes and misjudgements that may follow in the present project.

And for particular help with this project, thanks are due as follows:

to Andrew McNeillie, for signing it up and continuing to encourage it;
to Keir Elam, for persuading me (in a bar in Bologna) not to abandon it;
to Mel Duckworth, for the loan of her paper on the *Commedia* in Australian literature;

to Sarah Pringle, for introducing me to Okri's *Astonishing the Gods*;

to Bernard O'Donoghue, for reading the 'Understanding Love' section with his usual acute understanding;

to Karen Wilson of Blackwell, for steering the book to a conclusion;

to Fiona Sewell, for swift, meticulous and good-humoured copy-editing;

and to Dante Alighieri, the 'man with a beard', whom women in a Verona street thought could really bring back news of the afterlife (Boccaccio, *Trattatello* 1, para. 113).

# Introduction: How to Use This Book

'Dante in English' is a phrase that has been applied in a variety of ways. In the fifteenth century, Lydgate used it, rather obscurely, to pay tribute to Chaucer as vernacular author (*Fall of Princes* prologue, 302–5). A dozen years ago it was the subject of a concise and lucid essay on the reception of Dante's work by English-speaking authors from Chaucer to Heaney (Wallace 1993). Yet more recently, it has been the title of a lengthy anthology of verse translations and imitations from the fourteenth century to the twenty-first (Griffiths and Reynolds 2005). This book is 'Dante in English' in a slightly different sense. It is designed for those who are starting or about to start their reading of Dante in English, either independently or as students of courses on medieval literature and culture. It aims to place his work in its Italian and European contexts, to identify some of its major concerns, and to acknowledge the vitality of its presence in later literature and culture.

Rather than simply summarizing Dante's life or performing a descriptive trek through his works one by one, the book attempts to build up an integrated picture of an eventful career, a questing intellect, a complex imagination and a powerful influence. It will thus introduce Dante in four main ways. The first section outlines his life and career first in Florence and then in the places of his exile; the second surveys the texts he knew and the cultural traditions within which he worked; the third addresses key themes, episodes and passages in his writing, especially the *Commedia*; and the fourth explores aspects of the reception and appropriation of his work by later readers, especially in the English-speaking world. A broadly chronological approach will be taken in the first and second sections; and these are designed to provide initial overviews of the contexts, whilst keeping their relevance to Dante's texts in view throughout. The third and fourth sections follow a more thematic approach to the texts themselves and to their later reception. In these, the vast range of critical issues, views and debates on Dante's work and the ways in which it has been appropriated have to be treated selectively; and the choice of texts and topics to emphasize has been guided by the kinds of material and approaches that have worked for courses I have taught on the *Commedia* and on 'Dante in English' over the past few years.

Providing guidance for further reading is a daunting task when so much secondary material has accumulated on the subject, both in English and in Italian. I have indicated some directions by using asterisks (*) for my first references within a section to works that can be especially recommended to those about to take the next step in exploring the various topics. For the first and second sections, these include: translations of chronicles, political and social history and biography (e.g. Compagni 1986; Martines 1983; Bemrose 2000); and surveys of the intellectual and literary scene (e.g. Luscombe 1997; Minnis and Scott 1988; *CHIL*). Of the multitude of recent critical studies and resources that have a bearing upon the 'readings' in the third section, two can be mentioned as particularly valuable: Peter Hawkins's *Dante's Testaments* (Hawkins 1999) and the *Dante Encyclopedia* (*DE*), where some of the articles are brilliant essays in their own right – such as Baranski's on '*Commedia*: Title and Form', Barolini's on 'Ulysses' and Martinez's on 'Allegory'. For the further study of 'Dante's Readers' (my fourth section), Paget Toynbee's monumental *Dante in English Literature* of 1909 is still an invaluable resource (*DEL*), as for the wider European reception is Michael Caesar's *Dante: The Critical Heritage* (Caesar 1989); whilst the most enlivening critical discussions are David Wallace's overview of 'Dante in English' in *The Cambridge Companion to Dante* (Wallace 1993) and Steve Ellis's incisive study of the nineteenth- and twentieth-century appropriations in *Dante and English Poetry* (Ellis 1983).

All of this recommended material and most of the 'Works Cited' (pp. 267–80) are in English – but 'Dante in English' is only part of the enterprise. The ultimate aim of this guide is to provide readers with resources which they can eventually use for the reading of Dante's work in Italian and even Latin. Parallel-text editions provide the natural next step for those beginning to sample the texts in the original; and here Dante is well served. All three parts of the *Commedia* have appeared with facing prose translations in J. D. Sinclair's edition (rev. edn., 3 vols., London, 1948) and (with full commentary) in Charles Singleton's (6 vols., Princeton, NJ, 1973–5); and the most up-to-date and critically stimulating presentation of the poem in this form is by Robert Durling and Ron Martinez, who have so far completed *Inferno* and *Purgatorio* (2 vols., New York and Oxford, 1996 and 2003). The short poems (including those in *VN* and *Conv.*) were translated and edited by Kenelm Foster and Patrick Boyde in *Dante's Lyric Poetry* (FB); a revised version of Toynbee's edition of the letters with accompanying translation was published in 1966 (*Letters*); and excellent new parallel texts of the two major Latin works, *Monarchia* and *De vulgari eloquentia*, have recently been produced by Prue Shaw and Stephen Botterill in the *Cambridge Medieval Classics* series (nos. 4 and 5; *Mon.* and *DVE*).

In this book, the quotations from Dante's works are all in translation. For the Latin works I have used the versions by Toynbee (*Letters*), Shaw (*Mon.*) and Botterill (*DVE*); and for Dino Compagni's *Chronicle* the version by Bornstein (Compagni 1986). Translations of passages from all other vernacular texts (including the *Commedia*, *Convivio*, *Vita nuova* and lyric poems) are my own, unless otherwise stated. However, to remind the reader of the languages Dante used and their importance, I have occasionally given original words and phrases in parentheses; and in the third section, which involves the greatest amount of close reading, the first quotation in each subsection appears in both Italian and English.

For those who need neither translations nor parallel texts, there are many good Italian editions of Dante's vernacular and Latin works. An excellent annotated edition of the *Opere minori* ('shorter works') appeared in 1988 and subsequently in paperback (Dante 1988). Two especially good Italian editions of the *Commedia* are widely available: those by U. Bosco and G. Reggio (Dante 1979) and A. M. Chiavacci Leonardi (Dante 1991–7).

Hell is, nonetheless, where Dante starts his journey in the *Commedia*, and translations of the *Inferno* are where most readers start their reading. Therefore, to give modern English readers some examples of *Inferno* translations with which they might begin, this introduction concludes with five recent renderings of a passage in which Dante describes the problems of describing Hell.

Over the past dozen years (1994–2006), a number of poets have been trekking all the way through Dante's Hell and producing some striking records of the journey. Two very different versions appeared in 1994: Steve Ellis's vigorously colloquial, telegraphically terse and unrhymed *Hell* (with rarely more than seven words to a line); and Robert Pinsky's *The Inferno of Dante: A New Verse Translation*, which relies chiefly on consonantal or

'Yeatsian' rhyme to 'supply an audible scaffold of English *terza rima*' (Pinsky 1994: xxii). Another pair of very different verse translations were published in 2002: by Ciaran Carson and Michael Palma. Both use forms of *terza rima* (see glossary): Palma's handling of the rhyme is assured and fluent, whilst Carson responds to what he hears in Dante's 'relentless, ballad-like energy' (Carson 2002: xxi). The most recent version (2006) is by a professional Italianist and poet, Robin Kirkpatrick, who authoritatively discusses issues of metre and rhyme in his introduction, but whilst his verse attempts 'to register some of the patternings and variations of the original' and he stresses 'the importance of syntax to Dante's style', he considers the evidence of past examples of English *terza rima* translations to be 'not encouraging' (Kirkpatrick 2006: xciii–xciv). Three of the examples below may help to judge whether or not he is right.

Here, then, are five possible starting points, followed by the point from which they started. The first nine lines of canto 32 of the *Inferno*, in five different verse translations, are followed by Dante's original. Any or none of the five could be further sampled as an introduction to Dante; and those looking for a verse translation of the whole *Commedia* might try the versions by John Ciardi (New York, 1954–70) or more recently, Allen Mandelbaum (London, 1995). In any case, the reader would be well advised to read at least a few cantos of the *Inferno* (for instance 1–2, 5 and 15–19) before beginning to use the rest of this book.

## Samples of recent verse translations of the *Inferno*

1 *The Inferno of Dante: A New Verse Translation*, by Robert Pinsky (New York: Farrar, Straus and Giroux, 1994), p. 341:

> If I had harsh and grating rhymes, to befit
>   That melancholy hole which is the place
>   All the other rocks converge and thrust their weight,
>
> Then I could more completely press the juice
>   From my conception. But since I lack such lines,
>   I feel afraid as I come to speak of this:
>
> It is not jokingly that one begins
>   To describe the bottom of the universe -
>   Not a task suited for a tongue that whines
>
> *Mamma* and *Dadda* . . .

2 *Dante Alighieri: Hell*, translated, annotated, and introduced by Steve Ellis (London: Chatto & Windus, 1994), p. 191:

> If I had rough, grating verses
> that would suit the awful void
> all the other circles press on,
> I'd squeeze the juice of my idea
> more fully; but since I haven't,
> I worry here, starting to speak:
> it's no schoolboy lark, to describe
> the bottom of all the universe,
> no theme for a baby's prattle . . .

3 *The Inferno of Dante Alighieri*, translated by Ciaran Carson (London and New York: Granta Books, 2002), p. 222:

> Had I some wild barbaric rhetoric
> to suit the gloom of this appalling pit
> which takes the weight of stack on stack of rock
>
> I would extract more meaning from the pith
> of what I saw within; but since I don't,
> with trepidation do I take this path
>
> of words; for to describe the fundament
> of all the world is no mere bagatelle,
> nor is its depth for baby babble meant.

4 *Inferno: A New Verse Translation*, by Michael Palma (New York: W. W. Norton, 2002), p. 359:

> With harsh and clacking rhymes that could convey
> the nature of that dark hole of misery
> on which all other rocks converge and weigh,
> I would press out the juice more thoroughly
> from my conception. Lacking them, I fall
> to the work at hand with some anxiety.
> To try to describe the very floor of all
> the universe is nothing to attract
> an idle mind, no task for tongues that call
> to mama and papa . . .

5 *Dante Alighieri, 'The Divine Comedy' I: 'Inferno'*, translated by Robin Kirkpatrick (London: Penguin, 2006), p. 285:

> If I had rhymes that rawly rasped and cackled
> (and chimed in keeping with that cacky hole
> at which, point down, all other rock rings peak),
>     I might then squeeze the juices of my thought
> more fully out of me. But since I don't,
> not without dread, I bring myself to speak.
>     It's not (no kidding) any sort of joke
> to form in words the universal bum,
> no task for tongues still whimpering 'Mum!' and 'Dad'!

6 A. M. Chiavacci Leonardi (ed.), *Dante Alighieri: 'Commedia'* (2nd edn., 3 vols., Milan: Mondadori, 1997), vol. 1, pp. 945–7:

> *S'ïo avessi le rime aspre e chiocce,*
> *come si converebbe al tristo buco*
> *sovra 'l qual pontan tutte l'altre rocce,*
>     *io premerei di mio concetto il suco*
> *più pienamente; ma perch' io non l'abbo,*
> *non sanza temer a dicer mi conduco;*
>     *ché non è impresa da pigliare a gabbo*
> *discriver fondo a tutto l'universo,*
> *né da lingua che chiami mamma o babbo.*

# Abbreviations

| | |
|---|---|
| *Aen.* | Virgil, *Aeneid*. |
| BMS | Brieger, P., Meiss, M. and Singleton, C. S. (eds.) (1969), *Illuminated Manuscripts of the 'Divine Comedy'* (2 vols., New York and London). |
| Boccaccio, *Trattatello* | Ricci, P. G. (ed.) (1974), *Trattatello in laude di Dante*, in vol. 3 of V. Branca (gen. ed.), *Tutte le opera di Giovanni Boccaccio* (Milan), repr. separately as *Boccaccio: vite di Dante* (Milan, 2002). |
| *CHIL* | Brand, P. and Pertile, L. (eds.) (1996), *The Cambridge History of Italian Literature* (Cambridge). |
| CL | Chiavacci Leonardi, A. M. (ed.) (1991–7), *Dante Alighieri: 'Commedia'* (2nd edn., 3 vols., Milan). |
| *Conv.* | Dante, *Convivio*. |
| DE | Lansing, R. (ed.) (2000), *The Dante Encyclopedia* (New York and London). |
| *DEL* | Toynbee, P. G. (ed.) (1909), *Dante in English Literature* (2 vols., London). |
| *DVE* | Botterill, S. (ed. and tr.) (1996), *Dante: 'De vulgari eloquentia'* (Cambridge). |
| *ED* | Bosco, U. (dir.), Petrocchi, G. (ed.) (1970–8), *Enciclopedia dantesca* (6 vols., Rome). |
| FB | Foster, K. and Boyde, P. (eds.) (1967), *Dante's Lyric Poetry* (2 vols., Oxford). |
| *Inf.* | Dante, *Inferno*. |
| *Letters* | Toynbee, P. (ed.) (1966), *Dantis Alagherii epistolae: The Letters of Dante* (2nd edn., Oxford). |

| | |
|---|---|
| *Met.* | Ovid, *Metamorphoses.* |
| *Mon.* | Shaw, P. (ed. and tr.) (1995), *Dante: 'Monarchy'* (Cambridge). |
| *OCD* | Hammond, N. G. L. and Scullard, H. H. (eds.) (1970), *The Oxford Classical Dictionary* (Oxford). |
| *Par.* | Dante, *Paradiso.* |
| *Purg.* | Dante, *Purgatorio.* |
| *S Th* | Aquinas, *Summa theologiae* Blackfriars Edition (1964–76) (6 vols., New York). |
| Villani | Porta, G. (ed.) (1990–1), *Giovanni Villani: 'Nuova cronica'* (3 vols., Parma). |
| *VN* | Dante, *La vita nuova.* |

All references to the Bible use the conventional abbreviations for its books, and the translation used here is that of *The New Jerusalem Bible: Standard Edition* (London, 1985).

# Chronology of Significant Events, c.1200–1321

| Date | Dante's life and work | Other events |
|------|----------------------|--------------|
| 1209 | | Foundation of the Franciscan Order |
| c.1210 | Birth of Dante's father, Alaghiero di Bellincione | |
| 1215 | | Murder of Buondelmonte in Florence |
| 1215–18 | | Foundation of the Dominican Order |
| 1220–50 | | Reign of Emperor Frederick II |
| 1221 | | Death of St Dominic (canonized 1234) |
| 1225–30 | | Guillaume de Lorris writes first part of the *Romance of the Rose* |
| 1226 | | Death of St Francis (canonized 1228) |
| 1228 | | Mosaics in the Baptistery at Florence begun (Wilkins 1983: 144–5) |
| 1231 | | Death of Folquet of Marseilles |
| 1233–40 | | Giacomo da Lentini active as scribe to Emperor Frederick II |

| Date | Dante's life and work | Other events |
|------|----------------------|--------------|
| 1242 and 1247 | | Bonagiunta of Lucca mentioned in documents |
| 1249 | | Death of Pier della Vigna |
| c.1250/5 | | Birth of Guido Cavalcanti |
| 1260 | | 4 Sep., battle of Montaperti; Guelfs of Florence defeated by Sienese, imperial forces and Florentine Ghibellines |
| 1265 | **Between 14 May and 13 June, Dante born in Florence** | |
| 1266 | 26 Mar.?, Dante baptized in the Baptistery of St John, Florence | Imperial forces defeated at Benevento; Guelfs return to Florence (1266/7) |
| 1267 | | Birth of Giotto |
| 1269–78 | | Jean de Meun writes second part of the *Romance of the Rose* |
| 1270/3 | Death of Dante's mother | |
| 1274 | | Death of Thomas Aquinas |
| 1276 | | Death of Guido Guinizzelli; 11 July to 18 Aug., pontificate of Hadrian V |
| 1277 | 9 Jan., contracted to marry Gemma Donati | |
| 1277–80 | | Pontificate of Nicholas III |
| 1281/3 | Death of Dante's father | |
| c.1283–6 | | Murder of Francesca da Rimini |
| 1287 | | Death of Guido delle Colonne |
| 1289 | Cavalryman in battle of Campaldino; 16 Aug., at the siege of Caprona, near Pisa | March, death of Ugolino and his sons at Pisa; 11 June, Florence and Lucca gain victory against Arezzo at Campaldino |

| | | |
|---|---|---|
| **1290** | 8 June, death of Beatrice | |
| **1291** | | Fall of Acre ends Crusaders' rule in Palestine |
| **c.1291–4/5** | Composition of *Vita Nuova*; studies at friars' schools in Florence | |
| **1293–5** | | 'Popular' government of Giano della Bella in Florence |
| **1294** | March, meets the Angevin prince Charles Martel in Florence | 5 July–13 Dec., pontificate of Celestine V; 24 Dec., election of Pope Boniface VIII; deaths of Brunetto Latini and Guittone d'Arezzo |
| **c.1295** | Becomes member of a guild (listed as member in 1297) | Giano della Bella ousted and exiled by Florentine magnates |
| **1295–6** | Participates in discussions about elections and legislation | Dec. 1296, escalating violence between Black and White Guelfs |
| **1296–8** | Composition of *Il Fiore* (attributed to Dante, below, p. 110) | |
| **1297** | Dante listed in the records of the Guild of Physicians and Apothecaries | |
| **1299** | | May, Corso Donati, leader of the Florentine Black Guelfs, exiled |
| **1300** | 7 May, helps set up alliance between Florence and San Gimignano; 15 June, elected prior for two months; 24 June, agrees to exile for Guido Cavalcanti and others | 22 Feb., Boniface VIII proclaims Jubilee year at Rome; 23 May–28 August, pope's legate attempts peacemaking in Florence; 29 Aug., death of Guido Cavalcanti |

| Date | Dante's life and work | Other events |
|------|----------------------|--------------|
| 1301 | Participates in meetings of Florentine 'Council of 100'; 19 June, advises against support for the pope | 1 Nov., Charles of Valois enters Florence as papal 'peacemaker'; 5 Nov., Corso Donati returns |
| 1301–2 | Late autumn/winter, in Rome? | |
| 1302 | 27 Jan., sentenced to fine and exile; 10 Mar., sentenced to death; 8 June, at San Godenzo, 50 km from Florence, with White Guelf allies | |
| 1302–3 | Autumn–winter, at Forlì? | |
| 1302–5/6 | | Giotto's frescoes for the Scrovegni (Arena) Chapel at Padua |
| 1303 | | 11 Oct., death of Boniface VIII; 22 Oct., election of Benedict XI |
| 1303–4 | First visit to Verona | |
| c.1303–5 | Composition of DVE | |
| 1304 | Spring, to Arezzo in Tuscany | 20 July, defeat of Florentine Whites at La Lastra, outside Florence |
| 1304–6 | In Lombardy? | |
| c.1304–7 | Composition of Convivio | |
| 1305–6 | | 5 June, election of Clement V, first Avignon pope (consecrated 14 Nov.); Giotto's Arena Chapel frescoes at Padua completed |

| | | |
|---|---|---|
| **1306–7** | October, in Val di Magra then in the Casentino? | |
| **c.1307–10** | Composition of the *Inferno* | |
| **1308** | Autumn?, in Lucca (see pp. 35–6) | October, Henry of Luxembourg elected Holy Roman Emperor |
| **1309** | | January, Henry of Luxembourg crowned (as Emperor Henry VII) at Aix-la-Chapelle |
| **1310** | Sep./Oct., letter greeting Henry VII's arrival in Italy | 23 Dec., Henry VII enters Milan |
| **c.1310–13** | Composition of the *Purgatorio* | |
| **1311** | Spring, in the Casentino; letters to Florentines (31 Mar.) and Henry VII (17 Apr.) | |
| **1312–18** | Summer 1312?, second visit to Verona; at the court of Cangrande till 1318 | 6 March, Henry VII lands at Pisa; 29 June, crowned in Rome; opposed by papal forces under Robert of Naples; Sep./ Oct., lays siege to Florence |
| **1312–29** | | Cangrande della Scala sole ruler of Verona |
| **1313** | | 24 Aug., Henry VII dies of fever at Buonconvento, near Siena |
| **c.1313–21** | Composition of the *Paradiso* | |
| **1314** | May/June, letter to the Italian cardinals, electing a new pope at Avignon | 20 Apr., death of Clement V |

| Date | Dante's life and work | Other events |
|------|----------------------|--------------|
| 1315 | | 29 Aug., Uguiccione della Faggiuola defeats the Florentines and Tuscan Guelfs at the battle of Montecatini |
| 1316 | Possible date of letter to Cangrande (if authentic) | 7 Aug., election of John XXII (1316–34), the last pope of Dante's lifetime |
| c.1317 | Composition of *Monarchia*? | |
| 1318 | Late in the year, begins his stay at Ravenna, with Guido Novello da Polenta | |
| 1319 | Correspondence with Giovanni del Virgilio at Bologna begins | |
| 1320 | 20 Jan., reads the *Quaestio de aqua et terra* to audience of clergy at Verona | |
| 1321 | **13/14 Sep., Dante dies at Ravenna** and is buried in the church of San Francesco | |

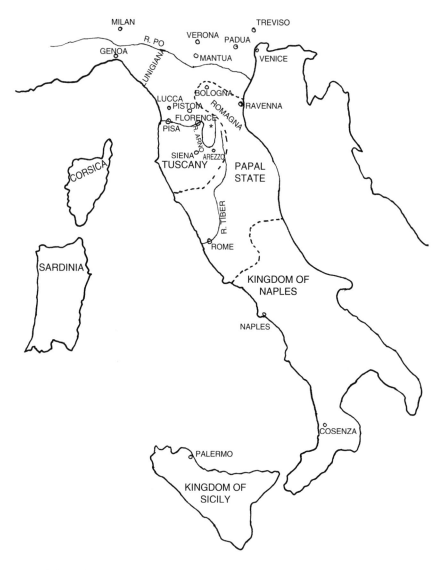

* CASENTINO (UPPER VALLEY OF THE ARNO)

Dante's Italy, c.1300

# Landmarks of a Life

Dante's face currently appears on the Italian 2-Euro coin, reflecting his dual European and national citizenship. As a medieval European intellectual, he used the international language of that community, Latin, for much of his work. Yet most of his poetry, including the *Commedia*, was written in what Boccaccio called 'our Florentine dialect' (*Trattatello* 1, para. 190–1). His voice thus carries a pronounced local accent.

The first section of this guide locates Dante's life and work mostly in the Italian places that he knew and mentioned, or where the evidence of surviving records puts him. It begins with some features of Florence, where the first 36 years of his life were spent (1265–1301). It then moves to the places of his exile, such as Verona, several regions of Tuscany, and Ravenna (where he died in 1321).

In the chronology of a life lived six centuries ago a number of uncertainties remain. We can, however, begin to place Dante's works and journeys in relation to some specific landmarks – many of them still recognizable. The first of these is the Baptistery in Florence, where Dante was given his name and where, near the end of his life and work, he hoped to return and receive the poet's crown (*Par.* 25. 1–9).

*An asterisk (\*) indicates my first reference in this section to works that are particularly recommended for further reading.*

# From the Baptistery to the Ponte Vecchio

## The sheepfold of St John and the city of Mars

The Baptistery of St John beside the Duomo was where Dante received his name. Already six or seven centuries old at the time of Dante's birth, it also stands out as a landmark in paintings of the later medieval period. A fresco of 1342 and several manuscript illustrations of the fourteenth century show its familiar octagonal shape – clad in white and green marble, surmounted by a pyramid of white and crowned by a lantern – standing out among the walls and towers of the city. Dedicated to St John the Baptist, the patron saint of Florence, it had originally served as the city's cathedral, and at the time of Dante's birth (between 14 May and 13 June 1265), it was the place where, on Easter Saturday (or the eve of Whit Sunday), every Florentine born during the previous year was baptized.

Florence's own origins, its civic pride and its urban myths were bound up with the Baptistery. Dante's contemporary, the chronicler Giovanni Villani, believed that the site in pagan times had been the temple of the Roman god Mars; and the granite columns of its interior are from a Roman structure (Villani 2). Villani also records a number of mementoes of Florence's early political triumphs being placed within or around the 'Duomo of St John'; and he notes how, in 1248, the building was miraculously preserved when a 120-metre tower that was about to collapse on it 'twisted away and fell straight along the piazza' (Villani 1906: 145).

Adornment of this ancient structure at the physical and emotional core of the city continued over the centuries. The marble cladding from Prato had been put on during the eleventh and twelfth centuries, and the white pyramidal roof is probably of the thirteenth century. Also of the thirteenth

*Plate 1*   Mosaics in the vault of the Baptistery at Florence, c.1271? © 1998. Photo SCALA, Florence.

century are the mosaics above the altar (perhaps completed around 1225–8). Inside the cupola (plate 1) is a much larger decorative project, possibly dating from around 1271. Five of the eight triangular faces of the cupola are occupied by horizontal bands of narrative: scenes from Genesis and the lives of Joseph, Christ and John the Baptist. Dominating the whole composition, however, is the scene of the Last Judgement, taking up the three faces of the cupola above the altar and centred upon the 8-metre-high figure of Christ in majesty.

The mosaics in the cupola combine awesome unity of design with a kaleidoscopic profusion of colour and detail. As a new addition to the Baptistery in Dante's time, they must have seemed exceptionally impressive; and it has been claimed that they 'were in Dante's boyhood and youth the most notable works of modern art in Florence' (Wilkins 1983: 145). The *Commedia*'s later imagining of Hell and Heaven may well have been influenced by the demonic figures in the Last Judgement mosaic or by the 'rose' of patriarchs and prophets on the altar arch; and these images with their gold background and brilliant colouring were indisputably landmarks in the visual culture of his city.

The Baptistery, John the Baptist and his predecessor Mars are all powerful presences in the *Commedia*. Looking at the holes in the grey rock of Hell where the bodies of corrupt popes are lodged, the pilgrim of *Inferno* is reminded of the structure of the font in his 'beautiful [Baptistery of] St John' and of an event in his own life that was connected with it (*Inf.* 19. 16–21). Dante connects the building with his family and its past, too, when, in Paradise, his great-great-grandfather, Cacciaguida, mentions having received his name and the Christian faith 'in your ancient Baptistery' (*Par.* 15. 134). And near the end of the whole journey and the poem the exiled narrator still hopes to 'return as poet' to the 'sheepfold' of Florence and receive the laurel crown 'at the very font of my baptism' (*Par.* 25. 5–9).

In the *Commedia*, Florence's patron saint is several times identified as St John the Baptist. Again in his encounter with his Florentine ancestor in Paradise, Dante asks Cacciaguida to describe the 'sheepfold of St John' as it was when he was alive (*Par.* 16. 25). One of the earlier Florentines in the poem identifies himself only as a citizen of 'the city that chose the Baptist in lieu of its former patron [Mars], who, because of that, will always torment it in his own way [i.e., through war and internal conflict]' (*Inf.* 13. 143–4).

For Dante and his Florentine contemporaries, the opposition between Mars and John the Baptist – the pagan god of war and the prophet and baptizer of Christ – was reflected in their city's early history and its subsequent conflicts. According to Villani, the marble statue of Mars 'as an armed knight upon a horse' had stood upon a column in the centre of this temple; and when Florentines adopted Christianity their respect for their old patron was so great that they removed him to a place of honour on the Ponte Vecchio (Villani 2.5). For some, this statue (possibly of a barbarian king) represented the baleful influence of Mars upon the city and its citizens; and Dante's ancestor, Cacciaguida, locates the source of Florence's troubles in the sacrifices it continued to offer to this 'mutilated stone that guards the bridge' (*Par.* 16. 145–7).

## Childhood, youth, gang warfare

In the early twelfth century, when Dante's great-great-grandfather Cacciaguida is said to have lived, Florence's population probably numbered no more than 20,000. The city was then enclosed by its original Roman rectangle of walls, and its southern and northern limits were marked by the statue of Mars on the Ponte Vecchio, and the Baptistery (*Par.* 16. 47). At the time of Dante's birth in 1265, however, there may have been about 50,000 inhabitants; a second circle of walls had been built in 1173 and extended across the river in 1258; and three more bridges spanned the Arno. By his death in 1321 Florence was one of the largest cities in Europe, with a population of perhaps 100,000 and a huge third circuit of walls (begun in 1284 and completed in 1334), enclosing six square kilometres of space. As Cacciaguida complains in *Paradiso* 16, much of this urban growth between his time and Dante's was due to incomers from the surrounding countryside. These new urban immigrants sought and contributed to Florence's increasing prosperity, which was based upon the produce of the countryside, long-distance trade in high-value goods, local industry (especially the manufacture of woollen cloth), banking and finance (*Hyde 1973: 152–8).

On several occasions in the *Commedia* Dante claims that his family was of noble rank and that they were of old Roman stock (*Par.* 16. 1–9; *Inf.* 15. 73–8). Whether or not this was the case, it did not prevent his five uncles and his father from actively engaging in business. It is even thought that his father, Alaghiero di Bellincione (c.1210-81/3), may have been a money-lender – which might account for the particularly dim view Dante takes of usury in the *Commedia* and elsewhere. Little else is known about his parents. His mother's name was Bella and she died a few years after his birth (between 1270 and 1273). His father remarried (some time between 1275 and 1278), and Dante grew up with three siblings: two brothers and a sister. The family home was in the south-east of the old city, in a *sestiere* (sixth division) named after one of the gates, the Porta San Piero, and it was here that, the poet was born.

A recent Italian writer on Dante has described him as the sort of person 'that one cannot imagine ever having been a child' (Dossena 1995: 127). In his work, however, Dante seems to show considerable interest in childhood. His early collection of love-poems and commentary, *La vita nuova* ('The New Life', probably completed 1294) describes how he saw for the first time, at the age of eight, 'the glorious mistress of my mind whom many called Beatrice' (*VN* ch. 1). Later, in the *Commedia*, his persona reverts a number of times to a childish state, including when he meets Beatrice again in the Earthly Paradise and she speaks to him as severely 'as a mother to a child' (*Purg.* 30. 79; compare *Par.* 1. 101–2).

There were various models in the Middle Ages for describing the stages of life (three, four, seven, or twelve) from childhood to old age. In the fourth treatise of his philosophical commentary, *Il convivio* ('The Banquet', 1304–7), Dante explicitly follows the four-stage scheme propounded by the scholastic philosopher Albertus Magnus in the early thirteenth century. Here the period of *adolescenzia* ('growing up') is said to occupy the first 25 years of life and is associated with the qualities of the sanguine 'humour' or temperament (especially heat and moisture) and with the season of spring (*Conv.* 4. 23. 13). Following this was the period of *gioventute* ('maturity') lasting 20 years and including the 'mid-point' of life (the age of 35), at which point, Dante says, he undertook the journey described in the *Commedia* (*Inf.* 1. 1).

The behaviour of male youth – especially those of noble families – in medieval Italian towns was a concern of city fathers, preachers and chroniclers; and it has also attracted attention from some modern historians (Crouzet-Pavan 1997: 173–221). Noble youths aspired to knighthood and status, and one way to achieve these was through participation in the military campaigns of the city-state. It is likely that Dante aged 24 took part as a cavalryman in Florence's victory against Arezzo in the battle of Campaldino in the upper valley of the Casentino (11 June 1289) and that a few months later he also witnessed the surrender of the garrison at Caprona (near Pisa) to the combined forces of Florence and Lucca. Both events are referred to at points in the *Commedia* (*Purg.* 5. 91–129; *Inf.* 21. 94–6).

Another way to achieve credibility in the streets, however, was through joining up with a gang of those who – as one of Dante's contemporaries put it – 'would ride around together' (*Compagni 1986: 25). Although youths were not themselves the root cause of the factional competition that was endemic to the social fabric of cities such as Florence, nevertheless 'the youth culture contributed to the violent form taken by that competition' (Lansing 1991: 186). Another contemporary chronicler, Dino Compagni, gives some vivid examples of youthful individuals and groups stirring up trouble and precipitating feuds within the city (Compagni 1986: 6, 23, 25; *Dean 2000: 183).

Dante was well acquainted with such examples and tendencies, as can be seen in his portrayal of turbulent Florentine figures like Filippo Argenti and Mosca dei Lamberti during his journey through Hell. He shows Filippo as a 'quarrelsome Florentine spirit' locked in a vicious brawl (*Inf.* 8. 31–63). Further down, in the eighth circle of Hell, among the mutilated souls of those who caused conflict, Dante's Mosca in a gesture of despair brandishes above his head the stumps of his wrists, from which blood runs down upon his face (*Inf.* 28. 103–11). Mosca is portrayed by several Florentine chroniclers as the moving spirit behind a dramatic family vendetta. In 1215, says Villani, a nobleman called Buondelmonte jilted a woman of the Amidei clan in favour of a wife from the house of the Donati. When the Amidei kinsmen met to decide how to deal with this affront, Mosca advised that 'a thing properly done has an end' (*Inf.* 28. 107). Hence, on the morning of Easter Sunday, Buondelmonte, as he rode all in white across the Ponte Vecchio, was set upon by a group including Mosca and stabbed to death at the foot of the statue of Mars (Villani 6. 38; Villani 1906: 121–2).

This 'sacrifice to Mars', the city's pagan patron, was for Dante, Villani and other Florentines a mythic event which marked the beginning of the city's factional conflicts (*Par.* 16. 136–47; Quinones 1994: 16–21). It also reflects the significant part played by youthful members of noble families in precipitating and pursuing such conflict. Mosca (who was born near the end of the twelfth century) would have been a young man at the time when he took a leading role in the murder of 1215; and Dante later on in the century would have been well aware of how, in a city where life was lived so much in the open, violence and vendetta could escalate from youthful brawls at public events such as weddings and funerals (Lansing 1991: 188).

Among Dante's own youthful circle of friends there are some elements of violence too. In his twenties he exchanged a sequence of harshly insulting sonnets with his wife's cousin, Forese Donati. The poet Guido Cavalcanti, whom the young Dante called his 'foremost friend' in the *Vita nuova*, was later exiled as a consequence of factional conflict and was described by Villani as 'too sensitive and passionate' (Villani 1906: 331). Dino Compagni describes Guido in the 1290s as 'a noble youth' (although he would have been at least in his thirties by then), 'generous and bold but haughty and private'; and he places this impetuous figure on several occasions at the forefront of the city's 'discord' (Compagni 1986: 23 and 26).

Yet Florence was not only the domain of Mars, of factions and youthful passions. It was also the city of the Baptist, of religion and learning, to which laymen such as Dante gained access from an early age.

# Learning in Florence

### Early education (or, why grammar is like the Moon)

Celebrating the 'size, condition and magnificence of the state of Florence' during the late 1330s, Villani makes several claims about the educational standards that had been reached by that time. He says that out of a population of around 90,000, between eight and ten thousand boys and girls were then learning to read; around a thousand to twelve hundred boys were studying basic commercial arithmetic in six schools; and five hundred and fifty to six hundred pupils learning Latin grammar and logic in four big schools (Villani 12. 94). Given their political and rhetorical context, these figures may need to be taken with quite a large pinch of salt. But they do reflect the value that was being attached to early education around Dante's time and the range of subjects that were being taught (Grendler 1989: 71–4; Gehl 1993: 24–6).

Basic reading would have been taught to many Florentine children of both sexes; and commercial arithmetic (the *abbaco*) would have been essential to those who were aiming to enter the city's flourishing business community. Latin grammar was the next essential skill or 'art' for anyone who wanted to reach high administrative office or participate in the scholastic culture of the time; and Dante aspired to do both. As he shows in his review of the fields of learning in part 2 of the *Convivio*, grammar was the first step in the command of the seven basic skills or 'liberal arts' (*Conv.* 2. 13. 7–9). The others were logic, rhetoric, arithmetic, music, geometry and astrology/astronomy; and these could lead on to the higher fields of learning, namely physics, metaphysics and theology. To describe this hierarchy of subjects, Dante uses a comparison with the Ptolemaic universe of his time: a set of planetary spheres with the Earth at their centre. Within this medieval model the sphere of the Moon was the nearest to the Earth, and beyond the concentric spheres of the planets and the 'fixed stars' lay the Empyrean, the 'highest Heaven' (*Conv.* 2. 14–15; and diagram 3, below, p. 125).

So why, for Dante, was grammar like the Moon? Because, he argues, of its density – the infinitude of words especially – and the constant variation over time of words, forms and constructions (*Conv.* 2. 13. 10). The other, less poetic reason was that grammar (like the Moon as the next sphere to the Earth in the medieval cosmic system) was the initial stage in the student's ascent through the universe of knowledge. The metaphor of the entry or 'gateway' (Latin *ianua*) also appears in the basic grammar-book that was used in Florentine schools. The *Donadello*, as it came to be called, got its name from the fourth-century Latin grammarian Donatus, whom Dante in *Paradiso* credits with 'composing the first "art"' and places even higher than grammar's sphere of the Moon, in the circle of the Sun (*Par.* 12. 137–8). This introduction speaks for itself in its 'Prologue': 'I am the door for the ignorant desiring the first art, without me no one will become truly skilled' (Gehl 1993: 88).

'Moral improvement' was intrinsic to the teaching of grammar, and this aim was reflected in the selection of basic texts for reading. Such texts included the *Distichs* – a sequence of moralistic two-liners attributed to the Elder Cato, whose descendant Dante places in a didactic role as the guardian of Purgatory; and the medieval Latin version of Aesop's *Fables*. Dante's debt to his basic schoolbooks – and his assumption of his audience's familiarity with them – is reflected in his direct references and allusions to the repertoire of pungent moral examples in the medieval *Fables*, which were being and were to be translated into the European vernaculars (*Conv.* 4. 30. 4; *Inf.* 18. 133–5, 23. 4–6). He also progressed to Latin texts for more advanced students of grammar, such as Boethius, Cicero and Virgil (below, pp. 67–72). The next stage of his education was provided by the friars in what he calls 'the schools of the religious'.

## The friars in Florence

Dante's philosophical encyclopedia, *Il convivio*, was written in the early years of his exile, and it reflects amongst other things the extent of his early education and intellectual interests. In the second part of the work – at the point where he is about to launch into an allegorical interpretation of one of his own poems – he speaks of the resources which helped him during the 1290s to survive after the death of Beatrice (*VN* chs. 29–31; *Conv.* 2. 12). Here he refers to his reading of Boethius's *Consolation of Philosophy* and Cicero's *On Friendship*; to his necessary command of Latin grammar; and to the intellectual quest that led him to discover other authors and their 'noble lady' (philosophy), who was to be found in 'the schools of the religious' (*Conv.* 2. 12. 7).

By 'the religious' (*li religiosi*) Dante means the orders of friars, and especially the Franciscans and Dominicans. In the religious and intellectual life of his time the orders of friars were a powerful presence. Outside Florence's twelfth-century walls, where many of the immigrants to the city lived, their convents and barn-like churches – designed as auditoriums for preaching – represented, here as elsewhere, 'the church's response to the challenge of town growth' (\*Murray 1972: 86). By Dante's time, convents and churches had been founded by seven of the orders of friars. The Franciscans (first authorized by the papacy in 1209) had arrived in the city in 1218. They had occupied the church of Santa Croce, to the south-east of the old walls of Florence, by 1228 and had begun a substantial new building programme there during Dante's lifetime. On the opposite side of the old centre – to the north-west – the Dominicans (whose rule had been formally recognized in 1216) had been established on the site of Santa Maria Novella since 1221, and the building of their church (begun in 1246) was completed in the mid-fourteenth century.

From these strategic positions, on opposite sides of the old city centre, both Dominicans and Franciscans wielded considerable power and influence. The Dominicans in particular recruited from the city's old aristocratic families; from the 1220s onwards they were active in combating heresy; and a few years after Dante's death they gained the distinction of being the first censors of the *Commedia* (below, p. 228). Support for the Franciscans is reflected in the frequency with which they are named as witnesses, executors and beneficiaries of wills. Following the Dominicans, they took over the office of inquisitor in the later thirteenth century; and they were also involved as advisors and negotiators in city politics (Lesnick 1989: 54–6, 60–2).

The impact of the friars upon the life of the urban laity is also evident from the growth of groups that were formally or informally associated with them. Their 'tertiaries' or third orders led a partly religious, partly secular life; and later in the fourteenth century it was even claimed that Dante himself had been a Franciscan novice (Buti 1858–62: 1. 438–9). There is no evidence for this, but the claim reflects the closeness of the mendicants to the community and the attractiveness of their way of life to the literate

11

Gramley Library
Salem Academy and College
Winston-Salem, N.C. 27108

laity. During the later thirteenth century such closeness was particularly apparent in the growth of the Florentine 'confraternities' (societies of lay penitents and devotees associated with the religious orders). Groups of pious adherents (both men and women) even lived in the areas around the friars' convents (*Holmes 1986: 61–2). As well as regulating the spiritual lives of their adherents, the friars also had a wider mission to the urban community of Dante's Florence. Through preaching, religious instruction and the circulation of devotional texts in the vernacular, they responded to the increasing demand of the laity for involvement in the learning and life of the church.

## Intellectual life: friars and the laity

By claiming that he frequented the schools of the religious soon after the death of Beatrice, Dante places his further education during his twenties, some time between 1291 and 1294–5. This includes the period when he was preparing the book of and commentary on his early love-poems, the *Vita nuova*, and precedes the years of his involvement in civic politics which led to his exile in 1301–2. If he had wished to study law in preparation for an administrative career, he could have found other schools in Florence or gone further afield to Bologna or Arezzo (*Davis 1984: 138–9). But what could he have found to support his interests in Boethius, Cicero and philosophy?

Both the Franciscans and the Dominicans had recognized early on the importance of universities for recruitment and training, and their *studia* (academic centres) were by Dante's time well established in cities such as Oxford and Paris (Lawrence 1994: 127–34). Florence, despite its prosperity, did not attempt to set up a university until the following century. Meanwhile, the cutting edge of intellectual life remained the friars' convents; and it is known that the Franciscan *studium* at Santa Croce and the Dominican one at Santa Maria Novella each ranked fairly high in its order's educational hierarchy (Davis 1984: 151, 155–6).

The two major orders of friars had in the course of the thirteenth century developed distinctive philosophical and theological traditions, associated with their major scholastic thinkers: the Dominican Thomas Aquinas and the Franciscan Bonaventura, whose primacy Dante acknowledges in cantos 10–13 of *Paradiso* (below, pp. 88 and 90–1). Such traditions would have been accessible to Dante at Santa Maria Novella and Santa Croce. The friars were committed to nurturing the lay community's devotion through their tertiary orders and confraternities as well as through public preaching and involvement in the city's affairs. Their more advanced intellectual resources would also have been available to some extent; and laymen like Dante would have been able to attend some of the lectures and disputations in the 'schools of the religious' (Davis 1984: 158–9).

The best-known lecturers at the friars' *studia* in Florence during the late thirteenth century were developing ideas with political themes and consequences. At Santa Croce during the late 1280s the prominent figures were Petrus Iohannis Olivi and Ubertino of Casale, who were to become the leading exponents of radical ideas on Franciscan poverty; whilst among the Dominicans at Santa Maria Novella around the turn of the century were theorists concerned with the politics of government and the city-state: Remigio de' Girolami and Ptolemy of Lucca (Holmes 1986: 81–5; and below, pp. 100–1). And political issues in the Florence of Dante's time were about to become increasingly urgent and divisive.

# From Florence to San Godenzo

## Division and conflict in Tuscany and Florence

Part of Dante's early life involved direct experience of warfare; and being a member of his city's knightly class he participated in its military ventures against opponents in Tuscany. He may have been involved in the Florentine expedition supporting the Sienese against Arezzo in the autumn of 1285; and we know that, at the age of 24, he saw action in both the eastern and western parts of the province: at Campaldino, near Arezzo; and at Caprona, near Pisa (16 August 1289).

Memories of these actions and of warfare in general recur in Dante's writing. Campaldino was a dramatic battle in which the Aretine cavalry initially overran the Florentines and their allies from Bologna, Lucca and Pistoia, but were subsequently cut off from their infantry and routed. In a lost letter, quoted by the Florentine humanist Leonardo Bruni in 1436 (in his *Life of Dante*), Dante describes the conflict as one 'in which I found myself, no longer a youth, at war, where I experienced great fear and eventually very great exultation, as a result of the varying fortunes of that battle' (Bruni 1996: 542). He was later to re-imagine the battleground of Campaldino as the setting for a more intense spiritual drama (*Purg.* 5. 91–129). Caprona was a castle on the southern slope of Monte Pisano, which since the spring of 1289 had been disputed between Pisan forces led by Guido da Montefeltro and a group of Pisan exiles with the support of Lucca and Florence. On 16 August it was recaptured with the help of four hundred Florentine knights, amongst whom was Dante; and the poet was later to compare the feelings of the surrendering Pisans to those of his own persona, facing a group of devils in Hell (*Inf.* 21. 91–6). Along with these acknowledged landmarks of conflict, Dante also incorporates other recollections of war into his writing. In the otherworlds of the *Commedia* he compares movements of groups to, for example, cavalry and infantry manoeuvring in response to given signals (*Inf.* 22. 1–11); knights heading a charge (*Purg.* 24. 94–7); and troops following a banner (*Purg.* 32. 19–24).

Amongst the Florentine cavalry and their allies on that stormy June day at Campaldino were two figures who, during the following decade, would be pitted against each other as leaders of opposing factions in the internal conflict that would beset Florence itself and lead to, amongst other things, Dante's own exile. These two were Corso Donati and Vieri de' Cerchi; and their exploits are mentioned in Compagni's account of the battle (Compagni 1986: 12–13). What, then, led to this eventual conflict? How did it relate to wider political interests and divisions within Tuscany and the Italian peninsula? And what bearing did it have on Dante's political career?

## Guelfs and Ghibellines

Terms used to describe the parties involved seem abstruse and often confuse rather than explain the issues. 'Guelf' (or 'Guelph') and 'Ghibelline' are names in currency from the early thirteenth century, and they originated in conflicts between German princes. In Italy they came to be attached to those amongst the various city-states who broadly favoured either the papacy or the empire, both of which directly controlled territory in the peninsula during the first half of the century. Following the death of Emperor Frederick II in 1250 and the subsequent extinction of his successors' claim to rule in southern Italy (by 1266), the terms 'Guelf' and 'Ghibelline' then 'take on a life of their own', denoting not organized parties under the direct control of pope or emperor, but rather 'a loose chain of local factions, co-operating up to a point under a convenient banner' (Hyde 1973: 132, 139–40). Their membership may have had some connection to social class, and 'while Guelphism attracted the solid *popolani* [mercantile groups including some aristocrats] of the average trading town, Ghibellinism was upheld in the main by inarticulate traditionalists and a handful of sophisticated intellectuals' (Hyde 1973: 141). It was with that latter handful that Dante would come to be associated.

By the 1290s, when Dante was moving towards a political career, 'Ghibellinism was a dead issue in Florence and everyone (or at least anyone who wanted any role in politics) was a Guelf' (*Najemy 1993: 80). Indeed, the only episode during the later thirteenth century when the Ghibellines held power in Florence (1260–66) was as a direct consequence of the most

15

catastrophic defeat in the city's history: the battle of Montaperti near Siena (4 September 1260), where the city's forces were overcome by a combination of the Sienese, imperial German forces, and Florentine Ghibellines who had been in exile since their attempt to take over the government in 1258. The large number of casualties at Montaperti meant that 'there was no Florentine household, small or large, without a member killed or taken prisoner' (Villani 7. 79; Lucchesi 1997: 91, n. 20), and the city was even said to have been faced with the threat of complete destruction (Villani 7. 81). Dante's uncle, Brunetto Alighieri, took part in the campaign; and nearly half a century later the memory of defeat was still raw, as several of the encounters in the *Inferno* clearly show (*Inf.* 10. 85–93, 32. 79–111).

When the Guelfs returned to Florence (after the defeat of the imperial cause in 1266) they were to dominate the city in one way or another for the rest of the century, first as its ruling council and then as a powerful corporation, the *parte Guelfa*. From September 1282, the ascendancy of what was called the *popolo* ('people') in Florence and other Italian cities involved the increasing participation in government of the wealthy guilds which 'represented a proportion of the inhabitants – the mass of the poor and some less esteemed trades which were not allowed to form autonomous guilds were strictly excluded' (Hyde 1973: 111–18). It thus led to a very limited form of 'democracy' which sought both to limit the trouble-making capacity of the old noble families (the *magnati*) and to develop a stable form of urban government under a *podestà* (head of the commune, appointed from outside); a *capitano del popolo* (responsible for public order); and first six, then seven 'priors', chosen from amongst the seven major and five middle guilds to act as effective rulers of the city.

This kind of governmental structure worked in favour of the new wealthy classes and against the old oligarchy, especially under the dictatorship of Giano della Bella, himself a member of an old family (*Par.* 16. 130–1). Giano took power with the support of the middle and lesser guilds from February 1293 and initiated a number of measures to limit the power and the violence of the 'magnates'. The apparent triumph of these *popolani* was short-lived, although the elective system of government remained in place and the lasting effect of their measures was that 'magnates, the violent nobles and their families were marked with a deep stigma' (*Larner 1980: 121–2). Giano della Bella was ousted by the magnates in March 1295 and sent into exile (Villani 9. 8).

It was during and just before the time of Giano's 'popular' government (1293–5) that Dante was extending his education at the schools of the friars and organizing his love-lyrics to Beatrice (who had died in June 1290) into the book he called *La vita nuova* ('The New Life'). A number of Dante's aristocratic friendships can be dated to this period: with the poet and Guelf nobleman Guido Cavalcanti (*Inf.* 10. 52–63; *Purg.* 11. 97–8); with the French Angevin prince Charles Martel (*Par.* 8. 31–148), who visited Florence in March 1294; and with Forese Donati (*Purg.* 23. 40–24. 99), into whose family Dante had married and with whom he exchanged a group of six sonnets (c.1293–6).

In one of the sonnets addressed to Forese Donati, Dante caricatures his friend as a glutton and spendthrift, heading for the debtors' prison or the thieves' gallows – a 'scar-faced character' who strikes fear and outrage into the prosperous, purse-bearing citizens. This portrait forms an apt prelude to the tensions and conflicts that dominated the second half of the 1290s and accompanied the poet's political career up to and beyond his exile in 1301/2. By this time, after the fall of Giano della Bella (1295), control of the city had reverted to the Guelf nobility and upper guilds; and they subsequently proceeded to fall out among themselves.

## Blacks and Whites

Two more problematic party names derived from this falling out: the 'Black' and the 'White' Guelfs. Originally, from 1286, these terms had been used by quarrelling members of the Cancellieri family in the neighbouring Tuscan city of Pistoia. The feud spread to the whole city and was then taken up by rival factions in Florence: the Blacks, headed by Corso Donati, 'a knight of great spirit', and the Whites, led by Vieri dei Cerchi, 'a very good-looking man but not very astute or articulate' (Compagni 1986: 22–3). The ensuing conflict in Florence was not one between 'old' and 'new' money, or between nobility and populace. Both Corso Donati and Vieri dei Cerchi had been, like Dante, among the Florentine cavalry at Campaldino in 1289; and the issue in Florence seems rather to have been what Compagni called 'competition for public office' between members of a broadly similar ruling class (Compagni 1986: 22, 38, 42). Eventually their choice of allies differentiated them more significantly: the Blacks, as will be seen, throwing in their lot with Pope Boniface VIII, and the Whites taking a more independent line and a more lenient attitude towards the Ghibellines (*Keen 2003: 35). But in the view of contemporaries much of the conflict appears to have been conducted at the level of the street brawls that tended to involve the younger generations of major families (above, pp. 7–8). Compagni describes the involvement of one of Dante's friends, Guido Cavalcanti, in an episode of escalating violence between the factions, following a scuffle at a funeral in December 1296, and concludes sombrely that 'as a result of this incident, the enmities began to spread' (Compagni 1986: 23).

## 'Ill-fated activities': Dante, the pope and Florentine politics

As the conflict developed, Dante's own political career got under way; and his participation in public discussion of such matters as elections of the priors and legislation against the magnates is documented in 1295 and 1296. Advancement in such a career depended upon membership of one of the seven major guilds (*arti maggiori*), and accordingly in the records of the Guild of Physicians and Apothecaries for 1297 there is listed the name of 'Dante d'Aldighieri degli Aldighieri, poeta fiorentino'. His recognition as poet here is worth noticing: his work by this time included the love-poems of the *Vita nuova* and the satirical sonnets to Forese Donati, together with some poems to the *donna pietra* ('Lady of Stone') and others of a more philosophical nature that would eventually feature in his encyclopedic *Convivio*. Perhaps also the commitment to both poetry and active politics was proving expensive for him: the documents also show evidence of substantial loans taken out by himself and his half-brother Francesco in the course of the year 1297 (Piattoli 1950: 64–5).

Florentine politics were to prove a costly investment for Dante in other ways too. As hostilities between the factions intensified over the winter of 1298–9, the leader of the Blacks, Corso Donati – whom his brother in the *Purgatorio* claims 'is most to blame' for his city's ruin (24. 82–90) – gained the support of the official Guelf party but 'overplayed his hand' by corrupting the *podestà* and was fined and exiled in May 1299 (Schevill 1963: 166). He was meant to be confined to an area to the far east of Tuscany – the Massa Trabaria in the Apennines – 'but he did not obey; he broke his bounds and went off to Rome' (Compagni 1986: 26). This move was to have momentous consequences for Florence and for Dante.

At Rome in 1299 the papacy was in the hands of Boniface VIII, who was to be portrayed on a number of occasions in the *Commedia* as an enemy of the Florentine Whites, of Dante and of the church (*Inf.* 6. 67–9, 19. 52–7; *Par.* 17. 46–51, 27. 22–54). Boniface, who reigned from late 1294 until his death in October 1303, was an energetic administrator – a canon lawyer and a member of a noble Roman family – who sought to strengthen the universal authority of the papacy in the face of national monarchies, especially that of

France (*Ullmann 1974: 270–7; *Tierney 1988: 172–92). One consequence of this was to be his declaration of a Jubilee or Holy year in Rome at the turn of the century (1300). The Jubilee 'caught the imagination of Europe' (*Duffy 1997: 119). Huge numbers of pilgrims (200,000 at a time) were drawn to Rome, and Dante – who may well have been among them – mentions the event both as an example of effective crowd-management (*Inf.* 18. 28–33) and as a time of especial grace (*Purg.* 2. 98–102).

At the same time, Boniface was concerned to buttress the papacy's authority in a more material way, by extending its political influence in Italy. One of his predecessors, Nicholas III (1277–80), had taken advantage of the weakness of imperial power in the peninsula to gain direct authority over the province of Romagna. Boniface was now looking to assert papal authority over Tuscany, as letters and statements of his in the spring of 1300 clearly indicate; and the activities of Corso Donati after his exile the year before helped to reinforce this direction in papal policy. Corso's exile had led to the White faction under his adversary Vieri dei Cerchi taking power in Florence, and this new regime then pronounced sentences against three Florentines at Rome, one of whom was of the Spini family, allies of Corso Donati and bankers to Boniface (*Holmes 1980: 19–21). This convergence between the interests of Florentine Blacks and the papacy helped to precipitate the crises of 1300 and 1301 which led to the defeat of the Whites and the exile of Dante.

By the spring of 1300, when Boniface was reprimanding the Whites for their treatment of the three Florentines at Rome, Dante seems to have been active on behalf of the new regime. A document of 7 May 1300 records his successful role in helping to confirm the alliance between Florence and the city of San Gimignano (Piattoli 1950: 80–2); and on 15 June he was elected to serve for a two-month term as one of his city's six priors, with the responsibility, amongst other things, for pursuing the condemnation of the three Florentines. In a lost letter quoted by Bruni, Dante attributes all his subsequent ills and troubles to 'the ill-fated activities of my priorate' (Bruni 1996: 542); and it is clear that, despite his prominent position, he was unable to prevent the growing rift with the papacy and his party's subsequent slide towards disaster. Rioting between the two Florentine factions had occurred at the beginning of May and an attempt had been made to calm the situation by exiling members of both, including Dante's friend Guido Cavalcanti. During the whole of Dante's priorate, the pope continued to intervene in the city's affairs through the appointment of the Franciscan cardinal Matteo d'Acquasparta as legate in Tuscany and peacemaker in Florence (23 May–28 August). It was not a successful mission: the cardinal was suspected of favouring the Blacks, and a crossbow-bolt was shot at the window of his lodgings (Compagni 1986: 25). Dante and the other city officials were blamed by the pope and accused of being 'hardened and persistent in evil-doing'; and shortly after the end of Dante's term as prior, the cardinal 'finally abandoned his task, excommunicated the rulers of the city, and left' (Holmes 1980: 26).

## The 'lance of Judas' and the 'bow of exile', 1300–2

The endgame for Dante and the Florentine Whites took over a year to unfold. Despite Dante's later pronouncements against Boniface and the contemporary papacy, it seems unlikely that he or those of his party wished to provoke the papacy into action during this period; indeed, up to the last there were attempts to negotiate, including a mission to Rome during October 1301, in which Dante himself may have taken part. But other forces were at work, and Dante's contemporary and colleague Dino Compagni summarizes the situation as follows:

> The citizens of Florence, divided like this, began to slander one another throughout the neighboring cities and in Pope Boniface's court at Rome, spreading false information. And words falsely spoken did more damage to Florence than the points of swords. They [the Black Guelfs at Rome] worked on the pope, telling him that the city would return to the Ghibellines . . . and they reinforced these lies with a great deal of money. The pope was persuaded to break the power of the Florentines, and so he promised to aid the Black Guelfs with the great power of Charles of Valois, of the royal house of France . . . The pope wrote [in October 1300] that he wanted Messer Charles to make peace in Tuscany, opposing those who had rebelled against the Church. This commission of peacemaker (*paciaro*) had a very good name, but its purpose was just the opposite, for the pope's aim was to bring down the Whites and raise up the Blacks, and make the Whites enemies of the royal house of France and of the Church. (Compagni 1986: 33–4)

Domination of Tuscany was part of Boniface's overall plan for Italy; and Charles of Valois, with a force of 500 knights, having duly crossed the Alps in early July 1300, marched through Tuscany bypassing Florence in mid-August, and arrived in Rome in early September. The next stage of his itinerary was probably planned in conjunction with Corso Donati, the exiled Florentines and the pope, in order to confuse and surprise his opponents in

Florence (Orvieto 1969: 132). He began travelling north from Rome again in the later part of September, but instead of heading directly for his objective he seems to have made a large loop eastwards through Umbria and Marche, descending into Tuscany from the Apennines in early October, reaching Siena on 15 October and, after some negotiation, entering Florence unopposed on 1 November 1301.

Events then moved swiftly, and the collapse of the White Guelf regime is vividly described by Dino Compagni, who, as one of its last priors, was himself at the eye of the storm (Compagni 1986: 39–52). Amid scenes of disorder, Corso Donati, leader of the Blacks, got back to the city by 5 November; and a new set of priors – all from his party – took office on the 8th, following the resignation of Compagni and his colleagues. Boniface's putsch was complete, and Charles of Valois had performed his task with minimal force, or – as Dante was later to put it – 'using only that lance with which Judas jousted, he wielded it so as to burst Florence's guts' (*Purg.* 20. 73–5).

At this stage of the crisis, in the late autumn and winter of 1301–2, we do not know for sure where Dante was. He is recorded as contributing to public discussion on at least three occasions in September. He may have remained for some time in Rome, as part of the Florentine delegation who were there in October (Compagni 1986: 54). It is possible that he could have returned to Florence for a while during the interval between the coup d'état in November and his sentencing to exile, along with three other members of the old regime, early in 1302. The sentence was pronounced on 27 January by the new *podestà*, Cante dei Gabrielli da Gubbio, who had accompanied Charles of Valois on his entry into Florence (Compagni 1986: 39, 46, 48). The accusations and the judgement appear in the document as follows:

That the above-mentioned [Palmieri degli Altoviti, Dante Alighieri, Lippo Becchi, Orlanduccio Orlandi] or certain of them, during or after their terms as priors, had, by themselves or by means of others, committed corruption in public office, acts of illicit gain and unjust extortion of money or goods;

That they or certain of them received money, promises of money or other benefit in return for the subsequent election of priors or standard-bearers [of justice, another elective post] . . . or for the election of officials in districts of the city or territory of Florence . . . ;

That they or certain of them, during or after their terms of office, had committed or caused to be committed the above crimes by giving, promising or paying sums of money or goods or through the accounts of certain merchants;

That they had obtained from the office of the Commune of Florence sums that were greater than or different from those provided for;

That they had perpetrated frauds or corrupt dealings involving money or goods, to the detriment of the Commune of Florence;

That they had caused money to be given and spent to oppose the supreme pontiff [Boniface VIII] and Lord Charles [of Valois], to obstruct the latter's arrival [in Florence, Nov. 1301], contrary to the peace of the Commune of Florence and of the Guelf party;

That they had obtained money or goods from private persons or groups through threatening confiscation of property or action against them by the priors, the Commune and the people;

That they had committed or caused to be committed fraud, deception, malicious acts, corruption of public office and outrageous extortion, and had worked to divide the city of Pistoia into factions and destroy its previous harmony, by causing the governors of the city to be elected only from a single party, by contriving the expulsion from the city of the Blacks who were faithful servants of the Church of Rome, and by detaching the city from its alliance with the city of Florence and from its loyalty to the Church of Rome and to Lord Charles [of Valois], peacemaker in Tuscany.

. . . Wherefore, we determine that each and every one of the said Palmerio, Dante, Orlanduccio and Lippo – in order that they may reap as they have sown and receive due retribution for their actions, being considered to have admitted their guilt through their contumacy – in accordance with the law, the statutes of the Commune of Florence, the ordinances of justice . . . and our own judgement should be fined the sum of 5,000 florins, to be given and paid to the treasurers of the Commune of Florence . . . and that they should restore what they have notoriously extorted to those who can furnish legitimate proof of such; and that if they do not pay the penalty within three days of this sentence, all the goods of the non-payer shall be subject to confiscation and destruction as communal property. And if any of them do pay the penalty, they must nonetheless remain outside the province of Tuscany for a full two years; and in order that the memory of the [deeds of] the said Palmerio, Dante, Orlanduccio and Lippo be preserved in perpetuity, their names are to be written down in the statutes of the people, and, being falsifiers and corrupters of public office [*falsarii et baracterii*], they shall – whether they pay the penalty or not – at no time hold any office or take any remuneration for or from the Commune of Florence in the city, the territory or elsewhere. (my translation; original in D. Ricci 1967: 204–7)

All this seems ferocious enough and reflects the judges' aggressive management of the laws about exclusion (*Starn 1982: 68). But worse was to come. On 10 March 1302 the *podestà* issued a further sentence against Dante and 13 others who had failed to appear before him; and this concludes that: 'if at any time any of the abovementioned shall come within the domain of the said commune [of Florence], any so doing shall be burned to death with fire (*igne comburatur sic quod moriatur*)' (my translation; original in D. Ricci 1967: 208).

Exile, for a citizen of Dante's Florence, was a traumatic and desolating experience (Starn 1982: 121–38; *Martines 1983: 150). What he was to call 'carità del natio loco' (feeling for one's native place, *Inf.* 14. 1) was an especially powerful force among the close-knit urban communities of his time. Dante's immediate reaction to the harsh sentences handed down by his Florentine adversaries in 1302 is not recorded. His deeper responses are, however, reflected throughout the works of his exile. They are evident, for instance, not only in his letters to and about the Florentines, but also in his philosophical and literary treatises (*Conv.* 1. 3. 4–5; *De vulgari eloquentia* ['On Vernacular Eloquence'] 1.6); and in his love-poetry (at the end of his *canzoni*, *Tre donne* and *Amor da che convien*; FB 1. 180–1 and 210–11). Above all, such feelings run their course through the whole of the *Commedia*. The *Commedia* was written during the later years of his exile (perhaps c.1307–21), but it takes as the fictional date of the journey of 'Dante' (the persona) the spring of 1300, the year of Boniface's Jubilee, the year when the poet was approaching the mid-point of human life (traditionally the age of 35) and three months before he took on the political office as prior that was to result, as we have seen, in his sentence of exile.

Throughout the *Commedia* recurs the sense of loss that was also expressed in the early works of his exile – as when at the end of a love-poem he speaks of Florence as if she herself were a scornful lady who 'lacking in love and denuded of pity, has barred me from her presence' (*Amor da che convien* in FB 1. 210–11, lines 78–9) – or at the start of the *Convivio*, where he imagines his city as a mother rejecting her son (*Conv.* 1.3.4–5). The sense of physical deprivation is evident, for example in the *Commedia*'s references to the Baptistery, the physical and emotional core of Florence – references which culminate in the exiled poet's expression of desire for return and reconciliation towards the end of the poem:

> If it comes to pass that the sacred poem,
> to which both Heaven and Earth have set their hands
> and has thus made me over long years lean,
>     can overcome the cruel ban that bars me
> from the fair fold where as a lamb I slept,

> hated by all those wolves who stir up strife there –
> with altered voice, then, and with altered fleece
> I shall return a poet, at the source
> of my own baptism putting on the crown.
>
> (*Par.* 25. 1–9)

Such a hope is, appropriately enough, expressed at the start of a canto in which Dante is to be asked to affirm the theological virtue of hope. Nor did it seem too much for the writer to expect. At around the time these lines were written (c.1319–20), Dante, in response to the offer of such a crown from a professor of literature at Bologna (Giovanni del Virgilio), would express a similar wish for recognition from his fellow-citizens (below, p. 50). It was a wish – like that of return to Florence – that would never be fulfilled.

# Landscapes of Exile

## Descent into the valley

The exiled Dante's representation of his native city in the *Commedia* is deeply ambivalent (below, p. 138). Intense hostility and contempt towards Florence are expressed here, along with an intense desire (as in *Par.* 25. 1–9) to return to her 'sheepfold'. Such hostility also extended to many of his fellow exiles. In canto 15 of the *Inferno*, the soul of his intellectual guide Brunetto Latini (who himself had been exiled from Florence in the 1260s) contemptuously condemns the poet's compatriots both within the city and outside it (*Inf.* 15. 71–2). With similar contempt, Dante's ancestor Cacciaguida describes the Florentine Whites who accompanied the poet in the early years after the 'bow of exile' had struck:

> 'And what shall weigh most heavy on your shoulders
> will be that vicious, stupid company
> with whom you will descend into that valley.
>    In rank ingratitude, fury, malice,
> they'll turn on you; yet not long after that
> it's they, not you, will have to blush for shame.
>    Their deeds themselves will show to all the world
> their bestial nature, and you'll find it best
> to form a faction for yourself – alone.'
>
> (*Par.* 17. 61–9)

However, the misery of exile seeks company; and, as the documents show, in the summer of 1302 Dante was still a member of a party of more than one. A meeting of the White Guelf and Ghibelline exiles took place as early as February, at the small hill-town of Gargonza, mid-way between Siena and Arezzo; and it may have been this sign of rapprochement between their opponents that led the Florentine Blacks on 10 March to pronounce the harsher sentence – of death by burning – on 14 of the exiles, including Dante (above, p. 23). Dante may have been at Gargonza, and his presence is recorded in June 1302 at the large abbey church at of San Godenzo, at the foot of the Apennines, some 50 kilometres to the north-east of Florence, and still well within Tuscany (Piattoli 1950: 110). 'Dante Allegherii' is listed in the document, along with powerful members of the White families, as agreeing to recompense the Ubaldini family of the Mugello (traditionally hostile to the Commune) for any damage or losses incurred to them during the imminent military campaign against Florence (Compagni 1986: 56). Also signatories to the agreement are four members of a great Florentine Ghibelline family who had not been in the city since 1258: the Uberti, whose most famous ancestor, Farinata, victor of Montaperti, is encountered by 'Dante' in canto 10 of the *Inferno*. Hence, just as the interests of the Florentine Black Guelfs had coincided with those of the papacy, so those of the Whites – and of Dante – came to converge with those of the Ghibellines.

Dante's subsequent travels during the first 10 years of his exile (1302–12) seem restless and circuitous. After that meeting in the church at San Godenzo, his journeys criss-crossing Italy led him to various destinations, some of which are documented to some degree, whilst others remain very uncertain (see chronology, above, pp. xxiv–v, and map, above, p. xxvii). Information about his wanderings is based largely on the surviving documents, and there are many gaps (Petrocchi 1984, 1994). As a recent account of Dante's exile argues, 'scholarly attempts to reconstruct [his itinerary] . . . have yielded conflicting scenarios' (*DE* 362A). In any event, it is clear that in the course of this decade the poet was moving across a great variety of landscapes and visiting a number of cities in central and northern Italy. With the lack of a secure base and the difficulties of travel – especially in the mountainous regions of the Apennines – it must have been an often disorientating experience, and one that is reflected in the composition over these years of another difficult journey: the *Inferno*, which was probably begun around 1307–8. The physical and mental stress of straying from the right path among the densely forested valleys and ridges of the high Tuscan Apennines could well lie behind the confusion and panic that beset 'Dante' in the dark wood and on the mountain in *Inferno*'s first canto.

Disorientation is also reflected in the images of wandering and drifting through which Dante represents himself as exile in two earlier works of this decade. In his treatise 'On Eloquence in the Vernacular' (*DVE*, c.1303–5) – which itself crosses 'the tree-clad shoulders of the Apennines' and 'roams through the wooded mountains and pastures of Italy' in search of the ideal vernacular – he speaks of Florentine exiles, still attached to the mother tongue of their city, as 'we for whom the world is now our homeland, as the ocean is for the fishes' (*DVE* 1. 6. 3, also 1. 14. 1, 1. 16. 1). And at the start of the *Convivio*, having portrayed himself as a rejected 'son' of Florence, Dante describes how

> through almost all the regions covered by this language (the vernacular) I have gone as a wanderer, almost as a beggar, reluctantly displaying the wounds of Fortune for which the wounded person himself is very often held to blame. Indeed, I have been a boat without sail or rudder, driven to various ports, harbours and shores by the parching wind that blows from grievous poverty; and I have changed in the eyes of many, who consider that not only has my person been diminished but that everything I have done or am yet to do has become of less value. (*Conv.* 1. 3. 5)

The extent of Dante's wanderings during the early years of his exile may be a little exaggerated here. But by the time he abandoned the *Convivio* around 1307 he had travelled widely between Verona and Sarzana; and he may have spent some time in places as far apart as Treviso (in the Veneto) and Lucca (in western Tuscany). And during these years he also underwent a gruelling emotional and political journey.

## Mugello and Lombardy, 1302–4

In the first months after the meeting at San Godenzo, the Florentine Whites and their new Ghibelline allies achieved some success in taking over strongholds around Florence (in the Mugello and the Valdarno) and near Pistoia; but these were soon recaptured by the Blacks and their allies (Villani 9. 52–3 and 60; Compagni 1986: 57). During the first year of these 'wars of the Mugello' Dante appears to have stayed quite close to the contested area; and a report based on a local chronicle places him at Forlì, very likely as an emissary of the Whites in the autumn of 1302. The court at which he was likely to have been a guest was that of Scarpetta degli Ordelaffi, whose badge, of green lion's paws, Dante mentions honourably in his account of the Romagna (*Inf.* 27. 43–5). Scarpetta was in Compagni's view 'a young man of well-balanced temperament', whom the Florentine Whites chose to command their forces in the Mugello during 1303 (Compagni 1986: 57). There is no firm evidence, however, that Dante either accompanied him on this venture or participated any further in the military or diplomatic activities of the Florentine Whites who had fallen with him 'into that valley' (*Par.* 17. 63; above, p. 25).

From about May or June 1303 for nearly a year, Dante was at some distance from the conflict, in Verona. His son Pietro, who spent much of his later life in Verona, confirms this; and Dante's own account of his exile that is voiced through his ancestor as a prophecy in *Paradiso* (above, p. 25) tells how his

> first refuge and hospitality
> will be the generous gift of the great Lombard
> who bears as arms the eagle on the ladder.
>
> (*Par.* 17. 70–2)

An eagle (literally, 'the sacred bird') upon a ladder was the heraldic emblem of the Della Scala or Scaligeri family of Verona, who had been rulers (initially elected but subsequently hereditary) of the city since 1262; and the 'great Lombard' to whom Dante here refers was Bartolomeo della Scala, *signore* from 1301 to 1304. Despotic government by such princely families was becoming widespread among the northern cities of Italy during Dante's time (Hyde 1973: 141–52; Larner 1980: 133–50; Martines 1983: 125–48). A number of these *signori* – like the Scaligeri in Lombardy and Guido da Montefeltro in the Romagna – were on the Ghibelline side; and Bartolomeo's youngest brother, Cangrande della Scala – who ruled Verona from 1312 to 1329 – was an active supporter of the imperial cause.

Dante was to spend much longer in Verona at a later stage of his career, as a guest of Cangrande della Scala from 1312 to 1318 (below, p. 44); but during 1303–4 there would still have been time for the city, its culture and its surroundings to make an impact on him. Verona's Roman past was prominent in its urban landscape. Its arena (c.100 CE) is the third largest of all surviving Roman amphitheatres and would still have been a striking feature in Dante's time, despite the damage caused by medieval quarrying and the earthquake of 1183. Overlooking the city to the east is the semi-circular theatre begun in the time of Augustus; over to the west (at the point where the river begins to loop north) is the first-century Arch of the Gavii; and nearer to the ancient city centre is the even more imposing double archway of the Porta dei Borsari. The city was thus perhaps even more visibly than Florence 'the daughter of Rome', and a sense of its past may well have reinforced both its rulers' inclination to the imperial cause and Dante's own developing 'idea of Rome' (below, pp. 98–9).

The old Roman forum of Verona also lies beneath its medieval centre, the market-place (now the Piazza delle Erbe), which adjoins the centre of power, the Piazza dei Signori. Signs of the dominance of the Scaliger family would have been especially evident here. Their power base in the city's merchant guild since the beginning of the dynasty in 1262 was acknowledged by the foundation in 1301 of the Casa dei Mercanti ('Hall of the Merchants') by Alberto I della Scala, father of Bartolomeo and Cangrande. And the project of tomb-building for the Scaliger princes that was to become such a monumental feature in the later fourteenth century had already begun (off the north-eastern corner of the Piazza dei Signori), with the plain tomb of Mastino I, founder of the dynasty, who had been assassinated near there in 1277.

By the time of Dante's arrival in Verona in the summer of 1303 the absolute position of the dynasty had long been consolidated and enforced. The 'honour, increase and good *status* of the lords Alberto and [his eldest son] Bartolomeo della Scala, general lords of the *popolo* and city of Verona' had been explicitly asserted in statutes 'read, approved and confirmed' before them, the *podestà*, the guild leaders and the Council of 800 on 27 November 1295; and this approval had been reinforced by some bloodcurdling penalties against any person who

> plots, conspires or consents publicly or privately in removing or diminishing anything of the lordship, captaincy and rectorate of the city of Verona of the lords Alberto and Bartolomeo della Scala . . . or presumes to commit anything in deed, writing or any other way against the persons of the lords and their sons, in any manner that can be imagined . . . The podestà is to raze his house to its foundations, uproot his trees and vines, confiscate his property . . . And if he comes into the hands of the commune of Verona, he is to be dragged through the city at a horse's tail, placed in a cask full of nails, and tied to a bridge over the Adige, where he is to remain until he dies, and then he is to be hanged. (Dean 2000: 232–3)

The scrupulousness of that 'and then' is impressive, in its way. Savage penalties against dissidents or political adversaries were not uncommon at the time, as the sentences against Dante by his fellow-Florentines show (above, p. 22) – but the ruthless despotic rule of the Scaligeri in Verona would have seemed quite strikingly different from the chaotic governance of contemporary Florence. How much of the regime of signorial punishment might then have translated into the *Inferno*'s 'terrible art of justice' (*Inf.* 14. 6)?

Other aspects of Verona's culture would also have made a strong impression. Such a well-established dynasty allowed for the development of a court culture; and it is around this time that Dante, in his treatise on vernacular writing (*DVE*), shows an interest in the civilizing and unifying power of the *curia* (court) (Davis 1984: 13). His more ambitious work on philosophy and ethics, the *Convivio*, could also have been begun during this period, and it bears a title which itself derives from another medieval Latin word for 'court' (*convivium*). At the level of more popular culture, one of Verona's regular festive events that Dante probably witnessed on the first Sunday of Lent in 1304 was the foot-race run for the prize of a green banner. This competition finds an echo in the powerful final tribute Dante awards to the memory of the Florentine writer Brunetto Latini at the end of canto 15 of the *Inferno* (15. 121–4).

The *Inferno* was probably begun in 1307–8 and was probably complete before Dante returned to Verona in 1312 – so other references there to features of the country around the city may derive from the poet's visit during 1303–4. Not far up the valley of the Adige from Verona is the spectacular landslip of the Lavini or Slavini di Marco, on the left bank of the river, near Rovereto; and this is turned into a means of visualizing the steep slope leading down to the seventh circle of Hell (*Inf.* 12. 4–10). Dante could have read about this in the topographical work of the Dominican Albertus Magnus (*Meteora* 3. 6, cited in CL 1.362), but it is also quite possible that he could have seen it for himself during his first stay in Verona. Even closer to Verona are the lower reaches of Lake Garda and the Scaliger fortress of Peschiera which are mentioned in *Inferno* 20, during a digression portraying the course of the river Mincio, flowing out of the lake and on to Mantua, the birthplace of Virgil (*Inf.* 20. 61–81; CL 1. 607). Landscapes of Lombardy and of north-western Italy (below, p. 34) thus form an important element in the imaginary world of Dante's Hell.

## Tuscany and elsewhere, 1304–9

The landscape of Tuscan politics was again in 1304 to exert its pull upon Dante and its influence, eventually, on the *Inferno*. In the autumn of 1303 Boniface VIII had died and been succeeded by a more conciliatory pope, Benedict XI, who in March of the following year sent Cardinal Niccolò da Prato to Florence as his emissary and peacemaker. Villani describes the cardinal as 'a Friar Preacher [Dominican], learned in Scripture, sensible, clever, wise, prudent and highly capable . . . [who] at first showed himself to be well-intentioned and even-handed' (Villani 9. 69). Representatives of the exiled Whites and even a few of the Florentine Ghibellines arrived in the city on 18/20 April, and the initial mood of optimism is vividly described by Compagni (Compagni 1986: 66).

It was probably this prospect of change and reconciliation that drew Dante back from Verona in the spring of 1304 and into active partnership again with the exiled Florentine Whites, on whose behalf he wrote (perhaps also in April) to the cardinal expressing good will towards the peace process (*Letters*, no. 1) A further letter and evidence from Bruni's 1436 biography seem to indicate that Dante was still in Tuscany in May or June of 1304, probably at Arezzo along with the *Universitas Alborum* (the White party), from where it was easy to monitor the situation in Florence (*Letters*, no. 2; Bruni 1996: 546). The signs were not good. As both Compagni and Villani make clear, the mood of peace and reconciliation within the city was short-lived (Compagni 1986: 69–72; Villani 9. 69 and 71) By the high summer Dante may have been distancing himself from his fellow exiles (Petrocchi 1984: 97–8). Two events at this time were particularly ominous: the death of the conciliatory Pope Benedict XI on 7 July; and the ill-fated attempt of the Whites to re-enter Florence by force and their subsequent disastrous defeat at La Lastra, just outside the city (20 July). Compagni, on the side of the Whites, saw the move on Florence as a 'bold and intelligent strategy' but acknowledged that in execution it was 'foolish' and 'premature'; whilst on the other side Villani held it to be through 'the will and intervention of God that they were thus stricken, in order that Florence should not be wholly laid waste, plundered and destroyed' (Compagni 1986: 74; Villani 9. 72). Dante in *Par.* 17 (65–9) was to look back on it as an instance of the shameful folly that would make it necessary for him to go it alone (above, p. 25).

Where, in 1304, the next stage of his solitary journey led him is not known for sure. There is very little independent documentation for the next two years of his exile. Boccaccio in his biography has the poet all over the place in this period: now in the Casentino, now in the Lunigiana, now in the mountains near Urbino; then at Bologna and Padua and thence to Verona (*Trattatello* 1, para. 74). Bruni in his 1436 *Vita di Dante* has him going straight to Verona after the defeat of the Whites at La Lastra, 'not wanting to waste any more time after the destruction of his hopes' (Bruni 1996: 546). More recent biographers agree that another journey northwards – with residence, perhaps, at Treviso and visits to Venice and Padua – is quite likely (*Bemrose 2000: 85; Petrocchi 1984: 98–9, 1994: 95–7).

Acquaintance with the Veneto, the north-eastern region of Italy, during 1304–6 would be consistent with a number of specific references to the area and its people in Dante's writing during and shortly after these years. As the late fourteenth-century commentator Benevenuto da Imola asserts, one of the poet's hosts then could have been the captain-general of Treviso, Gherardo da Camino (d. 1306). Gherardo is commemorated during the debate about the origins of nobility in the last treatise of the *Convivio* (4. 14. 12); and later, in the *Purgatorio*, the courtier 'Marco the Lombard' – in the midst of decrying the decadence of the contemporary world and of 'the region watered by the Adige and the Po' – finds space to celebrate 'good Gherardo' (*Purg.* 16. 124). In Treviso, too, Dante might by contrast have learned of an example of tyranny and cruelty: Ezzelino (or Azzolino) da Romano, who ruled over the March of Treviso till his death in 1259. Villani calls him 'the cruellest and most terrible tyrant there has been in Christendom', and Dante's *Inferno* shows him boiling in a river of blood (Villani 7. 72; *Inf.* 12. 109–10).

Padua, about 50 kilometres south-east of Treviso, is one of the major cities of the region that Dante could easily have visited at this time. Here he might at least have heard of the work of the Latin poet and proto-humanist Albertino Mussato, who, unlike Dante, was to receive the laurel crown a few years later (1315). Here too – if Benvenuto da Imola is to be believed – Dante could have seen Giotto's recently completed frescoes, especially those of Heaven, Hell and the Last Judgement (as well as the lives of the Virgin and of Christ) in the Scrovegni or 'Arena' Chapel, which were complete by around 1305–6. If so, Giotto's images of the damned could well have had some influence on the poet's representations of Hell; and Dante could have had the artist's command of gesture and expression in mind when describing divinely created art and its ability to make 'speech visible' (*Purg.* 10. 28–96). In any case he goes on explicitly to acknowledge Giotto's supreme earthly reputation in the following canto (*Purg.* 11. 94–6; below, p. 199).

The idea that Dante and Giotto may actually have known each other is one that has attracted a number of imaginative writers, from Vasari (*Lives of the Painters*) on, and it has some credence among modern scholars (Petrocchi 1984: 99; CL 2. 338). It is based not only on their contemporaneity and on Dante's reference in *Purgatorio* 11 (94–6), but also on Benvenuto da Imola's commentary, which notes Giotto's ability to reproduce any natural object realistically and shows the two artists sharing an ancient joke about the nature of human creativity:

*Plate 2*    Detail from the scene of Hell, Last Judgement frescoes at the Scrovegni (Arena) Chapel, Padua, painted by Giotto, c.1302–6. © 1990. Photo SCALA, Florence.

It happened once that while Giotto, still quite young, was painting [frescoes in] a chapel at Padua, in a place where there had formerly been a theatre or arena, Dante visited the place. Giotto showed him great honour and took him to his home, where Dante saw a number of the painter's offspring who were extremely ugly and – not to put too fine a point on it – very like their father. So he asked: 'Noble master, I am amazed that, since you are said to be unrivalled in the art of painting – how can it be that, whilst you create such fair shapes for others, your own are so truly hideous?' Giotto answered him at once with a smile: 'because I produce paintings by day but people at night' ['*quia pingo* (lit. paint) *de die, sed fingo* (lit. make, shape) *de nocte*'] This reply mightily amused Dante, not because it was a new one on him (it can be found in Macrobius's *Saturnalia*) but because it seemed to be born from native wit. (Benvenuto da Imola 1887: 3. 313)

Other features of the Veneto region are recollected in Dante's writing during and shortly after this period. His treatise on the vernacular shows a quite specific knowledge of the dialects of Brescia, Verona, Vicenza, Padua and Treviso, and recall (or invention) of a snatch of ugly verse in order to discredit the Venetians' pride in their language (*DVE* 1. 14. 5–6). A more respectful and vivid portrayal of activity in the great trading city forms an extended simile near the beginning of *Inferno* 21, which describes the business of repairing ships in the Arsenale at Venice (*Inf*. 21. 7–15). Earlier on, at the start of *Inferno* 15, the Veneto has provided another example of ingenuity to compare with the art of Hell. The description of the stone embankments that provide a path above the burning desert in the seventh circle evokes comparisons with those constructed by the Paduans beside the Brenta (*Inf*. 15. 7–9). Both these examples can be seen as part of Dante's own ingenious fiction to make the reader believe he was actually in Hell, and we do not have to assume that he actually witnessed exactly such activities in the Veneto. Nonetheless, the *Commedia* reflects a good deal of familiarity with the landscape of the region and with people whom Dante may have heard of or known during those years of exile leading up to his writing of the poem.

Definite evidence places Dante close to the border of Tuscany in the autumn of 1306. Two documents of 6 October 1306 mention 'Dante Alegerii de Florentia' as official representative of a noble family of the Val di Magra – on the western slopes of the Apuan Alps – in their negotiations with the local bishop (at Castelnuovo di Magra) over the control of castles in the area (Piattoli 1950: 116–25). Dante's employers and hosts were the Malaspini family, an ancient clan that held territory in the Lunigiana (on the borders of present-day Tuscany and Liguria) and exercised political and military influence in Tuscany and beyond. The Marchese Moroello Malaspina, who features on several occasions in Dante's work, was a particularly prominent and successful member of the family and became *podestà* of Bologna in 1298, *capitano del popolo* of Pistoia in 1306, and leader of the Tuscan Guelfs in 1307. If Dante was associated with the family in 1306 (he may have met Moroello much earlier in Florence, in 1288), this would further reinforce his detachment from the cause of the White Guelf cause, since Moroello had been attacking the Whites in the Pistoia area since 1302 and captured the city from them in 1306. Dante, perhaps with a touch of *schadenfreude* for his former allies, later has a damned soul rejoice in their defeat. In the circle of the thieves, Moroello is celebrated as a force of nature, 'a thunderbolt in the midst of murky, churning cloud', drawn by the god of war out of the Val di Magra and descending upon Pistoia from the savage peaks of the Apuan Alps (*Inf*. 24. 145–50). Dante was also to reply on Moroello's behalf to a sonnet from a contemporary Tuscan poet, Cino of Pistoia, and around 1308 would send him one of his own poems from the Casentino (*Letters*, no. 4, with the *canzone* 'Amor, da che convien'). He would also use the presence of another member of the Malaspini clan (Currado) in Purgatory, in order to celebrate at some length the family's fame and their 'prowess with the purse and with the sword' (*Purg.* 8. 121–32).

Such evidence about Dante's hosts during his exile raises questions about motives on both sides: what was in it for each of them? For the hosts, being protectors and patrons of a writer and rhetorician such as Dante (and one with some experience of politics) would have some immediate practical advantages: they might employ his skills in diplomacy and negotiation, as the Malaspini obviously did. Or in the longer term, did they expect their fame and name to be perpetuated in their guest's writing? The Malaspini and the Caminesi are not much mentioned now, but they would hardly be heard of at all if Dante had not included them in the cast of the *Commedia* and his other works. For Dante, on the other hand, there was not just other people's salty bread and the grim trek up and down their stairs (*Par.* 17. 58–60); there was also the opportunity to get a hearing for his work and even the possibility of help to return to Florence. The influence of the Malaspini in Tuscany could well have worked to the latter end, and it may be no coincidence that the poem sent by Dante to Moroello along with his letter concludes as a kind of appeal to return to Florence (above, p. 23).

A lingering hope of return to his native city in 1307–8 may also be suggested by the few pieces of evidence we have for Dante's journeys during those years. The letter to Moroello speaks of having left the Malaspini court and 'set foot by the streams of the Arno'. The attached poem (FB no. 89) speaks of being in the midst of the peaks and calls itself a 'song out of the mountains'. This may indicate that the poet was in the Casentino, the upper valley of the Arno on the opposite (eastern) side of Tuscany, where he was to return as a guest of the Guidi family in 1311.

By the end of 1308, however, it is possible that Dante had circled around to the west of Tuscany again, since a document dated 21 October mentions one Giovanni 'son of Dante Alighieri of Florence' as witness to a financial deal in Lucca (Piattoli 1950: 325–6). We cannot be wholly sure about this Giovanni di Dante: unlike his brothers, Pietro (d. 1364) and Jacopo (d. 1349); he does not appear further in any extant records, and he was not known as a writer – perhaps choosing a safer career in trade. Nor does his presence in the city necessarily mean that his father or family were there as well. Yet this scrap of evidence reinforces the vague prophecy that Dante voices through the soul of the Lucchese poet Bonagiunta in canto 24 of the *Purgatorio*. There, speaking as if at the fictional date of the *Commedia* (1300), Bonagiunta first fixes his eye on 'Dante', then murmurs 'something that sounds like "Gentucca"', and then in response to the pilgrim's invitation explains that she is a woman who will make Lucca 'pleasing to you' (*Purg.* 24. 43–8). 'Gentucca' was the name of several Lucchese noblewomen, and there is one whose age in 1300 and 1308 tallies with the description. The 'pleasure' that Bonagiunta mentions, however, is much more likely to be that of friendship and support than of a love-affair in Lucca.

It may also be no coincidence that this tribute to Lucca occurs at a point in the *Commedia* immediately before the text makes one of its most emphatic statements about Dante's role as a vernacular poet (*Purg.* 24. 48–63). The city had received two somewhat discreditable references in the *Inferno* (18. 115–26, 21. 37–49), but despite its alliance with the Black Guelfs it did not share anything like the degree of contempt that is there showered upon Florence and Pisa. Moreover, Moroello Malaspina, Dante's patron in the Lunigiana, was a respected figure among the citizens of Lucca, having recently commanded their forces in the attack on Pistoia – and it was not until March 1309 that Florentine exiles were banned from the city. Around 1307–9, then, Lucca may have provided an 'island of creativity' for the writing of the *Inferno*, which was under way by this time (Petrocchi 1984: 155; Bemrose 2000: 112).

If Dante had been in Lucca, he would have had to leave, along with the other Florentine exiles, in March 1309. One would like to think that he then found somewhere close at hand (perhaps again with the Malaspini?) where he could keep his head down over the next year or so and get on with the *Inferno*. But from 1309 until the autumn of 1310 is one of the most obscure periods of his exile; and several of his early biographers and commentators claim that at this time he went yet further afield. Giovanni Villani, the chronicler, in the oldest biographical sketch of the poet, asserts that Dante studied in Bologna 'and then in Paris' (Villani 10. 136); whilst Boccaccio sets out the following itinerary:

> Having seen his return route [to Florence] blocked on all sides and his hopes growing emptier by the day, he quit not only Tuscany but Italy itself, crossed, as he was able to do, the mountains that divide it from France and travelled to Paris, where he devoted himself entirely to the study of both philosophy and theology – regaining too the command of other fields of knowledge which, perhaps as a result of other preoccupations, had deserted him. (Boccaccio, *Trattatello* 1, para. 75)

This portrayal of Dante around 1309–10 as a kind of early EU visiting scholar is very attractive. Although it does not explain how he might have supported himself on this study trip, it does go some way towards answering the question of what the appeal of such a long journey would be. Dante, it has to be said, was not the most Francophile of poets, despite his receptivity to French culture and his friendship with Charles Martel (above, p. 17). Yet residence in Paris would have given him access to the richest intellectual resources available in Europe at the time and could have proved a vital stimulus to the continuation of the *Commedia*. Is it a possibility? Anglo-Saxon scholars seem especially reluctant to give it any credence. Bemrose asserts (2000: 14) that 'there is not a shred of evidence that Dante ever set foot outside central and northern Italy'; whilst the American *Dante Encyclopedia* does not even carry an article on Paris or its university. Some Italian commentators, on the other hand, seem rather more willing at least to entertain the idea; and perhaps Villani, Boccaccio and commentators such as Benvenuto da Imola and Francesco da Buti together may constitute at least a 'shred of evidence', along with the references to the Rhone valley, Arles and specific features of the University of Paris at points in the *Commmedia* (*Inf.* 9. 112–17; *Par.* 10. 136–8; Petrocchi 1984: 103; CL 1. xliii).

If Dante had been in France around 1309–10, he would have been closer to events which related to several of his major concerns: the papacy and the empire. Election of a French pope, Clement V, in 1305 had been accompanied by the transfer of the papacy from Rome to Avignon – a move that was 'of enormous significance', and a matter of concern to Dante and other Italian writers (Holmes 1986: 182–5). In the autumn of 1309 the establishment of the papacy in its new centre of power was followed by the preliminaries to a major council: the Council of Vienne, near Avignon in the Rhone valley (1311–12). Both Villani and Dante believed that Clement V was merely an ally (or worse) of the French king, Philip IV (Villani 9. 80; *Inf.* 19. 82–7). Both of them, however, knew that, at least initially, Clement resisted Philip's pressure to support a French candidate (Charles of Valois, the 'Judas' of Florence) as Holy Roman Emperor when the throne of the empire became vacant in 1308. It was also known in Italy that, following the coronation of Henry of Luxemburg (Henry VII) at Aix-la-Chapelle in January 1309, Clement had been quick to give his support, informally in June 1309, then through formal confirmation in July (Villani 9. 102). For Dante this potential alliance of pope and Holy Roman Emperor promised a new beginning.

## The garden of the empire: Dante, Henry VII and Italy, 1310–13

At evening on the first day of their ascent of Mount Purgatory Dante and Virgil are led towards a green valley, which is a temporary resting place for them and for a number of Italian and European rulers, two of them emperors (*Purg.* 7. 8). Their guide here is the thirteenth-century poet Sordello, who was born near Mantua and who in the previous canto has eagerly greeted and embraced Virgil as a fellow-citizen (*Purg.* 6. 74–5). This celebration of shared citizenship prompts from Dante an extended and well-known lament for the contrasting state of contemporary Italy, where sorrow has come to stay: the ship in a storm; 'no queen ruling provinces but a whore'; a land where, far from embracing each other, those who live in the same city are at each other's throats; a nation which is now like a wild, riderless horse since its people will not let an emperor sit in the saddle (*Purg.* 6. 76–96). From rebuking the unruly steed, Dante then turns to reproach its absent rider, the Holy Roman Emperor Albert I (elected in 1298 but never crowned in Rome), whilst calling for vengeance upon him for abandoning Italy and thus laying waste the 'garden of the empire' (97–105).

Dante's lament at the end of *Purg.* 6 refers to Albert's assassination (1308) as an act of divine judgement and to the need for his successor to pay due heed to this sign (100–2). It is thus likely to have been written some time between October 1308, when Henry of Luxembourg was elected emperor, and May 1310, when it became clear that he was indeed going to appear as emperor in Italy. It poses urgent questions about the true nature of community, citizenship and allegiance, at the local level of the city-state and in the wider context of Europe and the empire. As such, it forms a sombre prelude to the concerns expressed over the next two cantos in the so-called 'Valley of the Princes' (*Purg.* 7. 8) – concerns which demonstrate 'engagement with the political ills of a wider European order, stretching from England to Sicily and from Aragon to Bohemia' (Keen 2003: 171).

What did it mean, though, for Dante to call Italy 'the garden of the empire', and what kind of promise was there that it might be restored by an emperor such as Henry VII? The kingdom of Italy (*Regnum Italiae*) had been part of the Frankish empire under Charlemagne (800–14). Its link with the Holy Roman Empire in Germany had been re-established since 962 with varying degrees of success by the Saxon Otto I and his successors; and two of the Hohenstaufen emperors, Frederick I Barbarossa (1152–90) and Frederick II (1198–1250), made serious attempts to assert imperial power in the peninsula (Hyde 1973: 38–48, 94–104). Yet the rapid political and economic development of the city-states in northern Italy (especially during the period 1150–1250), the expansion of the papacy's territorial ambitions, and the establishment of the French Angevin empire in the south (from 1266 on) all combined to weaken the status and influence of the empire. By the time of Dante's political maturity and exile it was rather doubtful whether the emperor could exercise real power in Italy – let alone resolve internal conflicts like those diagnosed by the poet in canto 6 of the *Purgatorio*.

This, however, was what Henry of Luxembourg sought to do. Since his election in 1308, he had gained, at least for the time being, the support of Clement V at Avignon and agreement that he should eventually be crowned in Rome (in February 1312). In the summer of 1310 he sent his ambassadors to the parts of Italy that were still nominally under his control (the northern provinces, including Tuscany), signifying his intention to assert his rights and bring peace to the *Regnum Italicum*. In September of that year Clement V issued an encyclical urging the Italians to recognize and welcome the new emperor. In October Henry crossed the Alps by the Mont Cenis Pass and on 23 December entered Milan, where on 6 January he was invested with the ancient iron crown of the kingdom.

For Dante and a number of others it looked like a new beginning. A fellow White Guelf, Dino Compagni, described Henry's arrival in almost apocalyptic terms, as he passed 'from city to city, making peace as if he were an angel of God and receiving fealty' (Compagni 1986: 86–7). Dante, writing as 'a Florentine undeservedly in exile', addressed the rulers of Italy using even more rousing terms, in an encyclical of his own shortly after the papal proc-lamation (*Letters*, no. 5, September 1310). In this open letter he greets this 'welcome time, in which the signs of comfort and peace appear', seeing Henry VII as a rising sun, 'another Moses' and a new 'Caesar' who will restore fertil-ity and fruitfulness to what *Purgatorio* 6 called 'the garden of the empire'. He also exhorts the oppressed to hope and (important in view of what was to follow) warns against resistance to this divinely appointed authority. It was an occasion on which Dante clearly identifies the emperor in Christ-like terms and presents himself in a kind of prophetic role (*Scott 1996: 43–4). This was the first of three 'political' letters that Dante was to write in support of Henry VII during 1310–11. In the third of them, addressed to Henry himself the following spring (17 April 1311), he mentions having formally paid homage to the emperor, and it thus seems likely that he was either at Milan for the coronation in January 1311 or had met him earlier during his progress through Piedmont and Lombardy (*Letters*, pp. 90, 101).

By the spring of 1311, however, Dante was watching events unfold from the upper Arno valley in the Casentino, where he was probably the guest of Guido Novello di Battifolle at Poppi. This is where he may have composed much of the *Purgatorio* and where he certainly wrote two of his later political letters. In these his tone is markedly less confident. The first, dated 31 March 'in the first year of the most auspicious arrival of the Emperor Henry in Italy', is addressed to his fellow-citizens as 'the vile Florentines within the city' (*Letters*, pp. 66, 76, 77, 81). Florence, under Black Guelf rule, had been far from enthusiastic about the emperor's venture and had suggested as early as 1309 that 'it was enough for him to be king of Germany, whereas the trip to Italy seemed very uncertain and dangerous' (Compagni 1986: 86). By the time Dante wrote this letter, the Florentines had already (May 1310) put themselves at the head of the Guelf League of city-states with 4,000 cavalry, opposing the emperor's Italian campaign (Compagni 1986: 95–6; Menache 1998: 161). He thus heaps on them the kind of invective that he had already directed against the city in the *Inferno* and in canto 6 of the *Purgatorio*. Portrayed here as rebels driven by avarice, futile defenders of 'false liberty' and barbarian offspring of Fiesole (said to have been destroyed by Julius Caesar), the Florentines are warned about the imminent descent upon them of the imperial eagle, 'terrible in gold' (*Letters*, pp. 70, 79).

In the second of these letters, barely two weeks later, Dante actively encourages the eagle to strike. Writing to Henry himself on 17 April 1311, he urges the emperor not to delay in Lombardy, but to hit at the heart of the opposition: Florence: 'she is the viper that turns against the vitals of her own mother; she is the sick sheep that infects the flock of her lord with her contagion; she is the abandoned and unnatural Myrrha, inflamed with passion for the embraces of her father Cinyras' (*Letters*, pp. 97, 104). The allusion to Ovid's story of Myrrha (*Met.* 10) is a barb directed at the corrupt closeness of Florence's alliance with the papacy. Very shortly before this letter was written, the Tuscan communes had petitioned the Pope (1 April 1311) to prevent the 'king of Germany' from entering the province; whilst by the end of 1311 the Guelf League would vow at Bologna 'to return the province of Lombardy entirely to the party of the Holy Mother Church' with the aid of the pope and the French (Menache 1998: 164).

Over the course of 1311 Henry was having to deal with resistance from several cities in Lombardy. He arrived in Tuscany only in the spring of 1312, landing at Pisa – one of Tuscany's staunchly Ghibelline cities – on 6 March (Villani 10. 37). It is possible that Dante could at this point have taken a break from work on the *Purgatorio*, emerged from his retreat in the Casentino and, like other Florentine exiles, greeted the emperor's arrival at Pisa. But if so, he failed to follow up his previous year's message about dealing with Florence, and Henry departed for Rome on 23 April (Villani 10. 39). By this stage it was becoming depressingly clear that Henry no longer commanded the full support of the papacy. His arrival in Rome was accompanied by violence and disorder, and his coronation as Holy Roman Emperor (29 June) had to take place in the church of St John Lateran because Guelf troops prevented him reaching St Peter's. During the next few months he became embroiled in a conflict of authority with the pope (Clement V) and in hostilities with Robert of Anjou, ruler of the kingdom of Naples, the *miles Papae* ('soldier of the pope') and an ally of the Guelfs (Menache 1998: 166–70). As if in belated response to Dante's letter of the previous year, Henry at last made an abortive attempt to lay siege to Florence (18 September–31 October 1312), but was forced eventually (March 1313) to withdraw to Pisa again. Finally, after a few months of unproductive skirmishing in western Tuscany, he set off south in August 1313 to confront Robert of Anjou but got no further than Buonconvento, near Siena, where he contracted a fever. Here, on 24 August, he died (Villani 10. 47–52).

The mission of Compagni's 'angel of peace' thus ended in disarray and disaster. Nonetheless, the Emperor's good intentions were acknowledged, and his death was widely mourned in western Europe. Many in Italy and elsewhere blamed Clement V for the failure of the imperial venture; and some even accused him of having had Henry poisoned (Menache 1998: 172–3). In the prophecy about his exile half way through the *Paradiso*, Dante sets the virtues of his young Ghibelline patron, Cangrande della Scala of Verona, in contrast to Clement's duplicity, saying that they will become apparent 'before the Gascon betrays the noble Henry' (*Par.* 17. 82). As he wrote the final cantos of the poem, he celebrated once again the role of 'the noble Henry' who 'shall come to set Italy right before she is ready'; and he uses Beatrice's very last words to accuse Clement of treachery towards the emperor and to consign the Avignon pope to the lower reaches of Hell (*Par.* 30. 133–48).

Archaic as it may have been, the notion of the emperor as universal peacekeeper did not die with Henry VII at Buonconvento in 1313. Even a chronicler of the opposite party – Villani – acknowledged that the emperor's campaign in Italy drew the attention not only of western Christendom but 'even of the Saracens and Greeks', claiming that 'according to the experts, had his death not come so soon, he would through his brave and ambitious leadership have been able to conquer the Kingdom [of Naples] and take it away from King Robert [of Anjou]' (Villani 10. 53). The case for the empire continued to be argued by leading political theorists (such as William of Ockham and Marsilius of Padua) on into the fourteenth century; and there were a number of occasions even in the fifteenth and sixteenth centuries when 'religious controversy [such as the Papal Schism and the advent of Protestantism] seems to have revealed a fragility in other polities and restored some credibility to the Emperor's role' (*Black 1992: 92–108).

Dante's own continuing commitment to the imperial cause would be reflected not only in his allocation of a throne to Henry VII in the highest circle of Heaven (*Par.* 30. 133–8), but also in his treatise on universal monarchy, the *Monarchia*. It used to be widely held that the *Monarchia* was composed during Henry VII's Italian campaign or even designed to support it as 'a piece of imperial propaganda'; and several historians are still inclined to this view (Holmes 1997: 52–3; Black 1992: 55, 96). A wider consensus now, however (based on fuller assessment of the manuscript evidence), is that the work was written later in Dante's career – around 1316–17 – and that its thinking is not a political or propagandist aberration but is reconcilable with ideas that he continued to hold to the end (*Mon.* xxxviii–xli; Scott 1996: 49–55; Bemrose 2000: 186–8; *DE* 616).

For this crucial period of Dante's exile, then (around 1310–13), the main evidence we have about his immediate responses to the political hopes raised by Henry VII's advent are the three letters of 1310–11 and the political episodes and imagery of the *Purgatorio*, at least from canto 6 onwards (Scott 1996: 123, 133–4 etc.). After the indication in the two letters of spring 1311 that he was in the Casentino then, 'beneath the springs of the Arno', there is no precise evidence to indicate where he went from there or where he was during the later stages of Henry VII's campaign. Bruni – who knew about Dante's invective against the Florentines in the letter of March 1311 and his encouragement of Henry to strike against them – claims that 'nonetheless, devotion to his native city affected him so much that when the Emperor attacked Florence and encamped at its gates, he did not wish to be there' (Bruni 1996: 547). It could be that he remained in the Casentino throughout this period and that this relatively quiet, wooded and mountainous area of eastern Tuscany formed an 'island of creativity' for the composition of the *Purgatorio* (Petrocchi 1984: 155). There are certainly several striking and sustained evocations of the valley's landscape and its inhabitants (though not always complimentary ones) in the *Purgatorio* (5. 94–129, 14. 16–48).

42

As the 'last act of the Emperor's tragedy' (Petrocchi 1984: 154) began to unfold over the summer and autumn of 1312, Dante may have been quite a distant spectator. Yet, if he was then primarily engaged with the middle or later cantos of the *Purgatorio*, it would not simply have been as a way of escaping the brute facts on the ground. Those cantos themselves at several important points address thorny political problems, such as imperial and papal claims (*Purg.* 16), the ambitions of the French monarchy (20) and the leadership of the church (32–3). And the memory of Henry VII, the 'alto Arrigo', would later continue to inform the political vision of the *Paradiso* and inspire the political debate of the *Monarchia*.

There would also have been practical problems for the poet during the later stages of Henry's campaign. Bruni points out that he had made return to Florence yet more difficult by his recent denunciation of the rulers of the city – so that following the emperor's death: 'he lost all hope and spent the rest of his life in extreme poverty, living in various places around Lombardy, Tuscany and Romagna with the support of various princes, until finally he fetched up at Ravenna where his life came to an end' (Bruni 1996: 547). Bruni's reference to Lombardy reminds us of the 'first refuge' of Dante's exile at the princely court of Verona (*Par.* 17. 70–2). It was an attractive destination, and the poet might have made his way there as early as the summer of 1312 (Petrocchi 1984: 154; Bemrose 2000: 187–9). If so, this would have been the start of a relationship with the city and the court that was to last for much of the final decade of his life.

## 'So I turned to Verona': 1312(?)–18

Verona had several advantages for Dante as a place of refuge in the later part of 1312. Henry of Luxembourg had reached Rome in May and would turn his attention to Florence in September. Hope of return to Florence was certainly not yet lost, but it might have made sense for the poet – in view of his high-profile support for the emperor – to seek a securely Ghibelline environment. His host in the Casentino, Guido di Battifolle, was a supporter of the Guelfs and would eventually (in 1316) become Robert of Anjou's 'vicar' (representative) in Florence (Villani 10. 79). On the other hand, the rulers of Verona were firmly devoted to the imperial cause. On Henry VII's arrival in Lombardy (December 1310), Alboino della Scala and his younger brother, Cangrande, had declared their allegiance; and early the following year they had been appointed as imperial vicars of Verona. Following the death of Alboino – to whose lack of distinction

43

Dante had made a disparaging reference in the *Convivio* (4. 16. 6) – he was succeeded (in November 1311) by the altogether more glamorous and adventurous Cangrande, who, early the next year, had gained a further sign of Henry's favour by being appointed imperial vicar of Vicenza (11 February 1312).

Cangrande della Scala (1291–1329) had a relatively short but brilliant career as *signore* of Verona. In the prophecy about the years of his exile in *Paradiso* 17, Dante continues the tribute to his elder brother (Bartolomeo) by describing more fully the sparkling qualities of Cangrande, who had been only 12 or 13 at the time of the poet's first visit to Verona in 1303–4. Here, in a eulogy that may well date from near the end of his second stay in Verona (1312?–18), Dante has his crusading ancestor foretell 'notable deeds' on the part of Cangrande: 'sparks of valour' to be seen even before the year when 'the Gascon (Pope Clement V) betrays the noble Henry'; and generosity that will be acknowledged even by his enemies (78, 82–7). This ancestor (Cacciaguida) then concludes by admonishing Dante to:

> 'Rest hopes in him and in his acts of kindness;
> by him the lives of many will be changed:
> the rich will be cast down; the poor raised up.
>     Carry this news of him etched on your mind,
> but not to be disclosed'; and he said things
> incredible even if seen directly.
>
> (*Par.* 17. 88–93)

In his only direct reference to Cangrande in the *Commedia*, Dante thus uses the kind of prophetic and messianic language that are to be found in his other apocalyptic prophecies, such as those about Henry VII in the letter of 1310 (*Letters*, pp. 42–62). Other contemporaries were less impressed, but still acknowledged the energy and power of a ruler whose name ('Cangrande') means 'Great Dog'. Villani, after describing his death at a banquet following the capture of Treviso (July 1329), asks his readers to 'take note that this was the greatest, strongest and wealthiest tyrant there had been in Lombardy since the time of Ezzelino da Romano' (d. 1259; Villani 11. 138).

As the frequent references to his exploits in Villani's chronicle show, Cangrande was a dominant figure in Lombardy during the second and third decades of the fourteenth century: a major ally of the empire (of Henry VII and later of Louis of Bavaria), and a highly effective protector of Ghibelline exiles (Villani 10. 14 and 89, 11. 102). Such allegiances and activities would have made him an appropriate host for Dante in 1312–18. Dante may not, however, have been solely based in Verona throughout these six years. For two of them at least (c.1314–16), the ascendancy of Florence and the Guelfs in Tuscany was again seriously challenged. The Ghibelline leader Uguiccione della Faggiuola had been elected *capitano del popolo* at Pisa in 1313 immediately after the death of Henry VII; and he gained control also of Lucca in June 1314 (Villani 10. 54 and 60). He then defeated the Florentines and Tuscan Guelfs at the battle of Montecatini (29 August 1315) but was expelled from both Lucca and Pisa the following year, when he took refuge in Verona and continued in Cangrande's service until his death in 1320 (Villani 10. 70–3, 78, 86 and 121). Dante never mentions Uguiccione, although Boccaccio claims that Dante was Uguiccione's guest 'in the mountains near Urbino' and dedicated the *Inferno* to him (Boccaccio, *Trattatello* 1, paras. 74, 193). But the dramatic turn of events in Tuscany over which the Ghibelline leader presided could once again have revived the poet's hopes of a return to Florence and might even have led him to revisit Lucca, where he had been six years or so before (above, pp. 35–6).

If Verona was Dante's main base from about 1312 to 1318, it would have provided a receptive audience for some of his most important writing. It was around 1312–13 that he completed the *Purgatorio*, whose apocalyptic final cantos (32–3) culminate in a powerful prophecy of a divinely sanctioned world-leader and reformer. By 1314–15 he had begun work on the last *cantica* of the *Commedia*, the *Paradiso*; and his letters in those years reflect some urgent political and personal concerns. In April 1314, Clement V, the 'betrayer' of Henry VII, died at Avignon, and between May and June Dante addressed a public letter to the Italian cardinals, urging the papacy to return to Rome (below, p. 148). At the end of May 1315, he was actively considering an amnesty that had been offered to exiles by the Florentines on the 19th of that month. In a letter addressed to 'a friend in Florence' he indignantly rejects the terms of the amnesty (payment of a fine and a ritual of penance), refusing as the 'preacher of justice' to 'pay money to those that wronged him, as though they had deserved well of him'. This is not the path, he concludes defiantly, by which he will return home (*ad patriam*). Yet he cannot bring himself to close the door completely and expresses the hope that 'through yourself in the first place and then through other persons, some other [way] may be found which does not demean the fame and honour of Dante' (*Letters*, pp. 157, 159). *Monarchia*, too, is probably a work of the later Verona years (perhaps as late as 1317), and one that, with its insistence upon the necessity and rights of the empire, would have been well received

45

by the disappointed supporters of Henry VII. Its ideas about the papacy and temporal power (*Mon.* 3) were also highly topical, since August 1316 saw the election of the last pope of Dante's lifetime: John XXII, who proved to be a fierce defender of papal authority and an avowed enemy of both the poet and his Lombard patron (below, p. 48).

Another letter – which (if genuine) probably dates from 1316 – points explicitly to Verona and its ruler. This is the much-discussed 'Epistle to Cangrande', in which the author dedicates the *Paradiso* to the ruler of Verona and offers 'something by way of introduction' first to the *Commedia* as a whole and then to its third part, with some close reading of the opening of *Par.* 1 (*Letters*, no. 10; below, p. 226). Whether or not the letter is actually by Dante (and the scholars may never reach a consensus on that), its opening gives a vivid impression of Cangrande's reputation as it might well have been perceived by a poet in search of a patron:

> Even as the Queen of the South sought Jerusalem (1 Kings 10: 1–13; Matthew 12: 42) and as Pallas [Athene] sought Helicon (Ovid, *Metamorphoses* 5. 254), so did I seek Verona, in order to examine with my own trusty eyes the things of which I had heard. And there was I witness of your splendour, there was I witness and partaker of your bounty; and whereas I had formerly suspected the reports to be somewhat unmeasured, I afterwards recognized that it was the facts themselves that were beyond measure. (*Letters*, pp. 167, 196)

In this opening section of the letter, where Cangrande himself is most directly addressed, it has been pointed out that the issue 'of greatest note may be the extended proof [para. 2–3] that an inferior (that is, Dante) can legitimately call himself the "friend" of a social superior (Cangrande)' (*DE* 349B). The author is thus concerned both to assert his own worth, as one 'endowed with a certain divine liberty', and to defend himself against 'presumption' (*Letters*, pp. 169, 197).

The actual extent of Dante's friendship with Cangrande remains uncertain – except for the legends and anecdotes that proliferated from the fourteenth century onwards. So does the extent of Cangrande's interest in the *Commedia*, and so do the reasons for the poet's departure from Verona for Ravenna in 1318. By that time Dante – perhaps mid-way through the composition of the *Paradiso* – may have found the social and political atmosphere at Verona uncongenial for work on the remainder of the poem, and the cultural milieu at Ravenna might have been more attractive (Petrocchi 1984: 191–2). Certainly, Cangrande's main concerns were to establish local dominance in

Lombardy. According to Villani, he was busy attacking both Cremona and Padua during 1317–18 (Villani 10. 88–9, 91 and 100); and that would not have been a campaign of much interest to Dante. On the other hand they were both still in the same anti-papal, pro-imperial boat. Dante's main enemy at this time, Pope John XXII (*Par.* 18. 118–36), was also deeply hostile to Cangrande and had gone so far as to excommunicate him on 6 April 1318.

We should, however, be wary of the Pre-Raphaelite image of 'Dante at Verona' that was projected by Rossetti – that of the melancholy poet amid philistine courtiers and giggling ladies (*Ellis 1983: 108–12). Verona was far from being an intellectual or literary desert at this time. Like the neighbouring city of Padua, it was a centre of pre-humanist culture, and its Cathedral Library (where Petrarch would later rediscover letters by Cicero) was one of the major resources in Italy and in western Europe at the time (*ED* 6. 973–4). Indeed, Dante did not finally shake the dust of the city from his feet in 1318. On 20 January 1320 he would be back as a visiting lecturer to publish his geographical treatise (the *Quaestio de Aqua et Terra*), which was 'delivered in the presence of the intellectual elite of Verona' (*DE* 734A).

## 'To find peace with its tributaries': Ravenna 1318–21

Well before his arrival there (probably late in 1318) Dante had associated Ravenna with peace and quiet. Among the trees of the Earthly Paradise at the summit of the mountain of Purgatory, he had imagined a gentle breeze blowing with a sound like that of the south-east wind among the pines near the city (*Purg.* 28. 19–21) Amid a more violent wind in the second circle of Hell, his most famous tragic figure, Francesca da Rimini, recalls her birthplace:

> upon the shoreline, where the Po's main stream
> flows down to find peace with its tributaries.
> (*Inf.* 5. 98–9)

Francesca's own end – she and her lover 'staining the world with our blood' – was far from peaceful. Indeed, the whole province of the Romagna in her time (the late thirteenth century) was a byword for ruthless vendettas (Larner 1965: 1–2; Barolini 2000: 20–1). In Dante's circle of fraudulent counsellors (*Inf.* 27) the soul of former Romagnuol warlord Guido da Montefeltro anxiously asks if his countrymen are now at war or peace (*Inf.* 27. 28); and

47

the protagonist is able to reply that although the province 'is not and never was without war in the hearts of its tyrants', it was at peace at the time of his otherworld journey in 1300 (37–9). Immediately after this Dante turns to Francesca's birthplace again and adds that Ravenna has for many years been overshadowed by the eagle, the heraldic emblem of the Polenta family (*Inf.* 27. 40–1).

Francesca's father, Guido il Vecchio da Polenta, had become ruler of Ravenna in 1275, and his successors remained dominant as *signori* there until shortly after Dante's death. Throughout Dante's stay in the city it was ruled by Guido Novello da Polenta (the grandson of Guido il Vecchio), who had come to power in June 1316. Since Ravenna, as a city of the Romagna, was part of the Papal State, Guido Novello owed obedience to the pope's 'vicar', who from 1310 to 1318 was Robert of Anjou. This did not mean, however, that Dante in 1318 was entering a fanatically pro-papal Guelf environment. Robert's overall administration of the province had been corrupt and incompetent, and Guido had on at least one occasion directly opposed him. Indeed, so lukewarm had Guido Novello's support for the papacy been that eventually (in 1322) he was removed from power by the papal vicar and sent into exile. As ruler of Ravenna during this period (1316–22) he seems to have kept a low profile politically; and in contrast to other members of his family 'he openly cultivated peace, scholarship and the arts' (*ED* 4. 580b). Ravenna's peaceful state under the wings of the Polenta eagle at this time also contrasted sharply, as Dante would have been aware, with the turbulent state of Lombardy, which he had just left, and where the new pope (John XXII) and his vicars, Robert of Anjou and Philippe de Valois, were not very successfully attempting to assert their authority against the Ghibelline *signori* (Villani 10. 93–5 and 109–10).

Ravenna's urban landscape, like Verona's, still vividly evokes the city's Roman past. Established as a Roman *municipium* by Augustus in 49 BCE, it had expanded eastward during the following three centuries, and was chosen as an imperial residence by the Western Emperor Honorius in 404. The oldest monuments (such as the mausoleum of Galla Placidia with its superb mosaics, the church of Sant'Apollinare Nuovo, the Arian Baptistery, and the Mausoleum of Theodoric) date from the fifth and early sixth centuries: the end of the Western Empire and the rule of the Gothic kings. Under the Byzantine Emperor Justinian (527–65) the Western Empire (including Italy) was reconquered and Ravenna became the capital of the exarch (the Byzantine governor) from 540 till 751. Before he arrived in Ravenna Dante had celebrated Justinian's achievements by making him a spokesman for the imperial ideal in an early canto of the *Paradiso* (canto 6). Amongst the images of Byzantine power in the city he would very probably have noted especially the vivid portrayal of Justinian and his court at the side of the presbytery in San Vitale, and the equally impressive mosaics in the apse at Sant' Apollinare in Classe depicting the transfiguration of Christ and other subjects (Talbot Rice 1968: 160, 164–7, with plates 138, 140). The latter scene, in a church a short distance south of the city, takes an abstract form – representing the transfigured Christ as a jewelled cross in a starry disc, hovering above the Apostles, who are figured as sheep below. It may have reminded Dante of his own recently composed image of the illuminated cross in *Paradiso* 14; and like other mosaics in Ravenna, Florence and Rome it could have contributed to the imagining of the upper reaches of Heaven in the later cantos of the *Paradiso* (Schnapp 1986: 177–88 and plates 6, 7, 9, 12, 15).

Most of the second half of the *Paradiso* was probably written in Ravenna during the last three years of the poet's life. How much of a race against time this was we do not know for sure, but Boccaccio's dramatic story of the loss and miraculous recovery of the last 13 cantos perhaps implies that completion of the poem came close to the time of Dante's death (*Trattatello* 1, paras. 183–9). Nor is it known how much direct encouragement he received from his host, Guido Novello – although Boccaccio describes Guido as 'a noble knight' who, 'having been educated in liberal studies, rated men of worth very highly, and above all those who surpassed others in their learning' (*Trattatello* 1, para. 80). Dante's host seems to have been something of a poet, too: in a fourteenth-century manuscript, now at the library of the Escorial in Spain, a group of six elegantly plaintive *ballate* are clearly attributed to 'Messer Guido Novello de Opulenta [*sic*]'. These are thought to have been written before the time Dante was in Ravenna; and they perhaps reflect, in their dramatizing of the lover's inner conflicts and susceptibilities, something of the influence of Dante's *Vita nuova* (C. Ricci 1965: 514–19).

Ravenna also provided other sources of stimulus and support for Dante's final enterprise. Among a circle of literati from the professions (chiefly medicine and law) and associated with him at this time, there were several who wrote poetry. There was, for example, the Venetian Giovanni Quirini, who spoke of Dante as 'my teacher and master', and who addressed a sonnet to Cangrande (probably after Dante's death) expressing a 'longing' to see *Paradiso* circulated, reinforcing his plea with allusions from canto 9 of the poem (*ED* 4. 864, C. Ricci 1965: 514, 529, 530). In Ravenna itself, Dante's literary circle included both Tuscan exiles and some local professionals, of whom one of the better documented is the notary Menghino Mezzani, who lived until around 1375 and must have been quite young when he met Dante. He is first documented as a notary in 1317, and in later life his literary activity included a number of sonnets on political and other topics and some correspondence with Petrarch (C. Ricci 1965: 240–58). He wrote a Latin epitaph on Dante's death (*ED* 4. 864a), and brief summaries of the *Inferno* and the *Purgatorio* in verse which has been described as 'rather worse than usual'; and he was even said to have written some commentary on the *Commedia* (C. Ricci 1965: 258–9).

Fuller evidence of Dante's intellectual and literary contacts during this period is, however, to be found in his exchange of four Latin verse letters with a professor of classical poetry at the university of Bologna: Giovanni del Virgilio. Giovanni initiated this exchange in 1319 by writing to Dante, rebuking him for 'casting pearls before swine' and writing his great work not in Latin for the 'learned' (*clerus*) but in the vernacular (Dante 1902: 146–9). This first letter concludes by inviting the Florentine poet to write for this learned audience about recent political events and then be presented to 'the applauding schools' at Bologna, where he would receive the laurel crown. Dante seems to have been both amused and intrigued by all this, since he responded to the classicist by, appropriately enough, reviving a classical mode, the pastoral dialogue or 'eclogue', which Virgil himself had used. Here Dante expresses unease about the dangers of visiting Bologna, along with the hope (as in *Par.* 25. 1–9) still of returning to Florence, and finally responds to Giovanni's 'blaming of the words of the *Commedia*' by sending him 10 cantos of the most recent work, presumably the *Paradiso* (Dante 1902: 152–7). The third and fourth of these letters (Giovanni's reply and Dante's answer) are less specific about Dante's work and its reception, but by retaining the dialogue form they create the impression of a supportive social and intellectual group around the poet during this final stage of his career.

Such a group probably included other exiles from Florence and Tuscany; and manuscript notes to the eclogues identify several of Dante's pastoral figures as actual compatriots. There is also evidence that members of Dante's own family – his sons Pietro and Jacopo and his daughter Antonia – had joined him in Ravenna. Pietro, who was later to produce three versions of a commentary on the *Commedia*, is mentioned as *filius Dantis Aldigerii* in a document issued by a church court in Ravenna in January 1321 (C. Ricci 1965: 437–8). Jacopo, who in the early 1320s wrote a less ambitious commentary on the *Inferno*, was also probably in the city, since he sent a summary of the *Commedia* with a dedicatory sonnet to Guido Novello in 1322, very shortly after Dante's death (*DE* 533; C. Ricci 1965: 148–51).

Of the remaining women in Dante's life much less is known. His daughter Antonia and his wife Gemma may have been in Ravenna before his death (Petrocchi 1984: 199). Antonia entered a convent there, taking (as some kind of comment on her father's poetry?) the name of 'Sister Beatrice'; and she is referred to as 'daughter of the late Dante Alighieri' in a document of 1371, some time after her death (C. Ricci 1965: 443). Dante's wife, Gemma Donati, whom he had married around 1285, outlived him and is mentioned along with Pietro, Jacopo and Antonia in a transaction of 1332. It is not known whether she was with Dante in Ravenna or whether she followed him elsewhere during his exile. What kind of marriage it was can only be imagined – as it often has. Boccaccio asserts that it was arranged to console the poet for the death of Beatrice (*Trattatello* 1, paras. 44–5), but there is documentary evidence (from 1277) to show that the couple had been formally betrothed long before that (Petrocchi 1984: 12). The *Cambridge Companion to Dante* asserts that the marriage 'in point of fact, was far less unhappy than Boccaccio . . . thought', although it does not cite any evidence for this 'fact' (Mazzotta 1993: 3). Perhaps (to offer some more pure speculation) the problem that Gemma's marriage faced was the kind of infidelity that the poet's wife in Seamus Heaney's Dantean poem 'An Afterwards' dourly records:

> 'You left us first and then those books behind.'
> (Heaney 1979: 44)

Two very different journeys mark the years immediately before Dante finally left those books behind. The first, in 1320, led him back to Verona (above, p. 47). Here, according to the text itself, on 20 January, in the small church of Sant' Elena (on the northern side of the cathedral), he delivered to an audience of clergy his last work in Latin, the *Quaestio de Aqua et Terra* (Dante 1904: 422). This short treatise is based – like all medieval cosmography – on the concept of a universe with the Earth at its centre and with part of the Northern Hemisphere considered to be Earth's only habitable area (see diagram 3, below, p. 125). It addresses the question of 'whether water, in its own sphere, that is in its natural circumference, was in any part higher than the earth which emerges from the waters, and which we commonly call the habitable quarter' (Dante 1904: 390). It reflects Dante's aspiration to the status of a philosophic and scientific writer and his ambition

– as in the imagining of the cosmos in the three parts of the *Commedia* – to describe as precisely as possible the structure of the universe within which the human journey took place (*DE* 734A–735B).

Dante himself took several other journeys during these last years of his life: thus the *Quaestio* begins by saying that the scientific problem it addresses originated 'when I was in Mantua' (Dante 1904: 389). And it was a mission to Venice in the summer of 1321 that immediately preceded and may even have caused the poet's death. Dante's host, Guido Novello da Polenta, had for several years been in dispute with his powerful neighbour about trade and shipping; and matters appear to have come to a head in July 1321, when it looked as if the Venetians, in alliance with the ruler of Forlì, were about to attack Ravenna (*DE* 4. 580a–b). According to Villani, Guido Novello then in late July or early August dispatched Dante as ambassador to Venice in the hope of achieving an agreement, and the poet died shortly afterwards, possibly from an illness (perhaps malaria) contracted during the journey. Villani gives the date of his death as July 1321 (Villani 10. 136), but, from the evidence of those who were nearer at hand, it seems more likely that it occurred in September, probably between the 13th and the 14th of the month. He was buried in a stone coffin in the porch of the Franciscan church. Boccaccio says that Guido Novello ensured that 'poetic ornaments adorned his bier' (possibly the crown of laurel and a book, as the late fourteenth-century poet Antonio Pucci claims) and delivered a funeral eulogy (*Trattatello* 1, paras. 87–8).

It was the end and the beginning of the story. The legend of Dante's life and the cult of the poet-theologian were quick to develop, and this chapter will conclude by sampling three of the early tributes to his work.

Two of the epitaphs composed for the poet at this time were by members of his intellectual circle: the notary of Ravenna, Menghino Mezzani, and the Bolognese academic, Giovanni del Virgilio (above, pp. 24, 50). Giovanni – recollecting his recent exchange of letters with the poet, the debate about the vernacular and his bid to make Dante the laureate of Bologna – commemorates him as follows:

> Dante lies here: the theologian skilled in every form of teaching that Philosophy nourishes in her bright bosom, the glory of the muses, the most loved vernacular author; and his fame strikes from pole to pole. In both lay and learned terms [vernacular and Latin] he allotted places to the dead and spheres of authority to the twin swords [empire and papacy]. Of late he was celebrating pastoral life with his Pierian pipes; but envious Atropos [the death-bringing Fate], alas,

cut off that happy work. Florence, a cruel homeland to her poet, ungratefully yielded him only the sad fruit of exile; while kind Ravenna delights in having received him into the protection of the noble lord Guido Novello. In the year of Our Lord one thousand, three hundred and three times seven, on the ides of September, he turned again to his stars. (my translation; original in Dante 1902: 174)

The contrast between the 'cruel homeland' (*patria cruda*) of Florence and 'kind Ravenna' recurs in other tributes; and Boccacccio was to develop it at length in his biography of the poet (*Trattatello* 1, paras. 92–109). In a commemorative *canzone* of three stanzas (*Su per la costa, Amor, de l'alto monte*) written shortly after Dante's death, his friend, correspondent and 'dearest brother' Cino da Pistoia (1270–c. 1336) moves, like Giovanni del Virgilio, from celebrating the poet's lofty achievements to condemning the actions of his native city:

> Up there, Love, on the crags of that high peak,
> using the skills and style of poets' speech,
> who can still climb,
> now that the wings of genius lie broken?
>   I know for sure the waters have run dry
> within that spring where all who gazed might see
> their flaws exposed,
> should they look carefully upon that glass.
>   O, just, true God who pardons graciously
> all those who reach repentance at the end,
> take this keen soul,
> who tended all throughout life the plant
> of love, to Beatrice's arms at last.
>
> [. . .]
>
>   My poem, seeing Florence so denuded
> of all her hopes, go to her now and say
> she may well grieve,
> for now indeed the goat's kept from the grass.
>   And thus the prophecy that so foretold
> has come to pass, Florence; take it to heart;
> and if you can
> know your great loss, weep for its bitterness;
>   whilst wise Ravenna, which now guards

> your treasure, celebrates it joyfully
> and wins great praise.
> May God almighty with his vengeance then
> bring desolation on your unjust race.
> (my translation of the first and third stanzas;
> original in Contini 1960: 2. 689–90)

As befits a poet who was deeply versed in Dante's 'new style', Cino (below, p. 121) develops his tribute through a series of allusions to the *Commedia*. The 'high peak' of the first line recalls not only the mythical mountains of Apollo and the Muses (*Par.* 1. 16–18) but also Mount Purgatory, where Dante encounters, amongst many others, the souls of contemporary poets (*Purg.* 24, 26). The 'keen soul' (my translation) which Cino commends to the keeping of Beatrice at the end of the first stanza is, in the original, *quest'anima bivolca* – literally 'this ploughing soul'. The phrase echoes the simile through which Dante (as adventurous and challenging poet addressing the readers who can still follow him) compares his venture to that of Jason when he ploughed the earth to sow the dragon's teeth (*Par.* 2. 10–18; below, p. 204). Cino's turning of the poem towards Florence at the opening of the final stanza is reminiscent of Dante's conclusions to several of his exile poems, notably his 'song from the mountains', which also describes Florence as 'denuded', though of pity rather than hope (above, p. 23). Representing the Florentines as a goat 'kept from the grass' later in the stanza is a brilliantly barbed touch, since the 'prophecy' which is thus 'fulfilled' was actually the wish of Dante's Brunetto (*Inf.* 15. 72; below, p. 137). The stress upon exile at the end of this tribute is also personally appropriate, since Cino himself had experienced banishment from his native city, Pistoia, from 1303 to 1306 and had mentioned his own exile in a sonnet addressed to Dante (FB no. 88a).

   To conclude the obituary tributes, here is a voice from within Florence itself, and one that was in sympathy with the Black Guelfs who had exiled Dante. Born in some time before 1276, Giovanni Villani, the chronicler, was a near contemporary of Dante, although he outlived Dante by more than twenty years. Villani was particularly active in Florentine politics during the 1320s and was elected prior on three occasions between 1316 and 1328. His *Cronica* was a lengthy enterprise (1322–48), which was continued by his younger brother Matteo and his nephew Filippo (Aquilecchia 1979: ix–xxii; Green 1972: 9–43; *DE* 858–9). Villani's political opposition to Dante is evident even in the tribute translated below, especially when he deals with the poet's views of Florence. Yet Villani was by no means fanatical in his support for the Black Guelfs, and in his assessment of Dante (in effect the earliest biography of the poet) he can hardly be ranked amongst Cino's 'unjust race' of Florentines. He is probably wrong about several things (including the month of Dante's death and the place of his burial); yet he remains the first guide to the landmarks of Dante's life. It therefore seems appropriate to give this Florentine writer, writing in the poet's own vernacular, the final word:

In the July of this same year [1321] Dante Alighieri of Florence died in the city of Ravenna in the Romagna after returning from a mission to Venice in the service of the Polenta rulers with whom he was staying; and he was buried at Ravenna with great honour in the robes of a poet and a great man of learning, in front of the cathedral porch. He died in exile from the commune of Florence and at the age of about fifty-six. Dante was a Florentine citizen of ancient and honourable descent from the district of Porta San Piero and was a neighbour of ours. The reason for his exile from Florence was that, when Lord Charles of Valois of the House of France came to Florence in 1301 and threw out the Whites (as has been mentioned already under that year), this same Dante had been one of the main governors of our city and was of that party, although he was a Guelf. Thus, guiltless of anything else, he was expelled and banished from Florence along with the White party; and he went off to study at Bologna, and then at Paris, and then to other parts of the world.

This man was hugely erudite in almost all fields of learning, despite being a lay person. He was a supreme poet and philosopher, able to compose and versify perfectly as a [Latin] rhetorician, as well as being the noblest of the exponents of poetry in the vernacular. In verse [he was] supreme, displaying a finer and more polished style than has ever appeared in our language before his time or since. In his youth he wrote the book called *Vita nuova* on the subject of love, and then in exile he composed over twenty highly distinguished moral and erotic *canzoni*. Amongst other things, he also wrote three excellent public letters: one he sent to the rulers of Florence complaining about his unjust exile; another he sent to the Emperor Henry VII when he was besieging Brescia, rebuking him in an almost prophetic manner for his delay; the third was to the Italian cardinals when the papal throne was vacant following the death of Pope Clement [V], to urge them to agree on the election of an Italian pope. All these were nobly phrased in Latin with excellent use of sources and quotations from the [classical and Christian] authorities; and they were highly praised by wise and learned readers.

And he wrote the *Commedia*, where through accomplished verse, through the weighty and ingenious treatment of issues concerning morality, nature, astrology, philosophy and theology, and through fine and inventive figures, comparisons and poetic tropes – he compiled and described in a hundred chapters (or rather cantos) an account of the nature and condition of Hell, Purgatory and Paradise. He did this supremely well, as those who have acute understanding will acknowledge, inasmuch as they may read and understand this work of his. It is true that in that *Commedia* he indulged in invective and denunciation as poets tend to do, and in more places than was necessary; but perhaps it was the fact of his exile that made him do so.

He also composed the *Monarchia*, in which he discusses the role of the pope and the emperors. And he began a commentary in the vernacular [the *Convivio*] on fourteen of the moral *canzoni* mentioned above, but because of his death this did not get beyond three of them. Yet this will strike anyone who reads it as a noble, fine, ingenious and highly impressive work, since it is distinguished both by a noble style of writing and by fine philosophical and astrological arguments. In addition he composed a short work which is called *Of Eloquence in the Vernacular* where he sets out to write four books, but only two exist, perhaps because of his premature demise. Here in forceful and elegant Latin he finds fault with all the dialects of Italy.

This Dante, as a result of his great learning, was somewhat proud, haughty and disdainful, and like many unsociable men of learning he was not easily able to communicate with the unlearned. Yet on account of the other virtues, knowledge and worth of this great citizen, it seems right to set down an everlasting record of him in this chronicle of ours, in order that those noble works of his bequeathed to us in his writings may bear true witness to his memory and bring fame and honour to our city. (my translation from Villani 10. 136)

# Texts and Traditions

We began with Dante's dual citizenship – as a national and European poet and as a writer in both Latin and the vernacular. Our second approach to his poetic identity and its formation will focus much more closely on this duality: on the presence of local and foreign traditions within his culture; and on the presence of both Latin and vernacular in the texts and culture of his time.

The section begins with a survey of the various resources and media that were available to Dante. It then turns to pre-Christian culture: to the presence in Dante's world of classical authors and the Graeco-Roman traditions in philosophy and literature. It then addresses some aspects of the religious culture that the poet inhabited – attending first to the ways in which he might have accessed and read the Bible. It identifies some of the significant issues that he found in the work of Christian thinkers from Augustine to Aquinas and in the lives and writings of saints and visionaries from St Paul to St Francis. It samples some of the Latin and vernacular writing on historical, political and scientific topics that made knowledge potentially accessible to the laity. Finally, it outlines the vernacular traditions of poetry of which Dante was aware and within which he placed his own work.

*An asterisk (\*) indicates my first reference in this section to works that are particularly recommended for further reading.*

# Books, Authors, Libraries, Media

### Images of books

*Volume*, which is one of the Italian words for 'book', occurs in both the first and the last cantos of the *Commedia*. In canto 1 of the *Inferno* – at the moment when he recognizes Virgil as the poet who has come to rescue and guide him – Dante speaks of how he may deserve such help because of 'the great devotion that made me pore over your book (*volume*)' (*Inf.* 1. 83–4). Virgil is identified with the text of his epic, the *Aeneid*, which is to be one of the major sources for the *Commedia*. A much more mysterious *volume* is the one that appears through a metaphor in the very last canto of the *Paradiso*, as Dante's protagonist looks into the heart of the 'supreme' and 'eternal light' and sees there 'bound by love into one volume, all that is scattered through the universe' (*Par.* 33. 86–7). The image here is at one level a quite straightforward technological one, drawing on the process of bookbinding that very shortly awaited the completed *Commedia*; yet it also conveys the excitement of making the text.

There is a long tradition of imagining the book as not only a precious artefact but also an ambitious and even sacred enterprise. Such an image developed figuratively in various ways. The metaphor of the Book of Life written by God already features in the Old Testament, and Christianity, as a religion of the Book, develops it very fully (Curtius 1953: 308, 310–11). Particular forms of this metaphor were the ideas of the world or created Nature as a divinely inscribed book, open to inspired and instructed human understanding; and these are especially vital and persistent from the Middle Ages through to the early modern period (Curtius 1953: 319–24; *Gellrich 1985: 17–20, 29–30). Along with the notion of the *Commedia* itself as a book containing this world and the otherworlds, this idea of the whole of Creation as God's book also underlies Dante's metaphor of illumination and gathering into final unity in *Paradiso* 33.

As a poet, philosopher and avid reader, Dante drew upon the image of the book throughout his writing career. His early collection of love-poems with his own prose commentary, the *Vita nuova*, begins by invoking another long-established metaphor: finding the start of the poet's 'new life' signalled by a 'rubric' (literally a heading in red) at the beginning of 'the book of my memory' (opening of *VN* ch. 1). And in between those images of Virgil's book in *Inferno* 1 and God's book in *Paradiso* 33 there are numerous references, both literal and metaphorical, to the processes of reading and writing. They draw upon the more mundane features of paper, ink and lettering, as well as directly addressing the poem's readers and invoking awareness of illustrious authors and their texts (Curtius 1953: 326–32). The cumulative effect of such references, especially in the *Commedia*, is to create a powerful impression of textuality – of 'the work as a structure conscious of its own interpretive strategy' (Gellrich 1985: 144).

## Authors and authority

The *Commedia* is also densely peopled with the figures of named authors. The first of these is Virgil (*Inf.* 1. 79). Not long after this, at the start of the two poets' journey through Hell, they are briefly joined by the figures of Virgil's major fellow-poets in Limbo: the Greek Homer and the Romans Horace, Ovid and Lucan (*Inf.* 4. 79–102). Limbo – 'the place on the edge' – contains not only the 'fair college' (94) of the honoured classical poets but also the illustrious 'philosophic family' of Greek, Roman and Arabic thinkers, led by Aristotle, 'the master of all knowledge' (*Inf.* 4. 130–44). Aristotle's Christian heirs – such as the Scholastic theologians Albertus Magnus, Thomas Aquinas and Siger of Brabant – later appear along with a wide variety of named medieval Christian thinkers and writers in a full circle of light – the sphere of the Sun, the fourth circle of Dante's Heaven (*Par.* 10–14). Contemplative and monastic writers such as St Peter Damian and St Benedict are prominent in Dante's Heaven of Saturn (*Par.* 21–2), whilst the final guide for 'Dante' in the last three cantos of the whole poem is the greatest of the spiritual writers of the twelfth century: St Bernard of Clairvaux (*Par.* 31–3; below, pp. 89–90).

Redeemed writers in Dante's book are not, however, entirely confined to the Christian era. Solomon – the Old Testament king and the author (it was

60

then believed) of the Books of Wisdom and Ecclesiastes – is given a place and eventually a voice in the sphere of the Sun (*Par.* 14. 36–63); whilst his father David, 'the singer of the Holy Spirit', regarded as author of the Old Testament Psalms, appears at the very centre of the celestial Eagle's eye in the Heaven of Jupiter (*Par.* 20. 37–42). And crossing the border, in several senses, is the Latin poet Statius, whom Dante and Virgil encounter on the fifth terrace of Mount Purgatory. Like Dante, Statius is portrayed as an avid reader of Virgil's *volume*, which (as in Dante's case) points him towards conversion (*Purg.* 21. 94–102, 22. 37–42 and 60–81; below, p. 70). Along with these biblical, classical and Christian writers, vernacular authors (including poets) compose a tradition within which Dante includes himself. This vernacular tradition, as Dante makes clear both in *DVE* and in the *Commedia*, comprises not only those writing in various dialects of thirteenth-century Italian but also the earlier Provençal troubadours of the twelfth and early thirteenth centuries.

Dante's representation of such writers in the *Commedia* reflects his sense of his poetic inheritance and identity. His consciousness of authorship had already been markedly apparent in the *Vita nuova* of the 1290s, which develops a prose self-commentary on the writer's own love-poems and includes an essay on the development of vernacular love-poetry (*VN* ch. 25). Concern with authorship and authority is yet more explicit in *DVE* and the *Convivio* – works which 'struggle with the problem of conferring *auctoritas* [authority/authorial status] on Dante, poetry and the vernacular' (Ascoli 1993: 51). From the moment at which Dante in *Inferno* 1 identifies himself first as a reader of Virgil's *volume* to the point when the poet finally draws together the scattered pages of God's book, the *Commedia* engages in a process of authorizing the pilgrim as poet – a process which takes almost the whole of the poem to complete (*Hawkins 1999: 66–71).

Dante also authorizes himself to speak as a philosopher and theologian – a striking stance for a lay, vernacular writer of his time to adopt. His bid for philosophical and theological authority is evident in the *Convivio* and the *Monarchia*, as well as in the *Commedia*. Late in life, his concern to resolve a scientific problem with theological implications, the *Quaestio de Aqua et Terra*, led him to present his case from a position of academic authority at Verona in 1320 (above, p. 51). Academic authority, too, was what the Bolognese professor Giovanni del Virgilio was offering him at about the same time; and this was what he eventually conferred by describing Dante as a 'philosopher and theologian' (above, pp. 52–3).

## Other resources

Dante thus sought and received a degree of intellectual recognition for his ideas – but what were the resources that enabled him to develop them? What range of reading could he actually have done?

During his youth in **Florence** he had received some instruction in grammar (*Conv.* 2. 12. 4); and this would, at its more advanced levels, have introduced him to some well-known classical authors (above, p. 10). Well before his exile, in the early 1290s, he probably attended lectures in philosophy and theology at the schools of the Dominican and Franciscan friars, at Santa Maria Novella and Santa Croce in Florence (above, pp. 11–13). Evidence about book-collections and their origins, development and use at this time is difficult to assess. Nor can we be sure whether Dante, as a layman, would have had access to the friars' books. So, in speaking of 'Dante's library', we may have to include not only his possible use of texts in the possession of others (Davis 1988: 360–1), but also access to texts only through hearsay – through, for example, quotation and reference in public sermons, and attending lectures and disputations in the 'schools of the religious' (above, p. 11).

The Franciscans' collection at Santa Croce is the best-documented at this time. Around 1300 it is believed to have contained about 46 volumes (Davis 1988: 343). The range of subjects covered includes theology and biblical commentary, canon and civil law, logic and grammar. Authors represented include: philosophers, such as Aristotle (in Latin translation); Latin writers, such as Virgil, Horace, Ovid and Suetonius (often in the form of excerpts); Fathers of the Church, such as Augustine, Jerome and Gregory; scholastic theologians, such as Aquinas and Bonaventura; and medieval encyclopedists, such as Uguccione of Pisa (Davis 1988: 345–6, 1984: 149–54: *DE* 841B–842A). This gives some impression of the reading-matter that would have sustained the academic culture of the Franciscan convent, yielded material for preachers, and thus been passed on to attentive laymen such as Dante.

When describing his attendance at the schools of the friars, Dante identifies these as the place and occasion where Lady Philosophy 'truly reveals herself' (*Conv.* 2. 12. 7). This serves as a general tribute to the scholars who frequented the *studia* at Santa Croce, Santa Maria Novella and Santo Spirito around 1290 (above, p. 13), and acknowledges the opportunity for laypersons like himself to observe and participate. Amongst the literate laity themselves in a prosperous city such as Florence – especially the classes involved in law, politics and administration – there was also considerable scope for the exchange of ideas, books and poems.

Both before and after his exile, Dante could also have found such resources beyond Florence. Verona, Padua and Ravenna all offered various kinds of intellectual support and stimulus (see above, pp. 47, 49); yet the greatest centre of learning in Italy was considerably closer to Florence. **Bologna** was the oldest Italian (and European) university and was particularly prominent in the study of law and rhetoric. Whilst still in his early twenties (around 1286–7) Dante is thought to have been there for a few months (Petrocchi 1984: 22–4; Bemrose 2000: 13–14). He may also have visited the city again, just after his first residence at Verona, in 1304 (Villani 10. 136; Boccaccio, *Trattatello* 1, para. 74). If so, it would have been an important and perhaps unique opportunity to gather material for his major philosophical project, the *Convivio* (Scott 1996: 38). Bologna also beckoned during the last years of Dante's life, when he corresponded with Giovanni del Virgilio (see above, p. 50), who had offered him the equivalent of an honorary degree and a laurel crown (Dante 1902: 148).

Yet for various reasons the laurel crown was never awarded to Dante in Bologna or elsewhere. Despite his contacts with academia and the learned world of his time, he was, as an exile, constantly on the move and mostly on his own. The constraints of poverty and the need for mobility meant that his own collection of books would have been limited to a few classical and Christian authors and perhaps an anthology of scientific and historical material and one of vernacular (Provençal and Italian) material (Petrocchi 1984: 107). He clearly had opportunities for formal study in Florence, Bologna and elsewhere, but in many respects he was 'self-taught' (Bemrose 2000: 14). And an important part of this self-education would not only have been the practice of reading but also the habit of keeping his ears and eyes open.

## Hearing and seeing

Because of the vividness with which Dante projects the imagery of books, authorship and writing, we may be tempted to think of his resources solely in terms of words on the page; yet oral discourse and performance were still dominant features of intellectual and literary culture in his time and were sources that he drew upon substantially for characters, ideas, stories and illustrations. His representation of the contemporary social and political scene in the *Commedia* was much dependent upon such media; and its discourse has been described as the transfer on to a serious and elevated plane of worldly and local 'gossip' (*Catto 1980: 2). The lecture and the sermon were oral genres in which the Florentine friars excelled (below, p. 100). Some preachers of the time, as Dante's Beatrice alleges, could be merely curious, casuistical or facetious in the range of material that they dispensed from the pulpit and might thus leave their flocks 'fed with wind' (*Par.* 29. 94–126). Yet such accusations – rehearsed by a number of writers in the fourteenth century – are also a backhanded tribute to the strength of the popular appetite for preaching and the wide range of knowledge it transmitted.

Oral transmission was also the means by which texts by both clerical and lay writers reached a wider public. Around 1300, it has been argued, 'private reading must still have been a luxury, largely confined to retiring ladies and scholars. Books were scarce and it was ordinary good manners to share their contents among a group by reading aloud' (Clanchy 1993: 198). Dante's *Commedia* itself became not only a book to be read but also a poem to be heard, as a work that could be and was performed. The implications of oral performance and common currency are already apparent in certain features of the poem itself (below, p. 235). Dante's quick ear for manner of speech and turns of phrase is demonstrated in the dialogue of the *Commedia*, as well as in his discourse on the vernacular in *De vulgari eloquentia*, many of whose prolific quotations from poems and dialect speech would have been drawn not from reference works but from memory (Petrocchi 1984: 108).

A sharp eye is also evident in the scenes and images of the *Commedia*; and it is clear that for these Dante also drew on the resources of contemporary visual culture in Florence and elsewhere. Works of art that he could have seen in Florence or during his years of exile include the images of Heaven and Hell in the Baptistery at Florence and in Giotto's frescoes at Padua; the mosaics of the emperor Justinian and of Christ with the Apostles at Ravenna (above, pp. 4, 32–3, 49). Many further connections between Dante's imagery and that of the contemporary pictorial and sculptural arts can be traced; and his own 'painterly disposition' at points in the *Commedia* seems itself to have acted as a stimulus to later artists, from the early illuminators onwards (*DE* 250A–251B and below, p. 233).

Resources of and influences from visual culture at this time, however, were not solely confined to the work of famous artists such as Cimabue and Giotto (*Purg.* 11. 94–6), or to artefacts and buildings. We also need to be aware of the possible effects of more transient but equally visible (and audible) stimuli, such as the rituals, ceremonies and processions of the church and of civic spectacle: from the celebrations of the Jubilee at Rome in 1300 (*Inf.* 18.

28–33) to urban feasts and competitions (*Inf.* 15. 121–4; Dean 2000: 72–8). Urban spectacle at this time could also include dramatic elements which drew upon religious tradition, visual art and popular theatre. A striking example of such an event occurred at Florence two years after Dante's exile, and it is recorded in Giovanni Villani's chronicle as follows:

> During the very time that the Cardinal [Niccolò] of Prato was in Florence and was in favour with its people and citizens, who hoped he would be able to make lasting peace for them [above, p. 30], at the start of May 1304 – just as in the good old days of Florence's peace and prosperity, when companies and troupes of entertainers roamed the city, celebrating and making merry – so those who were best at doing so got together again in many parts of the city, with one district competing against another.
>
> Among all these, the citizens of Borgo San Frediano had long been in the practice of mounting novel and unusual entertainments, so they sent out a proclamation that if anyone wanted to get news about the next world, they should be present on May day upon the Carrraia Bridge and beside the Arno there. And on the Arno they set up platforms upon boats and skiffs where they presented a lifelike pageant of Hell, complete with fires, other punishments and afflictions, men disguised as truly horrible demons, and others in the guise of naked human-looking souls who were pitched into those various torments amid terrific cries, shrieks and struggles – all of which was hideous and terrifying to hear and see.
>
> This strange new spectacle drew a large audience of Florentines; and the Carraia Bridge, which was then built of wood resting on piers, was so overloaded with people that it gave way at several points and fell along with those upon it. Thus many were crushed and drowned and many were seriously injured; so the play became reality and as the proclamation had promised many through death came to get news of the next world, to the great grief and sorrow of the whole city, since everyone thought they might have lost a son or brother there. And this was an omen of future troubles that would shortly descend upon our city. (my translation; original in Villani 9. 70)

Dante would not himself have been able to witness this 'strange spectacle' and its grim conclusion, as he had been exiled from Florence for over two years by that time. However, it seems very likely that he would have heard about it, since he had returned to Tuscany from Verona in March of that year and was keeping a close eye on political developments in Florence (above, p. 31). It seems the sort of story that might well have appealed to the imagination of a poet who was soon to present the spectacle of devils chasing the souls of corrupt citizens into a river of pitch as 'a strange new game' (*Inf.* 22. 118). The theatricality of the event would also have been of interest, and there is evidence in the *Inferno* and elsewhere in the *Commedia* that Dante was aware of such traditions, both in vernacular drama and in civic spectacle (\*Armour 1991: 9–12). This recent vernacular example of 'news from the next world' could thus be placed among Dante's texts and traditions, alongside the ancient portrayals of the afterlife that he inherited from illustrious figures such as Virgil and other authors that he names.

# Pagan Culture

## Pagan poets: Virgil, Ovid, Lucan, Statius

In Limbo, on the fringes of Dante's *Inferno*, we find not only classical Latin poets (Virgil, Ovid, Horace, Lucan) but also a wide range of authors who wrote in Greek (Homer, Aristotle, Socrates, Plato) and Arabic ('Avicenna' [ibn-Sina] and 'Averroes' [ibn-Rushd]). Yet despite Dante's wide-ranging interest in languages, his actual reading of the classics would not have gone beyond a selection of the Latin writers. **Homer**, for instance, appears in Limbo (*Inf.* 4. 88), but for Dante and most of his western European contemporaries this 'supreme poet' (*poeta sovrano*) was no more than a name; and writers of Dante's time regarded him as an unreliable source for the story of Troy (*Minnis and Scott 1988: 114f). Yet with Homer, during the medieval period, 'the name had to be named' (Curtius 1953: 18).

**Virgil**, the writer to whom 'Dante' pays tribute in the very first canto of the *Commedia*, is hailed as 'the noblest of poets' by an anonymous voice as the two poets enter the hemisphere of light in Limbo (*Inf.* 4.80–1). Virgil's status as Dante's *altissimo poeta* rests on a long tradition. Virgil's major work, the 12-book *Aeneid* (26–19 BCE), became a school text in imperial Rome. Commentaries on it appeared in the late Roman period and were influential on the medieval reading of the poem. That of the grammarian Servius (late fourth century CE) survived in several versions during the Middle Ages. The Neoplatonist Macrobius in the early fifth century produced the *Saturnalia*, a seven-book dialogue on Virgil which established him as 'the Complete Rhetorician, the omniscient, infallible, unique scholar-poet' (*OCD* 635). Then the Christian bishop and interpreter of myths Fulgentius (467–532) allegorized the epic voyage of Virgil's Aeneas from Troy to Rome as the progress of human life, in his *Expositio Virgilianae Continentiae*. Fulgentius's method of interpreting Aeneas's journey through the underworld in Book 6 of the *Aeneid* has been summarized as follows:

> Fortified with the golden branch, which is the wisdom which opens the way to hidden truths, he [Aeneas/humanity] undertakes philosophical investigations (the descent into Hades). First of all there appear to him the sorrows of human life; then after passing, guided by Time (Charon), the troubled waters of youth (Acheron), he hears the quarrels and strifes that divide men (the barking Cerberus), which are stilled by the honey of wisdom. Thus he proceeds to a knowledge of the future life and a discernment of good and evil, and reflects on his passions (Dido) and the affections (Anchises) of his youth. (Comparetti 1966: 111)

As well as rendering Virgil's underworld more acceptable in this way, the early Christians also conscripted him to their cause on the basis of his Fourth Eclogue, a pastoral poem which begins with a reference to prophetic song, a 'Virgin', the return of the Golden Age, and some kind of divinely ordained rebirth and renewal (lines 4–7) (*Davis 1957: 7–8). Fathers of the Church, such as Augustine and Jerome in the fourth and fifth centuries, thus cited lines from it for this purpose (Comparetti 1966: 99–103).

During the Middle Ages Virgil's value as a school text and as a model of style remained high, and interest in his work gained impetus from the revivals of classical studies at the court of Charlemagne in the eighth and ninth centuries and the School of Chartres in the twelfth. Interpretation of the *Aeneid* as an allegory of the progress of human life continued to enhance the poem's moral status, for instance in the work of the twelfth-century humanist John of Salisbury, who claimed that Virgil 'expresses the whole body of philosophical truth in the guise of fables' and who interpreted the first six books of the *Aeneid* in terms of the six ages of man (*Policraticus* 6.22, 8.24). Dante was also to allude to this way of reading Virgil's poem at several points during his account of the noble life in the last treatise of the *Convivio* (4. 24 and 26).

Virgil's Fourth Eclogue continues to be cited as a prophecy of the birth of Christ, for example by Abelard in the twelfth century and Pope Innocent III in the thirteenth, as well as by Dante's Statius paying tribute to the author in *Purgatorio* 22. 70–2. Prophetic powers akin to those of the Roman Sybil are attributed to the Roman poet in a number of sources over this period (Comparetti 1966: 102, 309–13). Dante knew that the 'Virgin' of the Fourth Eclogue was not 'really' the Virgin Mary but the goddess of Justice (as he explains at the beginning of *Monarchia* 1.11); but, as the encounter between the poets in *Purgatorio* 21–2 shows, he was very much interested in Virgil's intermediary position between the pagan and Christian worlds. For Italians like Dante, the medieval Virgil was not only the 'Homer of the Romans' (as St Jerome had called him); he was also '*our* divine poet' (*Mon.* 2. 3. 6) and a major source for myths about the destiny and achievements of ancient Rome, such as those that Dante's ancestor imagines being narrated by the family fireside in the Florence of the 'good old days' (*Par.* 15. 124–6; Davis 1957: 100–38).

Unlike Virgil, his near contemporary **Ovid** (43 BCE–18 CE) does not feature significantly as a character in the *Commedia* – save for two brief appearances, as the 'third' of the 'noble school' of pagan poets in Limbo (*Inf.* 4. 90), and as one of the writers whose imagination is being outdone by Dante's own transformation of sinners into serpents (25. 97–9) Yet his status in medieval culture as a poet of the Roman Golden Age is comparable to that of Virgil. For Dante's contemporaries, Ovid provided the main Latin model for writing about love (particularly the three books of the *Ars Amatoria*) and the chief repository of pagan mythology, the *Metamorphoses* in 15 books, narrating and interweaving stories of transformation, and ranging from the origins of the cosmos to Julius Caesar's Rome.

Ovid's work, like Virgil's, was the subject of long study and much interpretation. By the twelfth and thirteenth centuries it had become so much a feature of literary culture that modern criticism has given this period the title of *aetas Ovidiana*, 'the Ovidian age'; and it has been argued that the 'faintness' of Virgil's voice when he first appears as Dante's guide in the *Inferno* (1. 63) in part reflects the pre-eminence of Ovid in the classical culture of the time (Jacoff and Schnapp 1991: 214, 289; Picone 1997: 54). It was certainly a time when commentary on Ovid proliferated and when the *Metamorphoses* was known to Italian writers, including Dante, as *Ovidio maggiore*, 'the greater Ovid', probably because of its combination of canonical status and encyclopedic scope (*Conv.* 3. 3. 7). As with Virgil's *Aeneid* and Fourth Eclogue, the *Metamorphoses* became subject to Christianizing allegorical interpretation, including the commentaries by Dante's friend Giovanni del Virgilio (written shortly after Dante's death) and culminating in the mammoth, moralizing glosses of the *Ovide moralisé* in the early fourteenth century (Minnis and Scott 1988: 316–17, 321–4, 360–6). Dante may have known and used some of the commentaries on the *Metamorphoses*, but his frequent reinvention of Ovid's myths of transformation in the *Commedia* is also based on direct knowledge and long study of this key text and his recognition of its value as 'a vibrant tale to which one can turn for inspiration in describing the reality of the underworld' (Hollander 1969: 202–20; Picone 1997: 67).

A less-well-known Roman poet who ranks among the top three or four of Dante's *bella scola* was **Lucan** (39–65 CE). Lucan's main surviving work is the *Bellum Civile* (sometimes known as the *Pharsalia*), an incomplete 10-book poem about the civil war between Julius Caesar and Gnaeus Pompey in 50–48 BCE. Lucan was a standard 'curriculum author' in the Middle Ages (Curtius 1953: 46, 260), and for at least one mid-twelfth-century commentator he was an innovative writer about the past: 'not simply a poet but a poet and historiographer combined' (Minnis and Scott 1988: 115). For Dante, he was 'the virtuoso of horror and turgid pathos, but he was also versed in the underworld and its witchcraft. In addition he was the source book for the Roman Civil War, the panegyrist of the austere Cato of Utica, whom Dante places as guardian at the foot of the Mount of Purgatory' (Curtius 1953: 18). Among the 'noble school' of classical poets in Limbo, Lucan is placed 'last' by Dante (*Inf.* 4. 90). This may be because he was the latest in time (of those in Limbo), or possibly because his work was thought to be the least consistent with the classical standards of epic (*DE* 573A). Yet, like Ovid, he will be addressed as a poet whose imagining of the strangest things that might happen to a human body Dante will now recall and claim to outdo (*Inf.* 25. 94–6).

For the fourth of Dante's leading Latin poets, we need to look beyond the 'noble school' of Limbo to an encounter that takes place high on the mountain of Purgatory. Here, in *Purgatorio* 21, Dante and Virgil are greeted by the figure of **Statius** (45–96 CE). Dante's Statius was best known in the Middle Ages as the author of two major epics. His 12-book *Thebaid* (published 91 CE) portrays the tragic rivalry of the sons of Oedipus (Eteocles and Polynices) and the destruction of Thebes; and the unfinished *Achilleid* describes the upbringing of the Greek hero Achilles and his life before his departure for the Trojan War. Dante knew of and refers to both these works (*Purg.* 21. 92); but it is the dark history of civic and individual self-destruction in the *Thebaid* to which he returns more often, especially in the *Inferno* (e.g., 14. 49–72, 26. 52–4, 30. 1–12, 32. 10–11, 33. 89; see *DE* 811B). In the *Commedia*, Statius also occupies a special position in relation to Virgil, since he not only, like other medieval poets, acknowledges the *Aeneid* as source of vital poetic nourishment (*Purg.* 21. 94–102), but also claims that Virgil's work (notably the Fourth Eclogue) had actually converted him to Christianity (*Purg.* 22. 64–73). Statius's alleged secret conversion and his life as a 'closet Christian' (*chiuso cristian*, line 90) are a dramatic fiction which Dante uses to explore the borderlands between paganism and Christianity. But it also reflects his role in literary tradition as the earlier poet's close follower, who became known in Dante's time as 'the second Virgil'.

## Classifying the classics

Like Virgil, Ovid and Lucan, Statius had long been one of the major authors in the medieval academic curriculum (Curtius 1953: 48–53). An outline of the classical canon, as envisaged in the century before Dante, is provided by the Benedictine monk and schoolmaster Conrad of Hirsau (c.1070–c.1150) in his *Dialogue on the Authors* (Minnis and Scott 1988: 37–64). Conrad's canonical sequence of 21 Latin authors proceeds in order of assumed difficulty for the medieval reader. Its final group includes the four who have just been mentioned: Statius, Lucan, Ovid and Virgil, along with two other members of the 'noble school' that Dante presents in *Inferno* 4: Homer and Horace. **Horace** (65–8 BCE) is identified by both Conrad and Dante as a satirist (Minnis and Scott 1988: 54, 56; *Inf.* 4. 90) and both his *satirae* (or *sermones*) and his Odes were known in the Middle Ages. However, his *Ars poetica* (*Art of Poetry*) was highly influential on the literary criticism of the period; and this was probably the main if not the only work of Horace that Dante knew and from which he quotes (*VN* 25. 9, *DVE* 2. 4. 4, *Conv.* 2. 13. 10; *Baranski 2001: 19–22).

Of the **Latin prose writers** grouped before the great pagan poets in Conrad of Hirsau's *Dialogue*, two in particular were influential upon Dante. These were **Cicero** and **Boethius**. The orator and politician Cicero (106–43 BCE) assimilated a wide range of Greek philosophical work into Latin culture, thus also acting as an important intermediary for medieval writers and readers. His writings on ethical issues and personal conduct (principles of morality, old age, friendship) are cited around fifty times by Dante (*DE* 170A, 172B–173A; Baranski 2001: 19–22). Along with a later Latin moralist, **Seneca** (c.1–65 CE), Cicero (as *Tullio*) is placed among the Graeco-Roman 'philosophic family' of Dante's Limbo (*Inf.* 4. 141), presided over by Aristotle (below, p. 73). Like Cicero, although much later, **Boethius** (c.480–c.525 CE) also acted as one of the conduits through which Greek philosophical traditions entered the mainstream of western medieval thought (below, p. 80). His dialogue with Lady Philosophy in *The Consolation of Philosophy* was one of the key texts of the Middle Ages, circulating with a number of commentaries and translated into several vernaculars. Dante cites it over thirty times and acknowledges it as one of the key works that led him towards the study of philosophy after the death of Beatrice (*Conv.* 2. 12. 2).

Amongst the ancient historians frequently cited by Dante is **Livy** (64/57 BCE–12/17 CE). Livy's history of Rome from its foundation to the time of Augustus was in 142 books, of which 35 have survived; and it was an authoritative text in the Middle Ages and Renaissance. In the comparison of the mutilated bodies of *Inferno* 28 to the casualties of various famous battles, it is invoked as an 'infallible' source for the battle of Cannae (lines 10–12). It is uncertain how much of Livy's work Dante knew directly; and on occasion he may be more indebted for his material on Rome to the later *History Against the Pagans* (417–18) by the Christian priest Paulus Orosius (Moore 1896: 280 and below, p. 99). The Roman historian is, however, named as a model of 'excellent prose' alongside the four canonical Latin poets – 'Virgil, Ovid of the *Metamorphoses*, Statius and Lucan' – during Dante's discussion of illustrious stylistic models in *DVE* (2. 6. 7).

The game of naming the 'great tradition' of classical authors was played by a number of writers throughout the Middle Ages; and there are variations on it throughout Dante's work: from chapter 25 of the *Vita nuova*, through *DVE* and the *Convivio* – especially *Conv.* 4. 24–8, where Statius, Virgil, Ovid and Lucan are drawn upon to illustrate the ages of man – to the 'noble school' of *Inferno* 4 and the trinity of pilgrim-poets in *Purgatorio* 21–2. It will be clear, however from the small selection of Dante's authors surveyed so far, that the classical canon was not simply a repository for models of style. The Graeco-Roman traditions could also offer (or be made to offer) material of moral and philosophical value.

Medieval Christian writers used various rhetorical figures to justify the study of pagan authors. Conrad of Hirsau, for example, speaks of groping for the gold amongst the dung in the writings of Ovid, and of using the worldly knowledge imparted by the pagan authors like a culinary herb – to be thrown out once it has imparted its flavour to the dish (Minnis and Scott 1988: 54, 56). Much earlier, St Augustine, writing *On Christian Doctrine* (2. 40. 60), had used the famous figure of the Israelites 'plundering the Egyptians' and converting their vessels and ornaments 'to a better use', and St Jerome, quoting Deuteronomy 21: 11–13, had made a similar point about 'domesticating' the classics (Bolgar 1954: 204). Conversion of the pagan writers' work 'to a better use' could also be achieved by selective breeding of ideas from the classical **philosophers** – as had been happening with increasing intensity during the century or so before Dante.

## Aristotle and his 'family'

Accompanied into the light of Limbo by the other five members of the 'noble school' of poets, Dante enters a 'noble castle' which encloses and celebrates two further elements of pagan culture (*Inf.* 4. 106–44). Here on the 'bright greensward' (111, 118) he first encounters the 'great spirits' of the pagan heroes, from Electra (mother of the founder of Troy) through Julius Caesar to Salah-ud-Din (c.1138–93), the chivalrous enemy of the Christians in the Third Crusade (lines 118–29). Placed a little higher even than these illustrious figures, Dante then sees 'the master of those who know, / sitting amid his family of philosophers' (130–2). All of these, from Socrates and Plato, through Cicero and Seneca to the Spanish Arab philosopher and commentator 'Averroes' (ibn-Rushd, c.1126–c.1198) 'look towards and pay tribute to' this un-named 'master'; and the text's use of the historic present here (lines 133 and 135) highlights the vitality of the imagined tradition that stems from him.

Unlike Homer, who was, as we have seen, not much more than a name for Dante and his contemporaries, that 'master', **Aristotle** (384–322 BCE), did not really need to be named. For Dante and his contemporaries – even those who had serious reservations about him – he was very often to be referred to simply as 'the Philosopher'. Of the three hundred or so occasions on which Dante cites him, around forty use simply this title. Thus, near the beginning of his philosophical voyage in the *Convivio* (2. 1. 13), Dante invokes the advice of 'the Philosopher' in the *Physics* to proceed in an orderly way from the familiar to the unfamiliar (even though he is actually here following Aquinas's commentary on the text). When discussing a question of cosmological science in the third treatise of *Convivio* (5. 7), he cites Aristotle as 'that glorious philosopher to whom Nature revealed her secrets most fully'; whilst in the fourth treatise Aristotle is exalted as the 'master and leader of human reason' and the authority on ethics (4. 6. 7–8). Most strikingly, the moral ordering of the whole *Inferno* is based upon Aristotle's *Ethics* (*Inf.* 11. 80; *DE* 64A).

As Dante's allusions suggest, medieval writers were aware of the enormous intellectual range that Aristotle had covered in a life of not much more than sixty years. The authority that Dante attributes to 'the Philosopher' extended to the disciplines of logic, metaphysics, psychology, ethics and aesthetics, as well as the natural sciences. For the scholars of the medieval west, knowledge of this body of Aristotelian work was channelled through Byzantine, Arabic and Jewish sources and through commentary and translation. By the mid-thirteenth century a substantial amount of Aristotle's scientific and philosophical work was available in Latin translation; and the scholastic commentaries on the *Ethics*, the *Metaphysics* and the *Politics* by the Dominican Albertus Magnus (1193/1206–80) paved the way for the systematic appropriation of Aristotelianism into Christian philosophy that was undertaken by Albertus's follower Thomas Aquinas (c.1225–74) (*Luscombe 1997: 61–85, 95–108).

This process of reception and appropriation was not always straightforward. A number of attempts were made by the ecclesiastical authorities to restrict the circulation of Aristotle's works in the earlier thirteenth century; and in the hands of some adventurous intellectuals (some of them known to Dante) certain Aristotelian ideas about the intellect, the existence of God, time, the soul and free will were later in the century to prove problematic (*DE* 62; Luscombe 1997: 68–9, 108–16). Dante himself seems to have used several translations, summaries and commentaries (including those by Albertus and Aquinas) to access Aristotle's ideas (*DE* 64A). He also shows some awareness of the contemporary controversies about them, notably in canto 10 of the *Paradiso*. For Dante, the key Aristotelian concepts were humanity's perfectibility through knowledge and its natural impulse towards citizenship; and these were inculcated close to home by his attendance at the 'disputations of philosophers' at the Florentine *studia* (Davis 1984: 163 and above, p. 11).

Aristotle in Dante's time was leading intellectuals to 'reconsider long-established definitions of and methods in the arts and sciences, and to analyse as never before their relationship with the queen of the sciences, theology' (Minnis and Scott 1988: 197). We shall return soon to the implications of this reconsideration for Christian thought in Dante's time. First it will be necessary to consider how he and his contemporaries read, used and interpreted Christianity's main canonical text.

# The Bible

## Scripture and text

Although the Bible is by far Dante's most frequently cited text, the modern Italian word for it (*Bibbia*) does not occur in the *Commedia*; and it is not until *Paradiso* that the terms 'Scripture', 'Holy Scripture', 'the Scriptures' or 'the new and old Scriptures [i.e., the Testaments]' emerge with obvious reference to it. In view of the traditions within which Dante was encountering the Bible, this is not surprising. Medieval scholars tended to refer to the text as *divina* or *sacra scriptura*, or even *pagina* (also the word for 'page'); and it is not until the early thirteenth century that the word *Biblia* (originally a plural noun in Greek) comes into common usage in editions, concordances and commentaries (Riché and Lobrichon 1984: 18–19).

The text of Dante's Bible was somewhat different from the one with which many English-speaking readers are familiar. For many of his five hundred or so biblical quotations and allusions, he, like other medieval writers, would have drawn upon his memory, or upon the oldest Latin version (the early Christian *Vetus Latina*) as preserved in the liturgy of the church (*Hawkins 1999: 40). He also knew and quoted from the 'Vulgate' (i.e., 'widely circulated') text, as established and translated from the Hebrew and Greek by St Jerome in the late fourth century (Curtius 1953: 72–3; *DE* 536). Dante certainly knew of French vernacular compilations of biblical texts (*DVE* 1. 10. 2) and of the various ways in which knowledge of those was transmitted in Italian vernacular culture. Revised versions of the Latin text had been produced in the early and high Middle Ages, and notable amongst these was an edition produced in Paris early in the thirteenth century by a committee of university theologians and booksellers (Riché and Lobrichon 1984: 56–65, 75–93).

## Reading the Bible

What would Bibles of Dante's time have looked like in scale and layout? Those produced in the early ninth century often measured 50 by 35–9 cm; monastic Bibles of the eleventh and twelfth centuries (sometimes produced in two or three volumes) ranged up to 60 by 40 cm; whilst the more widely circulated 'Paris Bibles' of the thirteenth century were mostly between 48 by 32 cm and 27 by 18 cm, although by then some more portable volumes were being produced, with one or two as small as 16 by 11 cm (Riché and Lobrichon 1984: 63, 69, 83). Medieval Bibles also contained a good deal of apparatus along with the canonical text. A page of a twelfth-century Gospel, for instance might have glosses amounting to a phrase, a line or several lines in smaller script, inserted between the lines of the biblical verses (Smalley 1952: pl. I). Surrounding this would be an imposing edifice of script, comprising blocks of lengthier commentary and reminding the reader to keep an eye upon the tradition of interpretation that had built up around the text.

Such traditions had long drawn upon Hebrew commentary. Christian commentators from at least the third century CE had engaged in dialogue with Jewish rabbinic scholars; and for his translation of the Old Testament, Jerome went to the original Hebrew text to verify the Greek 'septuagint' ('work of 70 [translators]') version (Curtius 1953: 72–3; Smalley 1952: 13, 21, 103, 361–2). In the Gospels themselves (especially that of Matthew) and in St Paul's Epistles, there is often an explicit concern to interpret events and institutions of the Old Testament in the light of Christian history; thus for St Paul, Adam 'prefigures' Christ and the 'old law' (of Moses) is 'a figure of the new' (Romans 5: 14,10: 4). The early Church Fathers, such as Clement of Alexandria (c.150–c.215), Origen (185?–254?) and Augustine (354–430) inherited and developed the reading of the Bible in 'figural' and allegorical terms (*DE* 375–6; Smalley 1952: 6–13).

The emergence of the cathedral schools, such as Laon and later Paris, in the eleventh and twelfth centuries was accompanied by increased production of text-books, anthologies and commentary on the Bible. The chief product of this effort was the commentary that was later called the *Glossa Ordinaria* but was known to scholars of the twelfth and thirteenth centuries simply as *Glosa*, 'the Gloss' (Smalley 1952: 56). With the rise of universities such as Paris in the early thirteenth century and the increasing dominance in them of the new orders of friars, biblical commentary, especially in the hands of the friars, comes to feature more largely in academic activities such as lecturing and disputations, as well as preaching (Smalley 1952: 270–81).

What then were the ways of reading the Bible that prevailed in Dante's time? Two developments are relevant here: first, whilst allegorical approaches to the Bible as well as to the pagan classical texts persisted, the value of the distinction between the 'letter' and the 'spirit' of the text was being challenged by Aristotelian theologians such as Thomas Aquinas (see below, p. 82), who 'would perceive the "spirit" of Scripture as something not hidden behind or added on to, but expressed by the text. We cannot disembody a man in order to investigate his soul; neither can we understand the Bible by distinguishing letter from spirit and making a separate study of each' (Smalley 1952: 293). Secondly, in late thirteenth-century biblical interpretation, a more 'literary' approach to authorship has been noticed: the writers of the Books of the Bible are no longer simply undifferentiated vessels of the Word, but come to be recognizable through style, genre and personality (Minnis and Scott 1988: 197).

What are the consequences of such developments for Dante's own reading of the Bible? He was certainly well aware of the long-standing tradition of reading the Scriptures for their allegorical senses, as he clearly shows when he is about to expound his own text at beginning of *Convivio* 2. The extent to which he deploys the panoply of allegorical readings of, for instance, Exodus and the Psalms in the *Commedia* is still a matter of debate (*DE* 29A–30A). In his polemical writing, however, he is also clearly influenced by the new trends in biblical scholarship and interpretation. Thus, when disputing the papacy's claims to temporal as well as spiritual supremacy in Book 3. 9 of *Monarchia*, he argues that the biblical text so often cited by his opponents (the disciples' 'here are two swords' in Luke 22: 38) needs to be read with regard to context, intention and the character of the speaker (Smalley 1952: 306–7).

Dante could have gained some knowledge of recent biblical commentary from his contacts with the schools of the Florentine friars – especially the Dominicans and Franciscans, who would have given him some impression of the new critical methods. Such teachers would also have sharpened his awareness of the wider philosophical and theological issues that preoccupied the thirteenth-century scholastic philosophers and their predecessors.

# Faith seeking Understanding: Christian Traditions of Thought before Dante

## Convergences and Conflicts

'I do not want to be a philosopher if it means resisting St Paul; I do not wish to be Aristotle if it must separate me from Christ' wrote Peter Abelard about two centuries before Dante (quoted in *Leff 1958: 114). St Anselm (1033–1109) put things more positively by describing his main philosophical works as 'meditation on the reason for faith' and 'faith seeking understanding' (Luscombe 1997: 44). Both reflect the fact that 'dependence of reasoning upon the dictates of faith is central to the whole of medieval thinking' and the awareness that 'reason of itself could never directly reach the truth; it acted in the light of faith; and was essentially an accompaniment to man in his transitory state as voyager in this world' (Leff 1958: 11, 19).

The established harmonies and developing dissonances between reason and faith, philosophy and theology, in medieval culture find echoes in Dante's work. In canto 18 of the *Purgatorio*, Virgil concludes the long discussion of human free will and the nature of rightly and wrongly directed love that occupies the middle cantos of the whole *Commedia*. Here he acknowledges that:

> 'as far as Reason's vision reaches
> I can inform you; after that, wait to hear
> from Beatrice alone, regarding Faith.'
> (*Purg.* 18. 46–8)

Limitations of reason's power are also evident in Dante's vision of Paradise (from *Par.* 2. 57 on); and Dante's choice of a classical poet (Virgil), a Florentine *inamorata* (Beatrice) and a mystical theologian (St Bernard) as his main guides and intermediaries reflect his ultimate priorities in the *Commedia*. Yet human reason is celebrated and utilized throughout the poem, from the tribute to Aristotle and his 'philosophic family' in *Inferno* 4, through the cantos on free will and the right direction of love in the middle of the *Purgatorio*, to the exaltation of scholastic philosophy alongside other forms of wisdom in the Heaven of the Sun (*Par.* 10–13). Several of Dante's other major works – notably the *Convivio* and the *Monarchia* – are broadly philosophical in content and approach; and contemporaries clearly regarded the poet as both theologian *and* philosopher (above, pp. 52, 56).

In the *Commedia* and the *Convivio* Dante, like his contemporaries, celebrates Aristotle as 'the Philosopher' (above, p. 73); but he is also strongly influenced by traditions deriving ultimately from **Plato** (428–348 BCE). In this he is also thoroughly typical of his time. In her account of the appearance of souls in the spheres of Paradise, Beatrice refers to Plato's view in the *Timaeus* (*Par.* 4. 49–60). Aristotle was the philosophical flavour of the thirteenth century, and a wide range of his works was becoming available in new translations (Leff 1958: 173–5; Luscombe 1997: 62–3, 205); and the only text by Plato that was widely available in Latin during Dante's time was about half of the *Timaeus*. Nonetheless the interaction of Platonism with Aristotelianism and with Christian doctrine is a significant feature of medieval thought at a number of points up to Dante's time.

Platonic thought, developing as 'Neoplatonism' from the third to the fifth centuries, shared several basic features with Christianity, such as belief in a supreme being and in the non-material nature of reality. The Neoplatonic notion of the process whereby 'all reality emanates from and returns to the One, which is itself beyond being' proved attractive and adaptable to Christianity. It was developed by a Greek Christian writer of around 500 who referred to himself as **Dionysius the Areopagite** (after the figure who had become a follower of St Paul in Athens; Acts 17: 19–34) and who applied the Neoplatonic concept to the hierarchies of angels (Luscombe 1997: 24–8). The works of this 'pseudo-Dionysius' (including the *Divine Names*, *Mystical Theology* and *Celestial Hierarchy*) were translated into Latin in ninth-century Paris by John Scotus Eriugena (c.810–77) (Leff 1958: 68). Along with other Neoplatonic writers, Dionysius continued to be influential on later medieval theology and mysticism (Luscombe 1997: 65). Dante acknowledged his authority and influence in several ways. Amongst the circle of lights representing various traditions of wisdom in *Paradiso*, Dionysius is placed next to Solomon and is described as a figure who in himself illustrates the Neoplatonic process of ascent, since 'down there in the flesh he perceived more deeply than any the nature and role of the angels' (*Par*. 10. 116–17). Later, in the first of two cantos where Beatrice addresses this subject (*Par*. 28), Dionysius's representation of the orders of angels is explicitly acknowledged as authentic, by contrast to the version of the hierarchy (from Gregory the Great) that Dante had followed in the *Convivio* (*Par*. 28. 130–5; *Conv*. 2. 5. 6).

Neoplatonist thought reached medieval readers of Latin through several other intermediaries. Cicero assimilated a wide range of Greek philosophical work, including the Platonic tradition, into Latin culture. **Macrobius** produced a commentary on the episode of the 'Dream of Scipio' in Cicero's *De Republica* which developed at length the Neoplatonic implications of the Roman author's text and itself helped to shape thinking about dreams and the cosmos up to and beyond the time of Dante. And Boethius, whose work influenced Dante in several ways (above, p. 71), was also both an important early translator of Aristotle and a follower of the Neoplatonists; whilst his views on being and existence stem from traditions going back to Plato himself (Luscombe 1997: 17–21). Yet before Boethius comes a thinker for whom Platonism was even more intimately related to Christianity and whose effect upon Dante and the *Commedia* was just as strong.

## Augustine and Augustinianism

Addressing God in his *Confessions*, **St Augustine** (345–430) acknowledges the importance of Platonism in the process of his conversion to Christianity: 'By the Platonic books I was admonished to return into myself. With you as my guide I entered into my innermost citadel, and was given power to do so because you had become my helper' (Augustine 1992: 123). Platonism is one of the main strands in Augustine's thought, and it provided, amongst other things, a stimulus to the mystical and introspective quest that develops in Books 6 to 8 of the *Confessions* (Leff 1958: 35–8; Augustine 1992: xix–xxi; Luscombe 1997: 9–10). It did not provide the ultimate answers to the questions with which Augustine grappled in the *Confessions* and his other works: the nature of divine creation (*Confessions* 12); the relationship between God and the created world; the mystery of the Incarnation of Christ (*Confessions* 7. 9). But it was clearly a major element in the 'Augustinian' tradition of Christian thought up to and beyond the thirteenth century.

Thus, for example, the Persian Arab philosopher '**Avicenna**' (ibn-Sina, 980–1037) in proposing the idea of an 'active' or 'agent' intellect as an external power operating upon the human soul was developing (from Plotinus) the Neoplatonist view of God as the 'First Intelligence'. But the concept would also have been seen as reconcilable with St Augustine's doctrine of learning as 'illumination' (Matthews 2005: 59). Augustinian Neoplatonism was also still a vital presence alongside the newer Aristotelian influences and interests during the century or so before Dante. The scientist and translator of Aristotle's *Ethics* Robert **Grosseteste** (1168/75–1253) extended the Neoplatonic and Augustinian idea of the illumination of the intellect into a unified physics and metaphysics of light. Somewhat later in the century (1262–3), in his commentary on Aristotle's *Metaphysics*, the Dominican **Albertus Magnus** takes a Neoplatonic stance with regard to God's 'intellect' and asserts along with Augustine that 'by his intellective thought . . . God causes everything, for . . . understanding is his being' (Luscombe 1997: 97). Also around the middle of the thirteenth century, the Franciscan **St Bonaventura** (c.1217–74) extended Augustine's emphasis on quest and illumination into the notion of mystical ascent, a 'journey of the mind to God'. His work of this title (*Itinerarium mentis ad deum*) is one of the formative texts for Augustinian thinkers in the later part of the century; and it may have provided a precedent for Dante's narrative of ascent in the *Commedia* (*DE* 120B–121A).

Yet Augustine himself – whose influence is evident throughout Dante's work, from the *Convivio* to the *Monarchia* and the *Commedia* – is represented only briefly and indirectly on two occasions in the *Paradiso* (10. 120; 32. 35). Dante's commitment to the 'idea of Rome' (as opposed to Augustine's hostility to the empire in his *City of God*) may lie behind this reluctance to give this authoritative figure a more prominent presence. Nonetheless, it is clear that 'the *Commedia* is inconceivable apart from Augustine's thought, either encountered directly or through the mediation of subsequent theology'; the ideas of civic conflict and ideal citizenship in the *City of God*, of the levels of vision in Augustine's Bible commentary (on Genesis), and of conversion in the *Confessions* are all essential to Dante's poem (*DE* 71B–72A). In the *Convivio* (1. 2. 13–14) Dante also acknowledges Augustine (along with Boethius) as a key precedent for 'speaking about oneself', as he is to do throughout the *Commedia*.

## Scholasticism and the 'schools of the religious'

Essential as it is, Dante's Augustinianism is only part of the intellectual landscape within which the *Commedia* grew. We also need to consider some further tendencies in 'academic' philosophy and theology during his time. Amongst these are the challenges and problems posed by the reception of

Aristotle and by what has been called 'the application of reason to revelation' (Leff 1958: 92).

Scholasticism requires schools. Earlier in the Middle Ages these had been provided by the monasteries and (especially in northern Europe) the cathedrals. By the early thirteenth century the universities (several of which had been founded in the later eleventh century) had become the leading centres of higher education. In Italy the *Alma Mater Studiorum* at Bologna was pre-eminent, especially for the study of law; and Dante formed important intellectual links with the city during his years of exile (above, pp. 50, 55). Its academic culture also contributed towards the development of the 'new style' of love-poetry, as Dante and his contemporaries recognized (below, p. 115). Bologna, however, was not at the theoretical cutting edge during this period; and it did not have a theology faculty until well after Dante's time (in 1364).

As Dante was well aware, it was the University of Paris that dominated the scene as far as the advanced study of theology and philosophy was concerned. Whether or not we believe Villani's and Boccaccio's claims that he himself spent some time studying there (above, p. 36), it is clear that he recognized its status, which was substantially due to the presence of scholars from the mendicant orders. The Dominicans had established themselves at Paris as early as 1217/18 and the Franciscans shortly after that, acquiring a house within the city in 1230 (*Lawrence 1994: 128–30). The two major theologians of the later thirteenth century – **Bonaventura of Bagnoregio** and **Thomas Aquinas (c.1225–74)** – were both Italian friars (respectively Franciscan and Dominican) who studied and taught at Paris. Their career paths, as well as their philosophies, were very different, although they were both appointed to chairs as 'regent masters' in their schools at Paris in the same year (1257). Bonaventura, as we have seen, was, like many Franciscans, strongly influenced by Augustine and Platonism. He studied in Paris, but his full-time tenure there was soon cut short by being called to take charge of the entire Franciscan Order, as minister general from 1257 to 1274 (Moorman 1968: 132–3, 245). On the other hand, Thomas Aquinas seems to have spent most of his relatively short career (from 1256 to 1274) in various academic posts in France and Italy, including two periods as regent master in the Dominican school of Saint-Jacques in Paris, where, during 1269–72, he composed the second part of his huge compendium of doctrine, the *Summa Theologiae* (Lawrence 1994: 136–7).

Dante's Aquinas acts as guide through three cantos of the *Paradiso* (10–11, 13). In making him the chief voice of Christian wisdom in the Heaven of the Sun, Dante pays tribute to what has been seen as Aquinas's pre-eminent contribution to medieval intellectual culture: 'his adaptation of Aristotelian philosophy to the requirements of Christian thought in such a way as to produce an original philosophical system'; and his 'building up [of] a natural theology, a theology based upon rational argument' (Luscombe 1997: 99; Leff 1958: 215). To summarize his thought as solely 'Christian Aristotelianism' is inadequate: his theory of existence, of 'God as the measure of being, and of ascent and descent in a scale of being', also owes much to the Platonic tradition and there are frequent references in his work to 'the Platonists' and their notion of universal forms (Luscombe 1997: 100, 102; Gilby 1960: 16, 52, 194 etc.). Yet in his theory of knowledge, he seems to prefer Aristotle's view of the process of abstraction from sense images over the Platonic view of the intellect as 'a spiritual power making no use of a bodily organ in its thinking' (*S Th* 1a. 84. 6). Following his master, Albertus Magnus, Aquinas was actively committed to the promotion of Aristotle's ideas on a wide range of philosophical issues, through his commentaries on the *Ethics*, the *Politics*, the *Metaphysics* and *De Anima*. He can therefore be seen as both contributing and responding to the challenge that the newly available works of Aristotle were presenting to western Europe in the fields of logic, metaphysics, psychology, ethics, politics and the natural sciences.

For a Christian culture – and especially for its governing authorities – the treatment of Aristotle's ideas on God, eternity, the soul and human happiness proved problematic as well as stimulating. Measures taken by or urged upon the University of Paris with regard to 'the Philosopher' (as Dante, Aquinas and others called him) reflect various degrees of unease throughout the thirteenth century. There were, for example, official moves to ban Aristotle's scientific works in 1210 and his *Metaphysics* in 1215, and an attempt to censor the *Physics* in the 1230s – alongside various warnings from the papacy to universities about the dangers of philosophy more generally (1228, 1231, 1245, 1263). Yet despite (or because of) these admonitions, the academic study of 'the Philosopher' flourished, and by the middle of the century the teaching of the arts faculty (regarded as a preparation for the study of theology) was dominated by Aristotelian texts (Leff 1958: 172–3, 225). The condemnations of doctrine issued by the bishop of Paris in 1270 and more extensively in 1277 were directed against what were considered to be erroneous teachings disseminated by philosophers in the arts faculty, and not against specifically Aristotelian ideas. They reflect, however, concern about the teaching of 'radical Aristotelians' at Paris, such as **Siger of Brabant** (c.1240–81/4), whose views on the human intellect were criticized by Aquinas and whom Dante's Aquinas describes as having 'logically demonstrated unwanted truths' or 'truths that stirred up resentment' (*Par.* 10. 138).

Why does Dante place the controversial Siger in such a prominent position, and why does he make Aquinas pay him this kind of tribute? Siger in the 1270s was moving away from the notion of a single universal human intellect, as promoted by 'Averroes' (ibn-Rushd), the great Spanish Arab commentator on Aristotle (*Inf.* 4. 144; *DE* 79B, 522A). At that time he was moving closer to Aquinas's position (and that of orthodoxy), which was 'basically, that each human being thinks as an individual, and does not simply share thought with a separate intellect' (Luscombe 1997: 111). So Dante at the end of *Par.* 10 may be suggesting or even celebrating some kind of consensus. He may also, however, be acknowledging, less comfortably, the sheer energy of philosophical enquiry and debate that, close to the fictional date of the *Commedia*'s journey (1300), was being prompted by the reception of the Aristotelian texts. Such energy was being reflected not only in speculation about metaphysics and psychology but also in fields as diverse as politics and the natural sciences. It is also evident beyond the academy in the transmission of Aristotelian and other philosophies to a wider audience, for example through preaching (Luscombe 1997: 136), or through ambitious and encyclopedic vernacular texts, such as Dante's own *Convivio* (c.1304–7).

# Saints, Contemplatives, Visionaries

## Guides and models: Dante's prophets and saints

Voices of Old Testament prophets are heard at a number of points in Dante's writing. Thus, the death of Beatrice in the *Vita nuova* (ch. 28) is announced by the first verse of the Lamentations of **Jeremiah**: 'How deserted she sits, the city once thronged with people! Once the greatest of nations, she is now like a widow.' When confronting the authority of the papacy in *Monarchia* (3. 1. 1), Dante adopts the voice of the prophet **Daniel** answering King Darius out of the lions' den to affirm that God's angel had 'sealed the lions' jaws; they did me no harm, since in his sight I am blameless' (Daniel 6: 22). And the visionary and prophetic stance of the *Commedia* is informed in several ways by Dante's reading of prophetic books such as **Isaiah** and **Ezekiel** (Hawkins 1999: 20–2, 37, 191). He also shows an interest in some more problematic and marginal visionary figures, such as Joachim of Fiore and Ubertino of Casale (below, pp. 93, 96).

Amongst the **early Christian saints**, women have a prominent role from very early in the *Commedia* – as might be expected in a work that is dominated by the figure of Beatrice. The **Virgin Mary** plays a crucial part in the poem, not only as the 'queen of Heaven' and the mediator between Christ and humanity, but also as the instigator and goal of Dante's journey (*Inf.* 2. 94–6, *Par.* 33. 1–39). The long development of the cult of the Virgin through the Middle Ages – including her presence in the liturgy, in hymns, in mystical writing and in lyric poetry – lies behind the representation of her as 'the noble lady in Heaven' (*Inf.* 2. 94) and the invocation to her which opens the last canto of the *Paradiso*; and it also informs the frequent and vivid portrayals of her as exemplary figure in the *Purgatorio* (*Botterill 1994:

85

152–65). Acting as intermediary between the Virgin and Beatrice in *Inferno* 2 (97–108) is the fourth-century martyr **St Lucy of Syracuse**, whom Dante seems to have regarded as a kind of patron saint (*Inf.* 2. 98). Lucy's name itself carries associations with light (*luce*); and there is evidence that she was known as a patroness of sight (Cassell 1991). She reappears as an enabler of Dante's journey in *Purgatorio* (9. 52–63) and in *Paradiso* (32. 136–8), where we are reminded of how she prompted Beatrice to come to her lover's aid and helped to redirect his vision.

Three of the **early Apostles** witness Dante's affirmation of Christian belief in the later stages of the *Paradiso*: St Peter (24), St James (25) and St John (26). Of these the most powerful voice is that of Dante's **St Peter**, founder of the church, who examines the pilgrim on the nature of faith in canto 24 and urges him to raise a prophetic voice to condemn the present papacy and look towards its revival (*Par.* 27. 65–6). The poet's prophetic voice in the *Commedia* also draws strength from two other Apostles: St John and St Paul. **St John**, the disciple of Christ who questions the pilgrim on the nature of love in *Paradiso* 26, was also believed to be the author of the Gospel that bears his name and of the final book of the Bible: Revelation. Commentaries on John's Gospel had been produced by several of Dante's authors (Augustine and Aquinas), whilst for **Revelation**, or 'Apocalypse', he might have known or known of the commentaries by Richard of St Victor (d. 1173, referred to in *Par.* 10. 131–2), by Bonaventura and by Peter of John Olivi (see below, pp. 94–6). Appropriation of the apocalyptic language and imagery of Revelation is evident at a number of points in the *Commedia* (*Inf.* 19. 10–11, *Purgatorio* 32, *Par.* 27. 58–60, 32. 127–30). Invocation of St John by name (e.g., *Inf.* 19. 10, *Purg.* 29. 105) thus lends authority to Dante's prophetic and apocalyptic vision (Hawkins 1999: 54–71).

From **St Paul**, a key passage for Dante is from the second Epistle to the Corinthians:

> I am boasting because I have to. Not that it does any good, but I will move on to visions and revelations from the Lord. I know a man in Christ who fourteen years ago – still in the body? I do not know; or out of the body? I do not know; God knows – was caught up into Paradise and heard words that cannot and may not be spoken by any human being. (2 Cor. 12: 1–4)

This elliptical account of 'visions and revelations' stands out sharply from the rest of Paul's apologia for his life and mission at the end of 2 Corinthians. It is not surprising therefore that it inspired a later narrative of a journey to

Heaven and Hell: the late fourth-century *Apocalypse* (or *Vision*) *of St Paul* is one of a number of otherworld visions preceding Dante's (*Gardiner 1989: 13–46; *Morgan 1990: 225–6). Dante implicitly compares his venture and vision to Paul's at several points of departure in the *Commedia*. When the pilgrim is contemplating the descent into Hell with Virgil, he twice cites the saint's example: as God's 'chosen instrument' (the new convert, destined to convert others, in Acts 9: 15); and, more famously, as a daunting parallel to Aeneas, who explores the underworld in Book 6 of Virgil's poem: 'I am not Aeneas, not Paul' he urges anxiously here (*Inf.* 2. 28 and 32). Yet by the beginning of the ascent in the *Paradiso* he is describing his experience and its purpose in terms that strongly recall the passage in 2 Corinthians 12 (*Par.* 1. 70–5). As the ascent through Paradise continues – with its own visions and revelations – parallels with St Paul's continue (e.g., *Par.* 28. 136–9). Although the saint's voice is never heard directly in the *Commedia*, his role as theologian and martyr is recurrently acknowledged in the later cantos (e.g., *Par.* 18.131–2, 21. 127–9, 24. 61–6). Like the prophets and St John, therefore, St Paul is a visionary precedent and model; like his 'brother' St Peter (*Par.* 24. 62) he is also an apostolic example for a writer who himself aspired to be a 'chosen instrument', a new convert, capable of converting others.

## The monastic example: from Benedict to Bernard

Dante's Paradise is itself described several times as a 'cloister' (*chiostro*, *Purg.* 15. 57, 26.128, *Par.* 25. 127). In the later cantos of the *Paradiso*, saints associated with the monastic and contemplative life come to the fore, alongside their apostolic forerunners. Augustine (above, pp. 80–1) devised one of the early rules for a religious community which had been adopted in the Middle Ages by both monastic and mendicant orders; and he is hence enthroned alongside two other authors of religious rules in the Celestial Rose (*Par.* 32. 34). More directly prominent, however, in voicing the ideals of this tradition is a group of three other saints: St Benedict, St Peter Damian and St Bernard of Clairvaux.

   In Dante's Heaven of Saturn, which is the 'cloister' of contemplative souls, the brightest of the lights is that of **St Benedict** (c.480–c.547; *Par.* 22. 28–30). He first identifies himself here through his association with the summit of a mountain: the peak of Monte Cassino, which was the site of the monastery he founded around 525 (*Par.* 22. 37–41). Benedict, whose first communities were based around Subiaco near Rome, was the founder of western monasticism; and his rule – which emphasized obedience, stability of residence and shared ownership of property as well as a life of prayer, labour and study – proved a highly durable pattern for this form of religious life throughout the Middle Ages. Dante recognizes this role not only by placing St Benedict beside two other authors of religious rules (St Augustine and St Francis) in the Celestial Rose (*Par.* 32. 34), but also by making him one of the voices that, in the *Paradiso*, call for and look to the renewal of the church's original ideals. Hence, whilst Thomas Aquinas and Bonaventura have deplored the departures of the mendicant orders from the apostolic principles of their founders (*Par.* 11, 12) and a number of voices, culminating in that of St Peter (*Par.* 27), do the same for the papacy, Dante's St Benedict in *Paradiso* 22 claims that the Benedictines' failure to keep his rule has led their abbeys to become caves of thieves and turned their monks' cowls into 'sacks of mouldy flour' (76–8). This he laments as part of a more widespread process of decay and betrayal of apostolic ideals that can only be reversed by some kind of apocalyptic intervention (82–96).

Such intervention has also been called for at the end of the previous canto by **St Peter Damian** (*Par.* 21. 127–32) The historical Peter Damian (1007–72) was one of the leaders of the eleventh-century religious movement which sought, after five centuries of Benedictine monasticism, to recover the institution's original apostolic and eremitical principles (*Little 1978: 72–5) As a monk, he followed the severer version of the Benedictine rule that had been instituted at another mountain hermitage – that of Camaldoli in the Casentino – by **St Romualdo** (c.950–1027), another reformist to whom Dante's St Benedict refers (*Par.* 22. 127–32; Little 1978: 71–2). Both Romualdo and Peter Damian aspired to the austere life of the early Christian Desert Fathers, although the latter was, as Dante notes, reluctantly persuaded to become a bishop and cardinal towards the end of his life (*Par.* 21. 124–6). Peter Damian referred to his mountain hermitage as 'the desert', as well as a 'refuge from the persecutions of the world', where people could be 'truly free and truly happy'; and he described it in words which may well have influenced Dante's imagining of ideal monasticism as a 'happy marketplace, where earthly goods are exchanged for those of heaven ... where a little bodily suffering can purchase the company of heaven and a few sparse tears procure everlasting gladness' (Little 1978: 72, 74). Of the writings of Peter Damian that might have influenced Dante's portrayal of his contemplative and reformist vision in *Paradiso* 21, probably the most relevant are his collection of letters, his treatise *Dominus vobiscum* (where the image of the ladder of contemplation features as it does in Dante's canto), and his *Praise of Eremitical Life*.

There are some parallels between the historical and fictional Peter Damian and the figure whom Dante chose to represent as his final intermediary in the *Paradiso*. **St Bernard of Clairvaux** (1090–1153) replaces Beatrice as mediator and interpreter of the visions experienced in the last three cantos of the poem. The historical Bernard was, like Peter Damian, a product and leader of the monastic reform movement of the eleventh century – a movement which around the turn of the century had produced three major new orders: the Carthusians, Premonstratensians and Cistercians (Little 1978: 84–96). As an early member and leading writer of the new Cistercian order (which he entered in 1112), he followed a strict interpretation of the rule of St Benedict. Like the other new orders and like Peter Damian in life and in Dante (*Par.* 21. 106–21), the Cistercians sought to pursue their austere lifestyle in remote wilderness areas (thus managing to achieve considerable prosperity as landowners). Like Peter Damian, Bernard also felt the pull of church politics: he was an advisor to several popes and a publicist for the Second Crusade (1145–8). He was also drawn into theological controversy, and during the enquiry into Peter Abelard's doctrine on the Trinity in 1140 he was instrumental in 'fixing' the verdict. Although he may have had 'no conscious malicious intent' in this case and was primarily concerned to defend the faith and the authority of the church, he obviously had little interest in the actual evidence of Abelard's teaching and took the view 'that a man's teaching was of less importance than his attitude, that a proud and contentious person ought to be condemned as a heretic in any case' (Evans 2000: 117–23).

Unlike Augustine, Anselm or (later) Aquinas, Bernard does not seem to have been a philosophically adventurous thinker. His theology has been described as an exercise in 'damage limitation': reactive rather than ambitious or systematic (Evans 2000: 72). He was not opposed to the study of the liberal arts or distrustful of reason; but he was insistent that reason should not seek to challenge the authority of faith. Abelard's he saw as a case in point, where, as he wrote: 'the human intellect usurps everything to itself, leaving nothing to faith; it wants to go too high in enquiries which go beyond its power' (quoted in Leff 1958: 154).

Bernard's hostility to Abelard thus points us towards aspects of his work that were influential upon Dante. The way in which he himself wanted to 'go high' was through meditation and contemplation which, by means of grace (as Augustine had emphasized), would lead to an ascent and return to

God, as outlined, for example, in Bernard's *Sermons on the Song of Songs* (Matarasso 1993: 69–70, 74). Essential for the mediation of grace was the role of Christ and the Virgin Mary; and Bernard's writing on this subject formed an important part of the mystical tradition that developed through the twelfth and thirteenth centuries. In dramatizing the various operations of grace that lead in the *Commedia* from the Virgin Mary through Beatrice to Virgil (*Inf.* 2), and then through Beatrice and Bernard back to the Virgin (*Par.* 33. 1–39), Dante shows awareness of Bernard's contribution to Marian contemplation and devotion, even though direct and specific influence from the latter's works is hard to identify (Botterill 1994: 148–93). But he also recognizes the saint's wider role as 'contemplative' and 'teacher' (*Par.* 32. 1–2); and this characterization seems to be informed by a sense of St Bernard's example as visionary, as eloquent preacher and interpreter of the Bible, and as monastic and ecclesiastical reformer.

## The new apostles: St Dominic and St Francis

Dante's saints tend to talk about each other quite frequently in the *Commedia*. Early in the *Paradiso* there is an extensive example of such saintly gossip: the biographies of **St Francis** and **St Dominic** in cantos 11 and 12, as presented by two illustrious members of their orders, the Dominican St Thomas Aquinas and the Franciscan St Bonaventura. The pairing of these two lives and the use of a voice from one order to pay tribute to the other's founder serves to emphasize several features of the Franciscan and Dominican examples. Dante and his contemporaries saw the foundation of these two major orders of friars in the early part of the thirteenth century (the Franciscans in 1209, the Dominicans 1215–18) as a joint enterprise of renewal in the church, reviving the apostolic ideal of voluntary poverty and missionary preaching, especially in the growing cities of western Europe, and thus extending the spirit of reform that had animated the ascetic and eremitical movements of the previous century (Little 1978: 113–69; Lawrence 1994: 1–25). The energy of this enterprise is reflected in the elemental imagery (of the rising sun and the mountain torrent) through which Dante portrays the initial actions of Francis and Dominic; and in the representation of the two saints as the fellow-helmsmen of the ship of St Peter and as the two wheels of the church's battle chariot (*Par.* 11. 49–54 and 118–23, 12. 97–108). The impression of shared apostleship had also been reflected in accounts of a meeting between the two saints in Rome and in the imagery of the joint encyclical published by the leaders of the two orders (Humbert of Romans and John of Parma) in 1255, concluding: 'These are the two shining stars that according to the Sibylline prophecy have the appearance of the four animals and in the last days will cry out in the name of the Lord in the way of humility and voluntary poverty' (Lawrence 1994: 68; *McGinn 1998: 164–5).

Yet, despite the collegial harmony that leads Dante's Aquinas to narrate the life of St Francis and his Bonaventura to relate that of St Dominic, there were marked differences between the two saints and the orders they founded. Dominic's mission developed out of a more combative background: the Christian reconquest of Spain and the campaign against the Cathars in southern France. His order, moreover, was characterized by discipline; and its recognition of the need for training in the skills needed for preaching led the Dominicans to establish themselves within the universities at an early stage (Lawrence 1994: 67, 84–8, 127–51). Francis was, in his way, an equally determined figure, as Dante's Aquinas acknowledges (*Par.* 11. 88–93). Yet he seems to have experienced some tension between the life of the active preacher in the city and that of eremitical solitude in the mountains, and much of the abundant Franciscan art and literature of the time depicts him and his followers within a wilderness or pastoral landscape, as Dante does in *Paradiso* 11. 43–51 (Moleta 1983: 16–20; Cook 1999: 165–8). He was also ambivalent about the demands of running a rapidly expanding religious organization and sceptical about the value of learning (Lawrence 1994: 37–9). The Franciscans – although they eventually became as prominent as the Dominicans in the intellectual culture of the thirteenth and fourteenth centuries – found it more difficult to reconcile their founding ideals with the practicalities of working within the church. They were also recurrently beset by controversy and conflict both within the order and with the papacy, particularly with regard to the interpretation and observance of their founder's precepts (Lawrence 1994: 48–64).

Like the Cistercians before them, the new orders of friars were rather too successful for their own good. Their intellectual and cultural pre-eminence, their popularity among the urban mercantile classes, their usefulness to the papacy and their ability to attract the patronage of royalty and aristocrats did not help to gain them friends among the rest of the clergy; hence their rivals in the church and the universities were quick to accuse them of greed, ambition and other failings (Szittya 1986: 3–61; Lawrence 1994: 127–65). Some of the frequent accusations of their adversaries may have been warranted; and the warning delivered by Dante's Aquinas to those in Dominic's flock who 'stray' in search of 'new pastures' reflects a concern about the temptations of worldly learning and advancement (*Par.* 11. 124–32). A more specific and urgent anxiety, however, is that which Dante's Bonaventura expresses about the strife within and around the Franciscan 'family' (*Par.* 12. 114–26).

Central to this conflict within Franciscanism was the interpretation of St Francis's precepts on and example of observing evangelical poverty. The appeal of willingly adopting poverty and thus following the path of the original apostles is clearly evident in the Franciscan art and literature of the thirteenth century. Gestures of renunciation are powerfully registered in the fresco-cycles and the early biographies of St Francis; and the notion of a passionate apostolic 'marriage' to poverty provides the dominant metaphor for Dante's own 'life' of the saint in *Paradiso* 11. Strict observance of this sort is not without its paradoxes and problems. The ideal to which St Francis and his radical followers aspired has been described as 'a very specific kind of poverty that only Christians of means could effectively embrace' – a condition in which 'the affluent Christian had a decided advantage over the poor one, for he was in a position to relinquish money, property, or social standing in such a way as to impress the community with the magnitude of his sacrifice' (Wolf 2003: 37, 83). Nor did the Franciscan phobia about handling money make it easy to run a large and growing international organization – as a number of popes recognized from 1230 onwards (Moorman 1968: 89–95; Lambert 1998: 86–107, 149–269).

Yet the original Franciscan ideal of strictly observed evangelical poverty attracted a number of charismatic and visionary followers, as appears to be recognized in *Paradiso* (11.82–7, 12. 130–2). The paths of several important radical or 'Spiritual' Franciscans intersected with Dante's, and their ideas and language may have influenced his thinking about renewal in the church. We shall be considering their importance for the *Commedia* shortly, but before that we must acknowledge the role of another problematic visionary who preceded those friars and who appears briefly and silently at the end of the cantos that have celebrated St Francis and St Dominic.

## 'The spirit of prophecy': visionaries and radicals

After Dante's Bonaventura has ended his narrative of the life of St Dominic and the ensuing lament for the troubles of his own Franciscan 'family' (*Par.* 12. 115–26), he concludes the whole canto by identifying a further circle of scholars, mystics and visionaries in the Heaven of the Sun. The very last of those that he mentions is one who 'shines' immediately beside him, namely 'the Calabrian abbot Joachim, who was endowed with the spirit of prophecy' (141).

**Joachim of Fiore** (c.1135–1202) began his career as a Cistercian monk but founded his own stricter order at San Giovanni in Fiore, high up in the mountains of southern Italy around 1190, and gained papal approval for it in 1196. He was on good terms with three popes, but official approval was not consistently bestowed upon him or his ideas, especially during the century after his death (Reeves 1969: 3). What Dante saw as 'the spirit of prophecy' in his work was an apocalyptic reading of Christian history, based on elaborate biblical interpretation. As he states in the prologue to his commentary on the Book of Revelation (Apocalypse): 'Insofar as God inspired me and I was able, I have completed the *Book of Concordance* [harmonizing the Old and New Testaments] in five volumes, the *Exposition on the Apocalypse*, divided by titles into eight sections, and the *Ten-Stringed Psaltery* in three volumes, besides other things I included in the minor works' (McGinn 1998: 140).

Joachim's scheme of history, as outlined in his *Exposition on the Apocalypse*, divides it into three periods, each dominated by one of the persons of the Christian Trinity. Thus the Age of the Father is said to have begun with Adam; that of the Son (Christ) with the long reign of Uzziah (Azariah), king of Judah (781–40 BCE); and that of the Spirit with the work of St Benedict, the founder of western monasticism (McGinn 1998: 134). The transitions between these ages overlapped considerably: thus the final Age of the Holy Spirit was begun by St Benedict in the sixth century but would not come to fruition until 42 generations after the birth of Christ (i.e., 1260). No one could know when the final Judgement, as described in the Book of Revelation, would actually occur, but Joachim and his followers were confident that they were living in the End Times. Signs of the End would, as Revelation shows, include persecutions and the appearance of the Antichrist; whilst in his *Book of Concordance* and *Exposition* Joachim also prophesied the advent of an 'Angelic Pope', based on the angel of Revelation 7: 2, and the founding of an 'order of perfect men' or 'hermits', like the witnesses of Revelation 11: 3–13 or the group who attend the Lamb just before the Day of Judgement and the destruction of the Gentile nations in Revelation 14 (McGinn 1998: 134–7; Reeves 1969: 47, 194, 245–6, 252–3, 401–10).

Joachim's apocalyptic scheme forms part of a commentary tradition that was long established, but his vision was distinctive in a number of ways. His use of illustrative diagrams was inventive and influential; and several of the images from the *Book of Figures* (prepared under his direction) probably lie behind the vision of the Eagle in *Paradiso* 18 and the interlinked circles of the Trinity in *Paradiso* 33. 115–20. His insistence on recognizing the active interventions of the Trinity in history was a challenging way of interpreting the Scriptures; and like Peter Damian, he was distrustful of the new learning and hostile to Scholasticism (McGinn 1998: 127–8). Not surprisingly, his work evoked strong responses. His attack on the Trinitarian doctrine of the Scholastic master, Peter Lombard, was condemned at the Fourth Lateran Council of 1215. His orthodoxy was affirmed by his own followers and by Pope Honorius III (1220), but among the major theological authorities later in the century, Bonaventura was uneasy about some aspects of his doctrine, and Aquinas was thoroughly opposed to the ideas of the three ages and its grounding in Joachim's reading of the Old and New Testaments (Reeves 1969: 28–36, 65–70, 179–81). Dante's placing of the Calabrian abbot directly alongside Bonaventura at the end of *Paradiso* 12 reflects a recognition of their shared though different commitment to apocalyptic theology (McGinn 1998: 196–7). Yet – like his elevation of Siger of Brabant at the end of canto 10 – it also seems to recognize an energetic and potentially dangerous trend of thought with which the figure had by his time become associated.

'Joachimism' was a vigorous and unruly tradition in Dante's time. Among the new orders of friars, certain elements among the Franciscans were particularly attracted to Joachim's vision of history. Like some members of other religious orders, they also saw in Joachim's 'spiritual order' and 'perfect men' a prophecy of the role that they aspired to in the church and in the Final Age. The most striking manifestations of Joachimism in the mid-thirteenth century were the presentations of the abbot's work as a revolutionary 'Eternal Gospel' by an overenthusiastic Franciscan in 1254 and by the popular millenarian Flagellant movement around the year 1260, which was scheduled to be the time of fruition for Joachim's 'Third Age' (Reeves 1969: 53–5, 60–2, 187–90; Burr 1993: 14–21). More influential upon Dante and his contemporaries, however, was the version of this tradition that was transmitted by a later generation of radical or 'Spiritual' Franciscans in Provence and Central Italy, whose thought 'represented a much more subtle blend of rigorist Franciscan observance and Joachimist eschatology' (Reeves 1969: 190–228; McGinn 1998: 203–21).

The intellectual leader of this later generation of Joachites was the Franciscan **Petrus Johannis Olivi**. Born at Sérignan in western Provence around 1248, Olivi studied theology at Paris, where, having heard Bonaventura lecturing at the Franciscan school, he may have first become interested in

Joachim's eschatology. In the 1270s he began to engage with the vexed issue of evangelical poverty (above, p. 92); and in 1283 his views on this and other subjects were condemned by a commission of the Franciscan order. Rehabilitated in 1287, he was appointed *lector* in the Franciscan school at Santa Croce in Florence, where he taught until 1290. We do not know the content of his teaching at Florence, which took place very close to the time when Dante was attending the 'schools of the religious' there (above, p. 11), but his main work on Franciscan poverty dates from before that (1279–83; Burr 1989: 43–51). His apocalyptic ideas were most fully developed towards the end of his life, in the later 1290s, through his commentary on Revelation (*Lectura super Apocalypsim*). Like most other commentators before him, Olivi saw the vision of Revelation as representing seven phases in the history of the church, but a distinctive feature of his approach is his identification of his own time as the culmination of the fifth period of decadence in the church, preceding the time of evangelical renewal in the sixth (*Burr 1993: 91–5). The fifth period, according to him, was a time in which 'practically the whole church from head to foot is corrupted and thrown into disorder and turned, as it were, into a new Babylon' (*Lectura super Apocalypsim*, quoted in Burr 1993: 85). The completion of this process in the early part of the sixth period would, he claimed, involve attacks upon the faithful by the 'carnal church', which he identified as 'the multitude of the reprobate who assault and blaspheme against the pilgrim church through unjust acts' and as a persecutory figure based upon the Great Whore (*meretrix magna*) of Revelation 17: 'stained with the blood or the slaughter of souls and the impious persecution of the spirit and of spiritual persons' (*Lectura super Apocalypsim*, my translations).

In his Apocalypse commentary, Olivi was careful not to identify the Great Whore of Revelation 17 directly or comprehensively with the church of his time. His interpretation of the passage, however, made it easy for those so inclined to do that (Havely 2004: 115–16). Amongst these in the early fourteenth century were the *beguins* of Provence and the *Fraticelli* of central and southern Italy, the radical heirs of the Joachite and Spiritual Franciscan traditions, whose appropriation of Olivi's ideas was attracting close attention from the papacy and its inquisitors from 1317 on (McGinn 1998: 218–21, 234–8; Lerner 1994: 186–204).

Dante never mentions Olivi anywhere in his work, although in view of the Franciscan's dangerous reputation at the time when the *Commedia* was being composed, this is one of the poem's 'most explicable silences' (*DE* 660). However, the episodes and imagery through which corruption in the church is portrayed at several key moments in the *Commedia* strongly suggest awareness of the apocalyptic thought and language of Olivi's Revelation commentary and the polemic of his followers: in the denunciation of Pope Nicholas III and similar 'pastors' (*Inf.* 19. 106–11); in the vision of the history of the church (*Purg.* 32. 109–60); and in St Peter's diatribe against the contemporary papacy (*Par.* 27.40–66).

Amongst Olivi's most articulate followers and defenders was an Italian Franciscan whose path was to cross Dante's on several occasions and whom the poet's Bonaventura mentions briefly during his account of Franciscan feuding in *Paradiso* 12 (121–6): **Ubertino da Casale** (1259–c.1341?). Ubertino is best known now perhaps for his appearances, as a rather creepy ascetic with a lurid imagination, in Umberto Eco's historical whodunit *The Name of the Rose* (Eco 1983: 51–64, 122–3, 220–31, 330–1). Eco's novel is set in 1327, late in Ubertino's life and 10 years after Pope John XXII had transferred him into the Benedictine order (Havely 2004: 165). Before that, however, Ubertino's career had been highly prominent and controversial. Like Olivi, he studied at Paris and taught for several years at the Franciscan school in Florence (in his case from 1285 to 1289), and he was active not only as a preacher and leader of the Spirituals in Tuscany, but as a diplomat and advisor who had the ear of cardinals and popes (*DE* 838). During the papal enquiry into Olivi's doctrine and the observance of the Franciscan rule at Avignon in 1310–11, Ubertino presented a number of submissions; and before that he had completed his best-known work, the *Arbor vitae cruci-fixae*, during a period of enforced retirement (in 1305). The *Arbor vitae*, the 'Tree of Crucified Life', is indebted to Joachim's notion of the Tree of History, whose 'branches were the works of Christ, its fruits the deeds of the elect' (Reeves 1969: 209). It was probably compiled from earlier works, some of which may have been known to Dante (Davis 1984: 153). Its fifth and final book is a commentary on Revelation that follows Joachim and Olivi in dividing church history into seven periods and world history into three ages, but it goes beyond Olivi in reading Revelation in terms of Franciscan experiences, including their recent confrontations with Dante's enemy, Boniface VIII (McGinn 1998: 206, 212–15; Burr 2001: 96–100).

Ubertino's *Arbor vitae* was not (for obvious reasons) widely circulated; but Dante's terse reference to him as an excessively strict interpreter of the Franciscan rule (*Par.* 12. 124–6) may reflect some knowledge of or about the Tuscan Spiritual's polemical and visionary writing on poverty, on corruption in the church, and on the life and ideals of St Francis. Other danger-ous Franciscan radicals of the time – such as the poet and satirist **Jacopone**

**da Todi** (1230/6–1306), the historian of the Spiritual movement Angelo Clareno (c.1255–1337), and the anonymous authors of the early fourteenth-century pseudo-Joachimist prophecies about corrupt popes (the *Vaticinia de summis pontificibus*) – are not explicitly referred to by Dante. But his vision of history and his way of imagining its processes converges at a number of points with theirs (Havely 2004: 57, 85, 175).

# History, Politics, Science

## Virgil to Villani: ancient history and modern chronicle

Various versions of the apocalyptic timetable envisaged by radical and orthodox commentators on Revelation contributed to Dante's vision of history.
But he was also concerned to interpret other evidence of the providential
plan in human affairs: the Roman empire's mission and purpose, and his own
native city's past in relation to its troubled present. And for this process of
interpretation a number of texts and traditions – from classical and early
Christian authors to contemporary chroniclers – provided him with sources
and contexts.

Dante's '**idea of Rome**' was formed substantially by his reading of classical
Latin authors, especially Virgil, Cicero and Lucan and excerpts from Livy
(above, pp. 70, 72). But his view of the empire's place in the scheme of
Christian history developed partly in response to the reading of Rome that
he found in the work of St Augustine (above, p. 81). Augustine's monumental late work *Of the City of God* (413–26) explores a number of his major
themes, such as thought and existence, time and creation, foreknowledge
and free will, and the nature of evil (Matthews 2005: 36–8, 77–8, 96–7,
111–13). As its title implies, the *City of God* is concerned with the Christian's
journey through and beyond the earthly state. The role Augustine thus
assigns to secular government is strictly limited (5. 17, 19, 21). Moreover,
far from being sanctioned by God as the source of justice and peace (as it is
in Dante's *Monarchia* 2. 11), the Roman empire is seen by Augustine to be
founded upon 'gross brigandry' (*City of God* 4. 4).

Basing his approach on the Aristotelian premise of humanity's natural
predisposition to citizenship (see above, p. 74), Dante first argues against
Augustine's pessimistic view of Rome towards the end of *Convivio* 4. 4. In

the following chapter of the *Convivio*, in *Monarchia* 2 and in *Paradiso* 6, he goes on to substantiate his argument about the empire's divinely ordained mission by citing a number of edifying and heroic examples from Roman history; and in this he draws upon and 'transforms' material from Augustine's follower, the Spanish priest, historian and geographer Paulus **Orosius**, writing in the early fifth century (Moore 1896: 279–82; Davis 1957: 55–65). The seven books of Orosius's *History Against the Pagans* ran from the Creation to 417 CE. In Dante's Paradise he appears as 'advocate' for the Christian scheme of history and as pupil of St Augustine among the distinguished circle of luminaries in Dante's Heaven of the Sun (*Paradiso* 10. 118–20; *DE* 571A). His representation of the role of the emperor Augustus in establishing world peace under Rome at the time of Christ's birth (in Books 3 and 6 of the *History*) is developed by later medieval chroniclers whose work Dante may also have known (Davis 1957: 64–7). Dante himself reformulates this providential argument at a number of points, in *Conv.* 4.5, *Mon.* 1. 16 and several of his political letters (Moore 1896: 279, n. 1). His confidence in the empire's divinely ordained mission up to and including the present was not shared by many, nor was it borne out by events in his time (see above, pp. 38–43). But it is reflected in the work of some contemporary chroniclers, including several whom he might have encountered during his visits to the Scaliger court at Verona (above, p. 47; Davis 1957: 73–80).

Dante also recognized and sought to recover the identity of **Florence** as 'the fairest and most famous daughter of Rome' (*Conv.* 1. 3. 4). The myths associated with Florence's Roman origin are also to be found in the work of Dante's contemporary, the chronicler **Giovanni Villani** (above, p. 54), whose *Chronicle* likewise calls the city 'the daughter and creation of Rome' (1. 41). Dante probably did not know Villani's *Chronicle* (*DE* 859A), but both writers share a sense of regretful contrast between the peaceful austerity of Florentine life in former days and the present times of prosperity and conflict (*Par.* 15. 97–135; Villani 7. 69). Dante may also have drawn upon the language of contemporary northern Italian city-chroniclers to express the concept of his city's 'good old days' and he may thus have passed on to the Florentine chronicler 'a view of the history of his city that tempered, although it did not essentially alter, his [Villani's] fundamental optimism' (Davis 1984: 87, d 92).

## Ideas of citizenship

Aristotelian ideas about citizenship were an important element in the climate of political thought during the early fourteenth century. The first partial commentary on Aristotle's *Politics* had been written early in the thirteenth century by Albertus Magnus (above, p. 81); and the first complete translation into Latin had appeared in the early 1260s (Luscombe 1997: 98). Problems and crises faced by Italian city-states around the turn of the century prompted a number of political writers to turn to this newly available text and incorporate it into their thinking. Amongst these was Dante's contemporary, **Marsiglio of Padua** (1275/80–1342), whose main work, the *Defensor Pacis* ('Defender of the Peace', completed in 1324, three years after Dante's death), was an influential and controversial work, especially from the point of view of the papacy and its critics (Black 1992: 56–71). Marsiglio argued for strong government by a single 'legislator', elected by the 'weightier part' of the community (1. 15), and he set a clear boundary between the secular ruler's jurisdiction and that of the church (Hyde 1973: 191–3). There are some convergences between Marsilius's political thought and Dante's and they may even have crossed paths during Dante's later years in Lombardy (*Ferrante 1984: 37).

Another Aristotelian political thinker who was closer to home for Dante (at least until his exile) was the Florentine Dominican friar **Remigio de' Girolami** (d. 1319). Remigio studied in Paris and taught at the school of the Dominicans in Santa Maria Novella, where he is documented as a *lector* over four decades, from 1286 to 1314. Like his Franciscan colleagues, Petrus Iohannis Olivi and Ubertino of Casale (above, pp. 94–6), he can thus be located as an active teacher in Florence around the time when Dante was taking an interest in the 'schools of the religious and the disputations of the philosophers' (*Conv.* 2. 12. 7; Davis 1984: 157–65). The direction of Remigio's thought and teaching was, however, very different from theirs, especially in its development of political ideas from Aristotle. Of his many works the ones that give such ideas particular prominence are *De bono communi* ('On the Public Good'), which responds eloquently to the factional conflict around the time of Dante's exile, calling for unity in the body politic; and *De bono pacis* ('On the Value of Peace', probably of 1304), together with nine sermons on peace (Davis 1984: 200–13). Although Dante never mentions Remigio by name, he would have taken note of the latter's political and civic concerns and interests, which in some ways anticipated his own. Themes common to both Remigio and Dante include: decadence and discord in Florence; wealth and nobility; and the problem of the papacy's temporal power and the validity of the 'Donation of Constantine' which had endowed it (Minio-Paluello 1956: 57–8). Both authors also combine an Aristotelian optimism about the state with the use of historical examples from

Augustine's *City of God* – for example, when listing the exemplary heroes of ancient Rome, as Remigio does in *De bono communi* and Dante in *Convivio* 4. 25 (Davis 1984: 202–3).

An even wider range of political and historical issues had been covered by an author who was the most powerful Florentine influence on Dante's work: **Brunetto Latini**. Born around 1220, Brunetto was of the generation before Dante. Like Dante, he underwent exile for political reasons; unlike Dante, he returned to a public career as a notary, politician and writer in Florence, where he died in 1294. His main work, the *Livres dou Trésor* (written in French prose during his exile in northern France during the mid-1260s) covers the world of science, history, philosophy and rhetoric – as well as the politics of governing a city-state, which occupies most of the work's third and final book. Dante portrays him, even in Hell, as still concerned about Florence and the city's betrayal of her inheritance as 'daughter of Rome' (*Inf.* 15. 61–78). The Brunetto of *Inferno* 15 also demonstrates the political value of rhetoric that the historical Brunetto derived from his reading of Cicero (Davis 1984: 169–79). We do not know whether Dante knew him personally, or was actually taught by him; nor do we know for sure if the poet attended lectures or sermons by learned friars such as Remigio de' Girolami. But both the Dominican Remigio – with his emphasis on citizenship – and the layman Brunetto – demonstrating the civilizing power of rhetoric – expressed ideas and concerns that were crucial to Dante's political vision.

## Experience of the world: scientific traditions and resources

From the midst of a flame, Dante's Ulysses speaks of 'the burning desire I had to gain experience of the world and of human vices and virtue' (*Inf.* 26. 97–9). The main means of learning about vices and virtue have been outlined in the earlier parts of this section; but what, for Dante and his contemporaries, were the main sources of knowledge about the natural world?

The **seven 'liberal arts'** of the medieval curriculum could lead on to the higher levels of learning, namely natural science (known as 'physics'), metaphysics and theology. To describe this hierarchy of subjects in the *Convivio*, Dante uses a comparison with the geocentric universe of his time: nine spheres surrounding the Earth and set in motion by the outermost of these, the *Primum Mobile*, beyond which was (in the Christian version of this scheme) only the light of God, the 'Empyrean', or, as Dante calls it, 'the unmoved Heaven' (*cielo quieto, Conv.* 2. 13.8; see diagram 3, p. 125). The branches of knowledge that we would regard as scientific (arithmetic, geometry, astronomy and natural science in general) are contained within this hierarchical progression, with the **basic skills** of the *trivium* (grammar, logic, rhetoric) below them and philosophy and theology above.

The liberal arts had their origins in the education system of late imperial Rome. They were thought to be essential foundations for the study of the Scriptures and theology by Augustine and by Boethius, who wrote textbooks on them; but by the twelfth century it was becoming clear that this framework, although it remained authoritative, was no longer sufficient to take account of the new scientific learning that was becoming accessible in areas such as algebra and optics (Luscombe 1997: 29–33, 66–7).

The seventh of the 'liberal arts' is named '**astrology**' by Dante (*Conv.* 2. 13. 8), whereas Albertus Magnus (above, p. 81), who is the source for much of his learning in this field, calls it '**astronomy**'. In practice, the two terms were interchangeable in the thirteenth century. The science of the movements of heavenly bodies and that of accounting for their effects on human affairs were both regarded as legitimate and related academic disciplines (Kay 1994: 1–2). The main sources for medieval astronomy (using the term in our sense) would have been Aristotle and the early second-century Egyptian, Claudius Ptholomaeus (Ptolemy) (Crombie 1969: 89–110). The 'Ptolemaic' or geocentric model of the universe, as accepted throughout the medieval period (Boyde 1981: 143–4), was developed from theory and calculations by Greeks of the third century BCE. Dante refers to both Aristotle and Ptolemy (e.g., *Inf.* 4, *Conv.* 2. 3. 5–6), but his knowledge of astronomy was derived from commentaries such as that of Albertus Magnus, from contemporary astronomical tables, and perhaps from basic instruments such as the astrolabe (*DE* 68A–69B; Crombie 1969: 103–10).

Astrology was also an ancient discipline, influential upon late Greek and Roman culture and accepted as valid by the ancient astronomers, including Ptolemy. For those of Dante's time, too, the influences of the planets and the stars provided an explanation for the huge range of variations in nature and human affairs (Boyde 1981: 250–2). The use of astrology for the purpose of divination – especially with regard to the fortunes of those in power – was already a matter of concern to the authorities during the Roman empire; and medieval theologians emphasized the ultimate primacy of the individual's free will over the power of astral influence (*DE* 66B–67A). Divination had its dark and disreputable side, as Dante showed through his portrayal of devious or fraudulent astrologers and soothsayers of classical and medieval times in canto 20 of the *Inferno*. Yet two of these – Michael Scot and Guido Bonatti of Forlì – were also contemporary astrologers whose work Dante might have used, alongside that of Ptolemy and others (Kay 1985: 1–14, 1994: 11–14, 244–6). The will of God can, as Dante argues in *Monarchia*, be seen as operating on worldly affairs through 'the disposition inherent in the circling of the Heavens' (*Mon.* 3. 16. 12). Astral influences are acknowledged to affect the formation of human character to some extent (*Purg.* 16. 67–76); and the astrological properties of the planets are frequently evident in the spheres of the *Paradiso*: from the Moon through Mercury, Venus, the Sun, Mars and Jupiter to Saturn (Kay 1994: 247–57).

Essential to the medieval understanding of the material world beneath the sphere of the Moon was the **theory of the elements**. The view that all things in the universe were composed from the basic elements of earth, water, air and fire is found in Plato's *Timaeus* (Crombie 1969: 46–7), but it was Aristotle who formulated a consistent theory of their characteristics and relationship which was generally accepted by writers of Dante's time (Boyde 1981: 57–65). The main source for these ideas was Aristotle's *De Caelo et Mundo* ('On the Heavens and the Earth'), the text of which, along with several of the Greek and Arabic commentaries, had been translated into Latin in the twelfth and thirteenth centuries (Crombie 1969: 59–60, 63). Influenced as he was by the prevailing Aristotelianism of the thirteenth century (above, p. 83), Dante refers specifically to this text as he does to others by 'the Philosopher', for instance in the *Convivio* (2. 3. 4 and 6), although he is probably drawing more directly upon the commentators, such as Albertus Magnus. In Book 2 of *De Caelo* Aristotle sets out the natural arrangement of the four elements in concentric spheres, according to their respective weight (with that of earth surrounded by the spheres of water, air and fire); and Dante investigated the apparent anomalies of this system in one of his last works, the *Quaestio de Aqua et Terra* (above, pp. 47, 51). The notion of elements seeking their place in the hierarchy – and especially that of the lighter ones (air and fire) moving naturally upwards – held great imaginative potential; and Dante turns this aspect of Aristotelian science into a way of understanding human spiritual progression on several occasions: in *Convivio* (3. 3. 1–11) and most notably when Beatrice explains to Dante how he is able to rise beyond the 'light elements' of air and fire in *Paradiso* 1. 97–141 (Boyde 1981: 66).

Other major branches of medieval science and a wide range of scientific authors – Aristotle among them – also contributed to Dante's imagining of the world and of humanity's progress through it. **Meteorology** dealt not just with the weather but with interactions between elements and their

103

characteristics (hot, cold, moist, dry) in created nature below the sphere of the moon. Here again (although the term occurs first in Plato, *Phaedrus* 270a), Aristotle was the main source: the four books of his *Meteorologica* had been translated from Arabic and Greek in the twelfth century and at least one of the Greek commentaries was available in Latin by the later thirteenth (Crombie 1969: 59–60, 63, 110–11). Dante refers to the *Meteorologica* by name in the *Convivio* (e.g., 2. 13. 21) and the *Quaestio de Aqua et Terra* (83), probably by means of Albertus Magnus's commentary. Within this tradition, storms and earthquakes (for instance) were held to be caused by moist or dry 'exhalations' (Crombie 1969: 111; Boyde 1981: 74–9). Dante exploits the potential of both the Aristotelian theory and the observed actuality of such phenomena at some dramatic moments in the *Commedia*: for example when describing a storm that is raised by the impotent rage of a devil at having lost a human soul (*Purg.* 5. 103–29).

The study of **light (optics)** was 'among the most advanced physical sciences of antiquity' (Crombie 1969: 112–22). The work of Aristotle in this field and of his Greek followers such as Euclid and Ptolemy was taken further by the Arabic scientists of the tenth and eleventh centuries, and then by Robert Grosseteste and his followers, such as Roger Bacon (c.1214–92/4). Grosseteste, as we have seen (above, p. 81), was strongly influenced by Neoplatonic and Augustinian ideas about the illumination of the intellect, and his approach to the subject was thus both physical and metaphysical (Luscombe 1997: 86–7; Boyde 1981: 207–9). Similarly, Dante shows an interest in and knowledge of the science that he and his contemporaries (such as Roger Bacon) called *perspectiva*, along with awareness of light's significance in other ways. Thus, in the *Convivio* we find him linking the science of optics, as Aristotle had done, to geometry (2. 13. 27), whilst discussing faulty vision with reference both to Albertus Magnus (the commentary on Aristotle's *De Anima*) and to his own experience of eye-problems (3. 9. 13–16). In the *Paradiso*, practical experiments and diagnoses involving the action and perception of light are on several occasions (e.g., in *Par.* 2. 94–105) drawn upon to demonstrate the defects and development of the wayfarer's wider vision (Boyde 1993: 61–139; Rutledge 1995: 151–65).

The perception of the physical world in Dante's work also draws upon practical and mythical sources of medieval **geography**: the maps and travel narratives of his time, as well as the more academic authorities on the subject, such as the early Christian historian Orosius (above, p. 99). This kind of material is deployed and questioned in the scientific argument of the *Quaestio de Aqua et Terra* (19). It also informs the actuality of the world that is recreated and explored in the *Commedia*. One of the most vivid examples of such exploration is Dante's reinvention of Ulysses, references to whom recur four times in the poem (*Inf.* 26, *Purg.* 1, 19, *Par.* 27). The final epic voyage of Ulysses at the end of *Inf.* 26 – seeking such full 'experience of the world' and almost reaching the mountain of Purgatory in the midst of the ocean on the far side of the globe – shows Dante exploiting traditional and contemporary myths, models and narratives in order to imagine ways into the afterlife (Boyde 1981: 107–11; Hawkins 1999: 269–75).

For other features, components and inhabitants of the material world – motion, minerals, plants, animals, human anatomy – information was available in a number of forms. Academic knowledge of what came to be called **mechanics**, **geology**, **chemistry/alchemy** and **biology** was based on Aristotelian, pseudo-Aristotelian and Arabic texts; and like other branches of science, these were transmitted to western Europe through translations into Latin that were produced mainly in Spain and Sicily (Crombie 1969: 51–79; Luscombe 1997: 66–7). Moral and mythical lore about stones and animals could be found in the collections called 'lapidaries' and 'bestiaries'; whilst medical uses of plants were described in the herbals (Crombie 1969: 34–6, 154–6). **Medical knowledge** and the study of anatomy were developing rapidly during the late thirteenth and early fourteenth centuries, especially in Italy. Following the earlier development of medical studies at Salerno, the universities of Bologna and Padua were centres of excellence in this period; and it was at Bologna that dissection of human corpses for teaching purposes began to be practised around the turn of the century. Dante had close connections with Bologna (see above, pp. 50, 63), and the political guild that he belonged to as a non-practising member bore the title of *medici e speziali* (physicians and pharmacists). He also places the Greek and Arab medical authorities, notably Hippocrates (469–399 BCE), Galen (130–after 201 CE) and Avicenna (ibn-Sina, together as a group among the learned souls of Limbo (*Inf.* 4. 143). None of this suggests that he had a particularly strong interest in medicine; but developments in anatomy as an applied science in his time (Crombie 1969: 171–9) can be seen alongside the more exalted medical and philosophical disciplines as part of the context for his imagining of the human body in the *Commedia* (*DE* 115B–118A).

As well as being transmitted through translation of major texts into Latin, knowledge of science was also often accessible to a wider readership in various forms of **compendia**. The Latin encyclopedias produced during the twelfth and thirteenth centuries by scholars such as Alexander Neckam, Bartholomaeus Anglicus, Albertus Magnus and Vincent of Beauvais ranged widely through scientific and other disciplines (Crombie 1969: 144, 150–1). By Dante's time this kind of compendiousness was also being attempted by works in the vernacular, notably in French and most strikingly by Dante's own fellow-citizen and 'teacher', Brunetto Latini (above, p. 101). The first book of Brunetto's *Trésor* touches on physical knowledge of the Earth and Heavens, and his contribution to the encyclopedic tradition needs to be recognized as part of his profound influence on Dante (Sowell 1990; Havely 1990: 33–4). Dante's own encyclopedic work in the *Convivio* may be seen implicitly to recognize the *Trésor* as a precedent and to complement it as an ambitious project in the Tuscan vernacular, which for both writers was the 'mother tongue'.

# The Mother Tongue and the New Style

## The vernacular and its uses

'Mother tongue' (*parlar materno*) is used to describe the vernacular as a medium for poetry when the Italian poet Guido Guinizzelli introduces a Provençal predecessor in Purgatory (*Purg.* 26. 117). What awareness did Dante have of the forms and uses of that tongue; and how was vernacular literature developing in Italy during the thirteenth century?

Much of the answer to these questions can be found in Dante's own writing, both in Italian and in Latin, before the *Commedia*. The earliest material is in part of the prose commentary to his collection of love-poems, the *Vita nuova* (ch. 25), where, while explaining the figurative devices of such lyrics, he briefly discusses the relationship of Latin to vernacular poetry and the developments in Provençal and Italian writing over the previous century and a half. He also devotes most of the first treatise of the *Convivio* (1304–7) to a defence of his decision to write this exposition of his philosophical poems in Italian (*Conv.* 1. 5–13). And the forms and uses of the mother tongue are the main subject of a Latin treatise, *De vulgari eloquentia* ('Of Eloquence in the Vernacular'), which he began in 1303 and broke off, in the midst of Book 2, chapter 14, probably in 1305 (*DVE* xiii–xiv).

Some striking and dynamic distinctions between kinds and levels of language are developed in the early stages of the *Convivio* and *DVE*. Learned, literary Latin is said in *Conv.* to be 'immutable and incorruptible', by contrast with the vernacular which is 'unstable and corruptible', as can be seen from the diversity of dialects in Italian cities, where in just fifty years it can be seen how 'many words have become obsolete, been newly coined or altered' (*Conv.* 1. 5. 7–9). The vernacular thus follows and is susceptible to 'use' and

107

'nature', whilst literary Latin, like classical Greek, is rigorously grammatical and 'artificial' (*Conv.* 1. 5. 14, *DVE* 1. 1. 2–3). Initially in the *Convivio*, literary Latin is acknowledged to surpass the vernacular, by virtue of its 'nobility, power and beauty' (1. 5. 7). However, in the process of justifying his use of the vernacular for this extensive project (in 15 books, only four of which were completed), Dante develops the idea of 'love of one's own language' (1. 5. 2) in such a gallant and eloquent way that the vernacular comes, in the course of his defence, to acquire a nobility of its own – that of nature (1. 10–13). By the end of *Conv.* 1 the power of 'this vulgar tongue of mine' is being seen as that which brought the writer's parents together and shaped his very identity; whilst the 'huge benefits' he has gained through its use oblige him, as an affectionate duty, to seek to achieve for it through verse the 'stability' that he had earlier identified only with learning and Latin (1. 13. 4–10). Paralleling this development, at the start of *DVE*, Dante places the vernacular, as the tongue that infants acquire from those who surround and nurse them, in contrast to the *grammatica*, the language that is learned through long study (1. 1. 2–3), concluding that: 'Of these two kinds of language, the more noble is the vernacular: first, because it was the language originally used by the human race; second, because the whole world employs it, though with different pronunciations and using different words; and third, because it is natural to us, while the other is, in contrast, artificial' (*DVE* 1. 1. 4). Interestingly, this claim is made in Latin. Latin was, and would long remain, the gateway to an administrative or academic career and the means by which a writer could reach a learned and international public; and there would continue to be close and complex interactions between it and the literary vernaculars well beyond the Middle Ages. So, although he wrote the *Convivio*, the *Commedia* and much else in what Boccaccio would call 'our Florentine idiom' (*Trattatello* 1. 190–1), Dante would continue to write letters, political and scientific treatises (*Monarchia* and *Quaestio*), and occasional verse in the *grammatica* that he uses for *DVE*.

Dante shows awareness of the diversity of dialects being used in the Italy of his time – 'a range of at least fourteen different vernaculars', he estimates (*DVE* 1. 10. 7). There is frequent reference, from *DVE* 1. 12 onwards, to what had been written so far, especially in Provençal, Sicilian, Bolognese and Tuscan poetry. What had such writing achieved by Dante's time? Perhaps because of its closeness to Latin, the Italian vernacular (unlike French or English) had been relatively slow to develop as a written language in the early Middle Ages; and its 'consciously artistic and linguistically autonomous use' is not clearly evident until the late twelfth century (*CHIL* 4). Apart from the work of chroniclers (above, p. 99) and love-poets (below, p. 113f.), there were other important kinds of writing by Italians in their mother tongue.

Devotional writing in Italian and other vernaculars was given impetus by the development of the Franciscan movement, whose founder, **St Francis** (1182–1226), wrote a famous litany in praise of creation, the *Laudes creaturarum*. The Franciscans' commitment to popularizing and performing religion is reflected in their popular preaching and in their development of the dramatic song-form of the *laude*; and the most accomplished exponent of this form was the radical friar **Jacopone da Todi**, a near-contemporary of Dante (above, p. 96; Moorman 1968: 266–77). In the later thirteenth century the curiosity of the urban mercantile class and their interest in being able to conduct and express themselves to best effect in positions of power are provided for by compendia of scientific and ethical material (*CHIL* 30–1; Holmes 1986: 80–1). Also of interest to this new readership were the collections of exemplary, legendary and entertaining tales, with titles like *The Book of the Seven Sages of Rome, Lives of Philosophers, Sages and Emperors, Stories of the Knights of Old*, and the 100 tales of the *Novellino* (1280–1300). Much of this new material was based on translation from Latin or French. It answered and stimulated 'the desire of the new middle class to acquire culture, to parade modestly appropriate quotations from the classics', culled from vernacular versions (*volgarizzamenti*) of texts, such as the rhetoric of Cicero (translated by Brunetto Latini) and the sayings of Cato (*CHIL* 30–1). And both the sophisticated tastes of minority readers and the appetite for popular storytelling were catered for by translations of the French narratives of Charlemagne, Tristan and Lancelot.

## French and Provençal literature

Book 1 of *DVE* (especially chs. 8–10) shows awareness of relationships between what are now called the Romance languages, especially those whose words for 'yes' are *oïl* (Northern French), *oc* (Provençal) and *sì* (Italian). Among these, 'the third part, which belongs to the Italians' is a relative newcomer, but is said to be laying claims to superiority, both because of recent developments in poetry (the 'new style') and because of its closeness to Latin (1. 10. 2). Yet this linguistic self-confidence is not borne out entirely by the rest of *DVE,* where Dante's quest for an 'illustrious' vernacular becomes 'a fruitless search for writing in Italian which rises above the municipal or the uncouth' (*CHIL* 3). The other two 'parts' of 'our language' mentioned in *DVE* 1. 10 (Northern French and Provençal) had a much longer and far more distinguished record, as Dante and his contemporaries well knew.

Northern French by this time had a standard literary dialect, and its prestige was recognized by writers in other countries, such as England and Italy. Of this language Dante acknowledges that: 'because of the greater facility and pleasing quality of its vernacular style, everything that is recounted or invented in vernacular prose belongs to it: such as compilations from the Bible and the histories of Troy and Rome, and the beautiful tales of King Arthur, and many other works of history and doctrine' (*DVE* 1. 10. 2). This is a little understated. It recognizes the importance of the early thirteenth-century prose versions of the Arthurian stories, notably the *Prose Lancelot* and the *Death of King Arthur*, which were to be cited in the *Convivio* (4. 28. 8) and in the *Commedia* (*Inf.* 5. 127–38, 32. 61–2, *Par.* 16. 13–15). What it does not acknowledge is the already imposing *verse* tradition of Northern French epic, romance and lyric, much of which was also known to Dante.

Knowledge of the eleventh- and twelfth-century French **epics of Charlemagne and Roland** is evident in the *Inferno* (31. 16–18). The villain of *The Song of Roland*, Ganelon, appears among traitors to their country in the ninth circle of Dante's Hell (*Inf.* 32. 122), whilst the poem's two heroes, Charlemagne and Roland, are leading lights among the spirits of the just in his Heaven of Jupiter (*Par.* 18. 43–5). Dante would also have been aware that French romance (including classic versions of the stories of Lancelot and Tristan) had been written in verse; and that this was the medium, too, for the great allegorical romance, the *Romance of the Rose*. Begun by **Guillaume de Lorris**, who (between 1225 and 1230) wrote the first 4,000 lines describing the beginning of the lover's quest, this romance was completed (between 1269 and 1278) in a further 18,000 lines by **Jean de Meun**, who shifted its ground from courtly allegory into 'an atmosphere of robust academic debate in which subjective allegories give way to a set of loquacious, pugnacious characters, most of whom are drawn from earlier philosophical works' (Horgan 1994: xiv). The *Romance of the Rose* was widely disseminated and imitated; and two very early translations of material from it are to be found in two Tuscan or Florentine poems of the late thirteenth century. The *Fiore* compresses the *Romance* into 232 lively sonnets, whilst the much shorter (and incomplete) *Detto d'Amore* uses the original's octosyllabic verse form to explore aspects of love through the encounters with the allegorical figures of Reason and Wealth (*DE* 299B–300B, 378A–381A). Both these versions have been attributed to Dante himself, writing perhaps in the late 1280s or early

1290s – and if this is the case, they would represent a phase of vigorous thematic and stylistic experimentation early in his career. In any event, they clearly indicate the strong influence of Northern French upon Tuscan culture – an influence that is also reflected, for instance, in Brunetto Latini's choice of language for his *Livre dou Trésor* (above, pp. 101, 106).

In *DVE* Dante also shows some knowledge of the poems written by the Northern French *trouvères* (1. 9. 3, 2. 5. 4, 2. 6. 6, and notes 32, 128); but, for several possible reasons, he prefers to prioritize the *langue d' oc* (Provençal/Occitanian) for its achievement in lyric poetry. Thus in *DVE* 1. 10. 2 he follows his remarks on Northern French by noting that: 'The second part [of this tripartite group of languages], the language of *oc*, argues in its favour that eloquent writers in the vernacular first composed poems in this sweeter and more perfect language: they include Peire d'Alvernha and other ancient masters' (*DVE* 1. 10. 2). It is part of Dante's poetic agenda to relate these 'ancient masters' (the Provençal troubadours of the twelfth and early thirteenth centuries) to the early Italian love-poets and ultimately to the proponents of his own 'sweet new style'. This has been suggested in his very first illustrations of love-poetry in the *DVE* (1. 9. 3); and it becomes abundantly evident from his quotations in Book 2, where a number of Provençal poets are linked to the Sicilian school of love-poetry (below, p. 113); to the new stylists such as Guinizzelli and Cavalcanti; to Dante's friend Cino da Pistoia (below, p. 121); and ultimately to 'Cino's friend', Dante himself (2. 2. 8, 2. 5. 4, 2. 6. 6). Some of them also feature in all three parts of the *Commedia*: Bertrand de Born in the ninth 'pouch' of the eighth circle in Hell, paying a grim price for fomenting conflict (*Inf.* 28. 118–42); the Lombard poet Sordello da Goito, who wrote in Provençal and greets Virgil as a fellow-citizen of Mantua (*Purg.* 6. 58–75); and Folquet of Marseilles, the love-poet who became a bishop and an assiduous persecutor of heretics (*Par.* 9. 82–108).

Above all, it is the figure of a Provençal poet speaking in his own tongue who, at the end of *Purgatorio* 26, completes the construction of a poetic tradition within which Dante places his own transformation of love-lyric. This is **Arnaut Daniel** (b. 1145/50), whom the spirit of Guido Guinizzellli introduces to Dante as *il miglior fabbro del parlar materno*, 'the better craftsman in his mother tongue' (*Purg.* 26. 115–17). Arnaut had been listed among the practitioners of 'illustrious *canzoni*' in *DVE* (2. 6. 6, 2. 13. 2); and Dante used the difficult *sestina* form, using six rhymewords in intricate permutations (as favoured by Arnaut), for one of his own most taut and bleak lyrics (FB no. 78, 2. 265). Dante gives Arnaut a parting address at the very end of *Purgatorio* 26 (140–7) which is rather like the *tornado* or *congedo* ('leave-taking signature') that concludes a Provençal *canso* or an Italian *canzone*. The vitality and continuity of the Provençal tradition within Italian poetry is thus formally reflected here – from *canso* through *canzone* to *canto*.

## From Sicily to Tuscany

Within this tradition of Provençal influence (as Dante recognizes in *DVE* and *Purg.* 24, 26), the poets of early thirteenth-century Sicily and later thirteenth-century Tuscany form a crucial link. Sicilian vernacular poetry is said to have gained prestige through its association with the imperial court:

> those illustrious heroes, the emperor Frederick [1194–1250] and his worthy son Manfred [c.1232–66], knew how to reveal the nobility and integrity that were in their hearts . . . On this account, all who were noble of heart and rich in graces strove to attach themselves to the majesty of such worthy princes, so that, in their day, all that the most gifted individuals in Italy brought forth first came to light in the court (*aula*) of these two great monarchs. And since Sicily was the seat of the imperial throne, it came about that whatever our predecessors wrote in the vernacular was called 'Sicilian'. (*DVE* 1. 12. 4)

The **emperor Frederick II** is also referred to respectfully as an authority (albeit one to be disagreed with on the subject of nobility) in *Convivio* 4. 3. 6, onwards. In the *Commedia*, he is placed in the sixth circle of Hell among the heretics (*Inf.* 10. 119), probably on the basis of rumours and accusations about his beliefs, or lack of them, following his conflict with the papacy (Abulafia 1992: 254, 260). His illegitimate son, Manfred – who became regent after Frederick's death and was killed in battle against the papal forces at Benevento (1266) – is encountered as a mutilated figure 'of noble appearance' on the threshold of Purgatory (*Purg.* 3. 103–45); and his mother Constance, through whom he inherited the kingdom of Sicily, appears in the Heaven of the Moon (*Par.* 3. 109–20).

Although important as a ferocious, though ultimately unsuccessful, opponent of the temporal claims of Popes Gregory IX and Innocent IV (Tierney 1988: 139–49) and as the last emperor of the Swabian Hohenstaufen dynasty, Frederick seems to have been somewhat over-promoted by later writers as a patron of intellectual and creative activity, and his 'court', unlike that of his Sicilian predecessors, was not a fixed cultural centre (Abulafia 1992: 251–4). Nonetheless, his intellectual interests and curiosity made a considerable impression upon contemporaries, as Dante's references to him in *DVE* and

*Convivio* indicate. Frederick corresponded with Jewish and Islamic scholars, and employed as his court astrologer and physician a prolific translator of Aristotle's scientific works and their commentaries, Michael Scot, who appears amongst the diviners and soothsayers as a shady practitioner of 'magical delusions' in *Inf.* 20. 115–17 (Kay 1994: 11–14, 244–6; Luscombe 1997: 65; above, p. 102).

The poets of the 'Sicilian school' associated with Frederick II drew upon the Provençal traditions of love-lyric, but they were unlike the troubadours in certain important respects. They tended to have day-jobs as lawyers or speech-writers; and for genres other than love-poetry they used Latin (*CHIL* 9–10). One typical example is **Guido delle Colonne** (c.1210–after 1287), a judge of Messina who wrote five *canzoni* (two of which Dante cites and praises highly in *DVE* 1. 12. 2, 2. 5. 4, 2. 6. 6), along with an abridged Latin version of the lengthy French account of the Trojan War, the *Roman de Troie* by Benoît de Sainte-Maure (*Barolini 1984: 92, n. 9; Havely 1980: 165–6). Both the Sicilian poets mentioned by Dante in the *Commedia* also combined love-lyric with the law. **Pier della Vigna** (c.1190–1249) is a tragic case. Having studied law at Bologna, he rose to a high position as judge, legislator and rhetorician at the court of Frederick II, but after several decades of service to the emperor he was accused of embezzlement, blinded and put in prison, where he took his own life (Abulafia 1992: 203–8, 265, 401–4). Dante represents him as a plaintive and voluble figure in the Wood of the Suicides (*Inf.* 13. 55–78); and the rhetoric of the fictional character's speech here may reflect something of the actual Piero's skill in his Latin letters written for the emperor and the elegant arabesques of his vernacular *canzoni* (*CHIL* 13–14).

More important for Dante's construction of an Italian poetic tradition is the vernacular work of a less well-documented and less politically prominent Sicilian, another lawyer-poet: **Giacomo da Lentini**, writing as the emperor's 'faithful scribe' between 1233 and 1240 (Langley 1915: 131–5). Giacomo's surviving work comprises, in a recent edition, over 50 poems: 16 *canzoni* strongly influenced by the idiom of the Provençal troubadours and 38 sonnets. It is uncertain how much of this Dante actually knew: in *DVE* 1. 12. 8 he speaks favourably of the refined manner and courtly vocabulary of Giacomo's *canzone* 'Madonna dir vo voglio', although he does not name its author here, or anywhere in *DVE*, and appears to think of him as writing in the dialect of Puglia rather than that of Sicily. On the poetic map of *Purgatorio* 24, Giacomo, as 'the notary', is located as one of the staging posts along the route to the 'new style' of Dante and his nearer contemporaries (49–57). This somewhat underrates Giacomo's achievement, as does the judgement of one modern historian, who describes the movement he founded as 'but a pale imitation of existing Provençal work' (Abulafia 1992: 254). To balance such views, it should be acknowledged that this Sicilian poet probably invented the sonnet (which does not appear to have existed in Provençal). Moreover, one of his most accomplished essays in this form – the sonnet beginning 'Io m'aggio posto in core a Dio servire' – plays wittily with the idea of transforming or sublimating erotic passion, in a way that anticipates the more serious explorations of the new-style poets:

> I am determined to serve God so well
> I shall go straight to Heaven, come the day,
> to that blest place where, I have heard them tell,
> glad souls are all eternally at play.
> Yet it would not be worth my while to dwell
> in Heaven with my lady far away;
> bliss there, unpartnered, would be more like Hell;
> without her there, I would not want to stay.
>
> But I should make it clear I do not mean
> to think of any sinful actions there;
> I only want her graces to be seen:
>
> her sweet face and her gentle gaze, so rare,
> would in my view complete the holy scene,
> as she rose up to brightness in the air.
> (my translation from Contini 1960: 1. 80)

The poet whose voice Dante uses to invoke both Giacomo's reputation and that of the early **Tuscan writers** who followed him is that of **Bonagiunta of Lucca**. Bonagiunta Orbicciani (mentioned in documents between 1242 and 1257) was probably also a notary, and his work reflects the impact of the 'Sicilian school' upon the city-poets of Tuscany during the later thirteenth century (Barolini 1984: 86). So strong indeed was the influence of the Sicilian style upon Bonagiunta that a contemporary Florentine poet accused him of acting like the crow who went to court dressed up in the feathers of the peacock, by stealing the 'plumage (or pens, *penne*) of the Notary [Giacomo da Lentini]' (Langley 1915: 135). In *DVE* 1. 13. 1 Dante is quite dismissive of the claims of this generation of Tuscan poets 'to the honour of possessing the illustrious vernacular', and he places Bonagiunta among a group of those whose poetry is 'fitted not for a court but at best for a city council'. Nor is the portrayal of Bonagiunta in *Purgatorio* 24 much more flattering. Here he is a well-disposed but bumbling predecessor, expiating the sin of gluttony and regretting the lumpy style that prevented him from recognizing the voice of writers like, say, Dante. The historical Bonagiunta does indeed seem to have been sceptical about the pretensions of the new style, since in a sonnet addressed to Guido Guinizzelli (below, pp. 115–17) he reproached the Bolognese poet for changing the manner of love-lyric into that of abstruse and obscure discourse and of 'wringing *canzoni* out of learned tomes' (Contini 1960: 2. 481; see also Edwards 1987: 58–9).

Along with 'the Notary' (Giacomo), Dante's Bonagiunta names another Tuscan poet as guilty of similar shortcomings in style and vision (*Purg.* 24. 55–62). **Guittone d'Arezzo** (c.1230–94) was a 'municipal' poet (to use Dante's deprecatory term) but one whose work shows an impressive range. He was deeply versed in Provençal lyric, upon which the knotty style of some of his *canzoni* perhaps is modelled; he wrote prolifically in the newer Sicilian sonnet form; and his letters form a considerable contribution to the development of Italian vernacular prose (*CHIL* 15–17). Unlike the Sicilians – but very like Dante – he also addressed political themes, such as the defeat of Florence at Montaperti (above, p. 16) and his own exile from his native city of Arezzo; as well as the issue of religious conversion (Barolini 1984: 96–112). Dante's references to Guittone are consistently rather dismissive (in *DVE* 1. 13. 1, 2. 6. 8, as well as *Purg.* 24. 55–62, 26. 124–6). And understandably so: this was a figure whom Gunizzelli had addressed as 'father' and looked to for guidance and who addressed Guinizzelli as a 'worthy son' whose work was worth correcting (Edwards 1987: 62–5). Guittone's was a substantial achievement that Dante needed to downplay in order to stake a claim for the new generation and the new style of those who followed Guinizelli, namely: Cavalcanti, Cino da Pistoia, and 'Cino's friend' (Mazzocco 1993: 148–9).

## The new style: Guinizzelli, Cavalcanti, Cino da Pistoia

> 'Those sweet verses of yours
> which, while the modern way of writing lasts,
> will make the very ink that writes them precious.'
> (*Purg.* 26. 112–14)

This is the answer that Dante gives when the voice of **Guido Guinizzelli**, speaking out of the flames in the circle of the lustful, asks the reason for the affection he is showing (94–111). Dante does not specifically include

115

Guinizzelli (1230?–76) among the practitioners of the 'sweet new style' that he has made Bonagiunta acknowledge two cantos earlier (*Purg.* 24. 57). But it is clear from his description of the Bolognese poet as the 'father' of those around Dante who 'have produced sweet and refined verses of love' (*Purg.* 26. 97–9) that he regarded him as the key forerunner of the school of Tuscan love-poetry to which Bonagiunta had referred. So also do his references to Gunizzelli as *il saggio* ('the wise one') in the tenth sonnet of the *Vita nuova* and as *maximus Guido* in *DVE* 1. 15. 6. And so does the response in *Purg.* 26. 112–14 (above).

Guinizzelli's vocabulary and style reflect the influence of French, Provençal and Sicilian poets, as well as that of Tuscan writers such as his own poetic *padre*, Guittone, and Bonagiunta (Edwards 1987: xxxiii–xxxvii). Like a number of the Sicilians, and Bonagiunta too, he was a lawyer; and he is documented as judge and jurisconsult in a number of legal records from the mid-1260s till his exile from Bologna in 1274 (Edwards 1987: xv–xvii). Bologna (above, pp. 50, 63) was the leading centre for the study of law throughout the twelfth and thirteenth centuries; and even when Bonagiunta criticized Guinizzelli for obscurity (above, p. 115), he ironically conceded that learning came from there.

Guinizzelli's verse (some fifteen sonnets and five *canzoni*) is notable for some vivid visual and kinetic effects as well as for its more 'learned' aspects. One of his sonnets, for example, represents the lover in its last six lines as a figure almost literally thunderstruck by his lady's glance:

> My eyes let it like bolts of lightning pass,
> striking through the loopholes of a tower,
> smashing and shattering all that lies inside;
>
> and I am left just like a bust of brass,
> hollow within, void of all sense and power,
> seeming a man only from the outside.
> (my translation from Contini 1960: 2. 468)

The sonnet anticipates the representation of the disruptive and destructive power of love in several of the Florentine poets of the new style, notably Cavalcanti (below, p. 118).

Gunizzelli's most ambitious and influential poem in the more extended *canzone* form was the one beginning *Al cor gentil rimpaira sempre amore* ('Love always seeks its abode in the noble heart'; Edwards 1987: 20–3).

Concisely (in just 60 lines) he seems here to encompass the transition between the old and new styles. The first 30 lines figure the power of love through the kind of imagery (elements, precious and magical stones) that figure largely in earlier Tuscan poetry. The next stanza develops the idea of nobility through virtue rather than lineage, in the way that poets up to Guittone had done (Edwards 1987: xl–xlii) and as Dante was to do at far greater length in *Convivio* 4. It is the last two stanzas of the poem that would have appeared as a new departure – beginning with the resonant lines:

> *Splende 'n la 'ntelligenzïa del cielo*
> *Deo crïator più che ['n ] nostr'occhi 'l sole.*

[God the Creator illuminates the [angelic] intelligence moving the Heavens, more than the sun does in our eyes] (41–2)

They lead on to a lively dialogue in which God reproaches the lover for idolatry in attributing divine qualities to the lady – only to be met with the reply: 'She had the appearance of an angel from your kingdom; so I can hardly be blamed for falling in love with her.' And that – as it ends the *canzone* – seems to clinch the matter. As a slightly subversive way of elevating love in relation to religion, Guinizzelli's conclusion has something in common with the trajectory of Giacomo da Lentini's sonnet (above, p. 114). It also anticipates portrayals of the lady as an angelic figure in poets of the new style such as Dante. The first *canzone* of the *Vita nuova* – a poem which Dante regarded as a new departure in his own cult of Beatrice (below, p. 177) – builds upon Guinizzelli's scenario in several ways. It contains within the lover-persona's address to 'Ladies who have understanding of love' and his tribute to Beatrice's 'noble status' (11) a variety of voices of praise: an angel, saints, God, and Love. A more direct tribute to Guinizzelli and his *canzone* follows in the next poem of the *Vita nuova*: the tenth sonnet, which begins: 'Love and the noble heart are the same thing, / As the wise poet claims' (*VN* ch. 20). And yet more explicitly Gunizzelli is named five times in *DVE*, and his *canzone* 'Al cor gentil' is quoted twice (1. 9. 3, 2. 5. 4). It was necessary for Dante to leave Guinizzelli and Arnaut Daniel behind in the circle of the lustful as he moved through the wall of flame that divided him from Beatrice (*Purg.* 27. 34–54); and it was important for Dante as poet to outdo this *caro padre*, as he outdid Brunetto, Ovid, Virgil and others.

Outdoing is also the name of the game for much of the time in Dante's relationship with the fellow-Florentine poet whom he addresses in various ways throughout his work: **Guido Cavalcanti** (1250/5?–1300). A few years older than Dante, Cavalcanti is first named as the author's best friend at the beginning of the *Vita nuova*, where his response to the first sonnet of the collection is said to have more or less initiated the friendship between the two poets (*VN* ch. 3.). Later on in *VN* this friendship is explicitly mentioned four more times, most notably on two occasions where the implications of writing in the vernacular are being explored (*VN* chs. 25. 10; 30. 3).

What was the character of this friend? A fair amount has been said and imagined about Cavalcanti's accomplishments and manner, both by four-teenth-century writers and by later authors for whom he was the second most familiar poet of the new style. The contemporary chronicler Dino Compagni portrays Dante's friend in his late thirties or early forties as 'courtly and bold, but scornful, solitary and studious' amid a setting of unseemly scuffles and street brawls during the late 1290s (above, p. 18). Villlani records the attempts of the Florentine authorities to head off the approaching showdown between the Whites and Blacks by exiling members of both factions, includ-ing Cavalcanti, in May 1300, shortly before Dante's own 'ill-fated' spell of authority began (above, p. 19); and in his account of Cavalcanti's death from illness (29 August 1300), he, like Compagni, portrays a somewhat turbulent character, 'learned and highly cultivated', but 'prickly and quick-tempered' (Villani 9. 42). Two later fourteenth-century Tuscan writers highlight Cavalcanti's learning. The storyteller Sacchetti involves him in a nicely staged but rather pointless practical joke (*Trecentonovelle* 68); and Boccaccio more interestingly portrays him as 'a leading debater in his time and expert in the natural sciences', a courtly and accomplished atheist (*Decameron* 6. 9). His reputation for subversive thinking may have been partly responsible for Ezra Pound's promotion of him over a long period (1910–66) as a proto-modernist rival to the more orthodox Dante (*Nelson 1986: xxxv; *Ardizzone 2002: 142–5, 155–63).

Unlike Gunizelli, Bonagiunta and the Sicilian poets, Cavalcanti did not combine poetry with the practice of the law. Like Dante he was of an origi-nally mercantile family with some claims to nobility and to a stake in the political establishment of Florence. Both his political and his poetic career seem to have got under way rather earlier than Dante's, during the 1280s when he served on the Council of the Florentine commune along with Brunetto and Dino Compagni (Contini 1960: 2. 487; Nelson 1986: xv, xix–xx). This relative seniority, along with some possible political differences, may perhaps have contributed to the complexity and uneasiness of Dante's later attitude towards him (*DE* 460).

118

Formally and stylistically, Cavalcanti's poetry spans an ambitious range. Like Guinizzelli he makes occasional forays into the grotesque style (Nelson 1986: 84–5; compare Edwards 1987: 54–7) and draws upon the Provençal tradition for the language of elegantly visualized compliment (Nelson 1986: 6–7; compare Edwards 1987: 34–5, 40–1). Also in the Provençal vein, he engages in exchanges of poems (*tenzoni*) with other writers on a variety of topics. He provided comment in verse on Dante's first sonnet in *VN*; he responded ironically to the famous 'wish-poem' (*Guido, I' vorrei*) that fantasizes about a group outing for Florentine poets and their partners on an enchanted boat (FB nos. 15–15a); and he corresponded again with him about the condition of one of their fellow-passengers on that trip, Lapo Gianni (Nelson 1986: 60–5). Dante was also probably aware of Guido's rather coy venture into the *pastourelle* form (knight meets shepherdess in a wood etc.) when he rewrote the scenario in the encounter between the pilgrim and Matelda in the forest of the Earthly Paradise (*Purg.* 28. 1–69; Nelson 1986: 74–5; Barolini 1984: 148; Dante 2003: 485, 589).

Dante shows awareness of Cavalcanti's more serious representations of the ennobling and destructive power of love – for instance in sonnets such as 'Who is she that comes with all looking towards her' (Nelson 1986: no. IV, prefiguring sonnets 14 and 15 in *VN*). He was also clearly influenced by a larger number of Cavalcanti's poems which develop the kind of erotic mayhem portrayed in Guinizzelli's sonnet about the lightning bolt, and which prefigure visions of disorder in sonnets 7–9 of *VN* (Nelson 1986: nos. V–XIII; Barolini 1984: 136–9). Dante also knew and referred to Cavalcanti's great *canzone*, *Donna mi prega* ('A lady asks me'), in which the poet, whilst acknowledging the Guinizzellian association of love with 'people of worth', also explores the dark side of a power that 'often leads to death' (Nelson 1986: 38–41). Dante's three references to Cavalcanti in *DVE* date from three years after Guido's death and are quite faint in their praise, whilst the citation of *Donna mi prega* itself occurs in the context of a technical discussion of prosody (*DVE* 2. 12. 8). As Dante must have recognized, however, *Donna mi prega* is Cavalcanti's most challenging and 'illustrious' poem; the one that probably contributed most to his reputation in the fourteenth century and later as a supremely learned poet. It is informed by the kind of radical Aristotelianism of which Dante was aware (above, p. 83) and it combines ideas and vocabulary from metaphysics, astrology, psychology and optics – a range of learning, accomplishment and 'expertise in the natural sciences' that impressed later writers such as Villani and Boccaccio (Nelson 1986: xlii–li; Ardizzone 2002: 16, 19, 22–3, 48–9, 64).

Although Cavalcanti's death in August 1300 occurred a few months after the fictional date for Dante's journey in the *Commedia* (where he might perhaps have accompanied 'Guinizzelli' in *Purg.* 26), he is still a powerful, if shadowy presence 'encoded' in the poem (Barolini 1984: 136). In the circle of the Proud in Purgatory, he is seen as part of a tradition of outdoing: one Guido (Cavalcanti) is said here to have bereft the other (Guinizzelli) of 'the glory of the [mother] tongue'; but both may be 'chased from the nest' by 'one who is perhaps now alive', that is, Dante (*Purg.* 11. 97–9). By this point the *Commedia* had challenged Cavalcanti in other ways too, notably when Dante confronts the Florentine factional rivalries with which both he and Cavalcanti had identified in canto 10 of the *Inferno*. Here, amongst the souls of those who have denied the immortality of the soul, he encounters Guido's father-in-law (the Ghibellline Farinata degi Uberti) and his father (the Guelf Cavalcante dei Cavalcanti), both of whom are now confined to the double 'bed' of a burning tomb (52–114). In the midst of the poem's harshest vision of public and political life so far (the exchange with Farinata), a more private and personal note is struck when the desperate face of the elder Cavalcanti emerges just above the edge of the tomb, beside the towering figure of his impassive companion, and after glancing around asks the agitated question:

> 'If, through this dark
> dungeon, you go, empowered by genius,
> where is my son? Why is he not with you?'
> I told him then: 'I've not come by myself;
> waiting there is one who will lead me through,
> perhaps to one Guido held in contempt.'
>
> (*Inf.* 10. 58–63)

Revealing, as it does, the cross-currents of emotion, ambition and acute parental anxiety that immediately afterwards (67–9) make Cavalcante fasten despairingly upon the past tense the protagonist has used to describe Guido, the episode is itself an impressive demonstration of *altezza d'ingegno*. Loftiness and haughty contempt are key elements here as elsewhere in the canto. The 'one' to whom 'Dante' in the last sentence says he is being led is Beatrice – but it is not immediately clear how or why Guido Cavalcanti should have 'held her in contempt'. One interpretation is that this reflects Guido's rejection of faith and grace: the kind of philosophic self-sufficiency that writers such as Compagni and Villani were to attribute to him (CL 1. 330). Another (not wholly contradictory) view would be that Dante is referring to what Beatrice meant at a time when Cavalcanti actually knew of her, within the context of the new-style love-poetry and her development as a mythic figure within the *Vita nuova*. Dante may thus be reminding himself and the reader of the essential differences between Cavalcanti's dark sense of the destructive power of love (expressed in *Donna mi prega*) and his own vision of its trans-formative potential (Barolini 1984: 142–8). By contrast with his great Florentine contemporary, Dante thus seeks 'to ground love not in the mechanical process of nature and its necessity, but in the inner freedom of an interior law'; and for this purpose Beatrice becomes 'a comprehensive metaphor designed to oppose Cavalcanti's theory of love' (Ardizzone 2002: 42, 45). In his view of the 'potency' of love, therefore, Dante seems quite literally to be going beyond his poetic *primo amico*.

Dante also describes another poet of the new style as a friend: his slightly younger contemporary from a neighbouring Tuscan city, **Cino da Pistoia** (1270–1336/7). Cino's early writings already appear to relate him quite closely to the circle of the Florentine new-style poets. For instance, there is a sonnet replying to a (now lost) poem by Cavalcanti which must have accused him of plagiarizing. Here Cino rates his own work modestly enough, but for the haughty Guido he places stings in the tails of several lines. In the first quatrain he suggests that he has not actually been able to find anything in Cavalcanti's work that is good enough to plagiarize (3–4). In the sestet he presents himself as one 'of low creative skill' (*uomo di basso ingegno*), disclaiming the status of *artista* – using the word, it seems, for the first time in Italian – and then adding mischievously: 'Né cuopro mia ignoranza con *disdegno*': 'nor do I try to cover up my ignorance with disdain' (Contini 1960: 2. 639). Perhaps written some twenty years before Dante's reference to Guido's *disdegno* in *Inferno* 10 (63) or Compagni's description of him as *sdegnoso* (Compagni 1968: 48), Cino's ironic barb could well be the earliest portrayal of Cavalcanti as a proud and stroppy *filosofo*.

Cino's friendship with Dante also developed at an early stage in his writing career. He may perhaps, like Cavalcanti, have been among the poets who responded to the challenge of Dante's vision of Love and Beatrice, as expressed in the first sonnet of the *Vita nuova*; and the two young poets may have met at Bologna (where Cino studied law) in 1287 (*DE* 171A). In the early 1290s he certainly wrote a consolatory *canzone* to Dante on the death of Beatrice (Zaccagnini 1925: 61–3); and a decade or so later Dante still thought well enough of the poem to place it in the great tradition of

illustrious *canzoni*, following ones by Guinizzelli and Cavalcanti and immediately preceding one of Dante's own (*DVE* 2. 6. 6).

On a number of other occasions *DVE* represents Dante as 'Cino's friend',
and by this time (c.1303–5) the two poets had quite a lot of interests and
experience in common. Both were undergoing exile at this time, although
Cino, as a member of an aristocratic Black Guelf family in Pistoia, was, unlike
Dante, to return to his native city after a period of banishment in Prato and
Florence (1303–6). They continued to exchange a number of sonnets about
the nature of love and their experience of it (Dante 1970: 192–204; FB nos.
85–85a, 87–87a). They both also wrote about exile: Dante, for example, in
*canzoni* such as *Tre donne* (Dante 1970: 174–9; FB no. 81), in prose works
like *DVE* and *Convivio*, and in a letter accompanying a sonnet addressed to
Cino (*Letters* no. 3; *DE* 353B). Cino, for his part, contributed through
several poems to what has been called the 'troping of the political condition
of exile' in Tuscan poetry of this time (Keen 2000: 22). Like Dante, he
became during the turbulent years of 1310–13 a supporter of the ill-fated
campaign to restore the authority of the empire in Italy, assisting at the
emperor's coronation in Rome and writing a dignified *canzone* to commemorate Henry's death not long after (above, pp. 41–2). During the following
decade, while Dante was occupied with the *Commedia*, Cino pursued the
career for which he had been trained as an academic jurist; and he continued
to teach and to produce both poetry and legal treatises long after Dante's
death in 1321. As late as 1330 he spent a year as visiting scholar at the
University of Naples, where the young Boccaccio attended his lectures.

Despite, or perhaps because of, his substantial output (18 *canzoni*, 13
*ballate* and 134 sonnets), Cino has not had a very good press among those
who have written on the new style. His poetic inspiration is said to have
'petered out shortly after the turn of the century' and his work has been
thought to be 'characterised by an attenuation of the more intense aspects
of his mentors' (*CHIL* 26). One authoritative writer on Dante's attitudes
towards poets and poetry dismisses the favourable references to Cino in *DVE*
as 'essentially a stopgap used to fill the space left by Cavalcanti' (Barolini
1984: 135). Some have even found him 'somewhat insipid and monotonous'
(Nelson 1986: xxxi). Yet, despite the fact that he is not mentioned as a surviving practitioner of the new style in *Purgatorio* 24, it is clear from the
presentation of him in *DVE* and elsewhere that Dante had considerable
respect for his work. So also (a little later in the century) did Boccaccio,
whose character Troiolo in the *Filostrato* (1335?) purloins four stanzas from
one of Cino's most famous *canzoni* in order to lament his loss of Criseida

(*Filostrato* 5. 62–5; Zaccagnini 1925: 215–17). So did Petrarch, whose lyric style Cino's is often thought to have prefigured and who was moved to commemorate his death in a sonnet (*CHIL* 26). Like John Gower, the contemporary whom Chaucer was to overshadow later in the century, Cino was master of the cogent, relatively plain and harmonious style, which is evident in his poems on the departure of Beatrice, on exile, and in commemoration of the emperor Henry – as well as in the *canzone* on the death of Dante with which the previous section ended (above, p. 53). Like Gower, too, Cino was particularly good at goodbyes.

With Cino da Pistoia, whose writing thus intersects with Dante's throughout the Florentine poet's career – and who was to survive him by more than a decade – we come to the end of this group of poets in the vernacular whom Dante read. It is now time to put Dante in the foreground.

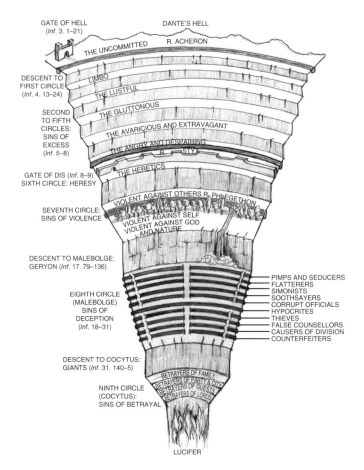

*Diagram 1*  Dante's Hell (cross-section).

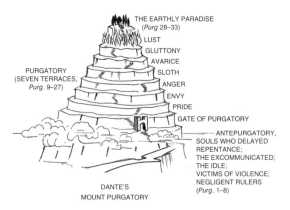

*Diagram 2*  Dante's Purgatory.

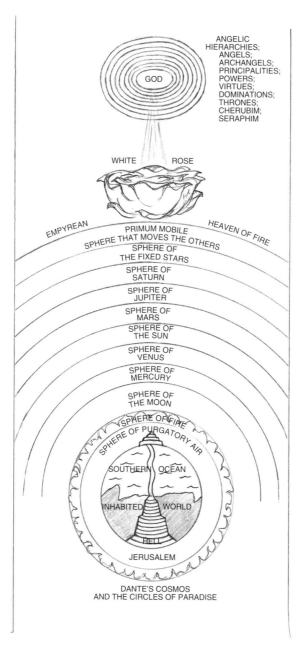

ANGELIC
HIERARCHIES;
ANGELS;
ARCHANGELS;
PRINCIPALITIES;
POWERS;
VIRTUES;
DOMINATIONS;
THRONES;
CHERUBIM;
SERAPHIM

GOD

WHITE ROSE

EMPYREAN PRIMUM MOBILE HEAVEN OF FIRE
SPHERE THAT MOVES THE OTHERS
SPHERE OF
THE FIXED STARS
SPHERE OF
SATURN
SPHERE OF
JUPITER
SPHERE OF
MARS
SPHERE OF
THE SUN
SPHERE OF
VENUS
SPHERE OF
MERCURY
SPHERE OF
THE MOON
SPHERE OF FIRE
SPHERE OF PURGATORY AIR
SOUTHERN OCEAN
INHABITED WORLD
HELL
JERUSALEM

DANTE'S COSMOS
AND THE CIRCLES OF PARADISE

*Diagram 3* Dante's cosmos, showing the spheres of Paradise.

# Reading Dante

Reading Dante's texts has already been necessary at many points so far. It would have been impossible to set aside the evidence of the poet's own writing when attempting to map the landmarks of his life or to survey the texts and traditions with which he worked.

This chapter now explores a range of major issues in the *Commedia* and Dante's other works. These include: the need for and function of guidance; political vision; the imagining of sin and sainthood; representations of love; and ideas about the journey, poetry and language.

The wider contexts for these issues will continue to be referred to, but the main emphasis will now be on close reading of the text. For this purpose a number of passages – including some substantial parts of cantos and *canzoni* – have been newly translated here. To remind the reader of the languages Dante used and their importance, I have continued to place important original words and phrases in parentheses; and the first substantial quotation in each main subsection appears in both Italian and English.

*An asterisk (\*) indicates my first reference in this section to works that are particularly recommended for further reading.*

# Seeking Guidance

## Fear, the dark wood and the light of other poets: Virgil

How and why does Dante in the *Commedia* express a need for guidance? The first canto of the poem is driven by the terms and images of terror – terror that will revisit Dante's traveller at a number of crucial points in his journey: at the entry to Hell; before the gates of Dis; flying through the abyss on Geryon's back; fearing pursuit by devils; and facing Satan himself at the lowest point of the universe.

In this first canto of the *Commedia* one of the Italian words for fear (*paura*) occurs more often than in any other canto of the poem: five times within the first 53 lines. Initially, it occurs on the first of several occasions when Dante insists on the truth of his vision by asserting memory's power to recreate the emotion he had found himself undergoing. 'Thinking about it', he says, 'brings back the fear' (*nel pensier rinova la paura, Inf.* 1. 6). The immediate cause of this terror is the dark wood in which the traveller has found himself lost – the 'valley' which 'pierced my heart with fear' (15). The fear is temporarily 'quieted' when, like the Psalmist (Psalms 120: 1) he lifts up his eyes to the hills (16–19), but is revived more intensely by the encounters with two of the beasts that block his attempts to ascend and once again strike fear into him (44, 53).

What makes this figure so acutely fearful? Dante represents himself here in the prime of life at the age of 35 during the spring of the Jubilee year, 1300. At this point he was politically active on behalf of the new regime in Florence and was soon that same year (15 June) to be elected to a term as one of the city's governing body (above, p. 19). Yet he was also on the edge of the abyss. In not much more than a year he would face the near total destruction of his career and reputation, the disorientation of exile and the threat of death by fire.

Disorientation and wandering had already been themes of Dante's writing in between the onset of exile (1301–2) and the commencement of work on the *Inferno* (around 1307–8). The *Convivio* and *DVE* both focus on this condition near their beginnings, and so do a number of the poems he wrote during the early years of his exclusion from Florence (above, p. 23). Yet being 'lost' at the start of the *Inferno* is for this fictional figure a still more terrifying experience. It seems to carry the threat of death as well as the hope of possible rescue (*Inf.* 1. 7–9); it is felt as a dark night in the soul (20–1) and as a time of acute loss and regret (55–7). At its worst – as the protagonist flees from the most savage of the beasts that drive him off the sunlit mountain – it becomes total breakdown. 'I rushed (literally "collapsed") downwards', he recalls (61); and the key word here (*rovinava*) is linked with verbs and nouns that he elsewhere uses to describe physical collapse. It is at this moment of disintegration that help is most needed, and it is 'offered' in the form of Virgil (62).

Virgil also appears to be a somewhat faltering presence, initially at least, and the protagonist is uncertain whether he is 'a shadow or a real person' (66). When he first appears he is described as 'one who seemed because of long silence to be faint (or 'hoarse')'; and this may refer both to his status as a voice of the long-distant pagan past and to Dante's own ignorance or neglect, till now, of what he stands for (63). Nonetheless, Virgil's speech quickly composes him into a more 'real' person than 'Dante' himself yet is: one with firm links to parentage, place and historical period; to Lombardy, Mantua and imperial Rome (68–72). Moreover, his identification of himself as the author of the poem about Aeneas who emerged from the fires of Troy to voyage to Italy and found a nation (73–5) constitutes the first statement of the theme of Rome that is to run through almost the whole of the *Commedia*.

'I was a poet' (*poeta fui*), says Dante's Virgil at the start of the *terzina* that identifies him as the author of the *Aeneid* (73–5). Virgil's fame for readers and writers of the Middle Ages rested on a long tradition of commentary (above, pp. 67–9); and he had much earlier been cited by Dante, alongside Lucan, Horace and Ovid, during his account of literary history in chapter 25 of the *Vita nuova*. It is significant then – as a foreshadowing of Virgil's lines about his poem in *Inf.* 1. 73–5 – that around 1307, when his work on the philosophical project of the *Convivio* is drawing to a close,

130

Dante pauses in the discussion of the noble life to give particular attention to Books 4–6 of the *Aeneid*, to its hero as a model of restraint and bravery, and to its author as 'the greatest of our poets' (*lo maggior nostro poeta*, *Conv.* 4. 26).

Virgil is addressed by Dante as *poeta* three times in the *Commedia*'s first canto and then frequently throughout the *Inferno* and the *Purgatorio*. The term is an illustrious one, reserved chiefly for classical authors, and it is not until relatively late in the poem (*Par.* 1. 29, 25. 8) that Dante begins to suggest that he, too, might be entitled to it. We are to be constantly reminded of Virgil's role as poetic model for Dante and others up to and well beyond his departure from the scene at the end of the *Purgatorio*. It is this role above all that authorizes his prophecy about the future of Italy in lines 100–11; that enables him to map the providential journey whose end he himself will never reach (112–29); and that makes him the 'master', 'teacher', 'father', 'mother' whose help the traveller seeks and whom he will follow for so much of the poem, beginning with the last line of *Inferno* 1: 'Then he moved on, and I kept close behind him.'

## Moved by love: Dante, Virgil and Beatrice

*Allor si mosse* ('Then he moved on'). Movement, led by Virgil, seems thus to be under way by the end of the *Commedia*'s first canto. Yet this movement comes to a gradual halt at the start of the next. It is held back first by the traveller's understandable pause to 'ready himself' for the journey as the daylight fades around him (*Inf.* 2, lines 1–5). It is further postponed by the poet's own rhetorical throat-clearing as he marshals his resources and invokes Muses, invention and memory (7–9). It then looks as if it may be prevented altogether, by a failure of nerve on the traveller's part. Nearly thirty lines of prevarication (10–36) make him doubt his worthiness to follow in the steps of illustrious otherworld voyagers like Aeneas and St Paul (32); and he looks ready, as he lingers 'upon that dark shoreline', to act like 'one who unwishes (*disvuol*) what he wanted' (40–2). Rebuilding this faltering resolve and regaining this loss of momentum will require more than the force of Virgil's own personality, 'magnanimous' as it is (44).

What Virgil conjures up for this purpose are words that were addressed to him by a 'bright and blessed lady', whilst he himself remained – not unlike the hesitant Dante at this present moment – in a state of suspended animation (*tra color che son sospesi*), in Limbo (52–3). The power behind these words is that of celestial light and angelic sound (55–7); and the very verb that marks their movement into utterance and action (*cominciare*, 56) is the one that earlier in this canto has ironically signalled Dante's reluctance to get started (*cominciare* 10, 39, 56).

Beatrice's words at this point represent a new start in several ways and within several time schemes. As recorded here by Virgil, they begin to reconstruct the process that had moved him to 'offer' himself as guide to Dante at the foot of the mountain in the previous canto. Being reported at this particular moment, they also form part of trio of speeches – those of the Virgin, St Lucy and Beatrice herself – that (Virgil claims), should themselves serve to rouse Dante out of his present state of inertia and stir him to action. 'Why then', he concludes, 'do you still linger?' (*perché, perché restai?* 121).

'Love moved me and now makes me speak' (*Amor mi mosse, che mi fa parlare*). At the end of the *terzina* in which Beatrice names herself to Virgil (70–2) she makes the key statement of the canto and perhaps even of the whole *Commedia*. The line concentrates the dynamism of speech and words, as they here trace an arc from the summit of Dante's Heaven to the borders of his Hell. Transmission of love through speech originates with the two lines with which the Virgin Mary, as the unmoved mover of Dante's journey, calls upon St Lucy (98–9). It continues when Lucy 'moves' towards and summons Beatrice herself (100–8); and when Beatrice becomes 'swift' to descend (109–12), to mobilize Virgil's 'eloquent words' (67). 'I am Beatrice, sending you on your way', she announces to Virgil when she names herself for the first time (*I' son Beatrice che ti faccio andare*), thus predicating her very identity upon the movement of love through words.

Words and speech in this canto also generate fresh movement. Further stages in the transmission of love through words are marked when Virgil ends his speech to Dante by affirming it as a 'promise of good' (126); when Dante's own speech then initiates a new 'beginning' (132), acknowledging the power of 'true words', 'your words' (135, 137); and when those words lead the traveller to follow his guide 'once he had moved on' (141).

A yet more dramatic new departure, however, is initiated in canto 2 of the *Inferno*. Here the key word is 'power' (*virtù, virtude*), and it is repeated at strategic moments three times in the canto. At first it applies to Dante alone and helps to express his hesitation and inertia when he asks Virgil to consider whether his 'powers are really sufficient' for the task in hand (11). Secondly, near the middle of the canto, it conveys something of the impact of Beatrice's intervention when Virgil first responds to and addresses her as *donna di virtù* ('powerful lady', 76). Thirdly and finally, it returns to Dante through the recovery of his 'wilted powers' (*mia virtude stanca*, 130) – a recovery that has been accomplished by means of the love that has moved both Beatrice and Virgil and made them speak.

# Writing the City

## Citizenship

Dante's Beatrice and Virgil are citizens of several cities. Virgil's citizenship of Mantua and of Rome is initially a key feature of his identity (*Inf.* 1. 68–71), and remains so throughout the *Commedia*. His first repetition of the word 'city' (*città*) is, however, imbued with a sense of exclusion (*Inf.* 1. 126 and 128). This is the seat of Christ's 'empire', to which Virgil as the inhabitant of a different state – the hemisphere of light and the castle on the borders of Hell – is denied entry. These are also the first uses of 'city' in the *Commedia*; and their connotations are appropriate for a poem that is so substantially concerned with exile. Beatrice, on the other hand, is identified as belonging to the very city from which Virgil is thus excluded. In *Inferno* 2 she tells Virgil that the place to which St Lucy goes to summon her is 'the place where I was sitting with Rachel of the Old Testament' (101–2). This is the circle of the celestial White Rose to which she eventually returns, having guided Dante to the outermost limit of Paradise, and which she will also then describe as 'our city' (*nostra città, Par.* 30. 130).

Before her elevation to the heavenly city, Beatrice was a citizen of Florence. Early in the *Vita nuova* (ch. 6) Dante refers to a poem he wrote about the 60 most beautiful women 'in the city where the Lord of all had placed my lady'. Like other works in the Tuscan new style, the *Vita nuova* is a text that locates love within the city – albeit a 'twilight city' (*Valency 1958: 209). Its action is marked by encounters within, departures from and returns to the 'city that I mentioned', namely Florence. Its core event, the death of Beatrice, is announced at the opening of chapter 29 by words taken from the beginning of the Lamentations of Jeremiah: 'How desolate remains the city that had been full of people! She who was queen of the nations has become like a widow.' Neither here nor elsewhere in the *Vita nuova* are the physical features of Dante's Florence actually visualized, but the deprived earthly city remains present as backdrop for events in the remainder of the text, after Beatrice has departed from it and 'become one of the citizens of eternal life' (ch. 35). The state of deprivation is reiterated here: Florence is the 'widowed city, stripped of all worth', 'the desolate city' (ch. 31); and in the penultimate sonnet, the phrase that describes her anticipates the first line of the inscription above the gates of Dante's Hell: *la città dolente*, "the grieving city" (*VN* sonnet 24. 6; *Inf.* 3. 1). Yet Florence in the *Vita nuova* is not identified with Hell. Chapter 41 begins with pilgrims travelling through the city to Rome and suggests that Florence would be the proper goal for such devotees, since it was 'the city where that most noble of ladies was born, lived and died'. And in the sonnet that follows, Dante addresses the pilgrims as if he were the priest of the new cult of Beatrice: 'She (Florence, 'the grieving city') has lost her Beatrice, and the words which a man may speak of her have the power to make others weep' (sonnet 24. 12–14).

Florence will be personified and feminized in various ways through Dante's writing between the *Vita nuova* and the *Commedia*. Deprivation is again the keynote in many of these references, although it is Dante who is represented as 'desolate' because of his exile from a city which is at times imagined as a lost mother. Thus at the beginning of the *Convivio* Dante characterizes Florence as 'the fairest and most famous daughter of Rome', from whose 'sweet embrace' he has been torn (*Conv.* 1. 3. 4). At around the same time (c.1304), near the opening of his Latin work on eloquence in the vernacular, he uses similarly affectionate terms when he asserts that he 'love[s] Florence so much that because I loved her I suffer exile unjustly' (*DVE* 1. 6. 3).

Later in the years of exile, this son or lover of Florence becomes more resentful towards the city that has rejected him. At the end of his last *canzone*, *Amor da che convien pur ch'io mi doglia* ('Love which forces me only to grieve'; FB no. 89), he speaks of Florence as 'my city' still, but it is one that 'has barred me from herself' and is 'empty of love and barren of pity' (77–9). The implied accusation of cruelty becomes explicit late in the *Commedia*, when Dante's ancestor Cacciaguida opens his prophecy about the poet's future by comparing Florence to the vengeful, jilted Phaedra as 'cruel and deceitful stepmother' (*Par.* 17. 46–8).

On a number of occasions later in his exile and in the *Commedia*, Dante imagines Florence yet more harshly as a sick or self-destructive body. In one of his fiercest political letters, addressed to Henry VII in April 1311 (above,

p. 40), he compares Florence, in her unholy alliance with the papacy, with other transgressive female figures from classical mythology: the incestuous 'Myrrha, inflamed with passion for the embraces of her father'; and the suicidal Amata, from *Aen.* 12. 593–607 (*Letters* nos. 97, 104). At around the same time, when diagnosing his city's political perversity as symptomatic of the wider ills of Italy, he compares Florence to 'that sick woman who can find no ease even on a feather-bed but tries to allay her pain by tossing and turning' (*Purg.* 6. 149–51). Behind this kind of personification lies the long tradition of representing the state as body, which had recently been reinvigorated though the influence of Aristotelian political thought upon contemporaries such as Remigio de' Girolami (above, pp. 100–1). Physical diseases were often at this time attributed to excess or superfluity; and this is how Dante often represents the causes and effects of political disorder in Florence (*Inf.* 6. 49–50, *Purg.* 20. 73–5, *Par.* 16. 67–9).

Yet more harshly and urgently, the civic divisions and conflicts that had led to Dante's exile are seen in his later writing as forms of self-destructiveness or even of self-devouring. An early example in the *Commedia* is the encounter between Dante and a fellow-citizen, Filippo Argenti, during the crossing of the muddy waters of the Styx (*Inf.* 8. 31–63). At the point when this 'ugly, accursed, filthy' soul reaches threateningly towards Dante, Virgil fends him off and orders him back to 'the other hounds', the souls who have already been shown in true civic spirit, ripping each other to pieces with their teeth (*Inf.* 8. 40–2, 7. 112–14). As these mud-encrusted figures close in on Filippo he performs a gesture that identifies him as the representative 'savage Florentine spirit', by 'turning his teeth upon himself' (*Inf.* 8. 62–3).

This vicious little scene, with its clinching act of auto-cannibalism, speaks a similar metaphorical language to that of a speech delivered later by a Florentine who is better disposed towards Dante: his 'dead master' Brunetto Latini in *Inferno* 15. Brunetto, who was himself important as a writer about the city (above, p. 101), prophesies a 'glorious conclusion' to Dante's present enterprise; but in doing so he also utters a stark warning about the malign and destructive effects that Florentine factions could still wreak upon him:

> '*Ma quello ingrato popolo maligno*
> *che discese di Fiesole ab antico*
> *e tiene ancor del monte e del macigno,*
>    *ti si farà, per tuo ben far, nimico;*
> *ed è ragion, ché tra li lazzi sorbi*
> *si disconvien fruttare al dolce fico.*

*Vecchia fama nel mondo li chiama orbi;*
*gent' è avara, invidiosa e superba:*
*dai lor costumi fa che tu ti forbi.*
    *La tua fortuna tanto onor ti serba,*
*che l'una parte e l'altra avranno fame*
*di te; ma lungi fia dal becco l'erba.*
    *Faccian le bestie fiesolane strame*
*di lor medesme, e non tocchin la pianta*
*s'alcuna surge ancora in lor letame,*
    *in cui riviva la sementa santa*
*di que' Roman che vi rimaser quando*
*fu fatto il nido di malizia tanta.'*

    'But there is still that churlish brutal crowd
who hurtled down on Florence long ago
from Fiesole and bear that stony soil
    still in their hearts. Your good work earns their hate;
and that's as well, since the sweet fig can't thrive
alongside fruit that sets the teeth on edge.
    They've long had worldwide fame as blinkered minds,
and they're a greedy, envious, stiff-necked bunch;
better keep clear of them and all their ways.
    For, since you're destined to achieve so much,
both of the warring factions will be keen
to snap you up; but herbs are not for goats.
    Let those beasts from Fiesole still graze
upon themselves, not nuzzle at that plant
(should any seed itself in all their litter)
    which shows new signs of growth from noble stock:
that of the Romans, those who still lived there
when Florence had become destruction's lair.'

                        (*Inf.* 15. 61–78)

Two metaphors in rapid succession reflect the 'cannibalistic' nature of Florence at the end of this speech. First, Brunetto's description of how the factions of Florence 'will be keen / to snap you up' (literally: 'will hunger after you', 71–2) may refer both to the desire of the exiled Whites of Dante's own party to enlist his support and to the Blacks' more straightforwardly destructive intentions towards him. Secondly, the speech's invocation of a self-destructive tendency that may lead the Florentine 'beasts' to 'graze / upon (literally: 'make fodder of') themselves' (73–4) sets the tone for imagining civic conflict in Florence and other Italian cities at several points later in the *Commedia* – for instance, the 'bestial' perpetuation of hostilities between the Pisan fellow-citizens Ugolino and Ruggieri (*Inf.* 32–3). Brunetto's speech about Florence – as befits a public orator in Hell – has an air of desperation about it. His rhetoric resembles the fierce invective that Dante was to heap upon Florence soon after this, in his political letters of 1310 and 1311, denouncing the city for its opposition to the emperor (above, p. 40).

Yet the encounter in *Inferno* 15 not only conveys a sombre vision of Florence's history and its obdurate, 'Fiesolan' character; it also hints at a possible way out of the claustrophobic 'lair of destruction'. It does so by means of a vivid and paradoxical image: that of the 'noble' plant, seeding itself in the midst of the 'litter' in which the 'Fiesolan beasts' live (73–7). At one level this can be taken personally: the noble seedling can be seen as Dante himself, with whose future Brunetto is obviously concerned here (65–6). At a wider, communal level, however, the tender and vulnerable plant deriving from the stock of ancient Rome could also be read as a tentative sign of possible civic recovery.

A similar paradox has already been explored during the previous encounter (*Inf.* 13–14). The preceding circle of Dante's Hell contains the forest of those who have destroyed their human selves and are now turned into trees. The final encounter here is with a minor shrub who turns out to be the soul of a Florentine who had 'hanged himself in his own house' (*Inf.* 13. 151) and who is fated to have his branches torn apart in a typically infernal cycle of destruction (111–35). Here, as in Brunetto's speech, Florence, destructiveness and self-destructiveness are linked. Unlike Brunetto, the Florentine suicide of *Inferno* 13 is anonymous; and that anonymity, along with his strange metamorphosis, suggests that he may be in some ways symbolically representative of his city's state. This representativeness is reinforced by his brief speech at the end of canto 13 (143–51), with its allusions to key features of Florence's urban mythology: the baleful influence of Mars as her first 'patron' (above, p. 5) and the destruction of the city by Attila. Yet even at this dark moment we are not entirely trapped within the nightmare of history. The destruction of Florence, the suicide acknowledges, has led to the 'refounding' of the city (148), even if one effect of this reconstruction has been to preserve a fragment of its truculent pagan patron, in the statue of Mars on the bridge over the Arno (above, p. 5). The tree-soul's request for its broken branches to be gathered (139–42) is answered by Dante at the opening of the next canto, and in a way that suggests the poet was aware of the significances that such a gesture could carry:

> Since deep affection for my place of birth
> moved me, I took up those scattered branches
> and gave them back to him whose voice had faded.
>
> (*Inf.* 14. 1–3)

This gesture of good faith on the traveller's part is also one of gathering together and reunification; indeed, it literally unifies, by spanning the break between cantos 13 and 14. After the laceration that has been inflicted and witnessed at the end of the previous canto, it enacts a brief ritual of restoration and reconciliation. Like Brunetto's metaphor of the noble seedling springing up beneath the hooves of the *bestie fiesolane*, it thus conveys the exile's tentative belief in the possible recovery of his city and the renewal of its civic ideals as 'the daughter of Rome'.

## Between two cities: Dante's Florence and Rome

But what did it mean for Dante and others to call Florence 'the daughter of Rome'; and what did the idea of Rome contribute to the poet's vision of civic renewal? It was believed that after the defeat of a conspiracy against the Roman republic led by Catiline (killed near Pistoia in 62 BCE), the Fiesolans who had supported the rebellion were evicted from their city and made to join a small core of Roman colonists in what would become Florence. This legend is invoked by the description of Florence as 'daughter of Rome' in the *Convivio* (1. 3. 4) and in the speech of Dante's Brunetto (*Inf.* 15. 61–2); and it is narrated more fully both by Brunetto Latini himself (Latini 1948: 1. 37. 1–2) and by Villani (2.1).

One implication of this opposition between the two cities is that Florence can be seen as a delinquent daughter whose 'Fiesolan' streak still leads her to defy the authority of her august parent. This is certainly how Dante portrays his city's resistance to the advance of Emperor Henry VII in his letters of 1310–11, when he describes his fellow-citizens as 'the wretched spawn of the Fiesolans', whose 'savagery is to be punished *yet again*'; and where he condemns Florence for 'seeking to wound her mother with viper-like ferocity, as she sharpens the horn of rebellion against Rome who had created her in her own image and likeness' (*Letters* pp. 75, 81, 97, 104). A similar contrast is evident around this time, in canto 6 of the *Purgatorio*, where Rome is made to speak like a grieving widow lamenting the loss of her husband the emperor (112–14), whilst Florence is imagined as the sick woman of Italy (149–51).

Other references to ancient Rome in the *Commedia* suggest Florence's need for this 'parentage'. In the *Paradiso*, during his reconstruction of the city's austere lifestyle during his time, Dante's ancestor Cacciaguida evokes a domestic scene in which a woman as she spins thread 'tells her household tales about the Trojans, Fiesole and Rome' (*Par.* 15. 124–6). Cacciaguida thus places the troublesome locality of Fiesole between two cities (Troy and Rome) which recall the mission of Virgil's Aeneas and imply a larger concept of citizenship. A few lines later, Cacciaguida speaks of 'the peaceful and pleasant life that citizens (*cittadini*) then led' (130–1); then – using the word for the first time in the poem – he exalts the concept of 'loyal citizenship (*cittadinanza*)' (132). His recollection of Florence within her 'ancient circle' of walls (97), thought to have been built during Charlemagne's empire, is a highly idealized picture, transmitted as it is from the sixth circle of Dante's Paradise. But this remote vision of the past still contained, for Dante and some of his contemporaries, a spark of continuing vitality. The *Commedia*'s tentative hopes that Florence could yet be a loyal 'daughter' thus form part of its larger 'idea of Rome'.

The earlier formation of Dante's providential idea of Rome can be discerned in the fourth treatise of the *Convivio* (chs. 4 and 5, written probably around 1307). In these two chapters his political vision takes shape in concise, lucid and accessible form. In chapter 4 the Aristotelian premise of humanity's 'sociable' nature leads first to the necessity for family and city; then, through 'requiring brotherhood with surrounding cities', to the need for kingdoms; and then, in the interests of peace between kingdoms, for there to be a single supreme monarch. This ruler 'because he held sway over everything would have nothing more to covet', and his authority would complete a kind of virtuous circle by maintaining peace between kingdoms and cities and enabling individuals to 'live well and happily, that being the purpose for which they were born'. Because he was thus the helmsman of the ship of human society and the instigator of its chain of commands, he would be called *imperadore*, 'commander' or emperor. Dante concludes this phase of the argument by asserting that 'the majesty and authority of the emperor is thus the ultimate associative ideal of humanity' (*altissima nell' umana compagnia, Conv.* 4. 4. 7). Finally, as the rest of chapter 4 and the whole of chapter 5 then demonstrate (citing Virgil's *Aeneid* and the Gospel of Luke), this unifying imperial role is divinely ordained to be performed by *la Romana gente*: the people of Rome.

Dante retained the basic pattern of this argument when, around 1316 or later – some time after the shipwreck of Henry VII's venture – he returned to defend the imperial cause more formally and elaborately in the *Monarchia* (above, p. 42). In the first of the three books of this tightly argued Latin treatise, he develops more fully the case for 'unity' rather than 'plurality', even claiming that 'to sin is nothing other than to spurn unity and move towards plurality' (*Mon.* 1. 15. 3). Harking back at the end of this book to a key metaphor of his earlier writing (*Conv.* 4. 4, *Purgatorio* 6. 77, *Letters* no. 6), he concludes that the ship of humanity must remain subject to storm, disaster and shipwreck, so long as 'transformed into a many-headed beast, you strive after conflicting things' (*Mon.* 1. 16. 4).

In order to avert such conflict and disaster, the only hope still in the *Monarchia* lies in recognizing and reviving the authority of Rome. The second book of the treatise is devoted to affirming the divinely ordained right of the Roman people to rule over the nations and prevent them 'raging furiously together' (Psalm 2, cited in *Mon.* 2. 1. 1). *Monarchia* 2 goes on to elaborate the providential argument that had been outlined a decade or so before in the vernacular of *Convivio* 4. 4–5. It continues to use biblical authorities for this purpose; and it concludes with a battery of texts from the Gospels (especially Luke) and the Pauline Epistles, as well as Exodus and Isaiah (*Mon.* 10, 11). Yet – building on the groundwork of *Convivio* 4. 4–5 – it also supports its case for the empire by drawing even more substantially upon the examples of Roman history, upon Rome's historians and upon the voice of 'our divine poet, Virgil' (*Mon.* 2. 3. 6), whose prophecies about Rome's mission are frequently cited at length, especially in chapters 3 and 6.

Among the voices of Rome in the *Commedia*, Virgil also takes precedence, but not in such an obviously polemical way. As we have seen, the theme of the foundation and mission of the empire is first stated by and with reference to him in the poem's first two cantos (*Inf.* 1. 73–5 and 106–8, 2. 13–27). Yet amongst Virgil's various roles as Dante's guide, preceptor and model in the *Commedia*, that of apologist for the imperial cause does not seem to be foremost. After his initial reference to the Rome of 'good Augustus' as the place where he lived (*Inf.* 1. 71), his only other invocation of the city's name in the *Inferno* is during the grim description of the 'Old Man of Crete' (*Inf.* 14. 94–114), who 'looks towards Rome as his mirror' (105) and seems to represent a somewhat enigmatic or even pessimistic reading of political history. Virgil's only use of the term *Romani* here is a paradoxical one: when he briefly associates the cunning Ulysses ('deviser of crimes' in *Aen.* 2. 164) with the treacherous device of the Trojan Horse, 'which formed the gateway through which emerged the noble stock of the Romans' (*Inf.* 26. 59–60). Through his very presence in the scenario of the poem, it is true, Virgil acts

141

at some important points as a catalyst for reactions to the idea of empire. Thus, his affectionate greeting and embracing of his fellow-citizen Sordello in *Purgatorio* 6 (71–5) serves to remind Dante of Italy's current and desperate disunity (76–87) and leads quickly on to the canto's extended lament for the absence of imperial rule (88–123). But on the whole the Virgil of the *Commedia* seems somewhat more reluctant to lend his voice to the expression of the imperial ideal than he is in *Convivio* 4 and *Monarchia* 2.

The main reason for this lies in the very nature of the poem. In the *Commedia* Dante creates a wide range of voices and figures through whom the heritage of Rome is explored. One of these in the *Inferno* is, as we have seen Brunetto Latini (above, p. 101). Another, in canto 16 of the *Purgatorio*, is the Lombard nobleman who conveys a dark vision of a 'blind', 'erratic' and 'corrupt' world (66, 82, 104) whose governance has been confused and distorted by 'the Church of Rome' (127). Dante's Marco Lombardo implies that the only hope for guidance here lies in the restoration of balance between the 'two suns' of papal and imperial authority, a balance which had once existed in 'the world that had been set to rights by Rome' (106–8). More comprehensively, in *Paradiso* 6, Dante devotes the whole of a canto to a single Roman voice, that of the emperor Justinian (527–65), who had reunified the empire after its division by Constantine and instituted the framework of laws that Marco Lombardo and Dante considered essential for the guidance of humanity. Justinian's vision of the pattern of imperial history and authority in *Paradiso* 6 focuses upon the heraldic image of the eagle – an image which re-emerges to embody the ideal of justice over two of the later cantos of the poem (*Par.* 19–20).

Ultimately, the most eloquent expression of the imperial ideal in the *Commedia* is through the voice of another 'citizen of eternal life' – to use the expression that has described her in chapter 35 of the *Vita nuova*. Beatrice, during her reappearance as Dante's guide in the later cantos of the *Purgatorio*, herself represents a kind of renewal of imperial authority, borne as she is on a triumphal chariot that is said to surpass those of ancient Rome (*Purg.* 29. 115–16). As she prepares Dante for the sequence of apocalyptic visions which transform this chariot and which mark the end of the *cantica*, she gives the concept of 'empire' a higher significance – as Virgil had done in the very first canto of the poem (*Inf.* 1. 124 and 127) – by promising him 'eternal citizenship of that Rome in which Christ is a Roman' (*Purg.* 32. 101–2). Such a transcendent significance does not render redundant the aim of earthly ordering, guidance and renewal that the ideal of empire also represents in the poem. Beatrice's interpretation of the apocalyptic visions of

*Purgatorio* 32 clearly envisages a form of restorative intervention in *historical* 'time' through some kind of imperial figure (*Purg.* 33. 37–44).

Beatrice's prophecies continue to ground themselves in human history to the last. Thus, in *Paradiso* 30 she will announce her own ultimate destination – the White Rose – in appropriately rapt and elevated tones: 'See our city, how widely it circles!' (130). Yet her last words in the canto, which are also her last speech in the whole poem, will turn to the pursuit of an earthly ideal: to Henry VII's attempt to bring peace to the cities of Italy and to the betrayal of that quest by Clement V (133–48). Her prophecy about the judgement that awaits both these historical figures contrasts two examples of temporal Roman authority: the emperor, for whom a 'great throne' is reserved in the White Rose of the Empyrean (*Par.* 30. 133–8); and the pope, who is due to be 'thrust down' deep into the dark fissures of Hell (146–8).

As the trajectory of Dante's pilgrim continues into the closing cantos of the *Paradiso*, he continues to be concerned, as Beatrice has been, with citizenship both on earth and in Heaven. His own vision of the White Rose at the start of *Paradiso* 31 is both an ascent into the heart of light *and* a determined attempt to direct some of that light downwards into the 'storm' (*procella*) of human life (28–30). This determination to remain almost to the last a citizen of both worlds then generates a powerful comparison which expresses the earthly traveller's awe, encompasses the huge scope of his journey, and brings Rome and Florence together for the last time in the poem:

> Barbarians – coming from those bleak tracts
> where the Arcadian nymph's constellation
> daily wheels round in her son's company –
>
> when reaching Rome at last, were lost in awe
> to see her mighty soaring monuments
> with Caesar's palace towering over all.
>
> How overwhelming then would be my awe,
> reaching God's court beyond our mortal earth,
> eternity beyond all reach of time,
>
> coming from Florence to a just, sane city.
>
> (*Par.* 31. 31–40)

# Confronting the Church

## The great mantle: Dante's vision of the papacy

Dante's vision of the imperial ideal and the history of cities such as Rome and Florence is inseparable from his concerns about the papacy. In his letter of 1311 to Henry VII he portrayed his native city in an unholy and incestuous alliance with her 'father' the pope against the emperor (above, p. 40). In *Purgatorio* 16, he envisages Rome's role in the world in terms of the proper balance between papal and imperial authority (above, p. 142). Very early in the *Commedia*, too, Rome is seen not only as the capital of the empire but also as 'the sacred seat of those who succeeded the mighty [St] Peter'; and the prophecies heard by Virgil's Aeneas in the underworld are said to point both to his own victory and to the mission symbolized by 'the papal mantle'(*Inf.* 2. 23–7).

As a symbol of papal authority, the mantle featured prominently at the beginning of the actual ritual through which a new pope was enthroned. Once the elected candidate had signified his acceptance, the archdeacon of Rome put a red robe upon him, gave him the name he would use as pope and declared 'I invest you with the Roman church' (*Ullmann 1974: 230). Dante was well aware of this symbolism (*Inf.* 2. 25–7), but the *Commedia*'s uses of the term 'mantle' (*manto*) in connection with the papacy and the higher clergy can carry problematic connotations. The first pope whose voice is heard in the poem is an abuser of his office who makes a direct connection between advancing the material interests of his family and being 'clothed in the great mantle' (*Inf.* 19. 69–72). Expiating avarice in Purgatory, another papal figure gives a more complicated turn to the imagery by emphasizing how heavily 'the great mantle weighs on those who try to keep it out of the mud' (*Purg.* 16. 103–5). And a satirical picture conjured up by an ascetic saint in Paradise shows opulent princes of the church whose fur-lined mantles when they ride extend to cover their horses, 'so that two beasts seem to move within one skin' (*Par.* 21. 133–4). Other traditional images of papal authority – such as the sun, the sword and the keys – undergo similar metamorphoses in the *Commedia*'s vision of the church and its recent rulers. It is through such means and others that Dante conveys the crisis of authority in the papacy of his time.

That crisis had several causes and effects. Intellectual developments in lay, urban culture, in philosophical and scientific theory, and in the idea of the 'purely human, natural State'(Ullmann 1974: 267–70) combined to challenge its claims to authority, as works like Book 3 of Dante's *Monarchia* show. Along with these, the papacy faced some pressing practical difficulties deriving from its role as an interested party in Italian and European politics and from the cumbersome structure of its bureaucracy and finances (*Barraclough 1968: 118–23). And for such a centralized organization, frequent changes of leadership and direction proved yet more damaging. Between 1252 and 1296 there were 13 popes, by contrast with only four from 1216 to 1252 (Duffy 1997: 118). The effects of such changes were intensified by dramatic differences in style of leadership. The idealistic Gregory X (1271–6) was succeeded (after three very short papacies) by the nepotistic Nicholas III (1277–80); and – most dramatically of all – in 1294 after a rule of little more than five months, the hermit-pope Celestine V abdicated and was replaced by Boniface VIII, a Roman nobleman and lawyer.

Knowledge of ecclesiastical law had become a key skill for the higher clergy of Dante's time, and it had become a crucial weapon for defending the interests of the papacy. The *Decretals* issued by Gregory IX in 1234 codified new ecclesiastical law according to the decrees of previous popes; and the experts on these (the 'Decretalists') played a leading role in underpinning papal authority (*Tierney 1988: 150–7). In view of the claims about papal power made by these lawyers (Tierney 1988: 156–7), it is not surprising that Dante in the *Monarchia* should give most of his attention to 'those who are called Decretalists' (*Mon.* 3. 2. 9). He thus seems to be well aware of how at this time 'the spirit of church government [was] legal' (Barraclough 1968: 122); and his portrayal of Boniface VIII in *Inferno 27* sharply reflects this perception. So do his repeated complaints that the higher clergy prefer to study the Decretals rather than the Gospels or the Church Fathers (*Letters* pp. 135, 145, *Par.* 9. 133–8); and so does his later reference to John XXII, the last pope of his lifetime, as 'you who write only in order to erase' (*Par.* 18. 130).

Initially in the *Commedia*, however, the papacy's temporal concerns are represented in more material terms. At certain points the poem portrays the church's response to the organizational and financial problems of the time driving its leaders towards avarice and towards the betrayal of their vocation through simony (the abuse of clerical power for profit). This gravitational pull draws a number of the clerics and popes of Dante's time down into the *Inferno*.

## Simonist succession: popes in Dante's Hell

Avarice characterizes Dante's clergy and papacy from an early stage in the *Commedia*. At the entrance to the fourth circle of Hell, which contains the souls of the avaricious, Dante and Virgil are confronted by the monstrous figure of Plutus, who embodies the appetite for material wealth and is described as 'the great enemy' (*Inf.* 6. 115), an 'accursed wolf' (*Inf.* 7. 8). Plutus's rasping outcry begins the seventh canto of the poem:

> *Pape Satàn, pape Satàn aleppe!*

Like the giant Nimrod's exclamation in *Inf.* 31.67, this is infernal gobbledygook. Yet it may convey some sort of meaning: the repeated *pape* differs in only one letter from the word for 'pope' (*papa*); and its appearance alongside the similarly repeated *Satàn* suggests a link between avarice, the papacy and Lucifer that will be further explored in the *Inferno*.

Meanwhile, the association between avarice and the clergy becomes explicit soon afterwards in *Inferno* 7, when 'Dante' notices how prominent tonsured heads are among the souls in this circle (36–9) and when Virgil confirms to him that indeed:

> *'Questi fuor cherci, che non han coperchio*
> *piloso al capo, e papi e cardinali,*
> *in cui usa avarizia il suo soperchio.'*

> 'Those whose crowns lack covering of hair
> were clerics once and popes and cardinals
> in whom the power of avarice reigns supreme.'
> (*Inf.* 7. 46–8)

There was nothing particularly new in the yoking together of the clergy, Rome and the papal court with avarice; this had been a subject for satire since at least the twelfth century (Little 1971: 22). Dante's two major representations of popes in the *Inferno*, however, demonstrate an urgent concern about avarice and its effects on papal authority. These two portrayals are that of Nicholas III in canto 19 and the more indirect encounter (reported by a damned soul) with Boniface VIII in canto 27.

*Inferno* 19 begins with a denunciation of Simon Magus, after whom the sin of simony is named, because he thought 'that money could buy what God has given for nothing' (Acts 8: 20). Along with him the 'trump of judgement sounds' for his 'wretched followers' in the church who 'adulterate the things of God in return for gold and silver' (*Inf.* 19. 1–5). Gold and silver thus set the tone for the first episode in which a member of the clergy is addressed in the *Commedia*. They appear again later in the canto, when popes like the one encountered here are said to be idolatrous worshippers of multiple 'gods of gold and silver' (112–14). In between, there are harsh references to papal appetites for worldly wealth (55); to this pope's love of the purse placing him in this particular 'purse' of Hell (71–2); to his 'ill-gained money' (98); and to the 'avarice' of 'pastors' like him which 'sickens the world' (104; *Armour 1994: 17).

Nicholas III (1277–80) is the pope in question here. He came to power very soon after Gregory X, who has been described as 'the best Pope of the later thirteenth century' (Duffy 1997: 118); and he used that power to advance the interests of his family, the Roman Orsini clan (*Inf.* 19. 70–2; Havely 2004: 52). Dante would have been aware of this contrast, and that may have been one of the reasons why he places Nicholas here, as the first in his anti-apostolic succession of corrupt popes. Simony, as an abuse of God-given power, seems in this case to be a more serious breach of trust than the civic corruption that Dante portrays two cantos later (*Inf.* 21–2), and it has been rightly asked why such popes are not placed lower in Hell (Scott 2004: 194–5). In any case, the canto pulls no punches in its account of this betrayal, reflecting its perversity through grotesque inversions, like the up-ending of the sinner's body (45–8, 73–5), and grim ironies, like Nicholas's mistaking of Dante for another pope – Boniface VIII, no less (52–7).

Boniface VIII (1294–1303) will eventually follow Nicholas III down into the crevices of *Inferno*'s eighth circle; but as his tenure of the office ended after the date Dante assigns to the journey (1300), he is not finally called to account in the poem. He is, however, condemned at several points. In *Inferno* 19, Nicholas III refers to him not as a bridegroom of the church but as a deceiver and abuser of his spouse (55–7). Later, in *Inferno* 27, a deceiving politician who has fallen victim to Boniface's even more practised deceptions portrays him as 'the great priest', the 'prince of the new Pharisees', burning with a 'fever of pride' (*Inf.* 27. 70, 85 and 97). Boniface's pontificate was not without its achievements: 'founding a university in Rome, codifying canon law and re-establishing the Vatican Archive and Library' (Duffy 1997: 119). He also, as the *Commedia* acknowledges at several points, inaugurated the Jubilee of 1300 as a time of especial grace for Christendom (above, p. 19). But the portrayal of this pope in *Inferno* 27 reflects the arrogant and impetuous tendencies attributed to him by others and displays the features that led him to over-state his claims about the temporal power of the papacy; to start a fight he could not win with Philip IV of France; and thus in the end to weaken the church's political position (Tierney 1988: 180–92). Some consequences of that weakening of position are evident in the *Commedia*'s portrayal of two further popes of Dante's time: Clement V and John XXII.

Both these last two popes held power early in the long period of the papacy's residence at Avignon in eastern Provence. Both were themselves also French: Clement V (1305–14) was a Gascon who before his election had been archbishop of Bordeaux; whilst John XXII (1316–34) was from Cahors and had been bishop of Fréjus and Avignon. Like other Italian writers, Dante saw the removal of the papacy from Rome as an exile or captivity and as a surrender to political pressure from the king of France. Clement's origins as 'a pastor without principle out of the west' are dwelt upon at several points in the *Commedia*, from *Inferno* 19 onwards; and for failing fully to support the imperial venture in 1312 (above, p. 41) he is scathingly described as 'the Gascon who betrayed the noble Henry' (*Inf.* 19. 83, *Par.* 17. 82, 30. 133–48). He and John XXII are also savagely condemned by Dante's St Peter, who portrays them as predators upon the church and as 'Gascons and Cahorsines preparing to drink our blood' (*Par.* 27. 59). The development of such a violently apocalyptic view of the papacy has been described as 'the most mysterious part of [Dante's] spiritual biography' (Holmes 1980: 37).

Indications of the poet's thinking about the papacy at an important moment in its history can be found in his letter to the cardinals who were assembled at Avignon in the summer of 1314 to elect a successor to Clement V (*Letters* no. 8). This letter begins by quoting the biblical verse (taken from the beginning of the Lamentations of Jeremiah) that he had earlier used to announce the death of Beatrice in the *Vita nuova*: 'How desolate remains the city that had been full of people! She who was queen of the nations has become like a widow' (*Letters* pp. 127, 143). Here the 'widowed city' is

Rome, which is said here to have been 'widowed and abandoned' by the departure of the pope to Avignon. Those in authority – the cardinals now charged with the renewal of the papacy – are then urged by the writer to return to the right path and not run astray like 'unruly oxen' dragging the Ark of the church 'away into the wilderness' (133, 145). Dante's stance here has been compared to that of one preaching 'a lay sermon', and of all his letters this is the one that 'comes closest to the tone and style of the *Commedia*' (*DE* 354B).

Two related features of the letter to the cardinals emphasize its relationship to the *Commedia* – of which in 1314 Dante was beginning the last part – and its importance for the poet's vision of the church. First, the stance he adopts is not only that of the layman addressing a kind of sermon to the cardinals, but also that of a prophetic truth-teller. The opening quotation from the Lamentations of Jeremiah already suggests this view of the writer's role, and so does his characterization of himself as a lowly figure who is forced to lift up his voice to rebuke those in authority (*Letters* pp. 131, 136, 144, 145–6). This stance had already been dramatized in the *Commedia* – for instance, in the *Inferno*, when denouncing corrupt popes (*Inf.* 19), and in the *Purgatorio*, when bearing witness to the decadence of the church (*Purg.* 32–3). Following the letter to the cardinals, it will be further defined through the authorizing of the poet's vision in the *Paradiso* – most notably when St Peter, after his violent condemnation of the present leadership of the church (above, p. 86), turns to Dante as the one who will pass on this prophetic message (*Par.* 27. 64–6).

Secondly, a key concern of the letter is the effect upon the church of the desire for material power and wealth. Immediately after its prophetic opening, it turns to the pernicious effects of the Pharisees' 'greed' (*cupiditas, Letters* pp. 127, 143). The cardinals are then compared to the merchants whom Christ drove out of the Temple (John 2: 13–17), and they are said to have become partners not of the now desolate church, the 'Bride of Christ', but of 'greed' (*Letters* pp. 133–4, 145). Confronting the panoply of their wealth and authority, the impoverished writer wryly acknowledges that 'I abuse no pastoral authority, seeing that I possess no riches' (132, 144). Clerical avarice is, as we have seen, at the root of the church's ills in the *Commedia*; and greed, both in the church and in the world, becomes 'the most insistent and powerful of all the themes' in the *Monarchia* (*Mon.* xxxi; Havely 2004: 154–5). Imagining its origins, effects and remedies will thus be crucial to Dante's vision of ecclesiastical renewal.

## Renewing the church: beginnings and endings

'Noble beginning, to what a wretched ending have you come!' This is how St Peter concludes his vision of the church, beset by 'ravening wolves in the guise of shepherds' and blood-sucking popes from Cahors and Gascony (*Par.* 27. 46–60). Peter speaks here as an Apostle and as founder of the church; and the rebirth of the original apostolic ideal is imagined – especially in the *Paradiso* – as a means through which this 'wretched ending' might possibly be averted. But what, apart from greed itself, had reduced the church to such a state? What action or event does Dante show precipitating this decline? Here we need to return for a moment to that first scene in which a pope is spoken to, in *Inferno* 19, and to an emperor who is addressed in the course of that speech:

> O Constantine, how many ills were born
> not out of your conversion but the gift
> received from you by the first wealthy father!
> (*Inf.* 19. 115–17)

These lines conclude the 'song' of rebuke performed by 'Dante' as newly confident pilgrim before Pope Nicholas III, who is 'planted like a pole', upside-down in the livid rock of Hell's eighth circle. They refer to the 'Donation of Constantine' through which the Roman emperor, out of gratitude for being cured of leprosy by Pope Silvester I in 314, was claimed to have transferred 'all provinces, palaces and districts of the city of Rome and Italy and of the regions of the West' into 'the power and sway of him and the pontiffs, his successors' (Tierney 1988: 22). The document conveying this gift was in fact composed by a Roman cleric around 760, but the forgery was not demonstrated until the mid-fifteenth century; meanwhile it had been put to various uses by the papacy – for instance, during the thirteenth century, in its claims to territories in Italy and its right to crown emperors (Ullmann 1974: 118, 133, 152; Tierney 1988: 142–4).

At several later moments in the *Commedia*, Constantine's gift is envisaged as a kind of second Fall. At the end of the *Purgatorio*, Dante witnesses a series of strange transformations in the chariot representing the church. One of these occurs when an eagle (symbol of the empire) descends upon the chariot, leaving it grotesquely 'covered with his feathers', whilst a voice from Heaven (presumably that of the Apostle Peter) exclaims: 'O little ship of mine, how badly you are burdened!' (*Purg.* 32. 124–9). Constantine himself is placed among the souls of the just in Dante's Heaven of Jupiter, and his 'good intentions' are recognized (*Par.* 20. 56). But the 'evil fruit' of his gift – the corruption of the papacy – is not forgotten; and his removal of the seat of empire from Rome to Byzantium here seems to compromise his authority and even his identity, since 'in order to yield to the pastor [the pope] he turned himself into a Greek' (57).

Dante was writing the *Monarchia* very close to the time in which he describes Constantine among the souls in Paradise; and here he also addresses the effects of the Donation. Again, there are references in all three parts of the work. The first, at the end of Book 1, recalls in some ways the violent symbolism of *Purgatorio* 32, although here the victim of the 'talon of cupidity' is the unity of the empire; and it is humanity in general that is subsequently seen transformed into a 'many-headed beast' (*Mon.* 1. 16. 3). In the context of Book 2, where the destiny of Rome and the empire has been affirmed, Constantine's action is viewed rather more harshly than it is in *Paradiso* 20; and Dante, in his address to the 'happy people' of Italy which concludes this book, wishes that the 'man who weakened your empire had never been born, or at least had never been led astray by his own pious intentions' (*Mon.* 2. 16. 8).

It is in the third book of the *Monarchia*, however – when he is confronting the church's claims to temporal power – that Dante addresses the effects of the Donation of Constantine most explicitly and extensively. Here (*Mon.* 3. 10) he identifies the founding principles of both the empire and the church, arguing that 'Constantine was not in a position to give away the privileges of empire, nor was the church in a position to accept them', and that the church is 'utterly unsuited to receiving temporal things' because an intrinsic part of its founding principle is Christ's commandment that the Apostles should not carry money (Matthew 10: 9–10). *Monarchia* 3.10 is thus a crucial passage not only in Dante's argument about the rights of the papacy and the empire but also for his vision of what lies at the heart of the church's authority and mission: its adherence – or return – to apostolic ideals.

The *Commedia*'s vision of renewal in the church is slow to take shape. In the *Inferno*, the main patterns of clerical activity are those of reversal and decline; and papal succession is seen as a process by which Boniface VIII and then Clement V will drive Nicholas III further down into the livid rock. Apart from Dante and his guide, there are few signs to point in any other direction. The hermit Pope Celestine V, upon whom hopes for a change in the papacy's direction had been placed (above, p. 145), is remembered only for his abdication, and is present as no more than the 'the shadow of him who through cowardice made the great refusal' (*Inf.* 3. 59–60). St Francis, who is to play such a powerful apostolic role in the *Paradiso*, appears only as a silent and defeated figure at the end of *Inferno* 27 (112–14). The word for 'church' (*chiesa*) occurs only once here, as part of a proverb through which Dante wryly considers the implications of keeping company with devils (*Inf.* 22. 14–15). And the words of the church emerge only in travestied form at the start of *Inferno*'s final canto, when the opening line of the ancient Good Friday hymn 'The banners of the King go forth' heralds not the appearance of Christ but that of the 'infernal King', Satan (*Inf.* 34. 1).

The word 'church' and the words *of* the church are, on the other hand, heard much more frequently as Dante ascends the mountain of Purgatory. Liturgical language – the use of prayers and psalms – is particularly frequent in the *Purgatorio* and continues to feature substantially in the *Paradiso* too (*DE* 570–1). Singing 'together with one voice' occurs frequently from *Purgatorio* 2 (46–8) onwards, and it powerfully conveys the impression of a restored community. So also do the variety of voices who address Dante as 'brother' (*frate*). Amongst these is the only pope to provide a narrative of salvation in the *Commedia*: Hadrian V, whose pontificate lasted scarcely more than a month (11 July–18 August 1276) and whom Dante encounters as a prostrate figure on the ground, among the souls expiating the sin of avarice (*Purg.* 19. 79–145).

The encounter with Hadrian V is a key moment in Dante's vision of the church's possible redirection and renewal; and *Purgatorio* 19 answers *Inferno* 19 in ways that release these possibilities. Both cantos dramatically represent the gravitational pull of avarice upon the popes portrayed; indeed it is Hadrian V who draws attention to the weight of the papal 'mantle' that is so difficult to 'keep from trailing in the dirt' (*Purg.* 19. 103–5). Yet, unlike Nicholas III, Hadrian is able to recognize the power of renewed 'love' (111) and divine 'justice' (120, 123) and thus to achieve what he calls here 'conversion' (106). Like the other souls in this canto, he is literally 'converted' (116), turned around and made to fix his gaze upon the ground, in order to expiate the avaricious obsession with 'things of the earth' (119). But he is also able to point the way forward for himself and those around him. He does so by rejecting the kneeling pilgrim's homage to his earthly authority and urging him vigorously and concisely to 'Straighten your legs, rise up, brother!' (133). This pope's speech thus seems to recognize the potential, at least, for the redirection and recovery of the community of the church.

Such recognitions are, however, overshadowed by the continuing awareness of the dire condition of St Peter's 'little ship'. The transformations of the chariot of the church that are witnessed by Dante at the end of *Purgatorio* 32 reflect the apocalyptic imagery and language of the Book of Revelation and of radical critics of the papacy in Dante's time (Havely 2004: 109–22). So, later on in *Paradiso* 27, does St Peter's invective about the state of Rome and the rapacious popes about to drink the blood of the Apostles and martyrs. Yet apocalyptic vision of this sort is also ultimately optimistic, since it looks to some sort of divine intervention and renewal (above, p. 96). In both these cases, Dante's Beatrice plays an answering prophetic role. In *Purgatorio* 33 she foretells the advent of a mysterious emissary of God – identified solely by the numeral 'five hundred and ten and five' – who will strike down those who have commandeered the chariot of the church (*Purg.* 33.43–5; *DE* 381A–383A). At the end of *Paradiso* 27 she prophesies in equally enigmatic terms how the power of the celestial spheres will be turned directly upon the earth, so as to reverse the direction that the 'fleet' of humanity is following (142–8).

In the *Paradiso* especially, Beatrice's confidence about the future of the church and of humanity is supported by a number of figures whose lives exemplify the renewal of religious life. Such figures become increasingly prominent as Dante ascends through the circles of this 'cloister'. In the early cantos, for example, he encounters Piccarda, the nun who addresses him as 'brother'; the courtier Romieu, who became a mendicant; and the poet Folquet, who became a Cistercian monk and a bishop (*Par.* 3, 6, 9). In cantos 11 and 12, St Francis and St Dominic are portrayed not only as the leaders of the new religious orders of the thirteenth century, but also as the two 'wheels of the chariot with which Holy Church was able to defend herself and gain victory in her civil war' (*Par.* 12. 106–8). Cantos 21 and 22 celebrate the contemplative life and the monastic ideal, giving voice in particular to the hermit and reformer Peter Damian and the founder of the Benedictine order. The original apostolic ideals which have been exemplified in the lives of Francis and Dominic and invoked by Peter Damian (*Par.* 21. 127–9) are embodied in Dante's sphere of fixed stars by Peter, James and John themselves (cantos 24–7). And finally, the dominant voice in the last three cantos of the poem (*Par.* 31–3) is that of St Bernard of Clairvaux, a moving spirit in the early years of the Cistercian order, an advisor to the papacy, an eloquent preacher, and the intermediary on Dante's behalf to the Virgin Mary (*Par.* 33. 1–39).

Dante's Paradise is seen as a 'city' (above, p. 143); but it is also imagined several times as a structure of the church, a 'convent' or 'cloister' (*Purg.* 15. 55–7, 26. 127–9). The White Rose is the image of sainthood which dominates the last three cantos of the *Paradiso*, and it is an image to which we shall return. Meanwhile we can note that Beatrice, returning home in *Paradiso* 30, presents it to Dante not only as the all-embracing 'city' of god and humanity (130), but also, just before that, as a white-robed assembly or, literally, 'convent' (*convento*, 129).

# Imagining Sin and Sainthood

## Early images: *Vita nuova*, lyrics, letters

Dante's Beatrice, as we have just heard, is a powerful voice in the *Commedia*. There and in the *Vita nuova* she is also powerful in the effects that her appearance, gaze and greeting have upon her lover. But what might she have looked like? Where, apart from the *Commedia*, does Dante portray such idealized figures, and how in his other writing does he imagine their opposites?

There are a few cues to the visualizing of Beatrice in the text of the *Vita nuova* or later in the *Commedia*. The initial vision shows her clad in a 'noble' blood-red colour (*sanguigno*): first as a child when the 8-year-old Dante sets eyes on her for the first time on May Day 1274 (*VN* ch. 2). Nine years later she appears again: first in a virginal guise, attended by two older women and 'dressed in the purest white'; and secondly in a more eroticized form, as a figure in his dream 'naked, except that she seemed to me to be lightly clad in a blood-red cloth' (ch. 3). Blood-red is also the colour in which she makes her final appearance in the *Vita nuova*, as a mutely reproachful spirit, to 'rekindle' her lover's grief for her death (ch. 39). It is also related to one of the three colours in which she manifests herself to Dante in the Earthly Paradise at the summit of Mount Purgatory: with a white veil, crowned with olive leaves, clad in a green mantle over a robe of flame-red (*Purg.* 30. 31–3). The colour which thus most closely identifies her (red) thus carries a variety of related symbolic associations: with nobility, passion and charity.

In the *Vita nuova* Dante also shows a keen interest in the actual process of depicting idealized figures. Its key *canzone* in praise of Beatrice, 'Ladies who have understanding of love', is itself presented in the chapters preceding

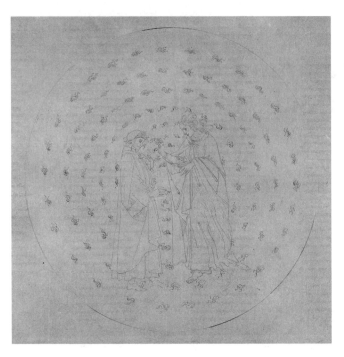

*Plate 3*  Dante and Beatrice in the sphere of Mercury (*Par.* 7), from Berlin, Kupfer-stichkabinett, MS Hamilton 201, illustrated by Sandro Botticelli, c.1480–95. By permission of Bildarchiv, Preußischer Kulturbesitz, Berlin.

it (17–19) as an exercise in how to do this (above, p. 117). A passage from near the end of the poem illustrates this vividly:

> *De li occhi suoi, come ch'ella li mova*
> *Escono spirit d'amore inflammati,*
> *che feron li occhi a qual che allor la guati,*
> *e passan sì che 'l cor ciascun retrova:*
> *voi le vedete Amor pinto nel viso,*
> *là 've non pote alcun mirarla fiso.*

> Out of her eyes wherever she turns her gaze
> spirits of love dart forth in fiery shape,
> striking the eyes of those who look on her,
> piercing straight through, till each reaches the heart.
> You, ladies, see Love figured in her face,
> on which no one may hold their gaze for long.

> (lines 51–6)

Here, the word that describes how Love is portrayed or 'figured' is *pinto*, which literally means 'painted' – thus reflecting how Beatrice has been represented so far in the poem, as an iconic and angelic figure. Later in the *Vita nuova*, after her death, Dante represents himself yet more explicitly as portrayer of Beatrice in angelic form. At the opening of chapter 34, he describes how, on the anniversary of the day in which she 'became one of the citizens of eternal life', he 'was sitting in a place where, in memory of her, I was drawing an angel'.

In the poems of Dante's early exile there are possible parallels to the idealized and iconic Beatrice of the *VN*. In the *canzone Tre donne* ('Three Ladies', FB no. 81), three downcast, weary and 'banished' women gather around the 'home' of Dante's heart and personify aspects of justice in the poem. And in the *Convivio*, as we shall see, the operation of love in the mind is embodied in the three *canzoni* addressed to the 'noble lady', Philosophy (below, pp. 182–4).

More difficult to find in Dante's earlier work are figures that might suggest how he began to imagine evil before his comprehensive portrayal of it in the *Inferno*. Several malicious or desperate figures do appear already in the *Vita nuova* – notably the Fury-like dishevelled women who foretell Dante's death and lament Beatrice's in the nightmare narrated in chapter 23. Yet these are hardly sinners on a par with those in Dante's underworld – nor is the cruel lady of his later 'stony' sequence of poems (FB nos. 77–80). However, the last and most ambitious of these *rime petrose* ('stony verses'), beginning 'I want to be as harsh in my speech as this fair stone is in her behaviour' (FB no. 80), has several possibly 'infernal' features. These include: the virtuosic harshness of the rhymes, diction and imagery (compare *Inferno* 32. 1–9); the wish to hear the cruel mistress 'howl for me in the burning ravine, as I do for her' (lines 59–60); and the fantasy of vengeful violence that concludes the poem (FB no. 80, lines 61–83).

It is, then, to Dante's early writing in this 'harsh' stylistic register that we could look for some foreshadowing of the *Inferno*. Such writing includes satirical verse of the kind to be found in the six abusive sonnets that he may have exchanged with his friend Forese Donati, perhaps around 1293–6 or even earlier (Durling and Martinez 2003: 612–14). There is some uncertainty about the attribution of these sonnets to Dante, as there is about his authorship of the sequence *Il Fiore* ('the Flower'), which summarizes the action of the *Romance of the Rose* in 232 sonnets (Casciana and Kleinhenz 2000). *Il Fiore* itself includes a fair amount of the original French romance's satirical material, for instance in its representation

157

of the clergy, wealth, poverty and avarice, and could thus be seen as pre-figuring some of the 'anticlerical' writing in the *Commedia* (Havely 2004: 12–16).

Vivid characterization of avarice can also be found in early work that is undoubtedly by Dante – notably in his moral *canzone Doglia mi reca* ('Grief brings boldness to my heart'; FB no. 83), which prefigures several of the *Commedia*'s concerns and harshly portrays the avaricious man in the restless pursuit of satisfaction through possessions, a goal that recedes before him into infinity (lines 64–73; Barolini 1993: 29–32, Boyde 2000: 154–5). The 'accursed miser' is also portrayed at points in the prose of Dante's *Convivio* – notably in 3. 15. 9 and at more length in 4. 12–13, where the 'inadequa-cies' of wealth are dwelt upon, as are the miseries of travelling merchants, whom every breath of wind in the leaves makes tremble with fear (*Conv.* 4. 13. 11). Such images reflect a continuing preoccupation in Dante's writing: the restless avaricious man again makes an appearance at the start of the *Inferno* when the distraught protagonist, driven back from his ascent by the wolf, is compared to

> one who has pursued a winning streak
> and, coming to the point where loss sets in,
> at once is plunged in grief and misery
>
> (*Inf.* 1. 55–7)

– which is the 'first economic image of the *Commedia*' (Armour 1994: 10).

Recognition of such features in Dante's early writing, however, should not blunt our awareness of the shock effect that the images of sin and sinners in the *Inferno* must have had when they were first encountered. When the poem began to circulate, its readers would already have had some familiarity with scenes from Hell in the visual art of churches and even in theatrical spectacle (above, pp. 4, 65–6). In some of the Latin visions of the otherworld (above, p. 87), they might even have come across life-stories of individual sinners that they could compare with, those of in, say, *Inferno* 5, 6 and 10. But those earlier vignettes would not have presented them with the degree of specificity with which such figures as Francesca, Ciacco and Farinata are presented. Still less would readers have been prepared for what meets Dante and Virgil on the edge of the abyss in *Inferno* 16–17: the 'foul image of deception' itself.

## Geryon: the image on the edge

> And that foul image of deception
> appeared before us, beached its head and forelimbs,
> yet did not bring its tail over the edge.
>     Its face looked like the face of honesty
> with good will manifest, but just skin-deep,
> while the whole trunk was scaly like a snake.
>     Its forepaws to the armpits sprouted hair;
> and all its back, its breast and both its sides
>     brightly adorned with knots and little wheels.
>
> (Inf. 17. 7–15)

In the first line of this description the original reads: 'E quella sozza imagine di *froda*', and most modern English versions (such as Durling and Martinez 1996: 261) translate the last word quite understandably as 'fraud'. Yet the most common meanings of 'fraud' in modern English – with their connotations of false accounting, or general charlatanry – fail to cover what this monstrous figure represents, nor do they convey the full extent of what Dante and Virgil are about to encounter when Geryon carries them down to the third and lowest section of Hell.

'Fraud' in the older English sense of 'quality or disposition of being deceitful' (*OED fraud* 1) could, however, be appropriate here. This wider meaning of deliberate and persistent deception seems to be what Virgil has in mind when, in his account of the categories of sin, he contrasts *frode* with *forza* ('violence') as the sin which is 'more repugnant to God' (*Inf.* 11. 25–6). This is because wronging others through deception rather than force is an abuse of reason and hence 'an evil distinctive to man' (*Inf.* 11. 25) as well as a denial of one's essential humanity. As Dante views it in *Inferno* 11 and as he imagines it from *Inferno* 16 onwards, it becomes 'an unbridgeable gap in society through its destruction of the natural bonds that should unite all citizens' (*DE* 420A).

Appropriately for such a figure, Geryon has a complex ancestry. Like Dante's Charon (*Inf.* 3), Minos (*Inf.* 5), Cerberus and many other Infernal monsters, he takes his name and some of his nature from classical mythology. In the first place, the tenth of the Twelve Labours of Hercules – an enterprise comparable to Dante's here – was to capture the oxen owned by the three-bodied Geryon and in doing so to kill him. Brief reference to that story is made by Virgil, who on Aeneas's entry into the underworld mentions him, along with other threatening shapes, as 'the three-bodied shade' (*Aen.* 6. 289, also 8. 202). Yet in keeping with his portrayal of evil as a travesty of divine creativity, Dante takes a Trinitarian approach to his 'foul image' and gives his Geryon not three bodies, but three natures in one body: the human face, the bestial paws, and the dragon-like trunk and tail, armed with a scorpion's sting.

Dante's Virgil is appropriately, as a pagan poet, the first to name Geryon, when he gives him instructions about how to carry the two poets on his back down to the eighth circle of Hell (*Inf.* 17. 97–9). At the opening of this canto, however, Virgil has announced the monster's appearance more enigmatically by proclaiming 'Behold the beast' (*Inf.* 17. 1). Here he is using terms which invoke the Christian biblical and exegetical traditions: the emergence of the Beast that comes 'out of the abyss' or from the sea in Revelation 11: 7 or 13: 1; the human-faced, scorpion-tailed creatures that rise again 'from the Abyss' to afflict the world (Revelation 9: 2–11); the fishing up of Leviathan in Job 40: 20; and the various medieval traditions about the appearance of Antichrist (Friedman 1972).

With his hybrid nature and complex mythic ancestry, Dante's Geryon concentrates key aspects of evil in the *Inferno*. Anxious awareness of how easily human reason could yield to animal instinct had meant that 'such composite monsters had become common motifs in sacred iconography, especially in sculpture and on capitals of columns in churches, etc.' (CL 1. 515). In the *Inferno* itself, before the descent to the eighth circle, the debasement of human nature through sins of excess or violence has already been represented through a number of human/bestial figures: from Minos the judge of the underworld, snarling and lashing himself with a long, curling tail (*Inf.* 5. 4 and 11–12) to the irate Minotaur and Centaurs by the river of blood (*Inf.* 12) and the predatory Harpies in the Wood of the Suicides (*Inf.* 13). And Geryon's appearance also prefigures some of the distortions and debasements that are yet to come in the eighth and ninth circles: humiliating games between corrupt politicians and cunning bestial devils (*Inf.* 22); snakes exchanging identities with thieves (*Inf.* 25); or Satan himself, shaggy-haired, bat-like and compared to an 'evil worm', gnawing at the core of the world (*Inf.* 34. 49–51, 73–5 and 108).

A further feature of this 'foul image' is the way in which it reflects Dante's sense of his own enterprise and artistry. Such implications already begin to be evident as Virgil and the narrator prepare for Geryon's arrival at the end of *Inferno* 16:

> He said to me: 'Soon there will surface here
> the thing that I expect and you imagine;
> soon it must manifest itself to you.'
> Faced with a truth that looks quite like a lie,
> always keep quiet as long as you can
> in case you undeservedly get blamed.
> But I cannot hold back here; by the words
> of this *Commedia*, reader, I now swear,
> hoping they will not lose their lasting fame,
> that I saw through that thick and murky air
> a figure swimming up towards us then
> that would strike even the boldest heart with wonder.
> (*Inf.* 16. 121–32)

The narrator/poet is here preparing a wonderful deception: a figure that he has, as Virgil says here, 'imagined' or 'dreamed up in his thoughts' (the Italian verb at the end of line 122 is *sogna*), and one he wants to persuade the reader that he actually saw. Admittedly 'the foul image of deceit' here is, as we have seen, the kind of 'lie' that even St Augustine would have considered permissible: a fiction that serves the wider truth of Dante's poem. But Geryon is also a celebration of his author's own audacity and inventiveness. 'Geryon's canto' (*Inferno* 17) has been shown to be more than usually patterned with the tools of the poet's trade: it 'teems with tropes' and it contains at its centre a highly self-conscious interruption to the narrative – the episode in which Dante turns aside to meet the usurers (34–78) – which itself is composed as 'a series of frames' (Cherchi 1988). Geryon's skin itself – 'adorned with knots and little wheels' (15) – is a work of art, as the immediately following comparisons claim:

> Such varied hues, in background or raised patterns,
> were never worked in oriental cloths
> nor in those webs that once Arachne wove.
> (*Inf.* 17. 16–18)

Ingenuity and audacity are the key features here. Arachne, according to Ovid (*Met.* 6), challenged Minerva to a contest of skill in weaving and produced compelling images of the crimes and deceptions of the gods, and was transformed for her pains into a spider; and she is to be imaged again as a cautionary example of over-reaching pride in the *Purgatorio* (12. 43–5). But here in the Geryon canto we are not reminded of her 'folly', nor of her grim fate at the hands of the angry goddess: she appears here, rather, as a supreme

*Plate 4* Geryon and the poets, descending the abyss into *Malebolge* (*Inf.* 17), from Paris BN, MS it. 2017 f. 199r, illustrated by the *Vitae imperatorum* Master, c.1440. By permission of Bibliothèque nationale de France.

example of human craft, to be surpassed only by a creature of Dante's own imagination.

Later artists responded strongly to Dante's assertion of creativity in this episode. The knots and little wheels on Geryon's back reflect the deviousness and intricacy of the deceits that he represents; but they also mirror the ingenuity Dante himself has to exercise when negotiating the increasingly dense labyrinth of the *Inferno*. The connection between the 'little wheels' (*rotelle*) of Geryon's patterning, his wheeling descent to the eighth circle (*Inf.* 17. 98 and 131), and the intricate pattern of linked concentric rings that comprise that circle is graphically suggested by the work of a north Italian artist who illustrated the *Inferno* for a manuscript around 1440 (see cover illustration and plate 4). Such a response seems to have recognized the extent of the *novità* that Dante has anticipated at the end of *Inferno* 16 – the strange new invention that he has bred out of classical and biblical traditions and is now using as a vehicle to further the enterprise of his journey.

Geryon is thus a powerful example of how, when imagining evil, Dante outdoes his traditional sources. The precariousness of his venture, balancing between due audacity and over-reaching pride, is evident in the fearful way he imagines the novelty of the experience of flight on the monster's back at the end of the Geryon canto (*Inf.* 17. 100–36). Yet even here the poet is busy invoking and outdoing Ovid and classical myth:

> I do not think there can have been greater fear
> when Phaethon let drop that chariot's reins,
> so that the sky – as still now seems – was scorched,
> nor when poor Icarus felt on his back
> the feathers loosen as the wax dripped off
> and all the while his father wailed: 'Too high!'
>
> (*Inf.* 17. 106–11)

The story of Phaethon's ill-fated attempt to drive the chariot of his father the Sun had been told with dizzying panache by Ovid (*Met.* 2; Humphries 1955: 28–40); and Dante returns to it as an example of human over-reaching and loss of control in both *Purgatorio* (4. 70–2) and *Paradiso* (31. 124–6). Even more disturbing is the myth of Icarus, whose fall from the sky is attributed by Ovid not only to his own rashness in failing (like Phaethon) to keep a 'middle course', but also to the 'fatal art' of his father Daedalus, the maker of the wings with which they flew (*Met.* 8; Humphries 1955: 187–90). Both allusions, as Dante develops them here, are double-edged in their effect. They convey the trepidation of the traveller-narrator venturing into unknown territory, alongside the poet's confidence in his ability to surpass the fictions of the classical writers.

## Shaping shape-shifters: the thieves

Other complex images of sin in the *Inferno* are represented with a similar blend of apprehension and authorial confidence. Amongst these, the portrayal of the thieves in cantos 24 and 25 stands out for several reasons. Theft here is a more serious affair than brigandry or even usury, which are placed among the sins of violence above in cantos 12 and 16. Cantos 24 and 25, by contrast, are concerned with theft as an act of deception, a breach of trust and hence a more serious threat to the community and the body politic. Hence, one of the main figures portrayed here, the 'bestial' Vanni Fucci of Pistoia, is from the city where the 'Black' and 'White' names

163

for the Guelf factions originated; and as a leader of the Blacks he takes malicious delight in prophesying further trouble for Dante and his former party (*Inf.* 24. 140–51). His own body is thus shown undergoing repeated processes of destruction and disintegration that are similar in their significance to the mutilation of those condemned for dividing communities (*Inf.* 28).

The immediate causes of this destruction are among the most strange and terrifying inventions in the *Inferno*. As Dante and Virgil reach the point where they can see into this *bolgia* – the seventh of the ten 'evil pouches' into which the eighth circle of Hell is divided – they are faced with a sight that the narrator says still makes his blood run cold: 'a fearful seething mass of serpents' (*Inf.* 24. 82–4). A bite in the neck from one of these reduces Vanni Fucci to a heap of renewable ash (97–102), whilst two others suppress the blasphemous speech and gesture with which he opens the next canto (*Inf.* 25. 1–9). Yet more strangely, a dragon-like creature embraces and merges with a thief to extinguish both their identities and produce a single 'perverse image' that moves off 'slowly', as if burdened with its own horror (49–78).

The final shifting of the 'ballast' contained in this grim hold is stranger still. About half of the canto (from line 79 on) is then devoted to showing how the natures of thief and serpent can not only be merged but exchanged. Another dragon-like serpent leaps in a flash upon one of a pair of Florentine thieves, fixes its teeth into 'the place where our nourishment is first received' and then drops motionless in front of him (85–7). Smoke then issues from the serpent's mouth and the thief's wounded navel and mingles, forming a kind of linking element through which each seems to transmit its features to the other (91–135). This kind of metamorphosis seems to go well beyond the debasement of the human into the bestial that is portrayed in the *Inferno* before and after these cantos. It generates a confusion that makes it difficult for the reader to know what is happening to whom, or indeed who (or what) *is* who.

The metamorphoses of the thieves, like the representation of Geryon, posed a challenge to the illustrators of the *Inferno*; and one to which several made striking responses. The early phase of the merging of thief and serpent is captured with a considerable degree of bizarre naturalism by the Ferrarese miniaturist Guglielmo Giraldi and his assistants, around 1478 (BMS 1. 331–2; see plate 5). This image responds to Dante's simile of ivy twisting itself around a tree (in *Inf.* 25. 91–135) by showing the green of the serpent's back merging into the flesh-tones of the thief's body. The yet stranger

L fine dele fue parole il Ladro
le mam alzo con amliedue le fiche
qridando tolle dio cha te le fquadro
Da mdi in qua in fur le ferp anmche
rerchuma gli fauolfe alhora al collo
come dicesse io non no che pui diche
Er unaltra a le braccia d'enlegollo
a huttendo fe ftessi si diniarzt
che non potea con esse dare un crollo

*Plate* 5  Thieves and Serpents (*Inf.* 25), illustrated by Guglielmo Giraldi and followers, c.1478. © Biblioteca Apostolica Vaticana, MS Urb. lat. 365, f. 66v.

exchange of natures between man and serpent is visualized by the anonymous (probably Tuscan) illustrator of a mid-fourteenth-century copy of the *Inferno* (BMS 1. 216; see plate 6). Here the process described by Dante in *Inf.* 25. 91–135 is portrayed at its mid-point: a dragon with human legs lies on its back, facing a half-erect, merman-like figure whose human upper body blends into a serpentine tail; whilst the two are held in a kind of diabolical dialogue by the plume of smoke that links the dragon's jaws with the thief's navel.

Even more sharply than in the Geryon episode, Dante himself seems to be conscious here of the challenge posed by the imagining of such evil. Like canto 17, cantos 24–5 are pervaded with allusions to the tools, traditions and techniques of the poet's trade. There are, for instance, references at several points to letters, paper and the possible inadequacies of the poet's pen when dealing with such 'strangeness' as has been witnessed here (24.100–2, 25. 64–6 and 143–4). There also seems to be an escalation of

165

*Plate 6*   Thief and serpent (*Inf.* 25), from Chantilly, Musée Condé MS 597, f. 170r, illustrated by an anonymous Pisan artist of the 1340s. By permission of the Musée Condé. © Photo RMN/© René-Gabriel Ojéda.

poetic self-consciousness as the full extent of that strangeness is communicated in canto 25: first with the address to the reader that introduces the initial, 'barely believable' metamorphosis (46–8); and then with the famous 'silencing' of the classical predecessors (Lucan, Ovid) that accompanies the second (94–9).

There is some disagreement amongst those who have considered the poetic self-consciousness of this episode closely. Is Dante thus conveying an uneasy sense of the risks he runs through such audacity (Hawkins 1980)? Or is he engaged in an 'elaborate program' here which requires the poet himself to be 'a kind of thief in order to renew the lineage of poetry' as well as to act like 'a thief in the Christological sense [1 Thessalonians 5: 2; Revelation 3: 3] . . . come not only to strive, imitate and surpass but also to judge' (Durling and Martinez 1996: 571)? Such questions are also implicit in the self-consciousness with which the poem presents images of both sin and sainthood as created by 'divine' art in the *Purgatorio*.

### Divine art in Purgatory

Once Dante and Virgil have entered the gate of Purgatory itself (*Purg.* 9) their progress becomes in some respects quite straightforward. They ascend the mountain through seven circles or 'terraces' (diagram 2, p. 124). The moral scheme here is based on that of the traditional seven capital sins – pride, envy, anger, sloth, avarice, gluttony and lust – and is thus rather simpler than the divisions, subdivisions and groupings of the *Inferno*. Throughout this stage of the journey, too – from canto 10 of the *Purgatorio* through to canto 26 – the poets are quite regularly presented with images of virtue and vice, designed to serve as examples for those who are expiating the various sins.

Yet this basic structure and the travellers' experience of it have their complicating features too. Examples of those sins and the corresponding virtues (humility on the terrace of pride, love on that of envy, and so on) are regularly portrayed, but they take different forms. They are first visual images, like the bodily forms of the penitent sinners themselves (*Purg.* 10, 12). But they can also be encountered as disembodied voices in the air (13. 25–36, 14. 130–41); then as inner revelations experienced by the protagonist (15. 85–114, 17. 19–39); and frequently in the later cantos they are heard as utterances performed by the penitent souls themselves (18. 97–105, 20. 19–27 and 103–17 etc.). This kind of variation avoids monotony in the narrative (CL 2. 537), but it also helps to generate a mounting sense of purgatorial purpose – for instance, when the examples of chastity form part of a hymn being sung by the souls of the lustful out of the heart of the flames on the final terrace (25. 121–35).

The initial examples of virtue in *Purgatorio* 10 are powerfully and sustainedly visual. Having, in canto 9, entered the gate guarded by an angel, Dante and Virgil have to use 'a little skill' (*un poco d'arte*) in mountaineering to negotiate a twisting cleft up the hillside (*Purg.* 10. 7–16). Emerging through this 'needle's eye' they reach a point where the mountain appears to 'pull itself back', forming the first terrace, a space only about five metres wide, but one that is initially described as 'more solitary than roads that lead through deserts' (21). This desolate but quite precisely measured space forms a stage for the images of humility. As the two poets move towards the inner side of the terrace where the mountain's wall rises again, Dante notices that at the foot of the slope there is a more gently inclined band of white marble worked with carvings by one whose skill, he says, surpasses not only that of the ancient Greek sculptors but the craftsmanship of Nature herself (28–33).

Detailed descriptions of the images themselves and their effects upon the viewer take up most of this canto (28–99). As with all the other groups of positive examples, the sequence illustrating humility begins with the Virgin Mary and the scene of the Annunciation, one of the most frequently depicted subjects of medieval religious art (34–45). Then Virgil prompts Dante to move on to the next scene, which is from the Old Testament (2 Samuel 6) and shows King David putting aside his regal dignity, joining the celebrating crowd and dancing in front of the Ark of the Covenant as it is brought into Jerusalem (46–69). Third and last is another crowd-scene, this time from Roman history, where the pagan emperor Trajan is shown performing for a humble widow the act of justice which – according to Christian legend and Dante's later portrayal of him in the *Paradiso* (20. 44–5) – would gain him salvation (70–93).

These images bring humility to life in several ways. They dramatize it as a dynamically active rather than patiently passive virtue: hence the Annunciation is represented not merely as the acceptance of the divine will but as humanity's 'key' to Heaven (*Purg.* 10. 36 and 42). They are also of such eloquence that they appear to speak or sing. 'You would have sworn that he was saying *Ave*', says Dante of the angel in the first scene (40). His ears deny that the crowd in front of the Ark are singing, but his eyes make him think that they are (59–60). Similarly, the banners accompanying Trajan appear to flutter in the breeze (80–1), whilst the depiction of the emperor and the grieving widow 'seems' to represent not a single moment in the encounter but a sustained conversation of three questions and three answers (82–93).

This effect of 'visible speech' (*visibile parlare, Purg.* 10. 95) is said to have been produced by the hand of God, who is subsequently referred to as 'maker' (*fabbro*, 99). Representations of God as the supreme 'artificer' or 'architect' (*Deus artifex*) were widespread before Dante's time; and it became commonplace to trace human arts and crafts to this ideal model (Curtius 1953: 544–6). The distance of human artistry from the divine ideal is acknowledged in this passage, when God is spoken of as 'one who never saw a thing that was new to him'; and when the 'visible speech' of the images of humility is said to be 'new to us, as it cannot be found here' (94, 96).

Yet the divine artistry here – 'visible speech' and all – has of course been imagined and portrayed in detail by a human artist: Dante. This episode could thus also be read as a celebration of the potential of *human* art. Expressions and gestures so eloquent that they seem to 'speak' were effects that human artists such as Giotto (named in line 94 of the next canto) might aspire to.

168

*Plate 7* Images of pride (*Purg.* 10), from British Library MS Add. 19587, f. 70r, illustrated by an anonymous Neapolitan artist of c.1370. By permission of the British Library.

A number of those who illustrated manuscripts of the *Purgatorio* during the fourteenth and fifteenth centuries reproduced the images on the terrace of pride, and it would be interesting to know what they thought their art was doing (BMS 1. 165–6, 2. 356–61). Several of these represent the divine art as a group of rather flat panels, but most represent the final image of Trajan's encounter with the widow 'as though it were an actual event in an undefined space that Dante witnesses' (BMS 1. 166). One of the most ambitious of these is in a Naples manuscript of around 1370 which reflects the influence of Giotto (BMS 1. 258; see plate 7). Here the artist has audaciously deconstructed Dante's terrace into what looks like a mountain pass, with the Angel and Virgin of the Annunciation confined to a rocky niche on the left and the scenes portraying David and Trajan forming an unbroken and increasingly dense procession that surges up the slope to the right. Dante's artistic challenge has been answered here, but not quite in the way that he seems to have imagined.

In Dante's *Commedia*, it is not just God's ability to convey visible speech through the images of humility that strikes with a shock of 'newness' (*Purg.* 10. 96). Newness and strangeness (the adjective *nuovo* and the noun *novità(de)* can convey both ideas) are characteristic of many of the poem's images of sin and sainthood – from Geryon to Beatrice. And only a few lines after the tribute to divine art, the images of the first penitent souls in Purgatory proper – as opposed to the souls outside its gates – are seen as *novitadi* ('strange new things') to which 'Dante' is eager to turn his eyes (*Purg.* 10. 103–5).

The physical appearance of those expiating the sin of pride is visualized only gradually – as if the narrator, despite his eagerness for 'strange new things', could not bear to keep his eyes on them for long. They are said 'not to look like people' (*Purg.* 10. 113), to be 'bowed down to the earth in torment' (116), to look like the bent and often grotesque figures supporting structures in buildings (130–5), and finally to be at the very limits of their strength (139). Here, as at a number of moments in the *Commedia*, the poet seems conscious of forcing the medium to extremes, and it is significant that the penitents' imagined phrase *più non posso* ('I can't bear any more') is the point at which the canto itself breaks off.

Dante may well have invested some personal concerns in imagining penitence for pride, as he appears to have done also with the images of humility here and those of deception in *Inferno* 16–17 and 24–5. The image of penitence for pride here is prefaced, like Geryon and the final metamorphoses of the thieves (*Inf.* 16, 25), through a direct address to the reader:

> I don't want you, reader, to be put off
> from following your good instinct just by hearing
> how God means us to pay this penalty.
>> Don't heed the form that suffering takes here;
> think of what follows; at the very worst
> it cannot last longer than Judgment Day.
>> (*Purg.* 10. 106–11)

But how are such readers *not* to take heed of 'the form that suffering takes' when it is so graphically portrayed? The power of Dante's created image of penitents may be so great as to risk dissuading them from penitence. To avoid this he has, in the midst of describing these contorted suffering figures, to pull another metamorphosis out of the hat, and to remind 'proud Christians' not only of their base origins but also of their potential destiny:

170

> Do you not understand that we are worms,
> born to become the angelic butterfly
> which breaks free, rising to the light of justice?
>
> (*Purg.* 10. 124–6)

The image of transformation here is part of a warning against pride (121–9). But it also makes clear that just as humans can debase themselves beyond the level of beasts (as in *Inf.* 24–5), so they are also ultimately capable of encompassing the scale that reaches upwards, all the way from worm to angel.

## Figuring Paradise

Imagining the end of the process of transformation that is suggested in those lines from *Purgatorio* 10 places Dante's poem under yet more pressure. The difficulty of representing the process of 'becoming more than human' (*Par.* 1. 70) and the ultimate states of sainthood and salvation constantly confronts the writer and the reader during the journey through the third part of the *Commedia*. Here, from the start, the narrator has to acknowledge the limitations of description when 'understanding . . . penetrates so deep that memory cannot follow after it' (*Par.* 1. 8–9); and Beatrice has to address the problems of his *falso imaginar* ('distorted perceptions', *Par.* 1. 89). A few examples from points throughout the *Paradiso* will help to illustrate how the final *cantica* of the poem negotiates these difficulties.

Corrections of Dante's vision and his 'distorted perceptions' continue to be necessary, especially during the first four cantos. The faces of the souls prepared to speak to him in the first circle – the sphere of the Moon – are like reflections seen in glass or water and are as indistinguishable 'as a pearl worn on a white forehead' (*Par.* 3. 10–15). They thus turn him into a Narcissus in reverse – believing that these are actually reflections of figures standing behind him – and he has to be assured by an amused Beatrice that the apparent 'reflections' are indeed 'real beings' to whom he may speak and listen (17–31). But are the souls that such faces represent really here? Did they then originate in the spheres of the planets and return to them after death, as Plato had claimed (*Timaeus* 41–2)? This is a set of questions which continues to preoccupy Dante after his first encounter with a soul in Paradise. Beatrice addresses it at the start of Canto 4, when she makes clear that the different spheres in which he will perceive souls as he ascends are to be understood as a kind of divine metaphor: a 'sign' of the different levels at which they participate in the 'eternal spirit' of divine love (*Par.* 4. 34–9):

171

'Thus we must speak to your intelligence,
since only through impression on your senses
can deeper understanding be received.'
(*Par.* 4. 40–2)

In the subsequent spheres of the *Paradiso* Dante's senses perceive souls chiefly through the sound of their voices and through patterns of light and motion. Thus, those placed in the sphere of Mercury are compared to a multitude of glittering fish in a clear pool, drawn through instinct and curiosity to the foreign body of the pilgrim (*Par.* 5. 100–5). Then, with a slight shift of metaphorical vehicle, a soul is said by Dante to be 'nestling in your own radiance' (124–5) and is urged to speak. This is the soul of the emperor Justinian (above, p. 142), and the increasing brightness of light before he begins to speak identifies him as an 'image of sanctity' (*figura santa*, 5. 137). Once his narrative (*Par.* 6) has been completed he becomes re-absorbed in to what will be a recurrent motif in this part of the poem: a wheeling 'dance' of 'rapid flames' (*Par.* 7. 7–9).

Movements and patterns of lights take a variety of forms later in the *Paradiso*, reflecting the natures of souls in the subsequent spheres. In the Heaven of Venus they initially appear like 'sparks within a flame' (*Par.* 8. 16–21). The 'high circles' to which the narrator directs his readers' gaze just before he ascends to the Heaven of the Sun (*Par.* 10. 7–9) also contain souls representing wisdom in the shape of a 'crown' or 'garland' encircling Beatrice and Dante – a 'glorious wheel' that moves harmoniously like the parts of a very recent invention, the mechanical clock (65, 92, 139–48; Gimpel 1988: 154). Such harmony in the sphere of the Sun is further enriched by the appearance of a second garland of 'joyful and affectionate' lights which circles around the first like a double rainbow and joins the continuing and expanding 'festival of dance, song and illumination' (*Par.* 12. 1–27).

One further effect of this harmony of the two 'wheels' of lights is to reinforce the complementarity of the two main voices that are heard in the sphere of the Sun. The Dominican Aquinas and the Franciscan Bonaventura are narrators of the lives of two major saints (Francis and Dominic) who are not themselves inhabitants of this sphere but are imagined later in the canto as the two 'wheels' of the church's chariot (*Par.* 12. 106–11). The emphasis on light and energetic movement extends also to the portrayal of those saints' lives and roles as leaders of the major religious orders of the century before the *Commedia*. St Francis is thus envisaged first, for example, as the rising sun (*Par.* 11. 49–57); whilst St Dominic is seen to have the elemental force of a 'torrent', cleansing and fertilizing the soil of the church (*Par.* 12. 97–105).

Light and movement continue to create symbolic patterns in each of the subsequent spheres: the cross of lights in the Heaven of Mars, where the souls are those who fought for their religion (cantos 14–17); the 'illuminated' text about justice whose last letter (M) reforms itself into an eagle in the Heaven of Jupiter (18–20); and the upward-reaching ladder in the sphere of the contemplative souls, the Heaven of Saturn (21–2). The eighth of the spheres in the cosmology of Dante's *Paradiso* is that of the 'fixed stars' (see diagram 3, p. 125). Encounters here – with the lights of the Apostles Peter, James and John and with the soul of the original patriarch, Adam – occupy more space in the text (about 5 cantos, from 22 to 27) than does description of any other sphere in this *cantica*. Here the foundations of Dante's religious belief are being asserted, and moments like that when the 'apostolic light' of St Peter encircles the pilgrim three times 'blessing me and singing' (*Par.* 24. 151–4) give his assertion visual confirmation.

Other moments of illumination in the Heaven of the Fixed Stars centre upon the figure and role of Beatrice. At the two points of transition – when entering the sphere at the end of canto 22 and when leaving it midway through 27 – Beatrice instructs Dante to do what he has not so far done in the journey through Paradise: 'look down' (*Par.* 22. 128, 27. 77–8), to see how far he has come from the small 'patch of earth' far below (*Par.* 22. 151–2, 27. 85–7). Extension of his vision thus continues to be an essential part of her task, and that includes the vision of Beatrice herself. In canto 23, as the advent of the Virgin Mary and the Apostles is close at hand, Beatrice makes a sequence of announcements greeting the reconciliation of Heaven and Earth through Christ (19–21, 35–9). These culminate in the assurance (46–8) that through his vision of this 'triumph' Dante is now able to 'open his eyes' to her smile and her beauty, which, as she has explained two cantos earlier, burn more brightly the higher they ascend, and which he would not then have been able to sustain (*Par.* 21. 4–12). At this moment, then, in *Paradiso* 23 the pilgrim Dante is thus able to sustain both levels of vision; but, as the opening of this *cantica* has warned, memory will not be fully able to keep pace with understanding on this journey, and the narrator-poet here declares himself momentarily unable to continue 'figuring Paradise' (49–69; below, p. 205).

Extension of the pilgrim's vision in doctrinal terms continues through the eighth and ninth spheres of the *Paradiso* – the Heaven of Fixed Stars and the 'Primum Mobile', the sphere which moves all the others. Dante here affirms the grounds of his belief through the encounters with the three Apostles (*Par.* 24–7) and gains knowledge of the nature of the angels from Beatrice (28–9). This process and the movement towards the end of the whole journey also continue to be marked by moments of visualized illumination. These include the celebratory circling of 'apostolic light' (*Par.* 24. 151–4), and more paradoxically the 'smile of the universe' that is suddenly transformed into the fierce glow of apostolic wrath accompanying St Peter's pronunciations on the papacy (*Par.* 27. 4–66).

The last three images of illumination and sanctity in *Paradiso* 30–3 show the poem pressing yet harder at the limits of what it is possible to signify in words. Beatrice's final correction of Dante's sight takes place shortly after she and he have emerged into the last Heaven, the Empyrean, 'which is pure light, light of understanding infused with love, love of the true good filled with joy, joy which transcends all pleasure' (*Par.* 30. 39–42). The initial image that conveys this state is the 'light in the form of a river' shedding sparks of flame into the flowers that grow along its banks (61–9). This is partly based upon the 'river of life, rising from the throne of God and of the Lamb and flowing crystal-clear' in the final chapter of Revelation (Revelation 22: 1–2). Here also, however, Dante outdoes his source through a final metamorphosis. On Beatrice's instructions he bathes his eyes in this stream and as he does so what is 'long' becomes 'round' (90), a wide 'circular figure' (103–5), a 'rose' filled with light (115–17, 124–6), which Beatrice recognizes as her 'convent' and native 'city' (128–30). The transformation of the linear into the circular at this point re-enacts the two main features of the whole 'figuring of Paradise': the line of Dante and Beatrice's ascent; and the circling of souls, saints, angels and the Trinity within and around the concentric spheres of the cosmos. The circular 'form of the White Rose', which is also the heart of the 'complete form of Paradise' (*Par.* 31. 1 and 52), then becomes the dominant image of sanctity over three cantos. Beatrice both introduces it and inhabits it; and it is further interpreted by the final intermediary of the *Paradiso*: the contemplative, St Bernard.

Like the river of light in the previous canto, the White Rose has traditional precedents, and Dante may have had in mind here the structure and luminosity of the rose-windows of medieval cathedrals (*DE* 882B). The combining of the image of the flower with the representation of the variety of figures that St Bernard describes within it – women from the Old Testament, saints from the New, founders of religious orders and many others (*Par.* 32. 7–36) – posed a challenge for most of the fourteenth-century illustrators of these cantos (BMS 1. 206). Later in the fifteenth century the Sienese artist

*Plate 8* The White Rose (*Par.* 30–2), from British Library MS Yates Thompson 36, f. 187r, illustrated by Giovanni di Paolo, c.1445–50. By permission of the British Library.

Giovanni di Paolo – one of the most accomplished of the *Paradiso* illustrators, working around 1445–50 – attempted a simplified solution (plate 8); and his version, with its elegant, elongated white petals forming 'panels' for the portraits, recalls the vivid altarpieces of the Madonna and saints that Dante must have seen and could also have had in mind when imagining this final figuring of human sanctity.

In the very last canto of the *Commedia* the narrator-poet again, as in *Par.* 23, undergoes a struggle with memory and powers of expression which itself is expressed through a number of images, metaphors and allusions (below, p. 206). The vision around which this struggle takes place is conveyed through the complex image of the Trinity as 'three circles of three colours and a single circumference' (*Par.* 33. 115–20). Again, Dante may be drawing upon an earlier image here: it has been suggested that he could have been influenced by the representation of the Trinity as three overlapping green, gold and red (or in some manuscripts green, blue and red) circles in the *Book of Figures* by the Cistercian abbot and visionary Joachim of Fiore, who had appeared in *Paradiso*'s Heaven of the Sun (*Par.* 12. 140–1; Reeves 1976: 65–6; above, pp. 92–3) Yet Dante's superimposed equal circles are yet more mysterious than Joachim's and much more difficult to represent or even understand.

The early illustrators of the poem found it difficult to deal with the image of the Trinity here. Dante does eventually see a sign of 'our effigy' which is 'painted' within the second of these three circles, thus 'representing' Christ (*Par.* 33. 127–32; Hawkins 2006: 112–13). As this image is said to be exactly the same colour as that of the second circle, it's not at all easy to visualize, but it offered some artists the solution of giving the figures of the Trinity human faces (BMS 2. 28B). Giovanni di Paolo avoided the problem altogether in his two images for the canto. The first simply shows St Bernard presenting Dante to the enthroned figure of the Virgin, whilst the second portrays the Virgin in glory, together with Neptune marvelling at the 'shadow of the *Argo*' (*Par.* 33. 94–6; Pope-Hennessy 1993: 186–91). Later in the fifteenth century, Botticelli represented eloquently the figures of Dante and Beatrice as they ascend through the spheres, and produced an impressive flock of angels to illustrate cantos 28–9 (Altcappenberg 2000: 276–81). But even he seems to have been struggling to convey the effects of light and movement in the *Paradiso*; and for the vision of the final canto he produced what in the end was perhaps the most appropriate response: a blank page (Altcappenberg 2000: 288).

# Understanding Love

## Praising Beatrice

The *Commedia* is in several ways a love-poem, and the relationship between love, motion and understanding is a crucial feature of Dante's journey. Beatrice's declaration 'Love moved me and now makes me speak' is a key phrase near the beginning of the poem (above, p. 132). Placed at the very mid-point of *Inferno* 2 (72), it conveys the dynamism of the Virgin's, Lucy's, Beatrice's, Virgil's and Dante's utterances. Like much else in that canto – the representation of powerful 'courtly' ladies and the poet's role as 'servant' to them – it is also inscribed with Dante's personal history, harking back to his early poetry in the *Vita nuova* and his developing recognition of Beatrice's significance there.

In the *Vita nuova* a crucial stage in that development was marked by the composition of the *canzone* that begins *Donne ch'avete intelletto d'amore*: 'Ladies who know the meaning of love'. This is the first *canzone* in the collection of lyrics that comprises the *Vita nuova*, and is probably Dante's first serious venture in the poetic form which he was to describe in *DVE* as 'far and away the most excellent' (2. 3. 3) and which was to become the basis of the *Commedia*'s canto structure. The poem also helped to establish Dante's reputation as a love-poet, 'expressing in words what Love dictates within' (*Purg.* 24. 49–54).

The new departure that this early *canzone* represented is also heralded by its 'prologue' in the commentary on the *Vita nuova* itself. In chapter 18 Dante describes a conversation about love and love-poetry with a friendly but sceptical female focus group in Florence. It leaves him then uneasily pondering the questions these women have raised about his work and wondering what move to make next:

'Since such bliss is in those words that praise my lady, why have I ever spoken of anything else?' Hence I determined to make the praise of that most noble person from then on the subject of my speech. But as I pondered this, it seemed that I had taken on too heavy an undertaking for my resources, so I did not dare to begin. And thus I remained several days eager to make utterance, but in terror of making a beginning. (*VN* ch. 19)

As in *Inferno* 2, the fear is of a noble and challenging undertaking (for which *impresa* is the word in both), and here too, the solution to the impasse is reached through several kinds of movement:

It then happened that, as I passed along a road beside which ran a sparklingly clear stream, I experienced such a desire to speak that I had to begin thinking about the form in which I might do so. And I thought that it would not be right for me to speak of her unless my speech was directed to women in the second person – but not to all women, only to those who are noble, and not just because they are women. I declare then that my tongue spoke as if moved of its own accord and said: 'Ladies who know the meaning of love'. These words I eagerly stored in my mind, since I meant to use them to get started. Hence, after I returned to the city I have mentioned and thought it over for a few more days, I began to write a *canzone* beginning thus:

> *Donne ch'avete intelletto d'amore,*
> *i' vo' con voi de la mia donna dire,*
> *non perch'io creda sua laude finire,*
> *ma ragionar per isfogar la mente.*
> *Io dico che pensando il suo valore,*
> *Amor sì dolce mi si fa sentire,*
> *che s'io allora non perdessi ardire,*
> *farei parlando innamorar la gente.*

> Ladies who know the meaning of love,
> I want to speak to you about my lady,
> not thinking that I could exhaust her praise,
> but using speech to clear my crowded mind.
> I say that, when I dwell upon her virtues,
> love makes its presence felt so sweetly that,
> if courage did not fail me in the task,
> my speech would make all fall in love with her.
>
> (*VN* ch. 19)

A few lines later, Dante's first *canzone* suddenly finds itself staging a conversation about Beatrice between an angel and God:

> An angel speaks to God's high understanding,
> and says: 'Lord, down on earth there can be seen
> miraculous signs and actions from a soul
> whose radiance spreads all the way to Heaven.'
> And Heaven, which lacks nothing but that lady,
> implores its Lord to have her brought up there,
> whilst all the saints demand her company.
> Pity alone pleads there on our behalf
> till God pronounces on our lady's future:
> 'Be patient, blessed souls, let me decide
> how long the one you hope for shall remain
> where there is one who is about to lose her
> and who will say in Hell: "Accursed souls,
> I have witnessed what those blessed ones expect."'
>
> (*VN* ch. 19)

The scenario here bears some resemblance to the celestial trajectory described in Guinizzelli's influential *canzone Al cor gentil* (above, p. 116), although it takes place much earlier in the poem and is far more ambitious in its claims. More importantly, it also foreshadows the chain of command that links the Virgin to Virgil and Dante in *Inferno* 2 (above, p. 132). *Donne ch'avete intelletto d'amore* goes on to affirm itself further as the new beginning that the poet has sought, by dramatizing the power of speech in, with and about Beatrice; a 'power' (*virtù*, *virtute*, lines 30, 38) that is felt through its effects on those who are 'worthy' to receive and respond.

The *canzone*'s vocabulary of praise for Beatrice's 'power' (*virtù*, *virtute*) also quite specifically prefigures the homage to her on her return to Dante's poetry in *Inferno* 2. At the start of his first speech to her in the canto, Virgil greets her as the 'woman of power (*donna di virtù*) by means of which the human race surpasses all other creatures beneath the smallest Heaven [i.e., on Earth]' (*Inf.* 1. 76–8; above, p. 133). Behind Beatrice's power, as she has acknowledged at the very mid-point of *Inferno* 2, is the moving force of 'love' (72). The process of participating in and understanding that movement occupies the *Commedia* up until its very last line; and in the *Inferno* the next important stage for the protagonist is the 'lesson in love' in *Inferno* 5.

## Love and the noble heart: *Inferno* 5

The souls in canto 5 are the first who, following the judgement of Minos at the beginning (*Inf.* 5. 4–15), are subjected to total damnation, and they are the first whose speech the poem records at length. Amongst them are first identified figures whose destructive and self-destructive passions had been subjects of earlier narratives: Semiramis, queen of Assyria in Orosius's *History against the Pagans* (above, p. 99); Dido in Book 4 of Virgil's *Aeneid*; Helen, Achilles and Paris from the classical and medieval legends about Troy; and Tristan from the great French and German romances (52–67).

Out of this imposing and tragic array of 'ladies and knights of days gone by' (71) the text focuses upon two who are noticeably 'light upon the wind' (75) – which probably means that they are being driven to and fro more rapidly than the others. These are Francesca and her lover and brother-in-law Paolo, both of whom had been killed by her husband, Giovanni Malatesta of Rimini, some time in the 1280s. We know very little about the historical Francesca, apart from what is said in this canto, but the story of the adulterous and (by the standards of the time) incestuous affair was developed by Boccaccio and others into a romance that exonerates her to some extent by claiming that she had been duped into the marriage (thinking she was actually marrying Paolo). Fascination with the lovers' powerful passion, their 'evil fortune' and 'sad destinies' (phrases from Byron's translation), was later to inform the Romantic readings and illustrations of this episode (below, pp. 236–40).

It is easy to understand how such a fascination could develop. Francesca is, like Beatrice in *Inferno* 2, powerfully moved by love, which she invokes in her first speech here:

> 'Love which sets noble hearts at once on fire
> took hold of this man through my body's beauty,
> snatched from me in a way that rankles still.
> Love that absolves no one beloved from loving
> took hold of me with such a power of pleasure
> in him that, as you see, it holds me still.
> Love sent us both united to our death,
> and lower depths await our murderer.'
>
> (*Inf.* 5. 100–7)

In his responses Dante is moved to and beyond tears:

> Then I turned back to speak with them once more,
> and said, 'Francesca, the pain you suffer
> wrings me with pity, forces me to weep.
>     But say, at that time when your love still spoke
> through sighs alone, when did it let you each
> know what was in your deep unspoken thoughts?'
>     She answered then, 'No greater pain can be
> than to recall our times of happiness
> in grief and loss – as he who leads you knows.
>     But if you now have such a strong desire
> to probe what lay at our love's very root,
> I'll tell you, though it makes me weep to tell.
>     One day we had, for pleasure, taken up
> the tale of Lancelot, subject to Love,
> and were alone, not fearing any wrong.
>     All the while what we read made our eyes
> turn from the text, our colour go and come.
> At one point only we were overwhelmed:
>     on reading how those longed-for smiling lips
> were kissed by such a lover as he was,
> he who is here and is with me forever
>     kissed my mouth, trembling as he did so.
> The book, the author were our go-betweens,
> and all that day we read no further there.'
>     Whilst one of these souls told me how this was
> the other wept, so that the power of pity
> flung me at once into a death-like trance,
> and I fell, just as a dead body falls.
>
> (*Inf.* 5. 115–42)

Reaction against the Romantic views of Francesca's tragic 'destinies' has yielded a sceptical reading of these speeches and their protestations about the power of love. One twentieth-century critic, for instance, noted her 'abundant use of the medieval casuistry of love', the 'studied elegance' of her speech, and her distortion of the connections that Gunizzelli and Dante had made between 'love and the noble heart' through her claim that 'passional love is the calling and destiny' of all such noble hearts (Poggioli 1965: 66–8). Another found Francesca's speeches 'inadvertently revealing . . . her self-centredness', developing 'histrionic self-consciousness' along with 'the ability to remember past events in a way that redounds to her credit', and is led by the 'falsity' he finds in her words to pose his own rhetorical question in conclusion: 'Is not Francesca Eve?' (Musa 1974: 22, 24, 28, 35). Such approaches open up complexities in the speeches of Francesca and of other self-justifying souls in the *Inferno*, although they risk replacing the Romantic reading with a reductively theological one.

Some more recent critics have resisted making a choice here between 'the theologian who condemns' and the romantic 'man who absolves'. More important and interesting for them are the problems that this episode creates early on in the journey through the *Commedia* for Dante as a writer about love. Thus one of the most recent Italian commentators has emphasized that the episode 'deals with a form of love . . . that an entire literature has celebrated'; and she argues that, although the *Commedia* rejects and will transcend the limiting view of love in poets such as Cavalcanti, 'that tradition in its turn was simply the expression of an ideal that had shaped humanity for centuries' (CL 1. 134–6). And the latest English translator of the *Inferno* concludes that 'for Dante – carrying forward the native love tradition in his devotion to Beatrice and his new attention to Virgilian ethics – *Inferno* 5 may be seen as the profound and ambiguous first move in a long redefinition of love and pity which only concludes with the final line of the *Paradiso*' (Kirkpatrick 2006: 335).

## Love in mind: *Convivio* 3 and *Purgatorio* 2

Dante had been redefining love well before starting the *Commedia*. After celebrating Beatrice as a sainted and celestial figure at the end of the *Vita nuova*, he had explored obsessive forms of passion in some of his love-lyrics, notably the poems to the 'stony lady' (above, p. 157). In writing about the 'illustrious vernacular' language early in his exile he had included love among the 'best subjects . . . worthy to be discussed in it', and he uses love-poetry to illustrate his arguments throughout the treatise (*DVE* 2. 2. 5–8). And his most ambitious project before the *Commedia* was his uncompleted vernacular work, exploring the love-affair between the soul and wisdom: the *Convivio* (c.1304–7).

The second, third and fourth parts of the *Convivio* are prose treatises prefaced by and commenting on love-poems. At the beginning of part 2, the *canzone* addressed to 'the intelligences who move the third celestial sphere [Venus]' begins by rather briefly regretting the departure of 'a lady in glory' (14–19), but spends most of its 61 lines describing the impact on the speaker of another lady, who is 'compassionate and gentle . . . wise and courteous in her greatness' and who has 'transformed' the speaker's life (FB no. 59). The implicit conflict here begins to be addressed in the following prose commentary, especially where the lady in glory is identified as 'the blessed and immortal Beatrice, about whom I do not intend to speak any further in this book' (*Conv.* 2. 8. 7). A few chapters later, he begins the 'allegorical' interpretation of the *canzone* by explaining that the need for consolation after the death of Beatrice had initially led him to frequent in Florence 'the schools of the religious and the disputations of those who teach philosophy'; and at the same time Philosophy is personified as a potential lover, a 'noble and compassionate lady' (*Conv.* 2. 12. 6–7).

The full significance of this 'second love', which 'stemmed from the compassionate appearance of a lady' (*Conv.* 3. 1. 1), is explored in the third treatise of the *Convivio*. Like *Conv.* 2, the third treatise is a commentary on a *canzone* (FB no. 61). Here, as the 'allegorical' interpretation of the poem begins, Dante declares that the lady described there is 'that lady of the intellect who is called Philosophy' (3. 11. 1), reinforcing the link between his personified mistress and the guiding presence in Boethius's *Consolation* (above, p. 71). The etymology of her name, he then explains, itself involves 'love' (that of wisdom), a love that is 'natural' to all (3. 11. 5–6). This 'loving use of wisdom' (*amoroso uso di sapienzia*) can lead all the way to paradise, since it finds its highest expression in God (3. 12. 12). Philosophy is thus enthroned here, in terms which echo the praise of the Virgin Mary, as the emperor of Heaven's 'spouse, sister and most beloved daughter' (3. 12. 14). And the final chapter of *Convivio* 3 draws upon a biblical source (Wisdom 7: 12) to exalt her as 'the mother of all and source of all origins . . . through whom God began to create the world and in particular set the Heavens in motion' (3. 15. 15).

The love-poem which is allegorized in *Convivio* 3 shows potential for this form of interpretation from its very first line: 'Love speaking to me within my mind' (*Amor che ne la mente mi ragiona*; FB no. 61). The prominence of speech within it reinforces its capacity to become the subject of philosophical commentary. This is particularly noticeable in the lines that provide material for the culmination of the commentary's argument in chapters 14–15 – the lines which describe the lady's manner of speech, its effect upon others and its origins:

> Clear signs are manifest in her appearance
> prefiguring the joys of Paradise
> within her eyes, in her enchanting smile,
> for there Love marshals them in his stronghold.

183

> They vanquish all our powers of understanding
> like sunlight dazzling a feeble eye;
> and since I cannot hold them in my view,
> few words describing them must now suffice:
>     Her beauty rains down flakes of fire,
> inspired and driven by nobility,
> the moving force of every worthy thought;
> erasing, like lightning
> the ingrained faults that give us such deep shame.
> For she casts down the proud and the stiff-necked:
> she was the word in the First Mover's mind.

Upward movement and progression are key features of *Convivio* 3's under-standing of this love-poem. Dante's commentary here celebrates the 'noble lady' of Philosophy, both as an aspect of God and as a guide to Paradise. In doing so it describes a hierarchical order, leading from the basic elements, minerals, plants and animals, through humanity to the angels and then on to God (*Conv.* 3. 3. 1–11 and 7. 3–7). This concept goes back to Plato and Aristotle, and it had recently been clarified further by Thomas Aquinas (Luscombe 1997: 102; above, p. 83). Love is linked to movement and capacity for achieving perfection within this 'scale of being'. Human beings, through love for Lady Philosophy as the image of God, can by that means be brought closer to the divine presence.

In the *Commedia* this kind of movement is dramatized at the beginning of the *Purgatorio*. Canto 1 prepares for this, but actual progress begins to get under way only in *Purgatorio* 2, with the sun rising, with Dante and Virgil looking out to sea 'like people thinking about a journey and already on the way in their hearts, although their bodies still linger'(*Purg.* 2. 11–12), and with the appearance out at sea of a fast-moving boat driven by the wings of an angel (13–42). In this boat are a group of souls who are on their way to Purgatory and Paradise, as their singing of the psalm about exodus, 'When Israel went out of Egypt', signifies (46; Psalm 113).

Movement in *Purgatorio* 2 is, however, still complicated by hesitations and delays. The souls emerging from the boat seem for the moment to have lost the impetus and initiative that impelled their journey and song and now 'gaze around' like strangers (52–4), even though the vivid image of morning sunbeams darting around them like 'arrows' is a reminder that there is a more purposeful pursuit to be mounted (55–7). Virgil's reply to their request for directions is the classic 'we're strangers here ourselves' (63), but the word he uses to identify himself and Dante (*peregrin*) has a number of possible meanings and can signify both confused unfamiliarity (as here) and purposeful pilgrimage.

Love and movement converge in the main encounter of *Purgatorio* 2. Seeing a friend, the musician Casella, among the newly arrived souls reaching out to embrace him, Dante responds in kind, but his arms three times close upon empty air. The frustrated love that this gesture conveys is then expressed in words by Casella, repeating 'love' (*amare*) for the first time as a verb in the *Purgatorio*, whilst at the same time raising the question of direction: 'why are you going this way?' (88–90). The pilgrim's response here is one of the *Commedia*'s most emphatic assertions about the purpose of Dante's progress through the otherworld:

> 'Dear Casella, in order to return
> where I now am, I have to make this journey.'
> (*Purg.* 2. 91–2)

Moreover, in response to Dante's subsequent question about his delay in reaching the shore of Purgatory (93), Casella points to a key event in the year (1300) in which Dante sets the action of the *Commedia*. This was the 'Jubilee' which was declared by Boniface VIII on 22 February and gave full remission of sins to pilgrims who visited Rome from the previous Christmas up till the Christmas of that year (Sumption 1975: 231–6). The *Commedia* has mentioned this event already (*Inf.* 18. 28–33); it was a 'formative episode' in the lives of several writers, including Dante and the Florentine chronicler Giovanni Villani (Sumption 1975: 235). Here in *Purg.* 2 (98–105), it is given as the reason why the angelic 'helmsman' is willing to take on board all the souls assembled at the mouth of Rome's river (the Tiber). The Jubilee thus acts as a powerful affirmation of the value of pilgrimage.

The relationship between love and the pilgrimage up the mountain becomes more problematic at the close of the encounter between Dante and Casella. At Dante's request for a moment of consolation (109–11), his musician friend performs as an 'amorous chant' a setting of one of Dante's own lyrics; and this is none other than the celebration of Lady Philosophy that has been commented upon in *Convivio* 3:

> ' "*Amor che ne la mente mi ragiona*:
> Love speaking to me deep within my mind . . ." '
> he then began, in such a melody
> that its sweet sound still plays within my ear.

My guide and I together with those souls
keeping him company appeared entranced,
as if we had no thought for other things.
    And as we stood so still and so beguiled,
gripped by his song – here that worthy old man
came shouting: 'Idle souls, what does this mean?
    Why all this lingering and this delay?
Head for the mountain, to slough off the scales
that keep your eyes from the clear sight of God!'
    And, as in fields a settled flock of doves,
gathered to feed on grains of wheat or tares,
quiet, not strutting proudly on display,
    will, if disturbed, all then take flight at once,
and leave their food behind them on the ground,
urged by an instinct yet more strong than greed –
    so then, I saw those newly arrived souls
break off that song, rush headlong up the slope
like someone hurrying off, not knowing where;
    and we too, moving on, did not delay.

(*Purg.* 2. 112–33)

Why is this *canzone* chosen, and why is it so brusquely interrupted by Cato, the ancient guardian of the lower level of the mountain? Does the conclusion of this episode expose a tension or contradiction between the love that had been celebrated in the song that Casella sings and the kind of pilgrimage that Dante and these souls are now being urged to make? Some critics have seen here a preliminary admission of Dante's 'error in abandoning Beatrice for Lady Philosophy', as he appears to do in *Convivio* 2 and 3, and a preparation for 'his ultimate rejection of his moral lapse' in *Purgatorio* 30–1, where Beatrice rebukes him for listening to siren voices and following false images of good (*DE* 230A–B). Others have argued that there is no such contradiction between 'philosophism' in the *Convivio* and 'theology' in the *Commedia* and that the different works represent different but reconcilable approaches to 'temporal happiness' and 'eternal salvation' (E. Gilson 1949: 159–61).

Cato's incursion into Casella's song and his scattering of its rapt audience could therefore be seen not as a rejection of the ideas about love and love of wisdom in the *Convivio* but as a revision of them. Its apparent harshness may be a reflection of the energy required to move on – to restore what Virgil later on, in his speech at the centre of the *Purgatorio* and the

*Commedia*, calls 'the defective love of good' (*Purg.* 17. 85). It is a reminder that is later to be paralleled and reinforced by, for example, the urgent calls of the souls expiating the sin of sloth 'not to lose time through lack of love' (*Purg.* 18. 103–4), and by Beatrice's recalling to Dante's understanding 'the desires for me that were leading you to love of that good beyond which there is nothing further to desire' (*Purg.* 31. 22–4).

## To the Heaven of Venus: *Paradiso* 1–9

Interactions between love, movement and understanding in the *Commedia*'s journey develop through and beyond the *Purgatorio*. In the early cantos of the *Paradiso* Dante and Beatrice ascend though the Heavens of the Moon and Mercury; and the pilgrim in company with his lover is made to confront and comprehend a number of knotty scientific, doctrinal and political issues. Prominent among these topics are: the significance of the Moon's uneven appearance (2); equality and hierarchy in Heaven (3–4); the doctrine of vows (4–5); the role and history of the Roman empire (6); the Fall, Incarnation and Atonement (7); and the nature of Venus and love (8–9).

The meanings of 'love' in relation to the understanding of God are addressed from the first canto of the *Paradiso* onwards. Here Dante begins to confront some of the difficulties of 'figuring Paradise' (above, pp. 171–6). One important way in which the poem starts to find its way through such difficulties is by representing the relationship between love and understanding through the imagery of fire, light and movement. Thus in canto 1, the beginning of the journey of understanding in Paradise is traced to the power of the '[divine] love which steers the Heavens' and which, the narrator says, addressing this power directly, 'raised me up by means of your light' (74–5).

Towards the end of the canto Beatrice goes on to explain this movement from another standpoint: in terms of the instincts that lead all created beings to seek their perfected states (*Par.* 1. 112–14). In the course of relating this explanation to the natural tendency of human beings who have 'understanding and desire' (*intelletto ed amore*, 120), she twice offers a vivid example and analogy: that of the 'instinct' that draws a flame upwards to seek what was believed to be its natural place, the sphere of fire (115, 141). In medieval cosmology this sphere lay between those of the Earth and the Moon (diagram 3, p. 125); and Beatrice is here not only stating a scientific 'fact' but also identifying the place that she and Dante have themselves just reached at the start of their journey through Paradise.

187

Fire and light continue to be prominent as ways of marking stages in this journey. In particular they signal the development of Dante's understanding by means of the 'sunlight', 'lightning' or 'sparks' of Beatrice's love (*Par.* 3. 1–3 and 124–30, 4. 139–42). Here, as elsewhere in the *Paradiso*, the text recognizes that such experiences are hard to comprehend, let alone to communicate; and this recognition, together with the awareness of the close relationship between love and understanding, flame and illumination, is concisely expressed by Beatrice's own words as she begins the fifth canto and prepares for the next stage of Dante's ascent:

> 'If I flame forth to you, burning with love
> far beyond what can be perceived on earth,
> and overpowering your eyesight's strength –
> be not amazed, for such effects are found
> in perfect sight when it both understands
> and steps towards the good thus understood.
> I can well see how the eternal light
> which, once seen, kindles firm eternal love
> illuminates your understanding now.'
>
> (*Par.* 5. 1–9)

Increasing radiance of light becomes a frequent way of representing not only the development of love and understanding but also the attitudes of the souls. Hence the 'more than a thousand radiances' that are drawn towards Dante immediately on his arrival in the sphere of Mercury (*Par.* 5. 103–8) are now pure light and voice, without even the faint lineaments of faces that had been visible in the sphere of the Moon (*Par.* 3. 10–18). They greet him unanimously as 'one who will increase love in us' (*Par.* 5. 105). The form that such 'love' takes first for Dante is the understanding conveyed by one single light and voice through the whole of the next canto. Here Justinian identifies the pursuit of 'honour and fame' as the chief goal of these souls (*Par.* 6. 114). This pursuit is, Justinian acknowledges, a deviation from the 'true love' of God (115–17), but the recognition of such a shortcoming does not, he is quick to add, lessen these souls' delight and harmony 'amid these spheres' (118–23, 126).

Awareness of the relationship between divine love and the varieties of human love becomes particularly intense as Dante and Beatrice approach the Heaven of Venus. The canto which precedes their ascent shows Beatrice touching upon some key aspects of such interactions: on the Incarnation as an 'act of [God's] eternal love' for humanity (*Par.* 7. 30–3); on God's *cor-*

*tesia* ('generosity') in bringing about the Atonement for the Fall (91); and on humanity's unique place as a creation which the 'supreme good' directly 'inspires and makes enamoured (*innamora*) of itself, so as ever after to desire it' (142–4).

The two cantos representing the Heaven of Venus (*Par.* 8, 9) redefine love in several ways. Dante's portrayal of souls here develops traditional interpretations of Venus's significance for humanity. In *Paradiso* 8, the kind of love that informs Dante's reunion with his friend the Angevin prince Carlo Martello (whom Dante had met in Florence) has a broadly political dimension and implies civic harmony, as Carlo's speech indicates (especially 115–48; Peters 1991). In the following canto the encounters with the Lombard aristocrat Cunizza da Romano and the Provençal poet, monk and bishop Folquet of Marseilles – although they too have marked political dimensions – relate to Venus's more obvious associations with sexual passion.

In both these cantos there is also constant awareness of how the Heaven of Venus relates to the love-poetry that Dante knew and wrote. Understanding of love here uses as points of reference the passionate Dido of Virgil's *Aeneid* 4 and of Dante's *Inferno* 5 (*Par.* 8. 9, 9. 97–8), the careers and relationships of two troubadours, Sordello (lover of Cunizza) and Folquet (*DE* 241A, 403A–B), as well as Dante's earlier writing. Thus the souls greeting the poet here quote the first line of his own *canzone* about the power of Venus, the loss of Beatrice and the advent of Lady Philosophy: *Voi che' ntendendo il terzo ciel movete* ('You who through understanding move the third sphere'; *Par.* 8. 37; FB no. 59). This poem had been the subject of commentary in *Convivio* 2, and the quotation here indicates – like Casella's singing of the *canzone* from *Convivio* 3 – that what is to follow will be a revision, not a rejection, of the doctrine of love in Dante's earlier philosophical work. A more indirect reference back to Dante's earlier writing on love is contained in Cunizza's admission of how 'the light of this planet overcame me', as she names herself and begins her account of her life (*Par.* 9. 33). Her use of the verb 'overcame' (*vinse*) at one level acknowledges the power of passion that had led her to become the lover of the poet Sordello and thus echoes Francesca's recognition of that power in *Inferno* 5 (132). At the same time, however, it unrepentantly celebrates what the light of Venus in the *Paradiso* now means: Cunizza now also 'shines out' *because* she was 'overcome' by that light (32–3).

Intensification of light is frequently the way in which souls in the *Paradiso* greet those who 'will increase [their] love' (*Par.* 5. 105). Since the beginning of the *cantica* it has also been the means through which the protagonist

189

perceives and understands Beatrice. At the start, the transmission of divine light through her eyes is in effect what 'raises' the pilgrim to the first sphere (*Par.* 1. 46–81). Imagery of sunlight, lightning, sparks of fire and flames combines with the language of love-lyric to confirm her leading role in the pilgrim's journey of understanding as it accelerates through the spheres. One early example of this combination is the description of Beatrice as 'That sun which first warmed my breast with love' (*Par.* 3. 1), which also takes us back to the beginning of the *Vita nuova*. Another is the tribute to her as the 'beloved of the Prime Lover . . . whose speech floods and warms me, so that I spring to life more and more' (*Par.* 4. 118–20). Here Dante uses the word 'beloved' (*amanza*) in a way that evokes the language of Provençal love-poetry, whilst also recalling the revivifying effect that Beatrice's words have had upon him near the very beginning of the *Commedia*'s journey (*Inferno* 2. 127–35). Further recognitions of the effect that she has had and will have upon him are densely packed into the brief description of her smile as one that 'would have made a man happy in the midst of the flames' (*Par.* 7. 18). This extravagant claim is validated in the poem itself by recalling the effect Beatrice's name had when Virgil invoked it to draw Dante through the wall of fire on the last terrace of Purgatory (*Purg.* 27. 35–54). It is also true with regard to Dante's relationship with Beatrice and other souls in Paradise, where he will in another sense be 'happy in the midst of the flames'. Indeed, as Beatrice very soon after this explains, the tempering experience of 'the flame of love' is essential for the true perception of doctrine such as that of the Incarnation and Atonement (*Par.* 7. 58–60).

Perception of and through Beatrice thus gives increasing impetus to the journey to the Heaven of Venus and beyond. Dante's arrival in this third sphere is marked not by any idea of movement – as has been imagined at both the previous stages of the ascent – but simply by the perception that his 'lady' has 'become more beautiful' (*Par.* 8. 13–15). Similarly, transitions to the subsequent spheres are signalled not by coordinates of space and time but by awareness of the role and radiance of Beatrice. It is in this way that Dante initially perceives his changes of state from the fourth Heaven through to the seventh – those of the Sun (10. 34–9), Mars (14. 79–87), Jupiter (18. 52–69) and Saturn (21. 1–24). The transitions to the last three spheres imagined in the *Paradiso* – those of the 'fixed stars', the 'Primum Mobile' and the 'Empyrean' – require yet more complex negotiation of the very processes of perception and understanding.

# The Shadow of the *Argo*: Travel, Poetics, Language

## Journey into exile: from the *Vita nuova* to the *Convivio*

*Homo viator* – humanity as traveller – was a powerful and long-established trope in medieval Christian culture, and Dante develops it at a number of points throughout his work (Ladner 1967). In the *Vita nuova*, the nature of love and the significance of Beatrice's role are at several key moments conveyed through the imagery of travelling and pilgrimage. The 'path of love' (*la via d'Amor*) is represented here also as a way of suffering that has religious connotations (*VN* ch. 7). One of the guises that the God of Love adopts here when appearing to summon the lover on a journey away from the city is that of 'a pilgrim thinly clad in shabby clothing' (*VN* ch. 9). What the narrator calls 'the road of sighs' (*VN* ch.10. 1) can, however, also be the path of poetic creation. In chapter 19, a later journey away from his city inspires the first line of Dante's first *canzone*, 'Ladies who know the meaning of love', enabling him to make a significant new departure in his writing (above, p. 178). New departures and directions in his poetry are also signalled by the idea and imagery of pilgrimage at the end of the *Vita nuova* (above, p. 135). And in the final sonnet of the *VN*, Beatrice becomes the object of a journey of contemplation undertaken by the poet's 'pilgrim spirit' (*peregrino spirito*, 41. 11; FB no. 57).

New directions were imposed on Dante by his exile from 1302 onwards (above, pp. 23–4). These are signalled and explored in his letters (*Letters* nos. 1, 3, 6, 9) and in poems such as the *canzone Tre donne* ('Three ladies'), 'the fullest expression outside the *Comedy* of Dante's reflections on his exile from Florence' (FB 2. 280). The connections between this experience and his developing concerns about the nature of language and poetry begin to be evident early in what has been described as his 'book of exile', his treatise

191

on *Eloquence in the Vernacular* written around 1303–5 (Shapiro 1990). Here, at the point where larger questions about 'original language' are being addressed, we are also reminded of the intensity and ambivalence of the exile's attachment to his own original 'mother tongue' (*DVE* 1. 6. 2–3). Dante's actual wanderings across the peninsula during this period also reinforce his imagining of a 'hunt' through Italy for the new language of poetry, the 'illustrious form of Italian' that he seeks in the later stages of *DVE* Book 1 (chs. 11–19).

Yet more challenging is the quest that Dante then embarks upon, around 1304–7, in the *Convivio*. In *Conv*. 1, his defence of the vernacular as a suitable language for the project is again closely linked to his identity as exile, as we can see from his vivid description of himself as an impoverished 'wanderer' across all the regions where that vernacular is used (1. 3. 4–5; above, p. 23). The word for 'wanderer' here (*peregrino*) can also mean 'pilgrim' and thus implies a more positive direction for Dante's life and work. Similarly, his identification of himself in this same passage as a 'boat without a sail or rudder, driven to various ports, harbours and shores' initiates a metaphor that is soon to surface in a much more confident context, when the next part of the *Convivio*'s enterprise gets under way: 'The moment calls for my ship to leave port; so having set the mizzen-sail of reason to catch the breeze of my desire, I set out upon the high sea in the hope of a prosperous voyage and a welcoming harbour' (*Conv*. 2. 1. 1). Dante is here 'speaking by way of introduction' or 'preamble' (*proemialmente ragionando*) and is thus using the traditional trope of the sea voyage that had accompanied the launch of a number of classical and medieval texts (Curtius 1953: 128–30). This kind of imagery will provide one way for him to project a sense of the journey and its purpose in the *Commedia*.

## *Inferno*: a cruel sea

The first brief metaphor of the *Commedia* is that of 'the road of our life', but its first extended simile is that of being cast ashore after a disaster at sea:

> *E come quei che con lena affannata,*
> *uscito fuor del pelago a la riva,*
> *si volge a l'acqua perigliosa e guata,*
>   *così l'animo mio, ch'ancor fuggiva,*
> *si volse a retro a rimirar lo passo*
> *che non lasciò già mai persona viva.*

As one who, gasping with exhaustion,
has struggled from the ocean on to shore
and turns back to those perilous seas and gapes,
    so, with my spirits still in disarray,
I looked back on that tract of wilderness
where no one can remain and stay alive.

(*Inf.* 1. 22–7)

Through the simile here, the experience of emerging from the 'perilous seas' (24), becomes comparable to the shipwreck of Aeneas and his companions at the beginning of the *Aeneid*, or to Dante's own representation of his exiled self as storm-driven vessel in *Conv.* 1. 3. 5. By contrast with those two episodes, however, the significance of the threat posed is less immediately clear. How has the 'dark forest' (to which this simile refers) suddenly become a dangerous ocean? What kind of 'voyage' on the part of Dante's protagonist has thus been interrupted; and how is it to be continued?

The journey through the *Inferno* itself is represented through the imagery of voyaging at a number of key transition points. On the banks of the Acheron, the demonic ferryman Charon denies Dante passage on the boat of damned souls whilst mysteriously (for those who have not already read *Purgatorio* 2) foretelling that he will be transported by 'a lighter vessel' (*Inf.* 3. 91–3). A small but speedy boat, steered by another demonic ferryman (Phlegyas), appears at the next major crossing point (the river Styx) and seems loaded only when the still living Dante steps aboard, bound for the gates of Dis and the next main sector of Hell (*Inf.* 8. 13–27). The fabulous monster Geryon, who ferries the poets across the next great gulf, is initially compared to a diver heroically freeing a trapped anchor, and is later likened to a ship beached on the shore or cautiously casting off from its mooring (*Inf.* 16. 133–6, 17. 19–20 and 100–1). Another important lift arranged by Virgil is at the hands of the giant Antaeus, who bends to set the poets down on the ice of the ninth circle and immediately raises himself upright again 'like the mast on a ship' (*Inf.* 31. 145). Such images and similes from the 'art' of sailing strengthen the impression of a higher power operating to control the movements of these monstrous figures and to direct Dante's underworld journey. They also reinforce the sense of control and direction behind the poem itself and thus relate to the writerly uses of the language and imagery of voyaging that are to become so potent in the *Commedia*.

An early example of this imagery occurs in the speech of an influential writer in Hell: Brunetto Latini. Brunetto begins his longest speech to the pilgrim by assuring him that if he follows his 'star', he will not fail to reach a 'glorious harbour' (*glorioso porto; Inf.* 15. 55–6). This prophecy can be interpreted at several levels. It can refer to the protagonist's progress towards Purgatory and Paradise under the protection or guidance of radiant, star-like figures such as St Lucy and Beatrice. But Dante's 'star' is also the constellation of Gemini, under which he was born and which was considered favourable to writers (*Par.* 22. 112–23). The 'glorious harbour' can thus also refer to Dante's achievement as a writer and to the completion of the *Commedia* itself. Brunetto's prophecy about Dante's future and the 'star' he mentions are recalled by the narrator at the beginning of a later episode, and one that is crucial to the development of the idea of the journey in the *Commedia*.

Near the beginning of *Inferno* 26, Dante looks down into the eighth 'pouch' of *Malebolge* and describes his reaction then and (from the writer-narrator's point of view) 'now':

> I sorrowed then, and sorrow yet again,
> as memory returns to what I saw,
> and rein my powers back more firmly now,
>    in case they lead where honour does not guide;
> so that if some good star or higher power
> endowed me with such gifts, I do not waste them.
>                   (*Inf.* 26. 19–24)

Dante is about to encounter the souls of those who have thus misdirected their intellectual powers and are able to express themselves now only through the tormented and tormenting tongues of flame. Dominant amongst these is the legendary schemer, orator and voyager Ulysses; and 'the whole prologue to the history of Ulysses is thus based by Dante – for the only time in the *Inferno* – upon his own personal history' (CL 1. 771). The personal significance of this prologue is emphasized by the stance that Dante adopts as writer-narrator here and by the reminiscence (in line 23 above) of Brunetto's earlier reference to the constellation guiding the pilgrim and the poet. It is further enforced by the extreme urgency of the protagonist's desire to see and communicate with the flame-enfolded souls. This urgency makes him almost fall off the bridge over this circle in his eagerness to look at them more closely, and it is also expressed through his eager pleading with Virgil, once he knows that one of these flames contains Ulysses (*Inf.* 26. 43–5 and 64–9).

Do the tone and empathy of this prologue to the encounter with Ulysses indicate that Dante has invested more of his personal concerns than usual in the representation of this deceiver's soul? And why should he have done so?

Despite Dante's eagerness to know about Ulysses, no direct conversation between the two of them takes place. At Virgil's solemn prompting (*Inf.* 26. 79–84) the 'greater spire' of the double flame that enfolds both Ulysses and his companion in arms, Diomedes, bends, moves to and fro 'like a tongue in speaking' (89), and delivers a single speech that occupies the remainder of the canto (90–142). It takes up the story of the Greek hero once he has returned home from Troy, having used his ingenuity to destroy the city from which the 'noble seed of the Romans' (in the form of Aeneas) was to emerge (58–60). Dante's Ulysses has thus, in a way, completed the *Odyssey* (which Dante would have known through Ovid's *Met.* 14 and other Latin sources). Yet as the opening of his speech makes clear, he remains restless, still 'burning' to meet the challenge of knowing the world and the qualities of humanity (97–9). It is this *ardore* that drives him to set off again in a single ship with a few companions on the 'deep open sea' (100). From the Pillars of Hercules (the Straits of Gibraltar), Ulysses and his crew thus begin the five-month voyage that will take them the on a course south-west across the ocean of which (it was believed) the southern hemisphere was entirely composed (diagram 3, p. 125; Hawkins 1999: 267; Boyde 1981: 107–9). Eventually, they sight a soaring mountain in the distance (133–5). This is the end of their journey, but not in the way that they expect. Out of this 'new land' a whirlwind emerges, strikes the prow of the ship, revolves it three times in the churning sea, then plunges it and the whole ship downwards 'until the sea had closed over us again' (142). At this point, too, Ulysses's speech and the whole canto come to a close.

This powerful sea-story has influenced a number of poets and storytellers, from Coleridge ('The Ancient Mariner'), Tennyson ('Ulysses'), Melville (*Moby-Dick*) and Poe ('MS. Found in a Bottle') through to T. S. Eliot's early draft of 'Death by Water' in *The Waste Land* and beyond. It has also intrigued and divided the commentators and critics. Most seem to recognize the strong parallels between Dante and the soul whose history he is reconstructing. Ulysses, like Dante, is an exile and wanderer, with political skills and an obsessive interest in the 'vices and worth' of humanity. He even has some features in common with Dante as writer and as poet: his ability to sway the minds and sharpen the resolution of his companions by means of his powerful speech. His eloquence is manifest in the speech that inspires his followers to accompany him 'beyond the setting sun, into the unpeopled world' (117). Dante would have been well aware of Ulysses's virtuosic demonstration of 'eloquence of speech and grace of gesture' during the verbal contest for the shield of Achilles in Book 13 of Ovid's *Metamorphoses* (Humphries 1955: 309–18).

But as with other encounters in the *Inferno*, detachment as well as involvement is evident here. Some critics have seen Ulysses as a figure damned for 'false counselling' before he ever sets off on his final voyage, which is thus to be seen as a heroic 'pre-humanist' quest for knowledge against all the odds and in the face of death. His quest seems thus to reaffirm what Dante has the Roman philosopher Seneca say late in the *Convivio*: 'Even if I had one foot already in the grave, I should want to continue learning' (*Conv.* 4. 12. 11). At the opposite extreme, however, are those who see Ulysses's *folle volo* ('mad flight', *Inf.* 26. 125) beyond the Pillars of Hercules as a cautionary example of over-reaching rationalism, hence as a condemnation of the *Convivio* as a whole and of the assumed 'philosophism' of Dante's earlier abortive intellectual journey (*DE* 844B–845B).

As when comparing the understandings of love in, say, *Convivio* 3 and *Purgatorio* 2 (above, pp. 182–7), it may be helpful to think of this episode as a revision rather than a rejection of Dante's earlier vernacular project, and thus to recognize a degree of productive tension and ambivalence in his attitude towards the voyage of Ulysses. The mythical Greek seafarer confidently forcing his way across the southern ocean towards the Mountain of Purgatory clearly contrasts with the hesitant pilgrim making his way there through the labyrinth of Hell. Moreover, the voyage of Ulysses will, at several stages of the *Commedia*'s journey, become a point of reference by which the protagonist is to measure his own progress (below, p. 198). But Dante's Ulysses also has affinities as epic traveller with mythic figures such as Aeneas and Jason. His disastrous fate and the inhumanity of his humanism (at least as far as family and crew are concerned) stand as a warning. Yet the excitement and audacity of his address to his crew as they launch into the uncharted ocean will find echoes in the tone and language of Dante's own claims to his followers about his poetic voyage – for example, the assertion that 'the waters I now venture on were never crossed before' (*Par.* 2. 7).

## 'The better waters': Purgatory and its poets

> On better waters my poetic craft
> now hoists its sails to run before the wind,
> and now behind lies all that cruel sea.
>
> (*Purg.* 1. 1–3)

At this point of new departure in the *Commedia*, the extended metaphor strengthens the relationship between poet and protagonist. The 'waters', 'sails' and 'boat' here are traditional metaphors that Dante has drawn upon at the start of *Convivio* 2 (above, p. 192) and will deploy yet again in the *Commedia*. But they are as much part of the visualized scene at the start of *Purgatorio* as the sapphire blue of the sky (13), the light of Venus and the stars (19–27) or the dawn rising over the sea (115–17). Dante's poetic 'vessel' has as much presence here as the 'actual' boat that is to bring souls such as Casella to the shores of the mountain in the next canto – so much of a presence indeed that readers, like a number of the poem's early illustrators, might easily be led to think that Dante and Virgil 'really' arrived in Purgatory by sea (BMS 2. 19–21, 24b, 25).

Confidence in the new enterprise is generated by several features of language, imagery and allusion here. Verbs of rising recur through the canto's first nine lines: the poet's boat hoists its sails (*Purg.* 1. 1); the ultimate ascent of the human soul is heralded (6); the poetry which has till now been confined to the world of the dead is summoned to 'rise again' (*resurga*, 7); and the Muse of epic poetry (Calliope) is called upon to 'arise' (*surga*, 9). Virgil presents Dante to the guardian of the mountain's lower slopes, the defender of the Roman republic, Cato, and describes him as one who, like Cato himself, seeks 'freedom' (*libertà*, 71–2). The beginning of that process is marked by the signs of dawn, by the poets' movement down towards the actual seashore, and by the performance of a ritual (ordained by Cato) through which Dante's face and eyes are freed of the 'grime' of Hell and he is girded with a reed that signifies humility and powers of endurance (94–108, 121–36).

The description of the muddy shallows from which this reed is to be plucked sets up some long and significant echoes:

> *Venimmo poi in sul lito diserto,*
> *che mai non vide navicar sue **acque***
> *omo, che di tornar sia poscia esperto.*
>   *Quivi mi cinse sì com' altrui **piacque**;*
> *oh maraviglia! ché qual elli scelse*
> *l'umile pianta, cotal si **rinacque***
> *subitamente là onde l'avelse.*

> Then we arrived upon that lonely shore
> which never yet had seen its waters sailed
> by any able then to turn for home.

And here he girded me, as was ordained;
but then, a miracle – for as he picked
that lowly plant, so it sprang up again
just as it was when he uprooted it.

(*Purg.* 1. 130–6)

The allusion in lines 131–2 is to Ulysses, whose vessel did indeed turn around, but only in the whirlpool that was to sink it (*Inf.* 26. 139–42). It is reinforced by the repetition of three rhymes (in 131, 133 and 135) that have also ended lines at the conclusion of *Inferno* 26 (137, 139 and 141) and by the phrase at the end of line 133, *com' altrui piacque*, which literally means 'as it pleased someone else [i.e., Cato or God]'; and this same phrase has also described the force that destroyed Ulysses and his crew (*Inf.* 26. 141). At the end of *Purgatorio* 1, then, 'the tragic myth of *Inf.* 26 returns, as in a distant dream, to give significance to this very different arrival' (CL 2. 34). Again, the implications for Dante in his various guises are complex; but one effect of the passage, for all its caution and concern with humility, is to reinforce the impression of the poetic voyager's confidence as he embarks upon the 'better waters' of the *Purgatorio*. Hence the canto's final comparison of Dante's voyage with that of Ulysses continues – although more tentatively – to elicit faith in the capacities of resurrected poetry and the renewed poet.

*Purgatorio* not only provides 'better waters' for the voyage of Dante's poem. It could also be called (to use Yeats's phrase from 'Sailing to Byzantium') Dante's 'singing school' for poetry and poets. He has encountered a number of writers and poets already in his journey through the *Inferno*. Virgil, as we have seen, has introduced himself and been celebrated by Dante as poet; Dante momentarily joins a group of classical poets in Limbo (*Inf.* 4. 79–102); and there are subsequently direct encounters with the souls of vernacular writers such as Pier della Vigna, Brunetto Latini and Bertrand de Born (*Inf.* 13, 15, 28). All these last three were to some degree poets (and Dante refers to two of them as such in *DVE*), but their poetry is not explicitly referred to or quoted in the scenes where they appear. The *Purgatorio*, on the other hand, is often specific in recognizing poets as poets, in quoting from their work at times, and in constructing a vernacular tradition within which Dante's own work can be placed.

Poetry in the *Purgatorio* is associated with other human arts and shares their limitations. The first poet to have his work quoted is Dante himself, whose *canzone* from *Convivio* 3 is sung by the musician Casella in *Purgatorio*

2 (above, p. 185). Whatever the deeper reasons for the interruption of this song, it is clear that Dante as pilgrim and as writer shares with the singer something of the immediate responsibility for the 'delay', about which Cato rebukes the performer and his hearers.

At a later point of departure in Purgatory proper, the complex relationships between human and divine art (above, p. 168) are further explored in the terrace of pride (*Purg.* 11). Here, the illuminator Oderisi da Gubbio speaks of fame as 'the empty glory humans seek', as no more than a mutable 'breath of wind' or a blade of grass bleached by the sun (*Purg.* 11. 91, 100–2, 115–17). Oderisi cites examples of this vanity and mutability amongst the painters and the poets of his and Dante's time. He first notes how the fame of Cimabue has been eclipsed by adulation for Giotto, whom Dante may have known (above, pp. 32–3) and who is 'now all the rage' (94–6). Turning then to 'the glory of [poetic] language', he traces a three-stage process whereby one Guido (Cavalcanti) supplants another (Gunizzelli) at the top of the literary tree and will in turn have to yield his place to 'one who will chase them both from the nest' (97–9; above, p. 120). It makes sense in this context to identify this third occupant as Dante himself and to read this brief, three-line episode as an expression of both audacity and humility on the poet's part. On one level it reflects the energy and ambition with which he silenced Ovid and Lucan in *Inferno* 25 (above, p. 166). On another level – in the context of Oderisi's speech about mutability – it recognizes Dante's own eventual subjection to the vicissitudes of 'empty glory'. Nor – despite the aggressive metaphor of ejection from the nest (99) – is the idea of poetic continuity and community to be excluded here: the first word that Oderisi speaks to his fellow-artist Dante in this canto is the key form of address in the *Purgatorio*: *frate* ('brother', line 82).

Poetic continuity and community are also evident in the role that continues to be played by Dante's guide and 'author', Virgil. Two encounters with poets in Purgatory illustrate this role. The first occurs during the later stages of the journey through Antepurgatory, when Dante and Virgil meet the Italian troubadour Sordello, who had died around 1269 (*Purg.* 6. 58–75). This is the first direct encounter with a vernacular poet in the *Purgatorio*; and Sordello parallels Virgil here as a writer who 'demonstrates in his own person the unity of a linguistic tradition that is rooted in Latin language and literature and that cannot be divorced from a political tradition rooted in the Roman Empire' (Barolini 1979: 399). This is also a relationship that emphasizes fellow-citizenship in several ways. Sordello and Virgil are both natives of Mantua (*Purg.* 6. 70–5); and their embrace prompts a long and impassioned lament about the division between and within Italian cities, including Dante's own (76–151). The poets then form a trinity of companionship which spans three cantos and acts as a standpoint from which political themes continue to be developed during the subsequent encounters with earthly rulers (*Purg.* 7–8).

From *Purgatorio* 21 on, an equally significant and even more long-lasting trinity of poetic companionship is shared by Virgil, Dante and the Latin poet Statius (above, p. 70). Like other fellow-pilgrims in the *Purgatorio* – including the artist Oderisi and several of the poets – Statius greets Dante and Virgil as 'brothers' (*frati*), as they make their way upwards from the terrace of avarice (*Purg.* 21. 13). The nature of his relationship with Virgil begins to become clear later in this same canto, when, having introduced himself by name (91), he speaks as a kind of 'grandson', rather than 'brother', of the earlier Latin poet, whose *Aeneid* he describes as 'mother (*mamma*) and nurse' (97–8). At this point he doesn't yet realize he is addressing Virgil himself, but once Dante has revealed to him that this is indeed the poet 'from whom you drew the power to sing of men and gods' (125–6), the bond between the two Latin writers is vividly acknowledged. Virgil responds to Statius's vain but human gesture of reverence by addressing him (in turn) as 'brother' (*Purg.* 21. 131) and then as 'friend' (*amico*, 22. 19 and 21). Statius then emphasizes the link between poetry and life when, having cited the prophetic lines from Virgil's Fourth Eclogue (above, p. 68), he affirms that 'Through you I became a poet, through you a Christian' (*Purg.* 22. 73). The link is also more indirectly reinforced by the imagery of Virgil's own question about Statius's conversion:

> 'what sun or star in Heaven
> shone through your darkness, made you trim your sails
> and set your course following the Fisherman?'
>
> (*Purg.* 22. 61–3)

where once again the metaphor of voyaging surfaces and conveys a powerful impression of the how apostolic guidance (identified with St Peter, 'the Fisherman') converges with poetic influence – the 'light' of Virgil's work.

The companionship of the three poets is to last until Virgil's departure some seven cantos later (*Purg.* 29), and it thus becomes interwoven with two encounters between Dante and two contemporary vernacular poets:

Bonagiunta of Lucca in canto 24 and Guido Guinizzelli in canto 26 (above, pp. 114–17). Two features of these encounters are especially important.

First, the old-school Tuscan poet, Bonagiunta, and the new stylist from Bologna, Guinizzelli, are literally and metaphorically left behind in the *Purgatorio*, but both of them are made to refer to Dante again as 'brother' (*frate*; 24. 55, 26. 115). The *Purgatorio*'s 'singing school' thus constructs a tradition within which certain 'father-figures' such as Guinizzelli, Guittone d'Arezzo and Virgil himself are to be outdone (above, p. 117). However, as the use of *frate* here and elsewhere suggests, this does not preclude recognition of how epic poets like Virgil, Statius and Dante and love-poets like Dante, Bonagiunta and Guinizzelli form part of a community.

Secondly, Dante's Bonagiunta and Guinizzelli both make specific allusions to poetry that resonate widely through Dante's work. Bonagiunta's 'murmuring' (*Purg.* 24. 37 and 47) – as he gets around to recognizing Dante long after he himself has been identified by Dante's friend Forese Donati (19–20) – eventually resolves itself into the articulation of the first line of the first *canzone* in Dante's *Vita nuova*: *Donne ch'avete intelletto d'amore*; above, p. 177; Valency 1958: 211–17; *Barolini 1984: 40–57). This is the second of three opening lines from Dante's own poems to be quoted in the *Commedia*; it is also the only direct self-quotation there from the *Vita nuova*. More importantly, it recognizes the impact of a poem that was already (even by the fictional date of the *Commedia*) circulating separately in manuscripts (CL 2. 710).

Finally, there is a dual resonance in the lines which are uttered as greeting to Dante's pilgrim out of the flames of the circle of the lustful:

> 'Blessed are you who from our country will [. . .]
> take knowledge for a better end aboard.'
> (*Purg.* 26. 73–5)

Dante's Gunizzelli is here echoing the opening of a sonnet in which the historical Guinizzelli had paid tribute to the work of another poet, Guittone d'Arezzo (CL 2. 776). The passage also incorporates Arnaut Daniel and Guinizzelli himself, both of whom wrote poems using the difficult rhyme 'embark' (Durling and Martinez 2003: 449). Moreover, the metaphor of 'embarking' or 'taking aboard' knowledge or 'experience' (74) reinforces the consciousness of poetic composition by drawing once again upon the language of voyaging. The 'freight' Guinizzelli speaks of is to be carried by the 'better waters' of the *Purgatorio*.

201

## 'The waters never crossed before': voyaging, vision and language in the *Paradiso*

> You who have set out in little boats
> eager to hear me, following
> behind my craft that sails on, powered by song -
>   turn round, head back again for your own shores;
> don't venture on this ocean's deeps, in case
> you lose track of me, cast yourselves adrift.
>   I take to waters never crossed before;
> Minerva fills my sail, Apollo steers
> and all nine Muses guide me by the stars.
>   You others, few of you, who for long years
> have reached for bread of angels which
> nourishes but does not sate us here –
>   you surely may set out upon the deep
> and salty ocean, following in my wake
> before the water closes over it;
>   and those brave souls who dared to sail to Colchis
> were not so struck with awe as you will be
> when they saw Jason there become a ploughman.
>
> (*Par.* 2. 1–18)

The language of voyaging in this passage powerfully conveys consciousness of the poetic enterprise and its challenging newness. At a similar point in the *Purgatorio* (1. 1–9) Dante had been concentrating on the redirection of his own resources, through the image of the poet's boat hoisting sail and the invocation of the Muses (above, p. 197). Here again, near the beginning of the *Paradiso*, the powers associated with creation and composition are invoked: Minerva, goddess of wisdom; Apollo, god of poetry; and all nine of the Muses (*Par.* 2. 8–9). This takes place, however, in the context of direct, second-person address to two groups of readers. The first – to those 'who have set out in little boats' – recognizes both the difficulty of 'figuring Paradise' that has been emphasized at the beginning of the previous canto (*Par.* 1. 7–9; above, p. 171) and the extreme demands that the poem will continue to place upon its audience (compare *Par.* 10. 7–27). The second group, addressed here as 'You others' (10–18), are those who are able to follow the poet because of their own long quest for wisdom in scripture and theology (the 'bread of angels' in line 11). This select band, too, are faced with a serious challenge, as Dante continues to call for the 'mobilization of the reader's forces' (\*Auerbach 1953–4: 273, 276). For such readers, the 'text projects itself as a discursive event', and they are involved (like the imagined readers of *Inf.* 9. 61–3 or *Purg.* 8. 19–21) in 'a happening of understanding' (\*Franke 1996: 40–1).

Combined with the language of voyaging in the address to this second group of readers are images of nourishment: bread, salt, ploughing. 'Alimentary metaphorics' had already been developed by Dante in the 'banquet' of knowledge to which he invited vernacular readers in the *Convivio* (Curtius 1953: 134–6). Various forms of appetite, literal and figurative, have also been shown driving both the protagonist and other souls in the *Commedia*; and the later stages of the vision in the *Paradiso* will be imagined (paradoxically) as a return to a very basic form of nourishment: milk (below, p. 206).

The imagery of nourishment in this address to Dante's readers is echoed on either side of the passage. Immediately afterwards, Beatrice and Dante are said to be moved upwards (with a speed as fast as the apparent motion of the stars) by means of the 'innate and everlasting thirst (*sete*) for the kingdom formed in the likeness of God' (*Par.* 2. 19–21); whilst shortly before, the desire of humanity to become 'more than human' has been exemplified by the myth of the fisherman Glaucus, whose curiosity led him 'to taste (*gustar*) the herb that made him a fellow of the other gods in the ocean' (*Par.* 1. 67–72). For this second example Dante dives once more into his sea of stories.

In *Paradiso* 1 (68–9) the brief, two-line allusion to Glaucus touches on a powerful myth of metamorphosis: the transformation of human into god through tasting. Dante's source here – as with other metamorphoses in the *Commedia* – is Ovid, who describes in much more detail the effects on the fisherman of chewing the grass that has brought dead fish back to life and drawn them into the sea again:

> 'its flavour
> Had hardly touched my tongue, when suddenly
> My heart within me trembled, and I felt
> An overwhelming longing; I must change
> My way of life. I could not stand against it,
> "Farewell, O Earth!" I cried, "Farewell forever!"
> And plunged into the sea, whose gods received me
> With every honor, and called on Oceanus
> And Tethys, to dissolve my mortal nature.
> They purged me of it, first with magic singing,
> Nine times repeated, then with river water

Come from a hundred streams, and I remember
No more, but when my sense returned I knew I was
A different kind of creature, body and spirit.'
(Ovid, *Met.* 13; Humphries 1955: 336–7)

Ovid's text is worth quoting at such length because his vivid version of the story spells out some of the implications that Dante is to explore and develop in the *Paradiso*. Initiating a change in one's 'way of life' through tasting something of miraculous power, the experience of 'magic singing' and of becoming mysteriously 'a different kind of creature', are all features of the visionary journey in this final *cantica*. They are also aspects of transformation that Dante's address to his readers in *Paradiso* 2 brings into focus. The 'bread of angels' will change his readers' lives as they follow in the wake of the 'vessel powered by song'; and they will also witness the writer-narrator becoming a different kind of creature, comparable to the mythic voyager Jason.

'Jason turning ploughman' (*Par.* 2. 18) is the mysterious example through which Dante imagines his relationship to his committed audience, and with it the first address to readers in the *Paradiso* closes. Again, Ovid's account of this strange transformation gives some clues to its meaning for Dante's poem. At the end of Book 6 of the *Metamorphoses*, the quest of Jason and the Argonauts has been described as an impressive new venture: a journey over 'an unknown sea'; a 'voyage / In the first ship for the gleaming fleece of gold' (Humphries 1955: 152). In *Met.* 7, Jason's first task on his way to obtaining the fleece is the taming of the fire-breathing bulls to plough 'fields that never before had known a furrow' and sow this ground with 'serpent's teeth'. His meeting of this challenge and that of the 'earth-born' warriors who spring up out of the serpent's teeth is witnessed by his followers first with dismay and then with relieved applause (Humphries 1955: 156–7). Yet Ovid's version makes clear that this is not simply the triumph of heroic brute force. The power behind the episode is that of the lovesick and resourceful magician Medea; and Jason's success is attributable not so much to his strength as to her skill. 'Magic herbs' here, as in the story of Glaucus, are the effective agents of change, and Jason uses them again, along with powerful incantatory 'words', to subdue the dragon that guards the Golden Fleece (*Met.* 7. 153; Humphries 1955: 158).

Dante's comparison of himself to Jason at this juncture reflects the audacity, the sense of newness of the enterprise and of confidence in the power of words that marked his portrayal of Ulysses (above, p. 196). Yet detachment as well as involvement marks Dante's allusions to Jason's quest, as both mark the later reference to Ulysses's 'mad voyage' across the southern ocean to Purgatory (*Par.* 27. 82–3). Like Ulysses, Dante's Jason is an impressive and heroic adventurer; and he is initially described in the *Commedia* as the figure 'who through courage and skill deprived the Colchians of the fleece' (*Inf.* 18. 86–7). Yet like Ulysses again, he is also – and crucially – a deceiver. Indeed, he is among the earliest examples of those who have sinned through deception, in the first section of the eighth circle; and he is placed there, as Virgil explains, because of his betrayal of women, including (specifically) Medea (*Inf.* 18. 96). Developing through the *Paradiso*, then, there may be an implied contrast – between Jason's infidelity to the woman whose magical skills secured him the Golden Fleece and Dante's reaffirmation of faith in the 'woman of power' (*Inf.* 2. 76) who visited the gates of Hell on his behalf (*Purg.* 30. 139) and is now his guide through the spheres of Paradise. Dante's process of understanding love and of 'figuring Paradise' in this *cantica* seems to oscillate between these poles of audacity and dependency.

Two further examples will illustrate this complexity of attitude towards the visionary voyage of the *Paradiso*. For the first, we return to the problems of communicating the vision that are articulated in *Paradiso* 23 (above, p. 173). Dante's confidence in the powers of 'the memory which does not err' (*Inf.* 2. 6) has been reaffirmed a number of times throughout the *Commedia* and has been reinforced often (as in *Inf.* 2. 7) by appeals to the daughters of memory, the Muses, whom Dante may have been the first Italian vernacular poet to invoke (Havely 1997: 64 and n. 12; *DE* 630B). However, as the opening of the *Paradiso* has recognized, memory will not be fully able to keep pace with understanding on this journey (*Par.* 1. 7–9). In canto 23 Dante is assured by Beatrice (46–8) that through his vision of the triumph of Christ he is now able to 'open his eyes' to her radiance, which shines more brightly the higher they ascend – but, as he does so, the narrator-poet declares himself momentarily unable to continue:

> For if I now could call on all those tongues
> that Polyhymnia and her sisters fed
> with all their sweetest, all their richest milk
>     to help me, they could not truly praise
> even a thousandth of that holy smile,
> nor of that holy face's radiance;
>     so now, when figuring forth Paradise,
> the sacred poem has to make a leap,
> as does a traveller whose way is blocked.

But if you think how this demanding theme
weighs on the human shoulder that supports it,
you would not blame it then for trembling.
This is no stretch of sea for a frail craft –
the waves that now this daring prow cleaves through –
nor for a helmsman out to spare himself.

(Par. 23. 55–69)

Polyhymnia, the Muse of lyric poetry – and hence of the love-poems that Dante had addressed to Beatrice and other women – is the most appropriate daughter of memory to recall and express this new moment of Beatrice's 'radiance'; but here she is mentioned only to be found inadequate to the task. Yet into this sombre admission of poetic shortcomings there flashes a moment of the old audacity, with the brief reappearance of the 'daring prow' (68), of the swift and confident 'vessel powered by song' with its Ulyssean or Jason-like commander (*Par.* 2. 3).

The slightly strange allusion to the Muses' 'milk' which has 'fed' (literally 'fattened') countless poets' tongues also signifies inadequacy at this particular moment (55–7). Yet it acts too as a reminder of the basic form of nourishment that becomes a key image of positive 'dependency' in the *Paradiso*. The souls at the end of this canto reach out to the Virgin 'like an infant when it has taken milk' (*Par.* 23. 121–2). Later, Dante himself, eager to transform his vision in the river of light (above, p. 174), is to be compared to a baby waking after its feeding time and 'turning at once and in haste towards the [source of] milk'; and humanity in the grip of greed is likened to 'a starving child that pushes away its nurse' (*Par.* 30. 82–5 and 139–40).

Finally, these two complementary figures – the audacious voyager and the dependent child – converge again at the point where the figuring of Paradise meets its ultimate challenge: that of conveying the vision of the Trinity in canto 33. Here Dante can only say that he *believes* he saw the 'knot' that unites the multiplicity of created beings because 'in saying so I feel a deeper access of joy' (*Par.* 33. 91–3). The strain to which this final vision subjects both memory and expression is here conveyed by framing the description of the mind in the presence of its creator within two familiar images:

*Un punto solo m'è maggior letargo*
*che venticinque secoli a la 'mpresa*
*che fé Nettuno ammirar l'ombra d'Argo.*
*Così la mente mia, tutta sospesa,*

*mirava fissa, immobile e attenta,*
*e sempre di mirar faceasi accesa.*

*A quella luce cotal si diventa,*
*che volgersi da lei per altro aspetto*
*è impossibil che mai si consenta;*

*però che 'l ben, ch'è del volere obietto,*
*tutto s'accoglie in lei, e fuor di quella*
*è defettivo ciò ch' è lì perfetto.*

*Omai sarà più corta mia favella,*
*pur a quel ch'io ricordo, che d'un fante*
*che bagni ancor la lingua a la mammella.*

Each moment since brings more forgetfulness
than twenty-five centuries since that voyage
and *Argo*'s shadow struck Neptune with wonder.

And so my mind, rapt in itself entirely,
gazed fixedly, motionless and intent,
kindling desire to gaze yet more and more.

Absorbed so in the presence of that light,
there is no way that can persuade the mind
to turn from it to any other sight;

for the supreme good, the goal of all desire,
is brought together there, whilst other aims
fail and fall short of what is there complete.

And now my speech itself will be less able
to tell what I recall than is a child
that bathes its tongue still at its mother's breast.

(*Par.* 33. 94–108)

In the original, *Argo* is rhymed with *letargo* ('forgetfulness'), and the first three lines of the passage convey the difficulty of recalling and imagining the vision, which at this point is comparable to the shadow seen by Neptune on the surface of the ocean. Yet the image of the first ship's shadow moving upon the face of the waters, to the surprise of the sea-god below, also evocatively recalls the new enterprise signalled by the allusions to seafaring and the voyage of Jason near the start of this *cantica* (*Par.* 2. 1–18), as well as the briefer reappearance of the 'daring prow', cleaving the waves in *Paradiso* 23 (67–9). In this way the apparent admission of the poet's inadequacy – the failure of memory to keep hold of what has been seen – can also be read, in this last recurrence of the language of voyaging, as an implicit reaffirmation of his audacity in seeking to show how the mind encounters its creator and

*Plate 9*  Neptune and the shadow of the *Argo* (*Par.* 33), from British Library MS Yates Thompson 36, f. 190r, illustrated by Giovanni di Paolo, c.1445–50. By permission of the British Library.

'goal of its desire' (*del volere obietto*). This was also one way through which a later illustrator could cope with the problems of visualizing this final canto (plate 9).

But following this gesture of audacity comes recognition of dependency; and after the allusion to the mythic voyage, the poem then reaches back into childhood. The intensely physical simile of the child 'that bathes its tongue still at its mother's breast' (*che bagni ancor la lingua a la mammella*) forces the reader of the Italian text to re-enact the movements of the child's lips and tongue (*Par.* 33. 108). It is also the last of many moments in the *Commedia* when the situation of the pilgrim and visionary has been imagined as the dependency of child upon parent. Frequently Dante's relationship with Virgil and others has been that of child to father and has comprised both dependency and detachment. Virgil and Guinizzelli have also on occasion been feminized as mother-figures (e.g., *Purg.* 26. 94–6, 30. 43–5), whilst Beatrice, although strongly maternal in her earlier association with the Virgin Mary (*Inf.* 2), has been a tough mother at the end of the *Purgatorio* (30. 79–81) and has adopted 'a predominantly masculine presence' there (Schnapp 1988: 155). Dante's 'childhood' in the *Commedia* has thus been a complicated and at times confusing experience; but one important and powerful effect of representing him in this way, especially in the *Paradiso*, is to make the reader return, as here, to the origins of being and of language.

Like the allusion to *Argo*'s shadow, then, the simile of the speechless infant at the breast in *Par.* 33. 106–8 conveys both an immediate sense of the limitations of expression and a profound concern with its processes. The vocabulary of speech and language here reinforces that concern. *Favella* ('speech', 106) rhymes with *mammella* ('breast'), and in the *Commedia* it has carried a wide range of meanings, from 'utterance' or 'way of speaking' to 'language' or 'languages' in general. *Lingua* (108) covers a similar range, although it is a more frequent term and one that, like 'tongue', can refer both to language and to the organ of speech and taste.

Both words reinforce Dante's concern with language as the medium of his art. An interest in the forms of speech and the meanings of words had been evident already in the *Vita nuova* – for instance in chapters 13 (4), 25 and 40. Language, its origins, forms and uses, had been the main subject of the early Latin work of his exile: *De vulgari eloquentia*, which explores the language of Adam, the myth of Babel and the varieties of the Italian vernacular (1. 4–19), and, in its second book, could be 'understood not as a mere treatise of style, but as an effort to fix the conditions . . . of the only conceivable perfect language – the Italian of the poetry of Dante' (Eco 1997: 46). That same Italian vernacular became quite literally a sexy subject in part 1 of the *Convivio*. There, in justifying its use for a work of this scope and scale, Dante defended it as a lover against its detractors and celebrates it as, amongst other things, the means by which his parents were brought together and to which he owes his own origin and identity (*Conv.* 1. 11–13).

Related ideas about language continue to develop through the *Commedia*. The nature and variety of speech are a concern in *Paradiso* 26, and we find in Adam's speech here (124–38) 'a somewhat different version of the genesis of human language' from that in *DVE* (Cremona 1965: 148–51). Here Adam also mentions the 'unfinishable project' of building the Tower of Babel (*Par.* 26. 125) and its architect, Nimrod (Genesis 11: 1–9). Nimrod had been described in *DVE* (1. 7. 4) as the 'giant' who 'led astray' humanity. He has appeared in the *Inferno* also as a malevolent giant speaking impressive gobbledygook (*Inf.* 31. 67–81); and has been portrayed by divine art in Purgatory, at the moment when his proud scheme fails and he stands at the foot of his great edifice 'in confusion' (*Purg.* 12. 34–6).

Further urgency is injected into the subject of language in the *Commedia* by the need to imagine and convey extremes: of confusion and coherence;

blindness and vision; evil and beatitude. Immediately upon entering Hell, the protagonist's very first sense impression is of the worst that can be heard from humans: 'confusion of tongues, horrible utterances, words of grief, cries of rage, loud and hoarse sounds' (*Inf.* 3. 25–7). Near the end of the journey through the *Inferno* – after he has passed by the wildly inarticulate Nimrod and been deposited by the eerily silent Antaeus on the ice of the final circle of Hell – Dante immediately faces the question of the language that could possibly be 'rough and harsh' enough to describe the 'wretched hole' that lies here:

> This is no enterprise to take on lightly,
> sounding the depths of the whole universe,
> nor is it for a tongue that still says 'Mum' and 'Daddy'.
> (*Inf.* 32. 7–9)

A growing up of language seems to be looked for both in Dante's conscious-ness of his task as poet here and shortly before in Virgil's indignant rebuking of Nimrod's nonsensical babble (*Inf.* 31. 70–5). This is in some ways accom-plished during the ascent of Purgatory – through the resurrection of 'dead poetry' (*Purg.* 1), through the choric utterances of souls which begin in canto 2, and through the community and partnerships of poets (above, pp. 199–201). Yet by the end of the *Paradiso* we have gone well beyond adulthood itself and, in a sense, beyond language. In the final stages of the *cantica* – as he compares his imminent silence to that of the child at the breast (*Par.* 33. 106–8) – Dante has returned to the mind of the child even *before* it has learned to 'say *mamma* and *babbo*'. And, shortly after that, even the attempts to lay hold of the vision that all these words seek to record must come to an end (142–5).

# Postscript: Dante's Readers

Readings of Dante are reflected in most genres of writing, a variety of media, and a wide range of cultures – all over a span of about seven centuries. This guide is intended for readers of Dante in English, but it would be impossible, in the space that remains, to survey the results of those later readings in even the English-speaking world.

This 'postscript' will thus be yet more selective than the previous three sections. It will identify some of the main forms in which Dante's work was received and appropriated and some of the main issues that concerned later readers. Most of the examples will be drawn from the cultures of the English-speaking world, but there will be some reminders of the wider horizons of reception – particularly in Italy.

To provide an initial map of the subject, the section begins with a chronology of significant events in Dante's afterlife. Then follow two brief surveys of how his work (especially the *Commedia*) was received in early commentary and criticism, and through illustration and performance. The last three sub-sections trace particular themes in the reception and appropriation of Dante's work: *Monarchia* and the *Inferno*; the *Purgatorio*; and the *Paradiso*.

*An asterisk (\*) indicates my first reference in this section to works that are particularly recommended for further reading.*

# Chronology of Significant Events in Dante's Afterlife, 1322–2006

| | |
|---|---|
| c.1322–5 | Summaries of the *Commedia* and commentary on *Inferno* by Jacopo di Dante (Dante's third son) |
| c.1323–33 | First complete commentary on the *Commedia*, by Jacopo della Lana in Italian |
| 1327/34 | *Monarchia* censured by Dominican friar Guido Vernani |
| 1328/9 | Pope's legate condemns *Monarchia* to be burnt, along with Dante's remains; official condemnation of the work was revoked in 1881 |
| c.1328–33 | Guido da Pisa's commentary on the *Inferno* in Latin |
| 1335? | Boccaccio's romance *Il Filostrato* shows influence of Dante |
| c.1340–58 | Commentary on the *Commedia* by Pietro Alighieri (Dante's second son) in Latin; three recensions |
| 1351–60 | Boccaccio's Life of Dante (*Trattatello in laude di Dante*), first two versions |
| 1373–4 | Boccaccio's public lectures in Italian, on the *Commedia* (*Esposizioni*), at Florence (Oct.–Jan.); text finishes at the start of *Inferno* 17 |
| 1375–80 | Benvenuto da Imola's commentary on the *Commedia* in Latin |

c.1380    Geoffrey Chaucer mentions and appropriates Dante in *The House of Fame*

1385–95   Francesco da Buti's commentary on the *Commedia* in Italian

c.1392    Matteo Ronto translates the *Commedia* into Latin hexameters

1416–17   Giovanni da Serravalle produces translation of and commentary on the *Commedia* in Latin at the Council of Constance

1428      Enrique de Villena completes translation of the *Commedia* into Castilian prose

1429      Andreu Febrer completes translation of the *Commedia* into Catalan verse

1436      Leonardo Bruni's *Life of Dante*

1444      Copy of Serravalle's 1416–17 translation of and commentary on the *Commedia* donated to Oxford University by Humphrey, duke of Gloucester

c.1445–50 Giovanni di Paolo illustrates the *Paradiso*

1467–8    Marsilio Ficino translates *Monarchia* into Italian

1472      First printed editions of the *Commedia* (Foligno, Mantua and Venice)

c.1480–95 Sandro Botticelli produces 92 drawings for presentation MS of the *Commedia* (Altcappenberg 2000; Columbia Digital Dante online)

1481      Edition of *Commedia* with commentary by Cristoforo Landino, Florentine humanist

1490      First printed edition of the *Convivio*, published at Florence

1502      Plain-text octavo edition of *Commedia* printed by Aldo Manuzio (Venice)

1515      Gian Giorgio Trissino's tragedy *Sofonisba* alludes to *Purg.* 1. 117 in final chorus

1529      Italian translation of *DVE* published at Vicenza

1554      *Monarchia* placed on Catholic Index of Prohibited Books

**1556–62**   Matthaus Flacius (Vlachich), Protestant historian, mentions and translates from Dante in *Catalogus testium veritatis*, published by Johannes Oporinus (Herbst) at Basel

**1559**   Oporinus publishes first edition of *Monarchia* at Basel; also a translation into German by Johann Herold

**1566–70**   Dante first cited by English Protestant polemicists (Robert Horne, John Jewel, John Foxe)

**1576**   First printed edition of *Vita nuova* and 15 *canzoni*, published at Florence

**1577**   First printed edition of *DVE*

**1587–8**   Galileo speculates on the dimensions of Dante's Hell (\*Caesar 1989: 301–3)

**1595**   Sidney's *An Apologie for Poetrie* shows knowledge of Landino's 1481 commentary on the *Commedia*

**1596**   First published translation of the *Commedia* in French (verse), by Balthasar Grangier

**1603**   Robert Parsons (Jesuit) attacks Protestant conscription of Dante in *Treatise of Three Conversions of England*

**c.1637**   Milton refers and alludes to Dante in his *Commonplace Book* and 'Lycidas'

**1641**   Milton translates *Inf.* 19. 115–17 into blank verse in *Of Reformation*

**1674**   René Rapin's neo-classical (Aristotelian) critique of Dante

**1716–18**   Thomas Coke of Holkham purchases six MSS of the *Commedia* in Italy

**1719**   Jonathan Richardson's verse translation of the Ugolino episode (*Inf.* 33. 1–77) in *A Discourse on the Dignity . . . of the Science of a Connoisseur*

**1726–76**   Voltaire's various writings and attacks on Dante (*DEL* 1. 204–13)

**c.1737–40** Thomas Gray's verse translation of the Ugolino episode (*Inf.* 33. 1–77)

**1753–77** Giuseppe Baretti (Italian resident in England) publishes critical work on Dante, including responses to Voltaire's criticisms (*DEL* 1. 256–74)

**c.1755–60** William Huggins's complete verse translation of the *Commedia* (lost)

**1767–9** First complete translation of *Commedia* into German prose, by Leberecht Bachenschwanz, a Dresden lawyer, 'condemned by modern critics in no equivocal terms' (Friederich 1950: 365)

**1773** Joshua Reynolds's painting of 'Ugolino and his Sons' exhibited

**1774–81** Detailed references to Dante and his influence in Thomas Warton's *The History of English Poetry* (*DEL* 1. 279–97)

**1780–2** First German verse translation of *Inferno* by Christian Joseph Jagemann, a former monk; described as 'iambic water-gruel' (Friederich 1950: 373)

**1782** Charles Rogers (art collector) publishes first complete English translation of the *Inferno* (blank verse)

**1784–91** Three-volume edition of *Commedia* by Andrea Rubbi (Venetian Jesuit), in the *Parnaso italiano* series

**1785– 1802** Henry Boyd (clergyman) publishes *Inferno* and then (1802) the first complete English translation of the *Commedia* (in six-line stanzas)

**1792–3** John Flaxman produces 110 drawings to illustrate the *Commedia* (engraved and printed at Rome in 1793)

**1800–5** Pencil and ink designs for *Inferno* and *Purgatorio* by Josef Anton Koch, Austrian artist resident in Rome; also watercolours of Paolo and Francesca (1805–10, 1823)

**1802–3**      August Wilhelm Schlegel discusses structure and number-symbolism of the *Commedia* in lectures on literature and art at Berlin (excerpt translated in Caesar 1989: 421–6); also translated episodes from *Commedia* and several of Dante's lyrics (Friederich 1950: 376–81)

**1805–6**      Henry F. Cary publishes translation of *The Inferno of Dante Alighieri* (blank verse)

**1806**      Henry Fuseli's painting of 'Ugolino and his Sons' exhibited

**1808**      First Italian editions of *Commedia* published in England (by G. Boschini and R. Zotti)

**1814**      Henry F. Cary publishes complete translation of *The Vision; or Hell, Purgatory, and Paradise, of Dante Alighieri* (begun 16 Jan. 1797, completed 8 May 1812) (blank verse)

**1815**      Hazlitt's discussion of Dante and other Italian poets in *Edinburgh Review*; Silvio Pellico's tragedy *Francesca da Rimini* staged at La Scala, Milan

**1816**      Leigh Hunt, *The Story of Rimini* (story of Francesca in four cantos)

**1818**      27 February, Coleridge's lecture on Dante; Ugo Foscolo's articles on Dante for the *Edinburgh Review*

**1818–19**      Niccolò Giosafatte Biagioli's edition of the *Commedia*, published in Paris

**1819**      J. A. D. Ingres's oil painting of Paolo and Francesca painted at Rome and exhibited at the Paris Salon (one of his 18 paintings and drawings of the subject); April, Keats's sonnet on *Inf.* 5 ('As Hermes once . . .')

**1819/20**      Byron's translation of *Inf.* 5. 97–142 ('Fanny of Rimini') and *The Prophecy of Dante* (1820, published 1821)

**1820–2**      Shelley, translation of *Purg.* 28. 1–51 (1820), *Epipsychidion* and *Defence of Poetry* (1821), *The Triumph of Life* (1822)

**1824–7**      William Blake's illustrations for the *Commedia* (102 watercolours, seven engravings)

**1832**      Gabriele Rossetti's *Spirito antipapale*, on Dante as radical reformer (translated in 1834 as *Disquisitions on the Antipapal Spirit*)

**1833–50**      Tennyson's *In Memoriam*, 'a sort of *Divine Comedy*', and *Ulysses* (published 1842)

**1837**      W. E. Gladstone's translation of the Ugolino story (*Inf.* 33. 1–78)

**1838–40**      Thomas Carlyle's discussions of Dante in *Lectures on the History of Literature* (1838) and *On Heroes, Hero Worship and the Heroic in History* (1840)

**1839**      A. F. Ozanam, *Dante et la philosophie catholique au treizième siècle*, scholarly approach to the intellectual context

**1842**      Margaret Fuller, translator and friend of R. W. Emerson, undertakes translation of *Vita nuova* but does not complete; Emerson publishes his version in 1843

**1843**      First published American translation of the *Inferno*, cantos 1–10, by Thomas William Parsons (in quatrains; Cunningham 1965)

**1846–62**      Various translations of the *Vita nuova* into English: Joseph Garrow (1846), Dante Gabriel Rossetti (1861), Theodore Martin (1862)

**1848–52**      D. G. Rossetti's poem 'Dante at Verona'

**1849**      J. A. Carlyle's prose translation of the *Inferno*, subsequently revised (by H. Oelsner) for the Temple Classics parallel text edition (1899–1901)

**1851**      John Ruskin's discussion of Dante as 'central man of all the world' in *The Stones of Venice*

**1855**      G. H. Boker's play *Francesca da Rimini* premiered in New York (revived in 1882 and 1901)

**1861–6**      Gustave Doré's wood-block engravings for the *Commedia* (*DE* 318A–B; Columbia Digital Dante online)

**1863–76**   George Eliot's novels allude to and quote from Dante: *Romola* (1863); *Felix Holt* (1866; prologue); *Middlemarch* (1871–2; epigraphs to chs. 19, 54); *Daniel Deronda* (1876; epigraphs to chs. 55, 64)

**1865**   May, celebrations in Florence of the sixth centenary of Dante's birth, reported for English readers by H. C. Barlow (Caesar 1989: 620–4), also in two Italian journals of 1864–5, *Giornale del centenario* and *Festa di Dante*; foundation of the Deutsche Dante-Gesellschaft, first of the Dante Societies

**1867**   H. W. Longfellow's translation of the *Commedia* (begun in 1845)

**1870–1**   Francesco de Sanctis's discussion of Dante in *Storia della letteratura italiana*

**1871**   Maria Francesca Rossetti, *A Shadow of Dante: Being an Essay Towards Studying Himself, his World and his Pilgrimage*), six editions up to 1894

**1874**   James Thomson, *The City of Dreadful Night*, poetic version of *Inferno* and 'a reverse image of Ruskin's utopian stones of Venice' (*Milbank 1998: 112)

**1876**   Tchaikovsky, *Francesca da Rimini*, op. 32, symphonic poem; foundation of the Oxford Dante Society

**1877**   Margaret Oliphant, *Dante* (introduction with passages of translation from *Inferno*, *Purgatorio* and *Paradiso*), six editions up to 1898

**1880**   Auguste Rodin's sculpture 'The Gates of Hell' commissioned

**1881**   Foundation of Dante Society of America (Longfellow as president); *Monarchia* removed from Index of Prohibited Books

**1884**   Christina Rossetti, *Dante: The Poet Illustrated out of the Poem*

**1888**   Società dantesca italiana (Italian Dante Society) founded in Florence

| | |
|---|---|
| **1896** | W. B. Yeats's three-part essay on 'William Blake and his Illustrations' in the *Savoy*: part 2 on Blake's 'Opinions on Dante' (Aug.) and part 3 on 'The Illustrators of Dante' (Sep.) |
| **1899–1901** | Temple Classics (parallel-text) edition of the *Commedia*, ed. P. Wicksteed and H. Oelsner, widely circulated and used by Ezra Pound, T. S. Eliot, W. H. Auden and Louis MacNeice |
| **1901** | Gabriele D'Annunzio's play *Francesca da Rimini* staged at Rome, subsequently in New York (1902) and Milan (1927) |
| **1906** | *The Dante calendar, representing incidents in the life of Dante Alighieri*, with quotations from Dante in English for each month; January, première of Rachmaninov's *Francesca da Rimini*, opera in two tableaux, with libretto by Modest Tschaikowsky |
| **1908–9** | Early short films on Francesca, Ugolino and La Pia (*Purg*. 5. 130–6) |
| **1910** | Pound's *The Spirit of Romance*, with chapter on Dante stressing the importance of *DVE* |
| **1911** | Milano Films 54-scene *Inferno* (Padovan/Bertolini), internationally successful |
| **1914** | R. Zandonai's opera *Francesca da Rimini*, with libretto by T. Ricordi, based on D'Annunzio's 1901 play; James Joyce's *Dubliners*, with a number of allusions to Dante (e.g., in 'Araby' and 'Grace'), published in London, whilst in Trieste Joyce is writing *A Portrait of the Artist*, which appropriates *VN* and the *Paradiso* |
| **1917–22** | T. S. Eliot's collections of poems, *Prufrock and Other Observations* (1917), *Ara vus prec* (1920) and *The Waste Land* (1922), with epigraphs, quotations and allusions from Dante, and the essay on 'Dante' in *The Sacred Wood* (1920) |
| **1917–60** | Pound's 116 *Cantos*, taking Dante's journey as model |
| **1922–39** | Joyce's *Finnegans Wake* ranges through the poem of 'the divine comic Denti Alligator' (thus described on p. 440; London, 1975) |

1924 Henry Otto's silent movie *Dante's Inferno* (Fox studios): cruel capitalist converted by reading Dante

1925 Yeats's *A Vision* sets out 'phases' of history, presenting Dante as 'poet [who] saw all things set in order' (p. 143; New York 1958) and opposing him to Pound

1927 Samuel Beckett takes his student edition of the *Commedia* on holiday to Italy; it will also be his holiday reading in 1971 and 1975

1929–30 T. S. Eliot's *Dante* (1929), his most extended critical essay on the subject, and *Ash Wednesday* (1930), appropriating *Purgatorio* and *VN* and quoting *Purg.* 26. 147; Beckett's essay 'Dante . . . Bruno . . . Vico . . . Joyce' (1929), on parallels between Dante and Joyce

1932 Auden begins epic modelled on the *Commedia* (abandoned in 1933; Spears 1985: 84; ed. McDiarmid 1978)

1933 Osip Mandelstam's 'Conversation about Dante' (published in 1960s)

1934 Beckett's story collection *More Pricks than Kicks* introduces the character of Belacqua (*Purg.* 4. 103–35), who is to reappear in his later novels *Murphy* (1938), *Watt* (1945) and *Molloy* (1951) and at the end of *Company* (1980)

1935 Harry Lachman's *Dante's Inferno* (Fox studios), with spectacular 10-minute Hell sequence

1938 Giuseppe Ungharetti's essay *Dante e Virgilio* on *Inf.* 3 and *Aen.* 6, published as 'Dante et Virgile' in *Innocence et mémoire* (Paris, 1969); Pound corresponds with Laurence Binyon about the latter's *terza rima* translation of the *Commedia* (published 1933–43; see Fitzgerald 1985)

1942 T. S. Eliot composes 'Little Gidding', the last of *Four Quartets* (published 1943–4)

1943–5 Vittorio Sereni's poems about his POW experiences in *Diario d'Algeria* (published 1947) evoke the *Purgatorio* (Robinson 1998)

**1944**     Spencer Williams, African-American film-maker, uses material from the Milano Films *Inferno* of 1911 in his fable of 'the Battle of GOOD AGAINST EVIL' *Go Down Death* (Looney 2004)

**c.1948**   Jorge Luis Borges completes *Nueve ensayos dantescas*, essays on Dante (published in 1982)

**1949**     Derek Walcott's early poem *Epitaph for the Young* published in Barbados; in 1977 Walcott acknowledges Dante among the 'visible, deliberately quoted influences here' (Balfour 1998: 224)

**1949–62**  Dorothy L. Sayers's translation of the *Commedia* published in Penguin Classics (*Paradiso* completed by Barbara Reynolds)

**1950**     T. S. Eliot gives a talk called 'What Dante Means to Me' to the Italian Institute (later published in *To Criticize the Critic* [Eliot 1965]); Walcott's radio play *Senza alcun sospetto,* based on latter half of *Inf.* 5 (Balfour 1998: 227)

**1951–2**   Salvador Dalí issues 100 lithograph illustrations, one for each canto of the *Commedia* (*DE* 244A–245A; Columbia Digital Dante online)

**1954**     MacNeice publishes *Autumn Sequel,* 26 cantos appropriating form and structure of the *Commedia* (Ellis 1998); John Ciardi publishes *The Inferno: A New Translation* (New York), a best-selling version in partial *terza rima,* followed by his *Purgatorio* (1961) and *Paradiso* (1970)

**1956**     Andrzej Wajda's *Kanal* traces an infernal journey by resistance fighters at the end of the 1944 Warsaw rising; part of the director's *Ashes and Diamonds* trilogy

**1959–75**  The *Commedia* provides 'a structuring informing model' for much of Pier Paolo Pasolini's work in film, fiction and poetry, from 'La mortaccia' (story, 1959) and *La divina mimesis* (novel, 1961) to *Salò* (film, 1975) (Rumble 2004: 153)

1960 Pound concludes the *Cantos* with quotation from Dante's *sestina*, 'Al poco giorno ed al gran cerchio d'ombra' (Canto 116)

1962 Giorgio Bassani's novel *Il giardino dei Finzi Contini* quotes the *Commedia*, but uses *VN* as its 'key text' (Woolf 1998)

1964 Antonioni's *Deserto rosso* ('Red Desert') alludes to Dante's Ravenna (Kirkham 2004)

1965 LeRoi Jones (Amiri Baraka), *The System of Dante's Hell*

1972 Wole Soyinka's collection of poems *A Shuttle in the Crypt* includes prison-poem, 'Purgatory'

1972–83 Beckett's late 'dramaticules' (especially *Not I* [1972]), where the *Inferno* 'comes to dominate [his] later theatrical imagination' (Elam 1994: 145)

1975–94 Canadian film-maker Bruce Elder directs a screen version of the *Commedia* running to over 40 hours: *The Book of All the Dead*

1976–83 Tom Phillips translates, designs and illustrates the *Inferno* (four prints per canto), published by Talfourd Press in 1983

1979– Seamus Heaney's collection *Fieldwork* (1979) begins a dialogue with Dante that continues through translation of the first three cantos of *Inferno* (early 1980s), to *Station Island* (1984), 'Envies and Identifications' (1985), *Seeing Things* (1991), *The Spirit Level* (1995), *Electric Light* (2001), possibly also *District and Circle* (2006)

1982 Sidney Nolan produces two sets of 30 illustrations for Dante's *Inferno* (Duckworth 2006)

1985 Gloria Naylor's novel *Linden Hills* reconstructs the *Inferno* in a prosperous African-American suburb

1986 David Lynch's *Blue Velvet*: the *Inferno* beneath the lawns of suburbia

1988 100-part *lectura Dantis* on the *Commedia* produced by the Dipartimento Scuola Educazione of RAI, Italian TV ('bookish television'; Iannucci 1989: 9)

**1989–91**   Federico Tiezzi directs theatrical version of the *Commedia* by three Italian poets at Prato and Bari: *Commedia dell'Inferno: un travestimento dantesco* (Sanguineti, 1989); *Il Purgatorio: la notte lava la mente* (Luzi, 1990) and *Il Paradiso: perché mi vinse il lume d'esta stella* (Guidici, 1991)

**1990**   Walcott's *Omeros*, 'a poem full of ghostly encounters', includes *Malebolge*-like sequence in Book 7 (Balfour 1998: 234–6); July, *A TV Dante* (Peter Greenaway and Tom Phillips) broadcast on Channel 4 – video version of the first eight cantos of *Inferno*; pilot version of *Inf.* 5 in 1984; series completed and shown in Netherlands, West Germany and Italy in 1988: 'A good old text is always a blank for new things' (Phillips's opening comment)

**1993**   Douglas Dunn uses *terza rima* ('Dante's drum-kit') for an extended poem about forms of afterlife: 'Disenchantments' in *Dante's Drum-kit* (pp. 31–46; London, 1993]); Ecco Press in USA publishes translation of *Inferno* by 20 poets (cantos 1–3 by Heaney), ed. Daniel Halpern

**1994**   Translations of *Inferno* by Steve Ellis (blank verse) and Robert Pinsky (partial *terza rima*)

**1995**   David Fincher's film *Se7en* cites and alludes to Dante (Iannucci 2004: 15–16)

**1997**   Issue on *Dante, Ezra Pound and the Contemporary Poet* published by the poetry magazine *Agenda*, ed. W. Cookson (vol. 34, nos. 3–4)

**2000**   Heaney's poem 'A Dream of Solstice', published on front page of the *Irish Times* (18 January), begins with translation of *Paradiso* 33. 58–61; Philippe Sollers publishes *La Divine Comédie: entretiens avec Benoit Chantre*, a 700-page conversation about the *Commedia*, raising such questions as 'Why does no one read the *Paradiso*?' (answer on p. 548; Paris, 2000)

**2001**   Conference and film festival *Dante and Cinema* organized by University of Toronto Humanities centre (30 March–7 April) (Iannucci 2004: vii); publication of *The Poets' Dante*, including essays and excerpts from Pound, Yeats, Eliot, Mandelstam, Borges, Auden, Robert Duncan, James Merrill, Heaney, W. S. Merwin and Pinsky (Hawkins and Jacoff 2001)

2001–2     Monika Beisner's illustrations to *Die Göttliche Komödie* published in Leipzig (Hawkins 2006: 149, cover illustration, and plates 1–4)

2002     Translations of the *Inferno* by Ciaran Carson and Michael Palma (both in forms of *terza rima*); *Divina Commedia* dance-mime show by Derevo company (at Edinburgh and London, Aug.–Sep.)

2003     *The Dante Club* by Matthew Pearl, a nineteenth-century murder mystery, set in Boston, featuring Longfellow and a cast of Boston Brahmins; *In the Hand of Dante* by Nick Tosches, involving the New York mob, Dante, Nick Tosches and an autograph MS of the *Commedia*

2003–5     Sandow Birk and Marcus Sanders, *The Divine Comedy* (San Francisco), a three-volume 'paraphrase' using 'California-inflected youth-speak' (Hawkins 2006: 154–9 and figs. 9, 11)

2004–5     Giulio Leoni's two crime novels in which 'Dante Alighieri investigates': *I delitti del mosaico* (2004) and *I delitti della luce* (2005)

2005     Jean-Luc Godard's *Notre musique*, version of Hell, Purgatory and Paradise, using news-reel footage and clips from westerns; Cristi Puiu's *The Death of Mr Lazarescu*, the infernal journey through the Bucharest health-system by the dying Dante Lazarescu (released in the UK in 2006; 'one of the best films of the year', *Independent, Information*, 19 August 2006)

2006     March, promenade production of *Inferno* at the Arches, Glasgow; translation of *Inferno* by Robin Kirkpatrick (blank verse); *Dante's Inferno: A Puppet Movie* (Sandow Birk and Paul Zaloom)

# Commentary, Criticism, Canonization

Dante himself wrote a considerable amount of 'self-commentary'. Before the *Commedia* we find him contextualizing and analysing his own love-poems in the *Vita nuova*, drawing examples from both his own and others' writing during his discussion of vernacular eloquence in *DVE*, and using his own *canzoni* as departure points for three of the four treatises in the *Convivio*. In the *Commedia* itself, some kinds of discourse function as commentary on episodes or issues in the narrative. Debate about the *Commedia* was well under way in Dante's own lifetime; and he himself wrote verse letters about his poem (above, p. 50). Debate also still rages about his authorship of the Latin prose letter to his patron Cangrande della Scala, in which the writer dedicates the *Paradiso* to the *signore* of Verona and offers 'in the capacity of commentator . . . a few words by way of introduction to the work' (above, p. 46). Whether or not Dante wrote this letter, it provides a starting point for discussion of commentary on and early reception of his work.

Language is one of the most important of the issues in the 'Epistle to Cangrande'. Dante wrote his prose treatises on the vernacular, politics and science (*DVE, Mon., Quaestio de aqua et terra*), together with his prose and verse letters in Latin, with a largely academic, administrative or learned aristocratic readership in mind. His decision to use Tuscan rather than Latin for the *Commedia* may seem to us to follow quite naturally from his achievements in vernacular love-poetry, but it was a contentious issue from the start. One academic correspondent, Giovanni del Virgilio (above, p. 50), was worried about the poem being 'sounded tritely on the lips of women' and 'croaked forth . . . at street corners' (Dante 1902: 146–9). Later, Petrarch in 1359 and some of the Italian humanists around the end of the *trecento* expressed concern about it being subjected to the 'windy applause of the masses' or the enthusiasm of 'cloth-workers, bakers, cobblers' and others. Even Boccaccio had misgivings on the subject and conceded that the *Commedia* might have been yet better if written in Latin (Havely 1997: 74–6; *Minnis and Scott 1988: 507–8).

At the same time, there was also recognition that the *Commedia*'s vernacular was a response to the demands of an aspiring and expanding lay audience, including 'women-folk' (*Letters* nos. 177, 201). Among the *Inferno*'s earliest commentators was the Carmelite friar **Guido da Pisa**, writing around 1328–33 (*DE* 463B–464A). Guido neatly combines his view of the *Commedia* as a work of prophetic authority with awareness of this wider readership when he stresses that Dante is here writing 'on a wall, that is, in an open and public place, for the benefit of all' (Minnis and Scott 1988: 470). And in the 1370s, Boccaccio concluded the introduction to his lectures on the *Commedia* by asserting that it had been begun in Latin but then fashioned to conform, 'at least in its outer shell, with the intellectual capacities of contemporary noblemen' (Minnis and Scott 1988: 519).

A number of other questions – about the form, style, content and status of the *Commedia* – are raised in the Epistle to Cangrande and developed in the early commentaries. The Epistle deals, for example, with the ways in which the meanings of this 'polysemous' text can be read; with the significance of its title, genre and style as 'comedy'; and with its subject matter, including its ethical, contemplative and prophetic features. Guido da Pisa also takes up such questions but in a different order: first developing the parallels between Dante and prophets such as Daniel and Ezekiel (suggested at the end of the Epistle) and then turning to levels of meaning, form of treatment, genre and the four 'senses' of allegory (Minnis and Scott 1988: 469–76; Caesar 1989: 122–30). Among the other most important and attentive early commentaries is that produced (in several versions) by the poet's second son, **Pietro Alighieri**; *DE* 20B–21B). In his prologue Pietro also deals amongst much else with the levels of allegory, form, genre and style, whilst emphasizing the poem's 'fictitious and imaginary' qualities, rather than its prophetic status (Minnis and Scott 1988: 476–84).

At least six other commentaries on the *Commedia* are known to have appeared within 20 years of Dante's death in 1321: some, like those of Guido and Pietro, acknowledge the status of the poem by writing about it in Latin; others address the vernacular in the vernacular. The critical industry continued to develop in both languages during the later fourteenth century – for example through Boccaccio's public lectures of 1373–4 on the first 16

227

cantos of the *Inferno*, and through the major commentaries on the whole *Commedia* by Benvenuto da Imola and Francesco da Buti (Minnis and Scott 1988: 442, 453–8; Caesar 1989: 6–9, 12–15, 176–82).

Commentaries like Guido's were often contained in manuscripts of the poem – but circulation of the *Commedia* itself was far wider. The *Inferno* was available to readers by around 1315 and the *Purgatorio* before 1320. Between then and the appearance of the first printed editions in 1472 a vast number of manuscripts were produced; and it has been estimated that the surviving number of those containing some part of the *Commedia* exceeds 800 (*DE* 199A). Some of these were de luxe copies, destined for wealthy clerical or aristocratic patrons – such as one of those containing Guido da Pisa's commentary and dating from the 1340s (Minnis and Scott 1988: 447), or the one which Giovanni di Paolo illustrated around 1445 (above, p. 175). Many more, however, were produced in large quantities for (and sometimes even by) less exalted groups of readers – such as notaries and merchants (*DE* 198B–200A; S. Gilson 2005: 7–8, 241).

The early popularity of the *Commedia* contrasts with the relatively limited circulation of Dante's other works. There are 46 extant manuscripts of the *Convivio* (with the first printed edition appearing in 1490), and 80 which contain some part of the *Vita nuova* (poems first printed in 1527 and the complete work in 1576). Of the Latin works, far fewer manuscripts survive: about 20 for the *Monarchia* (first printed in 1559); and only three for *DVE* (printed first in 1577). The early circulation of *Monarchia* – with its fierce critique of the church's temporal wealth and power – was, however, affected by some quite special circumstances: some time between 1327 and 1334 it was comprehensively censured by a Dominican friar and was condemned to be burnt (along with the poet's remains) by the pope's legate in 1328 or 1329 (Caesar 1989: 3, 110–14; Kay 1998: xxxi–xxxv).

Circulation of the *Commedia* during the later fourteenth and fifteenth centuries extended beyond Italy especially to Spain, France and England; and the ways in which it did so are strikingly varied. In Spain, not much more than a century after Dante's death, there are direct translations, both of the poem itself into the Castilian and Catalan vernaculars and of several of the commentaries (including Pietro Alighieri and Benevenuto da Imola) into Castilian (Friederich 1950: 14–28; *DE* 279B–280A). The first complete French printed translation of the *Commedia* did not appear until 1596, but Italian manuscripts and editions of the poem had appeared in France around the turn of the fifteenth and sixteenth centuries; several translations in manuscript date from that time; whilst French writers such as Froissart and

Christine de Pisan had been alluding to and citing Dante already in the later fourteenth century (Friederich 1950: 58–64, 85–6; *DE* 259 A–B).

We do not know the precise form in which the text of the *Commedia* first reached England, but the earliest writer in English to refer to it and its author is **Geoffrey Chaucer**, who first cites 'Daunte' as one of the authorities on the torments of Hell in a dream-poem of the late 1370s or early 1380s, *The House of Fame* (Havely 1994a: 13–15 and lines 445–50). Chaucer also alludes to and appropriates the *Commedia* on numerous later occasions, in his shorter works and the *Troilus* (below, p. 252), as well as in the *Canterbury Tales* (*Boitani 1983; Wetherbee 1984; Taylor 1989). Some of his imitations of passages or episodes from the *Commedia* – such as his version of the Ugolino story in the *Monk's Tale* (below, p. 245) or his rewritings of St Bernard's invocation to the Virgin (*Par.* 33. 1–21) – come close to translation, and as a 'great translator' himself he would have been interested in making the work of this illustrious vernacular author accessible to a wider audience.

Initially, that widening of access was to involve the clergy and academia, through the translation of the *Commedia* into Latin – the language in which some academics (such as Giovanni del Virgilio) thought it ought anyway to have been written. A Latin verse translation in hexameters was completed by a Venetian Benedictine monk, Matteo Ronto, in Tuscany around 1392 and is found in seven manuscripts, but it was not well received and 'the veil of oblivion very quickly descended over his works'(*ED* 4. 1037). A more influential Latin version was to be produced in the second decade of the fifteenth by a Franciscan bishop, **Giovanni da Serravalle**. At the Council of Constance (1415–17), convened to resolve the schism in the church, Serravalle gave lectures on Dante and was encouraged by two English bishops and an Italian cardinal to produce a translation of and commentary upon the *Commedia* (Friederich 1950: 190). He completed this enormous task speedily during the 'down-time' at this conference (Wallace 1999). His version was circulated in England and Germany during the fifteenth century and even as late as the seventeenth (Friederich 1950: 201, 342). By the start of the sixteenth century, then, the *Commedia* was quite widely available in translations, as well as in manuscripts, editions with commentaries, and the portable plain text published by Aldo Manuzio at Venice in 1502 (Parker 1993: 137–41; Richardson 1995: 241–4).

Yet Dante was not – and would not for some while be – an indisputably canonical poet. In sixteenth-century Italy, especially, he continues to be 'the poet of the powerful' (Richardson 1995: 247); and in northern Europe he

229

is, as we shall see, taken up by Protestant polemicists as a stick with which to beat the papacy (below, p. 243). But from the sixteenth to the later eighteenth centuries his reputation both at home and abroad was largely overshadowed by other Italian writers, notably Petrarch (Caesar 1989: 31–42; Parker 1993: 132, 216). For some writers over this period, including some Italians, the mixed genre and style of the *Commedia* presented serious aesthetic and critical problems (Caesar 1989: 26, 31–4, 35–42). Such concerns are expressed, for example, by the complaint about the *Inferno*'s 'base and filthie talke' in a late sixteenth-century English translation of an Italian book of manners; by Voltaire's mid-eighteenth-century comments on the *Commedia* as 'bizarre', a 'hotchpotch' and a 'monster' (*DEL* 1. 161–2 and 205–10). Over the course of the eighteenth century, developments in scholarship and changing attitudes towards 'Gothic' primitivism and emotionalism helped to challenge the neo-classical attitudes of critics like Voltaire (Caesar 1989: 43–9). British intellectuals, connoisseurs and aristocratic travellers came to include material on Dante as part of the package of Italian culture; and towards the end of the century the first full English translations of the *Inferno* and then of the whole *Commedia* at last began to appear (De Sua 1964: 1–21; Tinkler-Villani 1989: 59–172).

In the early nineteenth century, **Coleridge**'s criticism reflects some of the key attitudes and interests that were by now favouring Dante's rehabilitation. Coleridge's 1818 lectures convey an interest in the Middle Ages as different rather than inferior, together with a strong response to 'the passion and miracle of words' in Dante's time and to the *Commedia*'s 'picturesqueness', 'topographic reality' and 'absolute mastery over . . . the pathetic' (*DEL* 1. 620–1 and 624–5). By the time of these lectures the Romantic resurrection of Dante – or at least of the *Commedia* – was well under way, especially in Britain, France and Germany, and was even seen by some as becoming something of a cult. In the same year, **Byron**'s friend and companion John Cam Hobhouse records a member of the London publishing house of Longman pronouncing definitively that 'the world was sick of Dante' (Hobhouse's MS diary for 4 December 1818). For many, this surfeit resulted from only a limited intake of text. In a letter of 7 August 1820 to his mistress, Teresa Guiccioli, Byron remarked that Dante 'is now all the fashion', and he was himself notoriously obsessed with the story of Francesca; but, unlike Shelley, he showed relatively little interest in the *Purgatorio* or the *Paradiso* (below, p. 259). Around the same time the tetchy and erudite exile Niccolò Giosafatte Biagioli, who published an edition of the *Commedia* at Paris in 1818–19, was complaining (in a note on *Inferno* 5) that foreign readers were concentrating far too much on the sensational stories of Francesca and Ugolino alone.

For some Romantic writers, such as Coleridge, Dante was already a canonical author. The German critic and translator A. W. Schlegel, writing in 1802–3, described him as 'one of those gigantic figures of Antiquity who casts a shadow across our age . . . the first great Romantic poet' (Caesar 1989: 420; Friederich 1950: 375–83). In 1805–6, **H. F. Cary**, introducing his translation of the *Inferno* – the first part of what would become the standard version for poets such as Wordsworth, Coleridge and Keats – offered it to the public in order 'to facilitate the study of one of the most sublime and moral, but certainly one of the most obscure writers in any language' (*DEL* 469; Tinkler-Villani 1989: 173–238; Braida 2004: 27–55). One of the most influential critics among the Italian exiles in Britain during this period, **Ugo Foscolo**, in the second of his *Edinburgh Review* articles on Dante (September 1818), showed how the poet through traditional means had 'conceived and executed the project of creating the Language and the Poetry of a nation' (*DEL* 2. 165). Both of the Shelleys included the whole of the *Commedia* and the *Vita nuova* in their reading programme during 1818–20 (Feldman and Scott-Kilvert 1987: 1. 246–7, 295–7 and 351–7). In *A Defence of Poetry* (1821), **Percy Shelley** then placed Dante among 'modern writers' who are 'philosophers of the very loftiest power', asserting that he 'understood the secret things of love even more than Petrarch' and that his poetry as a whole 'may be considered as the bridge thrown over the stream of time, which unites the modern and the ancient world' (*DEL* 2. 225–6).

Some influential voices during the first two decades of the nineteenth century were thus insisting on Dante's canonical status; yet even in the England and Italy of Shelley's and Foscolo's time his 'cultural centrality was not assured' (*Pite 1994: 166). By the middle of the century, however – with the establishment of Dante as national poet and 'author of the schools', and with the development of the Victorian cult of Beatrice and the *Vita nuova* (translated by **Dante Gabriel Rossetti** and a number of others around this time) – that centrality was established (*Ellis 1983: 102–34; Milbank 1998: 1–6, 29–44). In 1851, **John Ruskin**'s key work on medieval and renaissance art, *The Stones of Venice*, identified the year in which the *Commedia* is set (1300) as the 'central year about which we may consider the energy of the middle ages to be gathered' and asserted that 'the central man of all the world, as representing in perfect balance the imaginative, moral, and intellectual faculties, all at their highest, is Dante' (Ruskin 1851: 2. 342, 3. 158).

The confidence of this assertion is backed by the evidence of publishers' returns. Between 1849 and 1864 the *Commedia* was by far the best-selling title on the list of one of the major Florentine publishing firms (Caesar 1989: 66–7). In 1865 the sixth centenary of the poet's death and the commemorations at Florence (then the capital of the newly reunited Italy) further stimulated demand for editions, translations, critical studies and popular introductions (Caesar 1989: 70–2). And, as a recent exhibition has demonstrated, 'from the end of the nineteenth century into the twentieth, numerous popular objects were produced to satisfy the appetite created by the fashionable cult of Dante, including calendars, diaries, almanacs and prayer books. Several books retelling Dante for children were also published' (Cambridge University Library 2006: 24–5).

The later nineteenth-century and modern reception of Dante in the English-speaking world has itself been the subject of a growing number of critical studies. Following the important work by Ellis (1983), covering the ground between Browning and Eliot, recent critical studies have included Milbank's *Dante and the Victorians* (1998), as well as several further monographs on responses to Dante by individual poets, such as Eliot, Heaney and Walcott (*Manganiello 1989; *Fumagalli 2001). Collections of essays dealing with all or some of this period have been edited by *McDougal (1985a), *Havely (1998) and *Haywood (2003). And to complement the already monumental collections of material edited by *Toynbee (*DEL*) and Caesar (1989), two more anthologies have recently appeared: one of critical writing on Dante by modern American, British, Irish, Italian and Russian poets (*Hawkins and Jacoff 2001); and one of verse translations and imitations mostly from 1800 onwards (*Griffiths and Reynolds 2005).

More attention is also being given to the impact of Dante's work on other media (the visual arts, film and television) and on other literary genres besides poetry (such as drama and the novel). Dante's presence in modern and contemporary poetry will be considered later in this section; but first the importance of other media, such as illustration and performance, also need to be reckoned with.

# Picturing and Performing the *Commedia*

Dante himself drew on the resources of contemporary visual and performative culture in several ways (above, pp. 64–6). There are also close connections between his poetry and the visual and performing arts from his own time to the present, as a forthcoming collection of essays will show (Braida and Calé). Here, meanwhile, we shall identify some of the ways in which the picturing and the performing of that poetry have developed and how on some occasions they have worked together.

Visual art that Dante could have seen before and during his exile included the images of Heaven and Hell in the Baptistery at Florence; Giotto's frescoes at Padua; and the mosaics of the emperor Justinian and of Christ with the Apostles at Ravenna (above, pp. 4, 32, 49; and plates 1 and 2, pp. 4, 33). His interest in this form of creativity is reflected, for example, in his account of 'drawing the figure of an angel' on the anniversary of Beatrice's death (*VN* ch. 34) and in his references to divine art and human art in cantos 10 and 11 of the *Purgatorio* (above, pp. 168, 199; and plate 7, p. 169). The way in which he expresses and represents these interests seems itself to have acted as a stimulus to later artists, from the early illuminators onwards (*DE* 250A–251B).

The *Commedia* posed a serious challenge to such artists from the start. The task of representing not only the metamorphoses of the thieves in *Inferno* 25 and the divine art of *Purgatorio* 10 but also the constant and various play of light in the *Paradiso* was one that few, if any, of the *Commedia*'s illustrators have been able fully to sustain. Amongst the 800 or so manuscripts containing all or part of the *Commedia* some 370 contain drawings, coloured initials or decoration, about 130 have miniatures at the start of each *cantica*, and 60 make some attempt to represent scenes canto by canto (*Owen 2001: 163). Of these only about 30 achieve anything like a full programme of illustrations. One of the finest of the early illustrated codices is a **Pisan** presentation copy of the 1340s (Chantilly, Musée Condé MS 597), which contains the commentary by Guido da Pisa (above, p. 227) and is limited to the *Inferno* (BMS 1. 52–70 and 216–19; Minnis and Scott 1988: 447; above, plate 6, p. 166). Around 1370 a talented and inventive **Neapolitan** artist produced 47 illustrations for the *Inferno* and up to canto 22 of the *Purgatorio*, handing over to another illustrator for the remainder of the *cantica* (London, BL Add. 19587; BMS 1. 258–61; above, plate 7, p. 169). Even more impressive in its detail and modelling of figures and landscape is the magnificent set of illustrations produced by a **Lombard** master probably for Filippo Maria Visconti, duke of Milan, around 1440 (Paris, BN MS it. 2017/Imola, Bibl. Com. MS 32; BMS 1. 318–21 and 2 with colour plate XVI). This comprises over 70 miniatures, but since it gives more attention than most to each canto (three illustrations for Geryon in *Inf.* 17, five for the thieves in *Inf.* 25), it does not get beyond the *Inferno*. Failure to complete the programme is not uncommon or surprising; even though artists were often working as a team and following traditional modes of portrayal, doing justice to all or most of the poem's 100 cantos would have been a daunting project.

Of the complete programmes, the most striking are those produced by known artists in the mid- and later fifteenth century. The de luxe copy presented to King Alfonso of Naples (London, BL Yates Thompson MS 36) was illustrated in Siena around 1442–50 by Priamo della Quercia or Nicola da Siena, who painted the *Inferno* and *Purgatorio* miniatures, and by **Giovanni di Paolo** and assistants, who, around 1445–50, painted those for the *Paradiso* (above, p. 175; BMS 1. 70–80 and 269–76; Pope-Hennessy 1993; above, plates 8 and 9, pp. 175, 208). Although not the most dynamic of the Dantean illustrators, Giovanni di Paolo was undaunted by the *Paradiso*, for which he produced over 60 miniatures. More ambitious, although not so well known, was the manuscript designed for Federigo da Montefeltro, duke of Urbino, and illustrated around 1478 (Vatican, MS Urb. lat. 365; BMS 1. 331–2). This contains 110 large framed miniatures, those for *Inferno* and *Purgatorio* being by the Ferrarese artist **Guglielmo Giraldi** and followers, who were much influenced by the perspective and modelling of figures in the work of Piero della Francesca (BMS 1. 331–2; Altcappenberg 2000: 314; above, plate 5, p. 165). These influences are put to good use, for instance, in the illustration for *Inferno* 18, where the two-way traffic of pimps and seducers, flogged on by athletic devils, recedes dizzyingly into the curve of the eighth circle's first *bolgia* (BMS 2. 214). As Owen points out, Giraldi creates 'a deep and complete landscape setting for his figures', which contrasts with the 'surprisingly traditional . . . flat and diagrammatic illustrations' produced on a much larger scale by **Sandro Botticelli** for Lorenzo di Pierfrancesco de' Medici between about 1480 and about 1495 (Owen 2001: 182]; Altcappenberg 2000: 23–9; above, plate 3, p. 156).

Botticelli's 92 surviving pen-and-ink drawings cover most of the *Commedia*. The manuscript they were designed for was probably meant to give equal prominence at each opening to the illustration and the text, and it may have been intended as a gift for 'a foreign dignitary' (Altcappenberg 2000: 23, 31, 340). Most of the drawings (85 sheets) went on a long European journey over the course of four centuries, travelling from Italy to France, then to Britain, and finally (1882) ending up in Germany (MS Hamilton 201 in the Kupferstichkabinett, Berlin). For most of this period until their reappearance in 1803 they do not seem to have been widely known, although their influence, and that of the manuscript traditions that Botticelli drew upon, was transmitted to the early printed editions through the engravings produced for the 1481 Florentine edition with commentary by Cristoforo Landino (Owen 2001: 182). The latter were based not wholly upon the drawings but on 'a collection of disparate material produced by Botticelli in connection with the *Comedy*' (Altcappenberg 2000: 331).

This long initial stage of picturing the *Commedia* – from the 1330s to the end of the fifteenth century – was shaped by a variety of traditions including that of **performing** the poem. The early illustrators may have been more familiar with the text through recitation rather than words on the page and some of their representations were perhaps 'influenced by theatrical images of the poem being performed in public' (Owen 2001: 178–80). Indeed, in a period when manuscript copies were multiplying and silent reading becoming more common, recitation was still an important medium for the circulation of texts, even to a literate public; and it is a 'reasonable, if strictly unprovable, assumption that Dante himself did recite at least his first two *cantiche* . . . in public and from memory' (*Armour 1991: 23). The poet clearly knew that his *canzoni*. such as the one Casella sings in *Purgatorio* 2 (above, p. 185), could be performed as well as read silently (*Ahern 1997: 221–6). There is also evidence that the *Commedia* quickly came to circulate among a wider audience; that members of the professional and mercantile classes who jotted down lines or phrases from the text were relying upon aural memory; and that various performances of the poem, as well as more informal domestic readings, were taking place during the fourteenth and fifteenth centuries (Ahern 1997: 226–9; S. Gilson 2005: 11). In Florence from 1373 to 1374 Boccaccio was appointed to lecture on the *Commedia* in the vernacular 'to all who [like those imagined readers of *Par.* 2. 2] desired to hear' (*omnibus audire volentibus*, according to the citizens' petition). Following common academic practice, the lecturer would read the text aloud before discussing it; and for Boccaccio's canto-by-canto series, that would have taken only about 10 minutes in each case (Havely 1997: 76–7).

Traditions of reading the *Commedia* aloud and of performing it from memory have continued into modern times, especially in Italy, where 'the natural "orality" of the text' survives (*Caputo 2004: 216). The poem reached the Italian stage in some forms in the seventeenth century – for example, through appropriation of its language in the final chorus of Trissino's tragedy *Sofonisba* in 1515 (*DE* 319) and in a better-known piece, Alessandro Striggio's libretto for **Monteverdi**'s *Orfeo*, premiered in 1607 (especially when the poet's otherworld journey begins in Act 3). The theatrical potential of some of the tragic material especially in the *Inferno* was frequently recognized, although not always successfully realized. Early examples were two versions of the **Ugolino** story (*Inf.* 32–3). The first was written early in the seventeenth century though not published till 1724 (*DE* 319B). The second was staged in 1779 at Bassano in northern Italy and described by the Irish antiquary and theatre historian Joseph Cooper Walker in 1799 (*DEL* 1. 542–5). This would have been the tragedy written by Andrea Rubbi, who was himself to produce a popular edition of the *Commedia* in 1784–91. The play does not, according to Walker or his sources, seem to have been a great hit: 'the horror attending the circumstances of a man dying of hunger through five long acts, disgusted the readers [i.e., performers] and the auditors, and the play fell to the ground' (*DEL* 1. 545).

Far more successful at the box-office was the story of Dante's **Francesca**, especially when developed into romance and tragedy, following Boccaccio's novelistic version (above, p. 180). Perhaps the best and most performable of the many plays on this subject written from the early nineteenth century onwards was the tragedy *Francesca da Rimini* by **Silvio Pellico**. Premiered at Milan in 1815 and featuring one of the great Italian actresses, Carlotta Marchionni, in her first starring role, the play was translated by **Byron** and his friend Hobhouse soon after they had arrived in Italy the following year (Havely 1994b). Although the English version has been lost, Pellico's play continued to influence a number of operas on the subject during the following century (Putignano 1994: 39–44).

236

*Plate 10*  Paolo and Francesca (*Inf.* 5), oil painting by Ary Scheffer, signed and dated 1835. © By kind permission of the Trustees of the Wallace Collection, London.

The romantic version of Francesca's story was also highly successful as a subject for Romantic visual art. Scenes of the lovers being observed by Francesca's jealous husband, or witnessed by Dante floating in an embrace on the storm of Hell's second circle (as in Keats's sonnet of April 1819), appear in a number of individual paintings and sketches, such as those by **Fuseli** (1776, 1786, 1808), **Ingres** (18 versions from about 1814 to after 1850) and **Ary Scheffer** (15 versions over the period from 1822 to 1855). Fuseli's 1808 sketch of Francesca and Paolo dancing on a terrace watched by her jealous husband in the shrubbery (at the Kunsthaus, Zürich) and Ingres's 1819 oil painting of them embracing whilst their cadaverous killer emerges from behind the arras (at the Musée Turpin de Cressy, Angers) are particularly dramatic forms of the 'lovers surprised' motif. Scheffer's is a more melancholic, Keatsian portrayal of the lovers, as martyred souls encountered in the second circle of Hell by Dante and Virgil. The 1835 version, now in the Wallace Collection, London (plate 10), was much admired, for instance by George Eliot (in a letter of 17 May 1854), and was widely circulated through engravings.

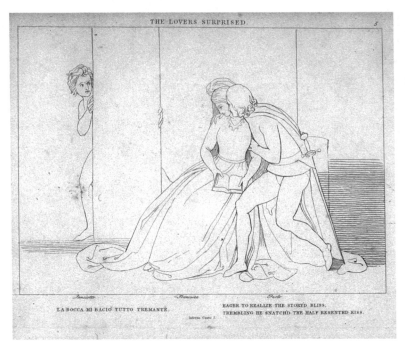

*Plate 11*   Paolo and Francesca, watched by Francesca's husband; drawing by John Flaxman RA, engraved by Tommaso Piroli, 1793. From *Compositions by John Flaxman, R. A., from the Divine poem of Dante Alighieri, containing Hell, Purgatory and Paradise* (1807) in the George Smith Special Collection, University of York.

Programmes of engravings for the whole *Commedia* also achieved wide circulation during the nineteenth century and beyond. A highly influential sequence of 110 neo-classical outline drawings was produced in 1792 by the English artist **John Flaxman**. The project was one of several programmes of illustrations (including those for Homer and Aeschylus) that resulted from his residence in Rome; and the whole Dante series was widely circulated, pirated and imitated, following its first (private) printing there in 1793 (*Miller 2003). To illustrate the episode in which the lovers, reading and kissing, are observed by Francesca's husband, Flaxman staged the action in a way that influenced many later versions of the scene, including those by Fuseli and Ingres (above, p. 237; see plate 11). Better known now – although not widely known until their exhibition in 1893 – were William Blake's great series of designs (102 watercolours, seven of them engraved), produced over the three years before his death (1824–7; Klonsky 1980: 6–8; Tinkler-Villani 1989: 261; Braida 2004: 151–78).

Blake's vigorous engagement with Dante is evident in his comments and his illustrations, both of which reflect his broader scepticism about aspects of Christian dogma (*Fuller 1988: 368). Indeed, Blake would probably have agreed with Shelley's assertion in *A Defence of Poetry* that for Dante and Milton the theological doctrines of their times 'are merely the mask and the mantle in which these great poets walk through eternity enveloped and disguised' (*DEL* 2. 226). His dialogue with Dante goes back at least as far as his own early visionary work, *The Marriage of Heaven and Hell* (engraved c.1790), in which as an argumentative traveller through the other world he encounters prophets, angels and creative devils. His approach to the *Commedia* in the designs of the 1820s is that of 'seeking to understand the poem by discovering his disagreements with it' (Pite 1994: 62). This does not mean that Blake's designs have to be interpreted solely through the symbolism of his other visionary works; indeed, it has been shown that much of his treatment of Dante's descriptions and imagery is close and 'literal' in its approach (Fuller 1988: 351). An example is the episode of Francesca in *Inferno* 5, for which Blake produced his only fully finished engraving (plate 12). He here represents the whirlwind of the second circle 'twisting and buffeting' the souls of the lustful (*Inf.* 5. 33). On the upper right in a circle of light we can see faintly the essence of the lovers' earthly existence: their first kiss and even the book. Dante himself is shown 'like a dead body' (142), with Virgil standing over him, while to the left the lovers flee away again into the storm. Blake's illustration is thus impressive in the depth and detail of its response to the text; indeed the whirlwind, breaking like a wave on the promontory where Dante lies, pointedly recalls the initial simile that has compared this circle to 'the sea in a tempest' (*Inf.* 5. 29).

More immediately successful than Blake's designs were the wood-block engravings produced by **Paul Gustave Doré** (1832–83). Like many illustrators (including Blake) Doré produced many more designs for the first *cantica* than for the other two. He published 75 plates for the *Inferno* in 1861, as against 42 for the *Purgatorio* and only 18 for the *Paradiso* (1864–6). Compared with Blake's – and as responses to Dante's text – his designs are often crude and cluttered (as in his various versions of Francesca); but he is also capable of some startling effects of spatial depth and distance (as in his rendering of the poets' descent on Geryon's back, *Inf.* 17); and he can at times reinterpret the text inventively (Cole 1995: 96–9). Doré's hugely popular images shaped the way in which the *Commedia* was visualized in the

239

*Plate 12*   William Blake, 'The Circle of the Lustful: Paolo and Francesca' (engraving, 1827; Rosenwald Collection 1943.3.5395). Image copyright © 2007, Board of Trustees National Gallery of Art, Washington.

following century; they still remain a standby for hard-pressed picture-editors and designers of book-jackets; and they are easily accessible online (the Columbia Digital Dante; below, p. 282). Their impact on early twentieth-century cinema provides a link between the visualization and the performance of the *Commedia* in the period. Contemporary critics and subsequent film historians noted the influence of Doré's designs upon the first major screen version of the poem – the Milano Films *Inferno* of 1911 – as well as on Henry Otto's *Dante's Inferno* of 1924 (Iannucci 2004: 6, 38, 40, 138, 143), whilst the spectacular and inventive dream-sequence midway through Harry Lachman's *Dante's Inferno* (1935) begins with the protagonist falling asleep over an edition illustrated by Doré.

Such links continued later in the twentieth century. Several modern illus-trators – such as **Salvador Dalí** (100 lithographs, produced in 1951–2; online at Columbia Digital Dante; below, p. 282); **Tom Phillips** (139 prints, 1976–83; Phillips 1983) and **Sandow Birk** (2003–5; Hawkins 2006: figs.

240

9, 11) – have had interests in film or TV. Phillips collaborated with the director **Peter Greenaway** on *A TV Dante*, screened by Channel 4 in 1990 (Vickers 1995; Havely 1998: 13); and his screenplay for an alternative TV version (set in a South African prison camp) has also been published (Phillips 1991). Several more avant-garde screen versions of Dante – those of **Brakhage** (*The Dante Quartet*, 1987) and **Elder** (*Book of All the Dead*, 1975–94) – have been described as 'artist's films' and seem to draw upon a variety of techniques, including hand-painting on to celluloid, to produce 'moving visual thinking' and 'elaborate sound-and image polyphonic montage' (Testa 2004: 191–3, 203). Bruce Elder's sequence has been described as 'the most ambitious Dante film-work ever attempted' (Iannucci 2004: xvii, 202); and, with a running time of over 40 hours, it could well be a purgatorial viewing experience.

Dante's presence on screen has been surveyed in a several modern collections of essays – notably Casadio's *Dante nel cinema* (1996) and Iannucci's *Dante, Cinema and Television* (2004) – and with recent Dantean movies like Jean-Luc Godard's *Notre Musique* (2005) and the highly praised *Death of Mr Lazarescu* (Cristi Puiu, 2005; below, p. 249) the critical record will need to be updated. Coverage of the modern illustrators and of theatre is more patchy – although there are helpful articles on both subjects in the *Dante Encyclopedia* and some lively comment on pop and cartoon versions in Peter Hawkins's *Dante: A Brief History* (*DE* 319A–324A, 502A–505A; Hawkins 2006: 153–63).

The vitality of Dante's continuing presence on the stage has been marked by a variety of performances over recent years. An Italian realization of the *Commedia* as theatre between 1989 and 1991 involved the avant-garde director Federico Tiezzi and three contemporary poets (below, p. 259). At Edinburgh and London in 2002, the Derevo company (based in Dresden) presented a dance-mime *Divina commedia* which featured four performers including a 'Traveller' figure – with elements from *commedia dell'arte* and (as the *Evening News* noted on 4 August 2002), influence from the Cirque du Soleil. In 2004–5 the comedian Arthur Smith's *Dante's Inferno* (appropriately at the Comedy Theatre, London) presented 'an account of my own descent into [alcohol-induced] hell', in which he characterized Dante as 'an Early Renaissance Tarantino' and concisely translated the opening *terzina* of the *Inferno* as: 'I'm old, I'm fucked, I'm in a forest.' Early in 2006 the *Inferno* was staged as a subterranean 'promenade production' at the Arches in Glasgow, in which 'an earnest and troubled Dante . . . meets us at a candlelit coffin as back-projected dirt begins to fill a grave. Hooking up with

[an] . . . austere Virgil . . . he pays witness to armies of sub-human creatures, half-naked and faceless in sackcloth, writhing in torment for their sins. Circling around us . . . they bring their misery uncomfortably close' (Mark Fisher, *Guardian*, *G2*, 15 March 2006). The 'strange new show' (*Inf.* 22. 118) still goes on.

# Controversy, Conflict, Crime

Dante was no stranger to controversy and conflict, and the reading of his work was contentious from the start. Civic feud and faction and disputes between the papacy, the empire and France affected his life and career and are reflected in much of his writing (above, pp. 134–54). The *Monarchia* – with its promotion of the rights of the Roman empire, and fierce critique of the church's temporal wealth and power – was the first of the poet's works in the firing line, drawing ecclesiastical censure and condemnation within 10 years of his death (above, p. 228). It continued to remain in the sights of papal apologists: the eight manuscripts that survive from the later fourteenth century 'show signs of having been regarded as dangerous (hidden amongst other kinds of writing; made anonymous) and stimulating (marginal notes and comments)'; and although Dante eventually became of use as a loyal son of the church, the *Monarchia* was placed on the Index of Prohibited Books in the mid-sixteenth century and remained there until 1881 (Caesar 1989: 3).

Meanwhile, during the sixteenth century Dante came to be recruited into the ranks of proto-Protestant 'witnesses to the truth', as, in **John Foxe**'s phrase, 'an Italian writer against the Pope' (Foxe 1570: 485; *DEL* 1. 58). Again the *Monarchia* was involved and played a substantial part in this process of conscription. It had been translated into Italian twice during the previous century (Caesar 1989: 216–18), but the first printed edition (by Johann Herbst [Oporinus] at Basel in 1559) and the first published translation (by Johann Herold, also at Basel in 1559) were both associated with Protestant polemic (Friederich 1950: 348–9). For Protestants in Germany and Britain who advocated 'magisterial reformation', with its privileging of secular rulers, the *Monarchia*'s assertions about the limitations of papal power had obvious appeal. In 1567, shortly before the pope revoked Elizabeth I's authority to rule, **John Jewel**, bishop of Salisbury, alluded to the *Monarchia* when inveighing against 'the Tyrannie of the *Bisshoppes* of Rome and their Barbarous Persianlike Pride' (Havely 2003: 136–7).

Antipapal and anticlerical material in the *Commedia* was also frequently cited by the Protestant polemicists of the sixteenth and seventeenth centuries. Bishop Jewel in 1567, for example, also notes that 'Dantes an Italian Poete by expresse woordes calleth Rome the Whore of Babylon' (*Boswell 1999: 28). He even gives a reference to 'cantione 32' (i.e., *Purg.* 32. 148–56) – although, like Foxe and others at this time, he almost certainly knew the *Commedia* only from the summaries and extracts translated into Latin by the Protestant historian **Matthias Flacius** in 1556 and 1562 (Havely 2003: 127–8, 134–5, 140). Other passages from the *Commedia* that came to be used as sticks to beat Rome included the denunciations of the contemporary papacy in *Inferno* 19 (90–117) and *Paradiso* 9 (126–42) and, with increasing frequency, Beatrice's attack (*Par.* 29. 103–8) upon vain and corrupt preachers who 'feed their flocks with wind' – a phrase which resonates through Protestant polemic of this period and emerges again in St Peter's outburst against Laudian clergy in **Milton**'s 'Lycidas' of 1637 (lines 119–27).

Milton certainly read the *Commedia* in the original; indeed, among all English poets he was one of the best Italianists. In 1638 he travelled to Italy and established close contacts with scholars and writers, particularly at Florence and Naples (Samuel 1966: 38–43). There is evidence, too, about his interest in Italian long before that. During his last year at Cambridge (1629) he is known to have been not only reading Italian authors but also writing poetry in Italian. His interest in Dante as a prophet of Reformation is evident in his *Commonplace Book* for the year 1637. Here he quotes from all three *cantiche* of the *Commedia*, and most of the passages quoted have to do with politics – especially ecclesiastical politics (*DEL* 1. 121–3). After returning from Italy, the first major work that he wrote (a year or so before the outbreak of the English Civil War) was the political treatise *Of Reformation: Touching Church Discipline in England*, which was published in 1641. Part 1 of this work traces the origin of corruption in the church to the Donation of Constantine (above, p. 150). To show (as the Protestant polemicists had gleefully done) that this was condemned 'even among men professing the Roman faith', the text then quotes 'three the famousest men for wit and learning that Italy at this day glories of'. The first of these is Dante; and Milton translates the lines addressing Constantine (*Inf.* 19. 115–17) into

'English blank verse', following up with a reference to 'the like complaint' in *Paradiso* 20. 55–7 (*DEL* 1. 124–5). Milton was a wide-ranging and responsive reader of the *Commedia*, which continued to resonate in his later work, including *Paradise Lost*; and he knew or knew of Dante's other works, such as the *Vita nuova*, *Convivio*, *DVE*, the letters and *Monarchia* (*DEL* 1. 122 and 127–8; Caesar 1989: 323–5; Samuel 1966: 34, 44). His most explicit uses of Dante's text, however, appear to be in political and controversial contexts. Political readings of episodes and figures in the *Commedia* can become narrowly and even perversely polemical, as the more sophisticated Catholic controversialists in the later sixteenth century were beginning to point out (Havely 2003: 144–5). But they can also, as Milton shows, enable later writers to relate the conflicts and controversies with which Dante was concerned to those of their own times.

Politics shaped the reception of one of the best-known prisoners in Dante's Hell: Count **Ugolino of Pisa**. The Ugolino who is encountered in the ninth circle of the *Inferno* (32.124–39, 33.1–90) embodies political betrayal and conflict in several ways. He is both a perpetrator of treachery to his city (33.85) and a victim of plotting and deception by Archbishop Ruggieri of Pisa, who imprisoned him, his sons and grandsons, subsequently starving them to death (*DE* 839). He is also – as Dante first sees him, and as he himself emphasizes – a punisher of betrayal, as he gnaws at the skull of his adversary Ruggieri, with whom he is 'frozen together in a hole' of the ninth circle (*Inf.* 32. 125–32, 33. 1–8, 15 and 76–8). 'Gnawing the traitor' (33.8) becomes what Dante calls 'a bestial image', conveying not only personal vengeance but also the recurring cycles of political violence that lead citizens 'encircled by the same walls and moat' to turn on and 'gnaw each other' (*Purg.* 6. 83–4; above, p. 138).

Ugolino featured as a pathetic and tragic figure in Chaucer's *Monk's Tale* (2407–62), and in Italian plays of the seventeenth and eighteenth centuries (above, p. 236). By the early nineteenth century Coleridge was referring to his story, alongside that of Francesca, as extremely 'well known' and as an example of Dante's 'absolute mastery over . . . the pathetic' (*DEL* 1. 625). Yet, together with the horror and pathos, recognition of the political implications of Ugolino's fate took a variety of forms from the fourteenth century to the twentieth. Chaucer's Ugolino had become not only a grieving father but also an example of the 'fall of princes'; and his fall in the *Monk's Tale* follows immediately after a more recent instance of the vicissitudes of Italian politics: the imprisonment and death in 1385 of Bernabò Visconti, lord of Milan, whom Chaucer himself had met in 1378 (2399–406).

When Ugolino's narrative returns to Whig Protestant England in the early eighteenth century – initially with the translations of the canto by **Jonathan Richardson** and **Thomas Gray** – it is 'not only [as] a pathetic story of a father's sorrow but also [as] a story of injustice, and, moreover . . . of injustice wrought by a churchman'; and several writers of the period underline its anti-clerical potential as an instance of 'Prelatical Revenge' (\*Yates 1951: 98; *DEL* 1. 196–204 and 232–4). Subsequently, Romantic libertarian concerns with imprisonment and other forms of oppression gave further vitality to Ugolino's afterlife. Significant numbers of paintings and drawings on the subject were produced in Britain and Italy during the late eighteenth and early nineteenth centuries and some of the most important of these – by **Reynolds**, **Fuseli** and **Blake** – provoked debate about ideas of liberty (Yates 1951: 108–10, 111–15). **Byron**'s poem about the imprisonment (and eventual release) of a Swiss patriot, 'The Prisoner of Chillon' (1816), drew upon Dante for this purpose, as Scott and Shelley recognized (*DEL* 1.444, 2. 388; Pite 1994: 199–229). In 1837, the young **W. E. Gladstone** honed both his skills in *terza rima* and his Italophile credentials by translating the story of Dante's prisoner and 'the foul traitor . . . hight Archbishop' who brought about his death (*DEL* 2. 603–5). And both **Thomas Carlyle** and **John Ruskin** pointed uncomfortable parallels between the form of that death and evidence of starvation closer to the Victorian reader's home (*DEL* 2. 511; Yates 1951: 100–1).

The forms of violence and oppression that appropriation of Ugolino and the *Inferno* addressed in this period were often those generated by industrialization and urbanization. An early example is Carlyle's *Past and Present* (1843), where a desolate social landscape in which 'two million . . . workers sit enchanted in Workhouse Bastilles, five million more (according to some) in Ugolino Hunger-cellars' is at several points during the analysis of the 'condition of England' compared with Dante's Hell, notably at the beginning of the whole work (*DEL* 2. 510–11). **George Eliot** may well have had such passages in mind when surveying the bleak Midland scene in the prologue to her most overtly political novel, *Felix Holt the Radical* (composed in 1865–6; Thompson 1991). George Eliot was wide-ranging in her appropriation of Dante here and in several of her major novels, including *Middlemarch* (epigraphs to chs. 19, 54) and *Daniel Deronda* (epigraphs to chs. 55, 64). Along with her characteristically Victorian appropriations of the *Vita nuova* and of *Purgatorio* as a source of moral self-help, there are some strikingly darker allusions to the *Inferno*, especially at the end of *Romola* (1863), where a grim re-enactment of the Ugolino episode takes place (Milbank 1998: 84–90; Thompson 2003: 202–4).

Less well known, although equally worth attention, are the allusions to the *Inferno* in American fiction that explores the industrial scene. Two striking examples appeared in the mid-nineteenth century. **Melville**'s story 'The Paradise of Bachelors and the Tartarus of Maids' (1855) describes a 'Dantean gateway' in the New England landscape, which leads to a scene that grimly portrays 'the work practices of industrialism and at the same time some of the sexual phobias and taboos of the age' (Melville 1993: xxxv, 195). The Pennsylvania novelist **Rebecca Harding Davis**'s most successful story was 'Life in the Iron-Mills' (1861), where a group of well-to-do visitors make some idle comparisons between a contemporary steel-foundry and the *Inferno* in a narrative which then moves towards 'the reality of Dante's vision' (Bigsby 1995: 155).

Dante continued to walk the streets of real and unreal cities imagined by late nineteenth-century and modernist writers – from Melville's *Pierre* (1852), through James Thomson's *City of Dreadful Night* (1874), which 'predicates a world in which any . . . social change is impossible', to Joyce's paralysed turn-of-the-century Dublin, and T. S. Eliot's London, where the commuter crowd of 'the Burial of the Dead' (1922) reincarnate Dante's neutral and suspended souls (*The Waste Land I*; Milbank 1998: 115, 206–13). In the brilliantly forged modernist poems of the Australian 'Ern Malley' (1943–4), Dante's Bertrand de Born is appropriated in a similar urban and Eliotic context, at the end of 'Sybilline' (1943):

> The evening
> Settles down like a brooding bird
> Over streets that divide our life like a trauma
> Would it be strange now to meet
> The figure that strode hell swinging
> His head by the hair
> On Princess Street?
>
> (from *The Darkening Ecliptic*,
> in Heyward 1993: 247)

As the creators of 'lucid Ern' must have recognized, Eliot drew upon the *Inferno* for several of the 'different voices' in his early poetry. The epigraph to 'The Love Song of J. Alfred Prufrock' (1917) quotes Guido da Montefeltro, speaking out of the flames in the eighth *bolgia* of the eighth circle of Hell (*Inf.* 27. 61–6); and Eliot returned to Dante's most eloquent infernal tongue – Ulysses – as the voice for a narrative that originally formed part of the 'Death by Water' section in *The Waste Land* (Eliot 1971: 63–9).

Near the end of *The Waste Land* (411–15 and note), Eliot alludes to the Ugolino episode in a way that suggests 'redemptive' consequences in 'the moment of a recognition of one's own isolation' (Milbank 1998: 214). His visit to Ugolino's tower on the way to the personal and purgatorial pilgrimage of *Ash Wednesday* (below, p. 256) might be taken as a sign that the political potential of this Dantean episode had at last been exhausted. But this is to reckon without the reinventions of Ugolino, some fifty years after *The Waste Land*, in **Seamus Heaney**'s *Field Work* (1979).

*Field Work* initiates Heaney's long dialogue with Dante, which continues through *Station Island* (1984) and *Seeing Things* (1991) to *Electric Light* (2001) (below, p. 261). Its closing translation of the whole Ugolino episode (Heaney 1979: 61–4) can be read in the context of poems that address the conflicts and violence of the 1970s in Northern Ireland – poems such as 'Triptych', 'The Strand at Lough Beg' and 'Casualty', as well as a number of those that pre-date *Field Work*. 'The Strand at Lough Beg: In Memory of Colum McCartney' (Heaney 1979: 17–18) draws obliquely upon the *Commedia*. Its epigraph describes the reeds on the shore of Purgatory (*Purg.* 1. 100–2), and its conclusion re-enacts the subsequent ritual of cleansing and girding (*Purg.* 1. 121–36); although the 'blood and roadside muck' that are cleansed here also evoke the violence of some later scenes (notably *Purg.* 5. 97–9; see *Wallace 1993: 254). The sequence of poems in *Field Work* thus seems to reverse the pattern of the Dantean journey, leading from the shores of Mount Purgatory back down to the souls of Hell's ninth circle, in 'An Afterwards' (Heaney 1979: 44) and 'Ugolino' at the very end. There is also a close and complex relationship between Heaney's 'Ugolino' and 'In Memoriam Francis Ledwidge, Killed in France 31 July 1917' (Heaney 1979: 59–60). The latter poem comes eventually to follow the beat of 'the sure confusing drum' that led an Irish Catholic to fight and die on the same side as his Protestant compatriots during the Great War; and its last line ('Though all of you consort now underground') is an uneasy interment of the ancestral figure and his comrades – foreshadowing the violence that is to break out immediately afterwards from the 'frozen hole' at the opening of 'Ugolino'.

Translating and appropriating Dante is also a means by which Heaney, like other poets, addresses questions about poetry itself (below, p. 255). Already in *Field Work* the Ugolino episode has also been recreated more sardonically, when the rival poets of 'An Afterwards' are shown 'Jockeying for position, hasped and mounted / Like Ugolino on Archbishop Roger' (Heaney 1979: 44). Implications for both poetry and politics re-emerge with the ghost of Ugolino in Heaney's later collection *The Spirit Level* (1995), where part 4 of 'The Flight Path' returns to 1979, and poses brutally awkward questions about political loyalty and writing. This section of the poem's homecoming ends by exploring what it meant, in the years of intense sectarian conflict and of the Long Kesh 'dirty protests', to be 'translating freely' the lines from *Inferno* 33 that describe how Ugolino's 'teeth, like a dog's teeth clamping round a bone, / Bit into the skull and again took hold' (Heaney 1995: 25). The repetition here of lines that Heaney had written 16 years or more earlier has several implications; and it sets up a powerful tension between the concern with artistic freedom and what can be seen here as the 'chewing over of political obsession' (O'Donoghue 1998: 250).

Experiences and memories of other twentieth-century conflicts have also led other major writers and artists to engage in dialogue with Dante at some points in their work. This has been particularly and diversely evident in the work of some Italian authors and directors negotiating the traumas and crises of the Second World War: in **Primo Levi**'s recourse to the *Inferno* in his 1947 prison-camp narrative *Se questo è un uomo* (*If This is a Man*; CHIL 546–7); in **Giorgio Bassani**'s fiction; in the poetry of **Vittorio Sereni**; and in the films of **Rossellini, Fellini, Pasolini** and others (Woolf and Robinson, in Havely 1998; Waller and Rumble, in Iannucci 2004). When producing his series of illustrations for the *Inferno* in 1982, the Australian artist **Sidney Nolan** found his work turning back to a traumatic event in the First World War: 'after Canto 18, he stopped illustrating the *Inferno* and drew instead images of Australian soldiers at Gallipoli, while still quoting Dante's words' (Duckworth 2006).

In twentieth-century cinema the *Inferno*'s 'city of pain' and its 'lost people' (*Inf.* 3. 1–3) have been reconstructed with various degrees of specificity, from **Henry Otto**'s *Dante's Inferno* (1924) and **Harry Lachman**'s social fable of the same name (1935) to **Andrzej Wajda**'s *Kanal* (1956), Pier Paolo Pasolini's *Salò* (1975), the opening urban sequence in the **Greenaway–Phillips** *A TV Dante* (1988/90) and the unnamed dystopian city of **David Fincher**'s *Se7en* (1995). In the USA, at least, the more adventurous infernal action moved out of town with **David Lynch**'s *Blue Velvet* (1986), where the entry to Hell lies not in some desolate urban or industrial desert, but beneath the neat lawns and picket fences of suburbia. On the other hand, the most recent European screening of the *Inferno* – the Romanian *Death of Mr Lazarescu* (**Cristi Puiu**, 2005) – returns to the city. Bucharest is the setting for the final journey of the dying Dante Lazarescu and a paramedic with aspects of Virgil and Beatrice, who 'embark on a descent into the health-care underworld that starts out ordinary, even drab, and ends up mythic' (Michael Phillips, *Chicago Tribune*, 12 May 2006).

Some of the most striking modern appearances of the urban and suburban *Inferno* have been in the work of **African-American novelists**. The importance of this 'intensely problematic' form of appropriation was perceptively noted over 10 years ago (Wallace 1993: 255); and attention has more recently been given to African-American film-making from this point of view (Looney 2004). Resonances of the *Inferno* are audible in the world of individual and social deprivation at the start of **Ralph Ellison**'s *Invisible Man* (1952) and throughout the scenes of urban violence in **Amiri Baraka**'s *The System of Dante's Hell* (1965). But again, it is in the suburbs that the most adventurous African-American exploration of the *Inferno* has taken place. **Gloria Naylor**'s *Linden Hills* (1985) is interestingly close in time to the infernal suburbia of Lynch's *Blue Velvet*. Here, Hell is populated by 'prosperous people': an upwardly mobile black middle class, who have moved 'out of the city of woe' and now live in eight descending crescents, leading downhill to the moated home of the estate's manager, the sinister funeral director Luther Nedeed. The problems of this group are explored through the journey of two young male outsiders (who are also poets) and through the narratives and identities which a number of the 'prosperous' inhabitants (including Nedeed's wife, imprisoned in a basement at the foot of the hill) are desperately seeking to recover (Havely 1998: 217–19).

In Naylor's and Lynch's versions of Dante's Hell the protagonists are also seen confronting and even investigating some kind of **crime**. Here it seems the American imagination has been particularly responsive – perhaps following precedents set by the American-Italian gothic of Hawthorne's *The Marble Faun* (1860). 'Abandon hope all ye who enter here' is how the disillusioned detective (misquoting *Inferno* 3. 9) greets his client at the start of **Ross Macdonald**'s mystery *The Zebra-Striped Hearse*, although the further 'hidden echoes' of Dante carry more significance in the novel (Macdonald 1962: 1; Ó Cuilleanain 2003: 115–21). In similar fictional and cinematic genres, investigators or criminals similarly come equipped with occasional Dantean credentials. The *Commedia* is consulted on the subject of the seven deadly sins in Fincher's *Se7en*; and in **Thomas Harris**'s *Hannibal* (1999), the erudite Dr Lecter delivers a lecture on canto 13 of the *Inferno* (Harris 2000: 228–31). Two more recent American novels have developed this tradition: **Matthew Pearl**'s *The Dante Club* of 2003, a historical whodunnit about serial murder in 1860s Boston; and (more ambitiously) **Nick Tosches**'s combination of pacey mafia thriller with a rather *un*-pacey medieval quest in

*In the Hand of Dante* (2003). In Dante's home country the most vigorous recent reinventions and appropriations of the *Commedia* have been in film and performance (above, p. 249, and below, p. 259). Recently, however, two successful Italian *gialli* (crime fictions) have been published by **Giulio Leoni**: *I delitti del mosaico* ('The Mosaic Murders', 2004) and *I delitti della luce* ('Crimes of the Light', 2005), both of them set in the Florence of 1300, where a series of murder cases urgently needs to be solved. And on this occasion – as in the *Inferno* – the investigator of crimes is none other than Dante Alighieri.

# *Purgatorio*: Poetics
# and Politics

The next two subsections will both follow a thematic rather than chronological direction. This section moves from the initial poetic energies derived from the *Purgatorio* by Chaucer and Shelley, through the political contexts and poetic concerns of Shelley's, Soyinka's and Heaney's purgatories, to the purgatorial poetics of Eliot's *Ash Wednesday* and 'Little Gidding'.

At the opening of the *Purgatorio* itself there is a strong sense of new departure in the writing as well as in the journey: the resurrection of 'dead poetry' (above, p. 197). One of the earliest poets to respond to this redirection in Dante's text was **Chaucer**, at the opening of the second book of his most ambitious completed work, the *Troilus* (c.1381–6). By this time, Chaucer had made Dante a significant part of his poetic agenda by naming him or alluding transparently to the *Commedia* at several earlier points of departure in his dream-poems. However, his most striking and complex Dantean opening is the reworking of *Purgatorio* 1. 1–12 in the prologue to Book 2 of the *Troilus*. As hope begins to dawn for the poem's protagonist, the writer summons up the resources of his 'art poetical':

> Owt of thise blake wawes for to saylle,
> O wynd, o wynd, the weder gynneth clere;
> For in this see the boot hath swych travaylle,
> Of my connyng, that unneth I it steere.
> This see clepe I the tempestous matere
> Of disespeir that Troilus was inne;
> But now of hope the kalendes bygynne.
>
> O lady myn, that called art Cleo,
> Thow be my speed fro this forth, and my Muse.
> (*Troilus* 2. 1–9)

On the face of it, this rewriting seems hesitant and tentative. Dante's image of his poetic craft – the *navicella del mio ingegno* ('the vessel of my [poetic] invention') which so confidently hoists sail in the first two lines of the *Purgatorio* becomes here the vulnerable 'boot . . . Of my connyng' which is literally split, between two lines; whilst Calliope, the Muse of epic poetry who is summoned to arise in all her power amongst the Italian poet's 'sacred Muses', is, in the *Troilus* proem, replaced by Clio, the Muse of history (or in some medieval traditions the Muse of beginnings). Nonetheless, this second *Troilus* prologue still signals a new beginning for the poem itself: a departure which is to take it in directions far different from those followed by Chaucer's main narrative source (Boccaccio's *Filostrato*).

New beginnings at the opening of the *Purgatorio* itself are also represented by the 'light and rapid vessel' in which the angel brings souls to the shore of Dante's mountain (*Purg.* 2. 13–51; above, p. 184). This appealed strongly to Shelley. In a letter to Leigh Hunt in 1819, he singles out three examples of 'exquisite tenderness and sensibility and ideal beauty' in Dante, namely: '*your* Francesca' (the Francesca that Hunt had rewritten in *The Story of Rimini*); 'Matilda gathering flowers' (the passage at the opening of *Purg.* 28 that Shelley was himself to translate, probably during the summer of 1820); and 'the spirit coming over the sea in a boat, like Mars rising from the vapours of the horizon' (*DEL* 2. 218–19). Shelley commandeered a variety of Dantean vessels – such as the 'magic ship' of the fantasy sonnet to Cavalcanti (above, p. 119) which he translated (*DEL* 2. 215–16), and the ship bound for Paradise, taking a course that 'no keel has ever ploughed before' (*Epipsychidion*, line 410) – but, so far as we know, he did not venture on translating this passage from *Purg.* 2. It was, however, according to Mary Shelley, his favourite episode in the *Commedia*, and one can readily grasp the attraction and significance that its combination of brilliant light, swift motion, wide horizons and new destinations would have held for him (M. Shelley 1980–8: 3. 160; P. Shelley 1964: 2. 112).

Bleaker conditions seemed to be shaping Shelley's poetic responses to the *Purgatorio* when he returned to Dante's Earthly Paradise in his last and unfinished poem, *The Triumph of Life* (1822) – a work which with its supremely confident use of *terza rima* has been seen as his 'most "Dantesque" poem' (Ellis 1983: 31; Griffiths and Reynolds 2005: 148–64). Its reworking of the *Purgatorio*'s procession becomes 'sad pageantry' (176), and the political idealism embodied in the desiccated figure of Rousseau, who acts as guide, is marked by disillusionment. Dante as poet is invoked late in the poem as one who:

'from the lowest depths of Hell
Through every Paradise & through all glory
Love led serene, & who returned to tell

'In words of hate & awe the wondrous story
How all things are transfigured, except Love'
(*Triumph of Life* 472–6)

– but the vision considered 'worthy of his rhyme' (480) becomes one of 'busy phantoms' proliferating through the world, using 'monarchizing worms' such as kings and pontiffs for breeding, feeding and preying upon humanity (495–547).

A similarly debilitating vision develops in **Wole Soyinka**'s 1972 poem 'Purgatory', which he reprinted in the section on 'Captivity' in *Poems of Black Africa* (1975). Here a judicial caning in a prison yard is staged as a 'freak show' for 'freaks' and an 'ancient pageant to divert / Archetypes of Purgatorio'. The prisoners who form the audience for this 'show' are the main subject of the poem. They include some who have been reprieved from death; whose 'rebirth' has become a sequence of 'tomorrows'; for whom 'purgatory' is the prison's 'calloused shelter of walls'; and whose state is 'a peace of refuge passionless / And comfort of a gelded sanity' (Soyinka 1975: 107–8).

Political conflict is the context for the reworking of *Purg.* 1. 121–9 at the end of **Heaney**'s 'The Strand at Lough Beg: In Memory of Colum McCartney' (above, p. 248). The question of whether art and poetry in such circumstances may be a means of eluding rather than understanding political realities is raised in *Station Island* (1984), which followed a few years after 'The Strand at Lough Beg' and drew into itself much of the thinking about and translating of Dante that Heaney had been doing in the early 1980s (Fumagalli 1996: 127). Here – in one of a number of Dantean encounters at a site of pilgrimage and penance – Heaney's persona is confronted with the resentful presence of the murdered 'second cousin' for whom the ritual at the end of the 1979 poem had been imagined. McCartney now responds harshly to the poet's claims about what had been seen and done on 'the strand empty at day break':

'You saw that, and you wrote that – not the fact.
You confused evasion and artistic tact.
The Protestant who shot me through the head
I accuse directly, but indirectly, you

> who now atone perhaps upon this bed
> for the way you whitewashed ugliness and drew
> the lovely blinds of the *Purgatorio*
> and saccharined my death with morning dew.'
>> (Heaney 1984: 83)

At the end of the previous purgatorial encounter, the protagonist had begged forgiveness for what he had called his 'timid, circumspect involvement' (Heaney 1984: 80); and he has no reply at all to the recriminatory speech here. However, he seems to be overdoing the self-laceration. The ending of 'The Strand at Lough Beg' with its evocation of partisan vocabulary ('shoot green', 'plait / Green') had hardly been 'evasive' or particularly 'tactful'. And the fact that the cousin's speech itself perfects the *terza rima* rhyme-scheme that had been evolving in the 1979 poem (and in 'Ugolino') strongly suggests that the use and value of Dante here may be to serve as rather more than a 'lovely blind'. Indeed, as Heaney himself seemed to suggest at the end of his own essay on Dante (*Heaney 1985: 18), *Station Island* is also framed as a community that has marked affinities with Dante's poets in the *Purgatorio*. The final encounter in the sequence is with the detached, self-exiled 'Old father' James Joyce (pp. 92–4). **Joyce** – who has been described as 'the greatest and least pious of all Irish Dantists' (Wallace 1993: 254; compare also 252–3) – now draws the penitent back on to the mainland, accompanying him some distance along what may well be the 'right path', whilst not forgetting to take the piss out of the pious pilgrim:

> 'don't be so earnest,
> let others wear the sackcloth and the ashes.
> Let go, let fly, forget.
> You've listened long enough. Now strike your note.'
>> (*Staion Island* p. 93)

The fact that Heaney, in his own later comments on the scene, notes that this is 'an encounter reminiscent of "Little Gidding"' (Heaney 1985: 19) suggests that he was aware of how **Eliot**, from the 1920s to the 1940s, had constantly returned to Dante and to *Purgatorio*'s poetics. At the start of Little Gidding's narrative section (lines 86–98), the meeting with the spirit of the 'dead master' in the desolate cityscape is based on Dante's encounter with Brunetto in *Inferno* 15 (*Charity 1974; Ellis 1983: 241–2; Manganiello 1989: ch. 6). But this section of 'Little Gidding' (II) concludes by suggesting the possibility of restoration through 'refining fire / Where you must

255

move in measure like a dancer' (lines 145–6). This is not a routine redemptive flourish, for it recalls and deploys the effects of Eliot's long reading of the *Purgatorio*, and particularly his repeated stealing of the 'fire that refines' the lustful poets, such as Guinizzelli and the Provençal Arnaut Daniel, in *Purgatorio* 26. 'I wished the effect of the whole', wrote Eliot in a letter of 1942, 'to be Purgatorial' (quoted in McDougal 1985b: 78).

Eliot's interest in Arnaut Daniel (above, p. 111) had been sparked by his own Dantean dialogue with Ezra Pound and especially by Pound's *Spirit of Romance* (1910), where the Provençal poet is presented as a key poet of the period (McDougal 1985b: 59). Eliot's third collection of poems (1920) originally had the title *Ara vus [sic] prec* ('Now I beg you'), from the last lines of Arnaut's speech out of the flames on the edge of Purgatory (*Purg.* 26. 145). Pound himself is addressed in the dedication to *The Waste Land* (1922) as *il miglior fabbro* ('the better craftsman'), the title that Dante's Guinizzelli bestows on Arnaut (*Purg.* 26. 117). At the end of *The Waste Land* itself, the first fragment to be 'shored' against the speaker's 'ruins' is one that later comes to be embedded in the blitzed landscape of 'Little Gidding' (145–6): *Poi s'ascose nel foco che gli affina* ('Then he was lost in the refining fire'; *Purg.* 26. 148; *The Waste Land* 427). In his note on this line, Eliot quotes the preceding three verses of Arnaut Daniel's speech, including *Ara vos prec*, which points back to the title of his 1920 poems, and *Sovegna vos a temps de ma dolor* ('Remember at due time my suffering'), which is the last line of the Provençal poet's appeal for a place in Dante's memory (*Purg.* 26. 147).

Arnaut Daniel's appeal next appears in truncated form (*Sovegna vos*) as the only non-English phrase in section IV of Eliot's *Ash Wednesday* (1930). *Ash Wednesday* is in several ways a 'purgatorial' poem, but, even in this austere context, the reading and response reaches beyond the *Commedia*. Eliot seems also to have had in mind here the later stages of the *Vita nuova* (Ellis 1983: 219); and this forms part of the wider dialogue with Dante that develops across the whole range of his poetry. This dialogue has drawn (in the early poems) upon voices from the *Inferno*, such as those of Guido da Montefeltro and Ulysses (above, pp. 47, 194). Those voices from the flames in Dante's eighth circle of Hell are answered by the phrases Eliot – in 'What the Thunder Said', *Ash Wednesday* and 'Little Gidding' – takes from Arnaut in the refining fires of *Purgatorio*. In this way Eliot seems instinctively to have grasped the complex 'inter-*cantica*' parallels and contrasts between *Purgatorio* 26 and *Inferno* 26–7 that scholars have noted recently (Durling and Martinez 2003: 454).

It would be impossible, in the space that remains, to do full justice to Eliot's or Heaney's responses to the *Purgatorio*. Nor can this section even begin on those of **Yeats** or **Pound** – let alone pluck 'dantallizing peaches' from the prose of **Joyce** or **Beckett** (though, for the source and meaning of Joyce's delicate phrase, see Wallace 1993: 253). These other major modern readings and rewritings have been well served in a number of important chapters and monographs, as follows:

**Beckett**: Fowlie (1985); Elam (1994); Haughton (1998).
**Eliot**: Ellis (1983); McDougal (1985b); Manganiello (1989).
**Heaney**: O'Donoghue (1998); Fumagalli (2001).
**Joyce**: M. T. Reynolds (1981); Wallace (1993: 252–3).
**Pound**: Wilhelm (1974); Ellis (1983); Kenner (1985).
**Yeats**: Ellis (1983); Bornstein (1985).

# A Conversation about the *Paradiso*

This final subsection will sample the responses of some twentieth- and twenty-first-century authors to the *Paradiso*. Again, it will follow a thematic rather than strictly chronological approach – and the chief participants in this imaginary and multilingual 'conversation' will be American/English (T. S. Eliot), Italian (Giovanni Giudici), Russian (Osip Mandelstam), Northern Irish (Seamus Heaney) and Nigerian (Ben Okri).

On 21 March 1920 **Eliot** wrote to Lady Ottoline Morrell: 'I have just finished an article on Dante – under difficulties, as you may imagine: and I feel that anything I can say about such a subject is trivial. I feel so completely inferior in his presence – there seems really nothing to do but to point to him and be silent.' Eliot was of course by no means silent about Dante. He published the 13-page article to which this letter refers (Eliot 1920: 159–71); a piece on 'Dante as Spiritual Leader' in the same year (*Athenaeum* 2, April 1920); and a substantial essay nine years later (Eliot 1929). He also discussed Dante in the Clark lectures at Cambridge in 1926 (Eliot 1993) and gave a talk called 'What Dante Means to Me' to the Italian Institute in 1950 (Eliot 1965: 125–35). Nonetheless, the notions of subservience and silence do inform Eliot's view of the *Paradiso* in the 1929 essay and especially his approach to the final canto.

In his 1929 *Dante* essay, Eliot argues that the *Paradiso* 'is a matter of gradual adjustment of our vision', and that it challenges our 'prejudice against beatitude as material for poetry'. In doing so, he also asserts that 'the eighteenth and nineteenth centuries knew nothing of it' [i.e., of *Paradiso* as defined in these terms]. This is a vast oversimplification – and Eliot shows some awareness here and in his later criticism that Shelley is at least one notable exception. It does, however, have some relevance to the Romantic

258

and Victorian Dante: to, for example, Byron's concentration on the *Inferno*; to Macaulay's view of the *Paradiso* as inferior to 'the preceding parts of the poem' (*DEL* 2. 397 and 402); to Carlyle's preference for *Purgatorio* as a hymn to self-help; and to the Pre-Raphaelites' love-affair with the Beatrice of the *Vita nuova*.

Does a comparable limitation also apply to responses to the *Paradiso* in Eliot's own time and beyond? If, as Ezra Pound said, 'Hell is *here*', is Paradise a transcendent twentieth-century absence? Much modernist and contemporary writing views Dante's Paradise as a state that is certainly not here and probably not there. **Samuel Beckett** repeats the conviction that 'there are no stars' and concludes the ironically titled novella 'The Calmative' with the following 'non-vision': 'in vain I raised without hope my eyes to the sky to look for the Bears. For the light I steeped in put out the stars, assuming they were there, which I doubted, remembering the clouds' (Beckett 1995: 67, quoted in Salvadori Lonergan 1997: 91).

Ironic readings of the *Paradiso* are also not hard to find among contemporary writers. The New York poet **Bruce Andrews** produced an anti-romantic version, called (with all due allowance for obscene double entendre) *Lip Service* (1989–92) – a 10-part work, corresponding to the 10 'bodies' of Dante's Paradise. This has been described as 'joylessly bereft of the personal, and . . . astonishingly difficult to take except in short doses . . . a bit like listening in on the powder-room of a somewhat sleazy night club' (Quartermain 2000: 122, 124). Less reductive than this is the stage version by the contemporary Italian poet, essayist and journalist **Giovanni Giudici**, entitled *Il Paradiso: perché mi vinse il lume d'esta stella* (quoting *Par.* 9. 33), and subtitled *sàtura drammatica* ('dramatic satire'). This is the last of three dramatic reinventions of the *Commedia* by Italian poets and was first staged by the avant-garde director Federico Tiezzi at Bari in 1991. One of Giudici's images is of the God of the *Paradiso* as a kind of 'infinite computer to which is linked a host of heavenly terminals' (Giudici 1991: 23) – a conception of the *cantica* to which we shall return. Giudici's *Paradiso* remains firmly based on Dante's text, but it also includes a number of Shandyesque dialogues between the Author, the Cleric and the Critic, together with several bit-parts for non-Dantean characters, such as Tiresias, Ezra Pound, and a 'Member of the Public' who turns up in the penultimate scene and turns out to be none other than Franz Kafka (Giudici 1991: 72). Giudici also rewrites Dante's conclusion: in his version the image of the dispersed Sybilline leaves (*Par.* 33. 65–6) is theatrically translated into a blizzard of loose pages, a whirlwind, and the appearance of the Sybil herself, hunched over a crystal

259

ball. Her response to the Chorus's question '*Che cosa vorresti, Sibilla?*' ('What do you desire, O Sybil?') is the single repeated infinitive '*Morire, morire*' ('To die, to die'); and this 'dramatic satire' thus ends by invoking the bleak little exchange that had been used as the epigraph to Eliot's *The Waste Land*.

Eliot's own view of the *Paradiso*'s ending is very different. In the 1929 *Dante* essay he sees in this 'last and greatest canto . . . a masterly use of that imagery of *light* which is the form of certain types of mystical experience'; and he finds its 'authentic sign of greatness' in the association between the vision of the Divine and the myth of the *Argo* passing over Neptune's head: 'It is the real right thing, the power of establishing relations between beauty of the most diverse sorts; it is the utmost power of the poet. *O quanto è corto il dire, e come fioco / al mio concetto!*' (Eliot 1929: 50). In this quotation of the canto's penultimate use of the inexpressibility topos, Eliot seems to be speaking as much for himself as he is for Dante. At this point in the 1929 essay we are not that far away from the wordless gesture envisaged in the 1920 letter: 'There seems really nothing to do but to point to him and be silent.'

Awareness of the nature and limitations of language and perception – and of the physics of light and movement – at this stage of the *Commedia* is also shared by the Russian poet and critic **Osip Mandelstam** (1891–1938). Mandelstam had been to Italy twice during his years as a student in Europe (1907–10) and he read other Italian poets, such as Petrarch, Ariosto and Tasso. As his wife records in her memoir, 'he chose Dante as the starting point for a discussion of his own poetics: For M[andelstam] Dante was the source of all European poetry, and the measure of poetic "rightness"' (N. Mandelstam 1999: 251). During his first arrest (for writing against Stalin) in 1934 and again in 1938 – the year of his final sentencing and death – copies of Dante accompanied him to prison and into exile. Nadezhda Mandelstam also recalls that he 'obtained an edition of the *Divine Comedy* in small format and always had it with him in his pocket, just in case he was arrested not at home but in the street' (N. Mandelstam 1999: 228). The 'discussion of his own poetics' is the essay or 'sketch' entitled 'Conversation about Dante'. It was written in 1933; and Dante continued to be reflected in the final phase of Mandelstam's poetry, as it is in the work of his friend Anna Akhmatova (*DE* 278).

Mandelstam's 'Conversation' is quirky, elliptical and at points fragmentary in the development of its ideas. His Dante is, like Eliot's, 'a master of the instruments of poetry' (O. Mandelstam 1991: 397); but, by contrast with

Eliot in the 1929 essay, Mandelstam sees these instruments as consisting not in 'tropes' but in the strategies of 'transmutation' and 'hybridization'. He engages in a vividly materialist reading of Dante, emphasizing the physicality of poetry, the physiology of reading and of form, and what he was to call, in one of his later poems of exile, 'the muttering lips' (p. 306). In one of the most-quoted passages from the 'Conversation' he speaks of how when learning Italian 'I suddenly understood that the center of gravity of my speech efforts had been moved closer to my lips, to the outer parts of my mouth' (p. 399). This physiological and material emphasis has other consequences, too: the association of walking with poetry; the speculation about how many shoes Dante wore out when composing the *Commedia* (p. 400). And in the 'Conversation's approach to the *Paradiso*, a further distance from Eliot's position is marked by the rejection of what Mandelstam calls the 'cult of Dantean mysticism' (p. 411).

Mandelstam's characteristic emphasis in the 'Conversation' is on poetry as performance rather than representation or reflection: 'not so much narrating as acting out' (O. Mandelstam 1991: 397). For him, the play of light and movement in the *Paradiso* is akin to ballet (p. 434) or drama (p. 450). The play of sound and light here is seen at one point in the 'Conversation' as 'approaching the wave theory'; and in the rough drafts (the 'Addenda') it is seen as prefiguring modern European theatre. The Dante of this *Paradiso* is a director, a conductor and (yet more playfully) a builder of a planetarium in which 'the prime mover himself is no longer the first principle, being merely a radio station, a communicator, a transmitter' (p. 450). Mandelbaum's notes, then, may be the germ of Giudici's more updated image of Dante's God as 'infinite computer' (above, p. 259).

Mandelstam's performative, playful reading of Dante has, since its reappearance in the late 1960s, been particularly influential on the work of **Heaney**, whose essay of 1985 centres upon a comparison of Eliot's and Mandelstam's readings of the *Commedia* and seems far more energized by the latter. Continuing response to Mandelstam is evident in Heaney's criticism: in *The Government of the Tongue* (1988) and in the Nobel lecture of 1995 (O'Donoghue 1998: 252–5).

During the later 1990s, Heaney's work emphasized other mythic and linguistic resources, such as Greek, Latin and Anglo-Saxon. His 2001 collection, *Electric Light*, however, cites and imitates Dante explicitly in the 'wish-sonnet' about Irish friends of the 1960s ('The Gaeltacht'; Heaney 2001: 44) and at a turning point in his elegy for Joseph Brodsky ('Audenesque'; Heaney 2001: 65). It has also been suggested that the three 'Little

Canticles of the Asturias' (Heaney 2001: 24–5) can be read as a kind of
*Commedia* in miniature – a pilgrimage that ends at Compostella with the
repetition of *stela*, and a scene that is in some ways reminiscent of the end
of Dante's journey in *Paradiso* 33 (Jamie McKendrick, *Independent on
Sunday*, 8 April 2001). The title and title-poem of the most recent collection,
*District and Circle* (2006), also suggest the Dantean underworld.

A recent work not included in *Electric Light* perhaps marks a more extensive response by Heaney to the *Paradiso*. This is a poem written for the
millennium, and published in the *Irish Times* for 18 January 2000 under the
title of 'A Dream of Solstice'. As its title implies, it marks the moment when,
at dawn on the winter solstice (21 December), the sun shines directly
through the 'roof-box' into the central chamber of the Newgrange burial
mound in the Boyne Valley north of Dublin – a Bronze Age site of historic
and political significance that had been recognized in section II of Heaney's
much earlier poem 'Funeral Rites' (from *North*, 1975). The verse-form,
approximating to *terza rima*, recalls that of Heaney's *Inferno* translations;
and it begins with a quotation and close translation of *Paradiso* 33.
58–61:

> Like somebody who sees things when he's dreaming
> And after the dream lives with the aftermath
> Of what he felt, no other trace remaining,
>
> So I live now.

The main narrative then describes the turning of the waters of the river Boyne
in this border country between north and south; the turning of the Earth
and the burial mounds; and the 'pilgrims, tourists, media folk' assembled on
the shortest day of the year, and at the end of the millennium. As the sun
rises, sending light into the passage grave 'like share-shine in a furrow', the
poem dissolves into a sequence of questions:

> . . .                    Who dares say 'love'
> At this cold coming? Who would not dare say it?
> Is this the moved wheel that the poet spoke of,
>
> The star pivot? Like his, my speech cannot
> Tell what the mind needs told: an infant tongue
>
> Milky with breast milk would be more articulate.

There are echoes here of Eliot and Eliot's Dante in the 'cold coming' and 'the moved wheel'. The poem's final image of the 'infant tongue', however, may also represent a further mediation of Dante through Mandelstam. 'A Dream of Solstice' finishes by evoking, as the *Paradiso* does, a pre-verbal state, and it does so with an intimation of possible new beginnings: a 'seedling' of light; a glimmer of 'Life's perseid in the ashpit / of the dead'.

A work which also evokes Mandelstam's reading of the *Paradiso* is a novel that appeared in the mid-1990s: **Ben Okri**'s *Astonishing the Gods* (1995). Okri's early reading included 'African, classical and European myths' and material from 'his father's library of western classics' (Bennett 1998: 364); and this recent novel takes the form of a mythic journey undertaken by a man who was 'born invisible' (Okri 1996: 1). With a sequence of guides, the traveller explores a magical island whose marvels are his 'personal wealth and paradise', but can be perceived as either 'wonderful' or 'infernal' (Okri 1996: 11). Yet the island's strange landscape, buildings and 'city of the Invisibles' (p. 31) probably owe less to Dante than to Calvino, whose quirky urban spaces are evoked here by, for example, the Invisibles' market-place of ideas (p. 74). Yet the appearance of a female guide towards the end of the journey (pp. 125, 153) and the pilgrim's final appearance on stage before the Invisibles and the three 'masters' (pp. 153–5) more specifically recall the *Paradiso* and Dante's encounters with the Apostles in *Par.* 24–6.

Other features of *Astonishing the Gods* recall how Dante's last *cantica* was imagined by Mandelstam and Giudici. In the paradoxical 'speech of silence' that follows those of the three masters, the 'acts of creativity' that enable Okri's Invisibles to 'astonish the gods' include 'our highest playfulness' (Okri 1996: 148). The second of the companions on the journey has been an anonymous and silent child (pp. 63–82), under whose guidance the traveller delights in 'play' and finds himself '[t]urning round and round like a child' (pp. 74, 80). The speechlessness of the *fante . . . alla mamella* had been compared to the 'tongue' of the poet as the *Commedia* draws to a close (*Par.* 33. 106–8). Several biblical sources (such as Psalms 8: 2; Matthew 18: 1–4, 21: 16) were probably evoked by Dante there; and this also seems to be the case when, near the end of the novel, Okri's traveller is 'overcome with light' and with 'the appreciation of the Invisibles', and himself becomes 'as a child' (p. 156). In a number of ways then, this modern conversation about the *Paradiso* seems to be informed by silence.

# Glossary of Literary Terms

These terms are used in this book or likely to be encountered in further discussion of Dante.

*ballata* (**plural** *ballate*) A form of lyric with short refrain (of 1–6 lines) and longer stanzas (often of 7–10 lines). As with other refrain-poems, the last line of each stanza rhymes with the first of the refrain. It would have been described by Dante in the fourth book of *DVE*, had he got that far (*DVE* 2. 4. 1). Dante wrote six *ballate* in all, including one in the *VN*.

*bolgia* (**plural** *bolge*), meaning 'pouch, purse, pocket'. One of the 10 subdivisions of the eighth circle of Hell (*Inf.* 18–29), which contains the first group of those who have sinned through various kinds of deception. (See: *Malebolge* below; diagram 1; and the cover illustration.)

*cantica* (**plural** *cantiche*) *Cantica* is in Latin the plural of *canticum* ('song'), hence the term could

mean 'group of songs'. The *Commedia* comprises three *cantiche* (*Inf.*, *Purg.*, *Par.*), containing respectively 34, 33 and 33 *canti* ('cantos'). Dante uses the term only once (*Purg.* 33. 140).

*canto* (**plural** *canti*), meaning 'song', is used to describe the 100 smaller units into which the *cantiche* of the *Commedia* are divided. Length of cantos varies between 115 and 160 lines and the average is 142 (*DE* 139A). Dante uses the term in this sense in *Inf.* 20. 2 and 33. 90; *Par.* 5. 16 and 139. It is also used to mean simply 'song' (e.g., *Purg.* 2. 131 and 5. 27) or 'poem/poetry', as in *Inf.* 4. 95 or *Par.* 1. 12.

*canzone* (**plural** *canzoni*) Like *canto*, the word can mean 'song' (as in *Purg.* 31. 134 and 32. 90). As a lyric form, the *canzone* descended from the Provençal *canso* and was devel-

GLOSSARY OF LITERARY TERMS

oped by the Sicilian and Tuscan poets before Dante. In *DVE* 2, Dante also calls it 'most excellent' and 'noblest' of poetic forms, and concludes that 'whatever is worthy of the highest form of the vernacular should be treated in *canzoni*' (2. 3. 10). Some of Dante's own *canzoni* are comparable in length to the *canti* of the *Commedia*, and it has been suggested that 'the roots of the canto are to be sought in Dante's vernacular apprenticeship' (\*Barolini 1993: 32). (See also: hendecasyllable.)

**Commedia** ('Comedy') is used by Dante twice to describe his poem (*Inf.* 16. 128 and 21. 2). His choice of title is problematic. The term may have been intended to convey the inclusiveness of the project; and 'comedy' as defined by a variety of classical and medieval commentators may have thus been 'the only manner of writing which, rhetorically, could offer Dante the space and liberty to accommodate a work as ambitious as his masterpiece' (\*Baranski in *DE* 185B–186B).

**contrapasso** The word occurs once only in the *Commedia* (*Inf.* 28. 142), but very frequently in criticism. The word comes from the medieval Latin noun *contrapassum*, which had been used by Aquinas to translate Aristotle's notion of 'suffering something in return' in the *Nichomachean Ethics*

(1132b21–1133b28) and as the equivalent of the law of punishment in kind (*lex talionis*) in the Old Testament (\*Charity 1966: 189–96; \*Gross 1985: 44; \*Armour 2001: 4–7). In the *Inferno* it becomes 'a highly metaphorical rendering back of suffering for the soul's entire career of sin' (Gross 1985: 44), and it operates in a more limited way in the *Purgatorio* (\*Pertile in *DE* 221B–222A).

**hendecasyllable** Literally meaning '11 syllables', the term actually applies to 'a verse-line of ten, eleven or twelve syllables whose last word-accent falls on the tenth syllable' (\*Robey in *DE* 477A). It is used by Dante throughout the *Commedia* and predominantly in his other vernacular poetry; he considered it 'the most splendid' form of line, 'both for its measured movement and for the scope it offers for subject-matter, constructions and vocabulary' (*DVE* 2. 5. 3, 2. 12. 2–3).

**Malebolge**, meaning 'evil pouches, pockets' (see *bolgia*). Part of the third and lowest level of Dante's Hell (*Inf.* 18–29), it holds the first and largest group of those who have sinned through *froda* (deception). The name is used on four occasions in the *Commedia*, all of them within the 12 cantos that describe this part of the *Inferno* (*Inf.* 18. 1, 21. 5, 24. 37, 29. 41).

**sonnet** Composed of 14 hendecasyllables (see above) divided 8: 6 ('octave' and 'sestet'), usually with a significant 'turn' (*volta*) or redirection in the ninth line, this concise and immensely adaptable verse-form may have developed out of the stanza of the *canzone* and is found first in the work of the Sicilian poets, especially Giacomo da Lentini (above, p. 113). Dante's output of 59 sonnets (or 291, if he was the author of *Il Fiore*), both before and after his exile, was considerable. It includes love-poems (25 of them in the *VN*), exchanges (*tenzoni*) about life and art with fellow-poets and friends, and even a diatribe against a pope (FB no.82; Scott 2004: 100–2).

*terza rima* Literally 'third rhyme', this rhyme-scheme was originated by Dante, and is used throughout the *Commedia*. Each rhyme occurs three times, except at the beginning and end of each canto, where the rhyme occurs only twice. It alternates once with the preceding rhyme and twice with the following one in the pattern *aba/bcb/ cdc*, etc. It thus generates a progressive pattern of interlocking tercets or *terzine* (singular *terzina*), each comprising three hendecasyllables (see above), and rhyming in the first 15 lines of each canto as follows: *aba/bcb/ cdc/ded/efe/*. The effect thus created is essential to the *Commedia*'s sense of 'forward movement' (*Robey in *DE* 808B–810B).

# Works Cited

Abulafia, D. (1992), *Frederick II: A Medieval Emperor* (London).

Ahern, J. (1997), 'Singing the Book: Orality in the Reception of Dante's *Comedy*', in A. A. Iannucci (ed.), *Dante: Contemporary Perspectives* (Toronto and London), pp. 214–39.

Altcappenberg, H. T. S. (ed.) (2000), *Sandro Botticelli: The Drawings for Dante's 'Divine Comedy'* (London).

Aquilecchia, G. (1979), *see* Villani 1979.

Ardizzone, M. L. (2002), *Guido Cavalcanti: The Other Middle Ages* (Toronto, Buffalo and London).

Armour, P. (1983), *The Door of Purgatory: A Study of Multiple Symbolism in Dante's 'Purgatorio'* (Oxford).

Armour, P. (1991), 'Comedy and the Origins of Italian Theatre around the Time of Dante', in J. R. Dashwood and J. E. Everson (eds.), *Writers and Performers in Italian Drama from the Time of Dante to Pirandello* (Lewiston, NY, Queenston, Ontario, and Lampeter), pp. 1–31.

Armour, P. (1994), 'Gold, Silver, and True Treasure: Economic Imagery in Dante', *Romance Studies* 23, 7–30.

Armour, P. (2001), 'Dante's *Contrapasso*: Context and Texts', *Italian Studies* 55, 1–20.

Ascoli, A. R. (1993), 'The Unfinished Author: Dante's Rhetoric of Authority in *Convivio* and *De vulgari eloquentia*', in R. Jacoff (ed.), *The Cambridge Companion to Dante* (Cambridge), pp. 45–66.

Auerbach, E. (1953–4), 'Dante's Addresses to the Reader', *Romance Philology* 7, 268–79.

Augustine, St (1992), H. M. Chadwick (ed. and tr.), *Confessions* (Oxford).

Balfour, M. (1998), 'The Place of the Poet: Dante in Walcott's Narrative Poetry', in N. R. Havely (ed.), *Dante's Modern Afterlife: Reception and Response, from Blake to Heaney* (London and New York), pp. 223–41.

Baranski, Z. (2001), 'Three Notes on Horace', in C. E. Honess (ed.), *DANTE: Current Trends in Dante Studies* (*Reading Medieval Studies* 21. Special Issue. University of Reading), pp. 5–37.

Barolini, T. (1979), 'Bertrand de Born and Sordello: The Poetry of Politics in Dante's *Comedy*', *PMLA* 94, 395–405.

Barolini, T. (1984), *Dante's Poets: Textuality and Truth in the 'Comedy'* (Princeton, NJ).

Barolini, T. (1993), 'Dante and the Lyric Past', in R. Jacoff (ed.), *The Cambridge Companion to Dante* (Cambridge), pp. 14–33.

Barolini, T. (2000), 'Dante and Francesca da Rimini: Realpolitik, Romance, Gender', *Speculum* 75, 1–28.

Barraclough, G. (1968), *The Medieval Papacy* (London).

Beckett, S. (1995), S. E. Gontarski (ed.), *The Complete Short Prose, 1929–1989* (New York).

Bemrose, S. (2000), *Dante: A New Life* (Exeter).

Bennett, R. (1998), 'Ben Okri (1959–)', in P. N. Parekh and S. F. Jagne (eds.), *Postcolonial African Writers: A Bio-Bibliographical Sourcebook* (Westport, CT), pp. 364–73.

Benvenuto da Imola, *see* Imola, Benvenuto da.

Bigsby, C. (ed.) (1995), *Nineteenth-Century American Short Stories* (London and Rutland, Vermont).

Black, A. (1992), *Political Thought in Europe, 1250–1450* (Cambridge).

Boitani, P. (1976), 'The *Monk's Tale*: Dante and Boccaccio', *Medium Aevum* 45, 50–69.

Boitani, P. (1983), 'What Dante Meant to Chaucer', in P. Boitani (ed.), *Chaucer and the Italian Trecento* (Cambridge), pp. 115–39.

Bolgar, R. R. (1954), *The Classical Heritage and its Beneficiaries* (Cambridge).

Bornstein, G. (1985), 'Yeats's Romantic Dante', in S. Y. McDougal (ed.), *Dante Among the Moderns* (Chapel Hill, NC, and London), pp. 11–38.

Boswell, J. C. (1999), *Dante's Fame in England: References in Printed British Books, 1477–1640* (Newark, DE, and London).

Botterill, S. (1994), *Dante and the Mystical Tradition: St Bernard of Clairvaux in the 'Commedia'* (Cambridge).

Boyde, P. (1981), *Dante Philomythes and Philosopher: Man in the Cosmos* (Cambridge).

Boyde, P. (1993), *Perception and Passion in Dante's 'Comedy'* (Cambridge).

Boyde, P. (2000), *Human Vices and Human Worth in Dante's 'Comedy'* (Cambridge).

Braida, A. (2004), *Dante and the Romantics* (Basingstoke and New York).

Braida, A. and Calè, L. (eds.) (forthcoming), *Dante on View* (Aldershot and Burlington, Vermont).

Bruni, Leonardo (1996), 'Vita di Dante', in P. Viti (ed.), *Leonardo Bruni: opere letterarie e politiche* (Turin), pp. 539–52.

Burr, D. (1989), *Olivi and Franciscan Poverty: The Origins of the 'Usus Pauper' Controversy* (Philadelphia).

Burr, D. (1993), *Olivi's Peaceable Kingdom: A Reading of the Apocalypse Commentary* (Philadelphia).

Burr, D. (2001), *The Spiritual Franciscans: From Protest to Persecution in the Century after St Francis* (University Park, PA).

Buti, Francesco da (ed. C. Giannini) (1858–62), *Commento sopra la 'Divina commedia' di Dante Allighieri* (3 vols., Pisa).

Cachey, T. J. (ed.) (1995), *Dante Now: Current Trends in Dante Studies* (Notre Dame, IN, and London).

Caesar, M. (ed.) (1989), *Dante: The Critical Heritage* (London and New York).

Cambridge University Library (2006), *Visible Language: Dante in Text and Image, An Exhibition in Cambridge University Library, 17 January–1 July 2006* (Cambridge).

Caputo, R. (2004), 'Dante by Heart and Dante Declaimed: The Realization of the *Comedy* on Italian Radio and Television', in A. A. Iannucci (ed.), *Dante, Cinema and Television* (Toronto), pp. 213–23.

Carson, C. (tr.) (2002), *The Inferno of Dante Alighieri* (London and New York).

Casadio, G. (ed.) (1996), *Dante nel cinema* (Ravenna).

Casciani, S. and Kleinhenz, C. (eds. and trs.) (2000), *The 'Fiore' and the 'Detto d'amore': A Late 13th-Century Translation of the 'Roman de la Rose' Attributable to Dante* (Notre Dame, IN, and London).

Cassell, A. K. (1991), 'Santa Lucia as Patroness of Sight: Hagiography, Iconography, and Dante', *Dante Studies* 109, 71–88.

Catto, J. (1980), 'Florence, Tuscany and the World of Dante', in C. Grayson (ed.), *The World of Dante: Essays on Dante and His Times* (Oxford), pp. 1–17.

Charity, A. C. (1966), *Events and Their Afterlife: The Dialectics of Christian Typology in the Bible and Dante* (Cambridge).

Charity, A. C. (1974), 'T. S. Eliot: The Dantean Recognitions', in A. D. Moody (ed.), *The Waste Land in Different Voices* (London), pp. 117–62.

Cherchi, P. (1988), 'Geryon's Canto', *Lectura Dantis Virginiana* 2, 31–44 [or Google: 'Geryon's Canto'].

Clanchy, M. (1993), *From Memory to Written Record: England, 1066–1307* (2nd edn., Oxford).

Cole, W. (1995), 'Literal Art? A New Look at Doré's Illustrations for Dante's *Inferno*', *Word & Image* 10, 95–106.

Compagni, D. (1968), G. Luzzatto (ed.), *Cronica* (Turin).

Compagni, D. (1986), D. E. Bornstein (ed. and tr.), *Dino Compagni's Chronicle of Florence* (Philadelphia).

Comparetti, D. (1966), *Virgil in the Middle Ages*, tr. E. F. M. Benecke (2nd edn., London).

Contini, G. (ed.) (1960), *Poeti del duecento* (2 vols., Milan and Naples).

Cook, W. R. (1999), *Images of St Francis of Assisi . . . from the Earliest Images to 1320 in Italy* (Florence).

Cremona, J. (1965), 'Dante's Views on Language', in U. Limentani (ed.), *The Mind of Dante* (Cambridge), pp. 138–62.

Crombie, A. C. (1969), *Augustine to Galileo* (2 vols., Harmondsworth).

Crouzet-Pavan, E. (1997), 'A Flower of Evil: Young Men in Medieval Italy', in G. Levi and J. C. Schmitt (eds.), *A History of Young People. Vol. I: Ancient and Medieval Rites of Passage*, tr. C. Naish (Cambridge, MA), pp. 173–221.

Cunningham, G. F. (1965), *The Divine Comedy in English: A Critical Bibliography, 1782–1900* (Edinburgh and London).

Curtius, E. R. (1953), *European Literature and the Latin Middle Ages*, tr. W. R. Trask (New York).

Curtius, E. R. (1973), 'The Ship of the Argonauts', tr. M. Kowal, in E. R. Curtius, *Essays on European Literature* (Princeton, NJ), pp. 645–96.

Dante Alighieri (1902), P. H. Wicksteed and E. G. Gardner (eds.), *Dante and Giovanni del Virgilio* (Westminster).

Dante Alighieri (1904), P. H. Wicksteed (ed. and tr.), *Latin Works of Dante Alighieri* (London), pp. 389–427 (translation of the *Quaestio de Aqua et Terra*).

Dante Alighieri (1966), P. Toynbee (ed.), *Dantis Alagherii epistolae: The Letters of Dante* (2nd edn., Oxford).

Dante Alighieri (1966–7), G. Petrocchi (ed.), *'La commedia': secondo l'antica vulgata* (3 vols., Milan).

Dante Alighieri (1967), K. Foster and P. Boyde (eds.), *Dante's Lyric Poetry* (2 vols., Oxford).

Dante Alighieri (1970), G. Contini (ed.), *Rime* (Turin).

Dante Alighieri (1979), U. Bosco and G. Reggio (eds.), *Dante Alighieri: 'la divina commedia'* (3 vols., Florence).

Dante Alighieri (1984), G. Contini (ed.), *Il Fiore e Il detto d'amore attribuibili a Dante Alighieri* (Milan and Naples).

Dante Alighieri (1988), C. Vasoli and D. De Robertis (eds.), *Dante Alighieri: opere minori* (5 vols., Milan and Naples).

Dante Alighieri (1991–7), A. M. Chiavacci Leonardi (ed.), *Dante Alighieri: 'Commedia'* (2nd edn., 3 vols., Milan).

Dante Alighieri (1996a), L. Rossi (ed.), *Dante: Il Fiore, Detto d'amore* (Milan).

Dante Alighieri (1996b), P. Shaw (ed. and tr.), *Dante: 'Monarchy'* (Cambridge).

Dante Alighieri (1996c), S. Botterill (ed. and tr.), *Dante: 'De vulgari eloquentia'* (Cambridge).

Dante Alighieri (1996d), R. M. Durling and R. Martinez (eds.), *The 'Divine Comedy' of Dante Alighieri I: Inferno* (New York and Oxford).

Dante Alighieri (2003), R. M. Durling and R. Martinez (eds.), *The 'Divine Comedy' of Dante Alighieri II: Purgatorio* (New York and Oxford).

Davis, C. T. (1957), *Dante and the Idea of Rome* (Oxford).

Davis, C. T. (1963), 'The Early Collection of Books of S. Croce in Florence', *Proceedings of the American Philosophical Society* 107 (5), 399–414.

Davis, C. T. (1984), *Dante's Italy and Other Essays* (Philadelphia).

Davis, C. T. (1988), 'The Florentine *Studia* and Dante's "Library"', in G. di Scipio and A. Scaglione (eds.), *The 'Divine Comedy' and the Encyclopedia of Arts and Sciences* (Amsterdam and Philadelphia), pp. 339–66.

Dean, T. (ed.) (2000), *The Towns of Italy in the Middle Ages* (Manchester).

Delcorno, C. (1975), *Giordano da Pisa e l'antica predicazione in volgare* (Florence).

De Sua, W. J. (1964), *Dante into English* (Chapel Hill, NC).

Dossena, G. (1995), *Dante* (Milan).

Duckworth, M. (2006), 'Everyday Infernos: *The Divine Comedy* in Australian Literature and Art', unpublished paper, given at International Medieval Congress, Leeds, 10 July 2006.

Duffy, E. (1997), *Saints and Sinners: A History of the Popes* (New Haven, CT, and London).

Durling, R. M. and Martinez, R. (eds.) (1996), *The 'Divine Comedy' of Dante Alighieri I: Inferno* (New York and Oxford).

Durling, R. M. and Martinez, R. (eds.) (2003), *The 'Divine Comedy' of Dante Alighieri II: Purgatorio* (New York and Oxford).

Eco, U. (1983), *The Name of the Rose*, tr. W. Weaver (London).

Eco, U. (1997), *The Search for the Perfect Language*, tr. J. Fentress (London).

Edwards, R. R. (ed. and tr.) (1987), *The Poetry of Guido Guinizzelli* (New York and London).

Elam, K. (1994), 'Dead Heads: Damnation-Narration in the "Dramaticules"', in J. Pilling (ed.), *The Cambridge Companion to Beckett* (Cambridge), pp. 145–66.

Eliot, T. S. (1920), 'Dante', in T. S. Eliot, *The Sacred Wood* (London), pp. 159–71.

Eliot, T. S. (1929), *Dante* (London).

Eliot, T. S. (1965), 'What Dante Means to Me', in T. S. Eliot, *To Criticize the Critic* (London), pp. 125–35.

Eliot, T. S. (1971), V. Eliot (ed.), *The Waste Land: A Facsimile and Transcript of the Original Drafts, including the Annotations of Ezra Pound/T. S. Eliot* (New York).

Eliot, T. S. (1993), R. Schuchard (ed.), *The Varieties of Metaphysical Poetry: The Clark Lectures at Trinity College Cambridge 1926 and the Turnbull Lectures at the Johns Hopkins University 1933* (London).

Ellis, S. P. (1983), *Dante and English Poetry: Shelley to T. S. Eliot* (Cambridge).

Ellis, S. P. (tr. and intro.) (1994), *Dante Alighieri: Hell* (London).

Ellis, S. P. (1998), 'Dante and Louis MacNeice: A Sequel to the *Commedia*', in N. R. Havely (ed.), *Dante's Modern Afterlife: Reception and Response, from Blake to Heaney* (London and New York), pp. 128–39.

Evans, G. R. (2000), *Bernard of Clairvaux* (New York and Oxford).

Feldman, P. R. and Scott-Kilvert, D. (eds.) (1987), *The Journals of Mary Shelley 1814–1844* (2 vols., Oxford).

Ferrante, J. (1984), *The Political Vision of the 'Divine Comedy'* (Princeton, NJ).

Fitzgerald, R. (1985), 'Mirroring the *Commedia*', in S. Y. McDougal (ed.), *Dante Among the Moderns* (Chapel Hill, NC, and London), pp. 153–75.

Foster, K. and Boyde, P. (eds.) (1967), *Dante's Lyric Poetry* (2 vols., Oxford).

Fowlie, W. (1985), 'Dante and Beckett', in S. Y. McDougal (ed.), *Dante Among the Moderns* (Chapel Hill, NC, and London), pp. 128–52.

Foxe, John (1570), *Ecclesiastical History* (2nd edn., London).

Franke, W. (1996), *Dante's Interpretive Journey* (Chicago).

Friederich, W. P. (1950), *Dante's Fame Abroad, 1350–1850* (Rome).

Friedman, J. B. (1972), 'Antichrist and the Iconography of Dante's Geryon', *Journal of the Warburg and Courtauld Institutes* 35, 108–22.

Fuller, D. (1988), 'Blake and Dante', *Art History* 11, 349–73.

Fumagalli, M. C. (1996), ' "Station Island": Seamus Heaney's *Divina commedia*', *Irish University Review* 26, 127–42.

Fumagalli, M. C. (2001), *The Flight of the Vernacular: Seamus Heaney, Derek Walcott and the Impress of Dante* (Amsterdam).

Gardiner, E. (ed. and tr.) (1989), *Visions of Heaven and Hell before Dante* (New York).

Gehl, P. F. (1993), *A Moral Art: Grammar, Society and Culture in Trecento Florence* (Ithaca, NY, and London).

Gellrich, J. M. (1985), *The Idea of the Book in the Middle Ages: Language Theory, Mythology and Fiction* (Ithaca, NY, and London).

Gilby, T. (ed. and tr.) (1960), *St Thomas Aquinas (1225?–1274): Philosophical Texts* (New York).

Gilson, E. (1949), *Dante* (New York).

Gilson, S. A. (2005), *Dante and Renaissance Florence* (Cambridge).

Gimpel, J. (1988), *The Medieval Machine* (2nd edn., London).

Giudici, G. (1991), *Il Paradiso: perché mi vinse il lume d'esta stella. Sàtura drammatica* (Genoa).

Green, L. (1972), *Chronicle into History: An Essay on the Interpretation of History in Florentine Fourteenth-Century Chronicles* (Cambridge).

Grendler, P. F. (1989), *Schooling in Renaissance Italy: Literacy and Learning 1300–1600* (Baltimore, MD).

Griffiths, E. and Reynolds, M. (eds.) (2005), *Dante in English* (London).

Gross, K. (1985), 'Infernal Metamorphoses: An Interpretation of Dante's "Counterpass"', *Modern Language Notes* 100, 42–69.

Halpern, D. (ed.) (1993), *Dante's 'Inferno': Translations by Twenty Contemporary Poets* (New York).

Harris, T. (2000), *Hannibal* (London).

Haughton, H. (1998), 'Purgatory Regained? Beckett and Dante', in N. R. Havely (ed.), *Dante's Modern Afterlife: Reception and Response, from Blake to Heaney* (London and New York), pp. 140–64.

Havely, N. R. (ed. and tr.) (1980, repr. 1992), *Chaucer's Boccaccio: Sources of 'Troilus' and the Knight's and Franklin's Tales* (Woodbridge and Totowa, NJ).

Havely, N. R. (1990), 'Brunetto and Palinurus', *Dante Studies* 108, 29–38.

Havely, N. R. (ed.) (1994a), *Chaucer: The House of Fame* (Durham).

Havely, N. R. (1994b), 'Francesca Frustrated: New Evidence about Hobhouse's and Byron's Translation of Pellico', *Romanticism* 1 (1), 106–20.

Havely, N. R. (1997), 'Muses and Blacksmiths: Italian Trecento Poetics and the Reception of Dante in "The House of Fame"', in A. J. Minnis, C. C. Morse and T. Turville-Petre (eds.), *Essays on Ricardian Literature: In Honour of J. A. Burrow* (Oxford), pp. 61–81.

Havely, N. R. (ed.) (1998), *Dante's Modern Afterlife: Reception and Response, from Blake to Heaney* (London and New York).

Havely, N. R. (2003), ' "An Italian Writer Against the Pope"? Dante in Reformation England, c.1560–c.1640', in E. G. Haywood (ed.), *Dante Metamorphoses: Episodes in a Literary Afterlife* (Dublin), pp. 127–49.

Havely, N. R. (2004), *Dante and the Franciscans: Poverty and the Papacy in the 'Commedia'* (Cambridge).

Hawkins, P. S. (1980), 'Virtue and Virtuosity: Poetic Self-Reference in the Commedia', *Dante Studies* 98, 1–18.

Hawkins, P. S. (1999), *Dante's Testaments: Essays in Scriptural Imagination* (Stanford, CA).

Hawkins, P. S. (2006), *Dante: A Brief History* (Oxford).

Hawkins, P. S. and Jacoff, R. (eds.) (2001), *The Poets' Dante: Twentieth-Century Responses* (New York).

Haywood, E. G. (ed.) (2003), *Dante Metamorphoses: Episodes in a Literary Afterlife* (Dublin).

Heaney, S. (1979), *Field Work* (London).

Heaney, S. (1984), *Station Island* (London).

273

Heaney, S. (1985) 'Envies and Identifications: Dante and the Modern Poet', *Irish University Review* 15, 5–19; repr. in P. S. Hawkins and R. Jacoff (eds.), *The Poets' Dante* (New York, 2001), pp. 239–58.

Heaney, S. (1995), *The Spirit Level* (London).

Heaney, S. (2001), *Electric Light* (London).

Heaney, S. (2006), *District and Circle* (London).

Heyward, M. (1993), *The Ern Malley Affair* (London and Boston, MA).

Hollander, R. M. (1969), *Allegory in Dante's 'Commedia'* (Princeton, NJ).

Holmes, G. A. (1980), 'Dante and the Popes', in C. Grayson (ed.), *The World of Dante: Essays on Dante and His Times* (Oxford), pp. 18–43.

Holmes, G. A. (1986), *Florence, Rome and the Origins of the Renaissance* (Oxford).

Holmes, G. A. (1997), '*Monarchia* and Dante's Attitude to the Popes', in J. R. Woodhouse (ed.), *Dante and Governance* (Oxford), pp. 46–57.

Horgan, F. (ed. and tr.) (1994), *Guillaume de Lorris and Jean de Meun: The Romance of the Rose* (Oxford).

Humphries, R. (tr.) (1955), *Ovid: 'Metamorphoses'*.

Hyde, J. K. (1973), *Society and Politics in Medieval Italy: The Evolution of the Civil Life, 1000–1350* (Manchester).

Iannucci, A. A. (1989), 'Dante, Television and Education', *Quaderni d'italianistica* 10, 1–31.

Iannucci, A. A. (ed.) (2004), *Dante, Cinema and Television* (Toronto).

Imola, Benvenuto da (1887), J. P. Lacaita (ed.), *Comentum super Dantis Aldigherii Comoediam* (5 vols., Florence).

Jacoff, R. and Schnapp, J. (eds.) (1991), *The Poetry of Allusion: Virgil and Ovid in Dante's* Commedia (Stanford, CA).

Jensen, F. (ed. and tr.) (1986), *The Poetry of the Sicilian School* (New York and London).

John of Salisbury (1990), C. J. Nederman (ed. and tr.), *Policraticus* (Cambridge).

Kay, R. (1985), 'The Spare Ribs of Dante's Michael Scot', *Dante Studies* 103, 1–14.

Kay, R. (1994), *Dante's Christian Astrology* (Philadelphia).

Kay, R. (ed. and tr.) (1998), *Dante's 'Monarchia', Translated with a Commentary* (Toronto).

Keen, C. (2000), 'Images of Exile: Distance and Memory in the Poetry of Cino da Pistoia', *Italian Studies* 55, 21–36.

Keen, C. (2003), *Dante and the City* (Stroud).

Kenner, H. (1985), 'Ezra Pound's *Commedia*', in S. Y. McDougal (ed.), *Dante Among the Moderns* (Chapel Hill, NC, and London), pp. 39–56.

Kirkham, V. (2004), 'The Off-Screen Landscape: Dante's Ravenna and Antonioni's *Red Desert*', in A. A. Iannucci (ed.), *Dante, Cinema and Television* (Toronto), pp. 106–28.

Kirkpatrick, R. (tr. and ed.) (2006), *Dante: Inferno* (London).

Klonsky, M. (ed.) (1980), *Blake's Dante: The Complete Illustrations to the 'Divine Comedy'* (London).

Ladner, G. B. (1967), '*Homo Viator*: Medieval Ideas on Alienation and Order', *Speculum* 42, 233–59.

Lambert, M. D. (1998), *Franciscan Poverty: The Doctrine of the Absolute Poverty of Christ and the Apostles in the Franciscan Order 1210–1323* (rev. edn., New York).

Langley, E. (ed.) (1915), *The Poetry of Giacomo da Lentino, Sicilian Poet of the Thirteenth Century* (Cambridge, MA, and London).

Lansing, C. (1991), *The Florentine Magnates: Lineage and Faction in a Medieval Commune* (Princeton, NJ).

Larner, J. (1965), *The Lords of Romagna: Romagnuol Society and the Origins of the Signorie* (London).

Larner, J. (1980), *Italy in the Age of Dante and Petrarch, 1216–1380* (London).

Latini, Brunetto (1948), F. J. Carmody (ed.), *Li livres dou tresor* (Berkeley and Los Angeles).

Lawrence, C. H. (1994), *The Friars: The Impact of the Early Mendicant Movement on Western Society* (London and New York).

Leff, G. (1958), *Medieval Thought: Augustine to Ockham* (Harmondsworth).

Lerner, R. (1994), 'Writing and Resistance among Beguins of Languedoc and Catalonia', in P. Biller and A. Hudson (eds.), *Heresy and Literacy 1000–1530* (Cambridge), pp. 186–204.

Lesnick, D. R. (1989), *Preaching in Florence: The Social World of Franciscan and Dominican Spirituality* (Athens, GA, and London).

Little, L. K. (1971), 'Pride Goes before Avarice: Social Changes and the Vices in Latin Christendom', *American Historical Review* 76, 16–49.

Little, L. K. (1978), *Religious Poverty and the Profit Economy in Medieval Europe* (London).

Looney, D. (2004), 'Spencer Williams and Dante: An African-American Filmmaker at the Gates of Hell', in A. A. Iannucci (ed.), *Dante, Cinema and Television* (Toronto), pp. 129–44.

Lucchesi, V. (1997), 'Politics and Theology in *Inferno X*', in John Woodhouse (ed.), *Dante and Governance* (Oxford), pp. 85–101.

Luscombe, D. E. (1997), *Medieval Thought* (Oxford).

Macdonald, R. (1962), *The Zebra-Striped Hearse* (London).

Mandelstam, N. (1999), *Hope against Hope: A Memoir*, tr. M. Hayward (London).

Mandelstam, O. (1991), 'Conversation about Dante', in J. G. Harris (ed.), *Collected Critical Prose and Letters* (London), pp. 397–451; repr. in P. S. Hawkins and R. Jacoff (eds.), *The Poets' Dante* (New York, 2001), pp. 40–93.

Manganiello, D. (1989), *T. S. Eliot and Dante* (Basingstoke).

Martines, L. (1983), *Power and Imagination: City States in Renaissance Italy* (Harmondsworth).

Matarasso, P. (ed. and tr.) (1993), *The Cistercian World: Monastic Writings of the Twelfth Century* (London).

Matthews, G. (2005), *Augustine* (Oxford).

Mazzocco, A. (1993), *Linguistic Theories in Dante and the Humanists: Studies of Language and Intellectual History in Late Medieval and Early Renaissance Italy* (Leiden, New York and Cologne).

Mazzotta, G. (1979), *Dante, Poet of the Desert* (Princeton, NJ).

Mazzotta, G. (1993), 'Life of Dante', in R. Jacoff (ed.), *The Cambridge Companion to Dante* (Cambridge), pp. 1–13.

McDiarmid, L. S. (1978), 'W. H. Auden's "In the Year of My Youth"', *Review of English Studies* 29, 267–312.

McDougal, S. Y. (ed.) (1985a), *Dante Among the Moderns* (Chapel Hill, NC, and London).

McDougal, S. Y. (1985b), 'T. S. Eliot's Metaphysical Dante', in S. Y. McDougal (ed.), *Dante Among the Moderns* (Chapel Hill, NC, and London), pp. 57–81.

McGinn, B. (ed.) (1998), *Visions of the End: Apocalyptic Traditions in the Middle Ages* (rev. edn., New York).

Melville, Herman (1993), A. R. Lee (ed.), *Herman Melville: 'Billy Budd, Sailor' and Other Stories* (London and Rutland, Vermont).

Menache, S. (1998), *Clement V* (Cambridge).

Milbank, A. (1998), *Dante and the Victorians* (Manchester).

Miller, C. (2003), 'John Flaxman's Working Copy of Dante's *Divina commedia*', *Italian Studies* 58, 75–87.

Minio-Paluello, L. (1956), 'Remigio Girolami's *De bono communi*: Florence at the Time of Dante's Banishment and the Philosopher's Answer to the Crisis', *Italian Studies* 11, 56–71.

Minnis, A. and Scott, A. B. (1988), *Medieval Literary Theory and Criticism c.1100–c.1375: The Commentary Tradition* (Oxford).

Moleta, V. (1983), *From St Francis to Giotto: The Influence of St Francis on Early Italian Art and Literature* (Chicago).

Moore, E. (1896), *Studies in Dante (First Series): Scriptural and Classical Authors in Dante* (Oxford).

Moorman, J. R. H. (1968), *A History of the Franciscan Order from its Origins to the Year 1517* (Oxford).

Morgan, A. (1990), *Dante and the Medieval Other World* (Cambridge).

Murray, A. (1972), 'Piety and Impiety in Thirteenth-century Italy', in G. J. Cuning and D. Baker (eds.), *Popular Belief and Practice (Studies in Church History* 8) (Cambridge), pp. 83–106.

Musa, M. (1974), *Advent at the Gates: Dante's 'Comedy'* (Bloomington, IN).

Najemy, J. M. (1993), 'Dante and Florence', in R. Jacoff (ed.), *The Cambridge Companion to Dante* (Cambridge), pp. 80–99.

Nelson, L. (ed. and tr.) (1986), *The Poetry of Guido Cavalcanti* (New York and London).

Ó Cuilleanain, C. (2003), 'Dante in *The Zebra-Striped Hearse*', *Quaderni di cultura italiana* 3, 107–24.

O'Donoghue, B. (1998), 'Dante's Versatility and Seamus Heaney's Modernism', in N. R. Havely (ed.), *Dante's Modern Afterlife: Reception and Response, from Blake to Heaney* (London and New York), pp. 242–57.

Okri, B. (1996), *Astonishing the Gods* (paperback edn., London).

Orvieto, E. (1969), 'Castel della Pieve e l'esilio di Dante', *Dante Studies* 87, 127–38.

Owen, R. (2001), 'Dante's Reception by 14th- and 15th-Century Illustrators of the *Commedia*', in C. E. Honess (ed.), *DANTE: Current Trends in Dante Studies (Reading Medieval Studies* 21. *Special Issue.* University of Reading), pp. 163–225.

Palma, M. (tr.) (2002), *Inferno: A New Verse Translation* (New York).

Parker, D. (1993), *Commentary and Ideology: Dante in the Renaissance* (Durham, NC, and London).

Peters, E. (1991), 'Human Diversity and Civil Society in *Paradiso* VIII', *Dante Studies* 109, 51–70.

Petrocchi, G. (1984), *Vita di Dante* (Rome and Bari).

Petrocchi, G. (1994), *Itinerari danteschi* (Milan).

Phillips, T. (tr. and ill.) (1983), *Inferno: The First Part of the 'Divine Comedy' of Dante Alighieri* (New York).

Phillips, T. (1991), '*A TV Dante*: Sketch of a Screenplay by Tom Phillips', *Eonta* 1 (4), 32–50.

Piattoli, R. (1950), *Codice diplomatico dantesco* (Florence).

Picone, M. (1997), 'Dante and the Classics', in A. A. Iannucci (ed.), *Dante: Contemporary Perspectives* (Toronto and London), pp. 51–73.

Pinsky, R. (tr.) (1994), *The Inferno of Dante: A New Verse Translation* (New York).

Pite, R. (1994), *The Circle of Our Vision: Dante's Presence in English Romantic Poetry* (Oxford).

Poggioli, R. (1965), 'Paolo and Francesca', in J. Freccero (ed.), *Dante: A Collection of Critical Essays* (Englewood Cliffs, NJ), pp. 61–77.

Pope-Hennessy, J. W. (1993), *'Paradiso': The Illuminations to Dante's 'Divine Comedy' by Giovanni di Paolo* (London).

Poppi, C. (ed.) (1994), *Sventurati amanti: il mito di Paolo e Francesca nell' 800* (Milan).

277

Putignano, L. (1994), 'Francesca da Rimini sulle scene del teatro d'opera italiano', in C. Poppi (ed.), *Sventurati amanti: il mito di Paolo e Francesca nell' 800* (Milan), pp. 39–44.

Quartermain, P. (2000), 'Paradise as Praxis: Dante and a Contemporary American Avant-Garde', in A. Goldoni and A. Mariani (eds.), *Testo e Senso 3 Dante: 'For Use Now'* (Rome), pp. 119–31.

Quinones, R. J. (1994), *Foundation Sacrifice in Dante's 'Commedia'* (University Park, PA).

Reeves, M. (1969), *The Influence of Prophecy in the Later Middle Ages: A Study in Joachimism* (Oxford).

Reeves, M. (1976), *Joachim of Fiore and the Prophetic Future* (London).

Reynolds, M. (1998), 'Ezra Pound: Quotation and Community', in N. R. Havely (ed.), *Dante's Modern Afterlife: Reception and Response, from Blake to Heaney* (London and New York), pp. 113–27.

Reynolds, M. T. (1981), *Joyce and Dante: The Shaping Imagination* (Princeton, NJ).

Ricci, C. (1965), *L'ultimo rifugio di Dante,* ed. E. Chiarini (Ravenna).

Ricci, D. (ed.) (1967), *Il processo di Dante* (Florence).

Richardson, B. (1995), 'Editing Dante's *Commedia,* 1472–1629', in T. Cachey (ed.), *Dante Now: Current Trends in Dante Studies* (Notre Dame, IN), pp. 205–35.

Riché, P. and Lobrichon, G. (eds.) (1984), *Le Moyen Âge et la Bible* (Paris).

Robinson, P. (1998) '"Una fitta di rimorso": Dante in Sereni', in N. R. Havely (ed.), *Dante's Modern Afterlife: Reception and Response, from Blake to Heaney* (London and New York), pp. 185–208.

Rumble, P. (2004), '*Dopo tanto veder:* Pasolini's Dante after the Disappearance of the Fireflies', in A. A. Iannucci (ed.), *Dante, Cinema and Television* (Toronto), pp. 153–65.

Ruskin, John (1851), *The Stones of Venice* (3 vols., London).

Rutledge, M. (1995), 'Dante, the Body and Light', *Dante Studies* 113, 151–65.

Salvadori Lonergan, C. (1997), '"*E quindi uscimmo a riveder le stelle*" – But There Are No Stars', *Journal of Anglo- Italian Studies* 5, 277–91.

Samuel, I. (1966), *Dante and Milton: The 'Commedia' and 'Paradise Lost'* (Ithaca, NY).

Schevill, F. (1963), *History of Florence* (New York).

Schnapp, J. T. (1986), *The Transfiguration of History at the Center of Dante's 'Paradise'* (Princeton, NJ).

Schnapp, J. T. (1988), 'Dante's Sexual Solecisms: Gender and Genre in the *Commedia*', *Romanic Review* 79, 143–63.

Scott, J. A. (1996), *Dante's Political Purgatory* (Philadelphia).

Scott, J. A. (2004), *Understanding Dante* (Notre Dame, IN).

Shapiro, M. (1990), *'De vulgari eloquentia': Dante's Book of Exile* (Lincoln, NE).

Shelley, Mary Wollstonecraft (1980–8), B. T. Bennett (ed.), *The Letters of Mary Wollstonecraft Shelley* (3 vols., Baltimore, MD).

Shelley, Percy Bysshe (1964), F. L. Jones (ed.), *The Letters of Percy Bysshe Shelley* (2 vols., Oxford).

Smalley, B. (1952), *The Study of the Bible in the Middle Ages* (Oxford).

Sowell, M. U. (1990), 'Brunetto's *Tesoro* in Dante's *Inferno*', *Lectura Dantis Virginiana* 7, 60–71.

Soyinka, W. (ed.) (1975), *Poems of Black Africa* (Oxford, Portsmouth, NH, and Ibadan).

Spears, M. K. (1985), 'The Divine Comedy of W. H. Auden', in S. Y. McDougal (ed.), *Dante Among the Moderns* (Chapel Hill, NC, and London), pp. 82–101.

Starn, R. (1982), *Contrary Commonwealth: The Theme of Exile in Medieval and Renaissance Italy* (Berkeley, Los Angeles and London).

Sumption, J. (1975), *Pilgrimage: An Image of Medieval Religion* (London).

Szittya, P. R. (1986), *The Antifraternal Tradition in Medieval Literature* (Princeton, NJ).

Talbot Rice, D. (1968), *Byzantine Art* (Harmondsworth).

Taylor, K. (1989), *Chaucer Reads 'The Divine Comedy'* (Stanford, CA).

Testa, B. (2004), 'Dante and Cinema: Film across a Chasm', in A. A. Iannucci (ed.), *Dante, Cinema and Television* (Toronto), pp. 189–212.

Thompson, A. (1991), 'George Eliot, Dante and Moral Choice in *Felix Holt, the Radical*', *Modern Language Review* 86, 553–66.

Thompson, A. (2003), 'Dante and George Eliot', in E. G. Haywood (ed.), *Dante Metamorphoses: Episodes in a Literary Afterlife* (Dublin), pp. 199–220.

Tierney, B. (1988), *The Crisis of Church and State 1050–1300* (repr., Toronto).

Tinkler-Villani, V. (1989), *Visions of Dante in English Poetry: Translations of the 'Commedia' from Jonathan Richardson to William Blake* (Amsterdam).

Toynbee, P. J. (1909), *Dante in English Literature* (2 vols., London).

Ullmann, W. (1974), *A Short History of the Papacy in the Middle Ages* (London).

Valency, M. (1958), *In Praise of Love: An Introduction to the Love-Poetry of the Renaissance* (New York).

Vickers, N. J. (1995), 'Dante in the Video Decade', in T. Cachey (ed.), *Dante Now: Current Trends in Dante Studies* (Notre Dame, IN), pp. 263–76.

Villani, Giovanni (1906), R. Selfe and P. H. Wicksteed (trs.), *Villani's Chronicle* (selections) (London).

Villani, Giovanni (1979), G. Aquilecchia (ed.), *Giovanni Villani: 'Cronica', con le continuazioni di Matteo e Filippo* (Turin) [selections].

Villani, Giovanni (1990–1), G. Porta (ed.), *Nuova cronica* (3 vols., Parma).

Wallace, D. (1993), 'Dante in English', in R. Jacoff (ed.), *The Cambridge Companion to Dante* (Cambridge). pp. 237–58.

Wallace, D. (1999), 'Dante in Somerset: Ghosts, Historiography, Periodization', in D. Lawton, W. Scase and R. Copeland (eds.), *New Medieval Literatures 3* (Oxford), pp. 9–38.

Waller, M. (2004), 'Back to the Future: Dante and the Languages of Post-War Italian Film', in A. A. Iannucci (ed.), *Dante, Cinema and Television* (Toronto), pp. 74–96.

Wetherbee, W. P. (1984), *Chaucer and the Poets: An Essay on 'Troilus and Criseyde'* (Ithaca, NY, and London).

Wilhelm, J. J. (1974), *Dante and Pound: The Epic of Judgment* (Orono, ME).

Wilkins, E. H. (1983), 'Dante and the Mosaics of his *Bel San Giovanni*', in A. B. Giamatti (ed.), *Dante in America: The First Two Centuries* (New York), pp. 144–59.

Wolf, K. B. (2003), *The Poverty of Riches: St Francis of Assisi Reconsidered* (New York and Oxford).

Woolf, J. R. (1998), 'Micòl and Beatrice: Echoes of the *Vita nuova* in Giorgio Bassani's *Garden of the Finzi Contini*', in N. R. Havely (ed.), *Dante's Modern Afterlife: Reception and Response, from Blake to Heaney* (London and New York), pp. 167–84.

Yates, F. A. (1951), 'Transformations of Dante's Ugolino', *Journal of the Warburg and Cortauld Institutes* 14, 92–117.

Zaccagnini, G. (ed.) (1925), *Le Rime di Cino da Pistoia* (Geneva).

# Electronic Resources

Have Mandelstam's and Giudici's prophetic images of Dante's God in the *Paradiso* as 'communicator, transmitter' and 'infinite computer' been fulfilled by the advent of the web and the resources it can provide on Dante and the *Commedia*? Or would all this have made Dante think of Arachne? In any case, new websites are being developed all the time, and some of the most reliable and accessible are listed below.

## Introductory

At the time of writing (30 August 2006), by far the easiest **portal** to the main resources is the website run by the **Dante Society of America**, at: www.dantesociety.org
Following 'Links' on the homepage will give quick access to a number of the best databases, such as: the Princeton Dante Project; the Dartmouth Dante Project; the Columbia Digital Dante; and an online concordance to the *Commedia*.

## Details of some individual sites

**The Princeton Dante Project** at: http://etcweb.princeton.edu/dante/pdp includes parallel texts of all the works, consultation of Toynbee's *A Dictionary of Proper Names and Notable Matters in the Works of Dante*, rev. C. S. Singleton (Oxford, 1968), maps and diagrams, and readings of the *Commedia* in Italian.

**The Dartmouth Dante Project** at:
http://dante.dartmouth.edu
includes over 70 commentaries on the *Commedia*, from Jacopo Alighieri's (1322–5) to Nicola Fosca's (2003–6). Helpful instructions on 'Using the DDP' are on the homepage.

**Digital Dante** at:
www.dante.ilt.columbia.edu/new
is particularly useful for a range of illustrations to the *Commedia*, by Botticelli,
Dalì and Doré; together with Pre-Raphaelite-style illustrations of *VN* by Evelyn
Paul (a follower of Rossetti).

**Dante Online** is the website of the Società dantesca italiana, at:
www.danteonline.it
which includes material on Dante's life, texts of the works and a list of
manuscripts.

## Audiovisual

For **illustrations**, Digital Dante (above) is an excellent resource but does not as
yet include early manuscript illustrations (apart from Botticelli's drawings of
1480–95). The **Bodleian Library, Oxford** has generously put about 150 digi-
tized images from a fourteenth-century manuscript (MS Holkham misc. 48)
online at:
www.bodley.ox.ac.uk/dept/scwmss/wmss/medieval/mss/holkham/
misc/048.a.htm

For **audio**, the Princeton Dante Project (above) provides a good, clear reading
of the *Commedia* in the original Italian by Lino Pertile. Reading of the whole
text in English by Robert and Jean Hollander is planned for this site, but at
present only a few cantos of the *Inferno* are available.

Meanwhile, Naxos have recorded the whole text in English, read by Heathcote
Williams from the translation by Benedict Flynn (*Inferno* on 4 CDs; complete
*Commedia* on 13). There is also a disc of *Inferno: Selections*: selected cantos
translated and read by poets including Fleur Adcock, Bernard O'Donoghue,
Steve Ellis and Jamie McKendrick, with some passages also read in Italian by
Emmanuela Tandelo and Diego Zancani (available from 'The Chaucer Studio';
order form at: http://english.byu.edu/chaucer). The Italian company 'Audio-
libri' have produced a 15-hour recording of the whole *Commedia*, read by
Claudio Carini on MP3 CD, and selected cantos from the readings of *Inferno*
and *Purgatorio* are also on two separate CDs (for information and orders, go to:
www.recitarleggendo.com).

# Index

4 446

Gramley Library
Salem Academy and College
Winston-Salem, N.C. 27108